Linguistic Modeling of Information and Markup Languages

Text, Speech and Language Technology

VOLUME 40

For further volumes:
http://www.springer.com/series/6636

Linguistic Modeling of Information and Markup Languages

Contributions to Language Technology

Edited by

Andreas Witt
Institut für Deutsche Sprache, Mannheim, Germany

Dieter Metzing
Universität Bielefeld, Germany

 Springer

Editors
Dr. Andreas Witt
Institut für Deutsche Sprache
(IDS)
68161 Mannheim
R5, 6-13
Germany
witt@ids-mannheim.de

Prof. Dr. Dieter Metzing
Universität Bielefeld
Fak. Linguistik und
Literaturwissenschaft
Universitätsstraße
33615 Bielefeld
Germany
dieter.metzing@uni-bielefeld.de

ISBN 978-94-007-3112-7   e-ISBN 978-90-481-3331-4
DOI 10.1007/978-90-481-3331-4
Springer Dordrecht Heidelberg London New York

Printed on acid-free paper

Springer is part of Springer Science+Business Media (www.springer.com)

Preface

The general markup language XML has played an outstanding role in the multiple ways of processing electronic documents, XML being used either in the design of interface structures or as a formal framework for the representation of structure or content-related properties of documents. This book in its 13 chapters discusses aspects of XML-based linguistic information modeling combining: methodological issues, especially with respect to text-related information modeling, application-oriented research and issues of formal foundations. The contributions in this book are based on current research in Text Technology, Computational Linguistics and in the international domain of evolving standards for language resources. Recurrent themes in this book are markup languages, explored from different points of view, and topics of text-related information modeling. These topics have been core areas of the research Unit "Text-technological Information Modeling" (www.text-technology.de) funded from 2002 to 2009 by the German Research Foundation (DFG).

Positions developed in this book could also benefit from the presentations and discussion at the conference "Modelling Linguistic Information Resources" at the Center for Interdisciplinary Research (Zentrum für interdisziplinäre Forschung, ZiF) at Bielefeld, a center for advanced studies known for its international and interdisciplinary meetings and research.

The editors would like to thank the DFG and ZiF for their financial support, the publisher, the series editors, the reviewers and those people that helped to prepare the manuscript, especially Carolin Kram, Nils Diewald, Jens Stegmann and Peter M. Fischer and last but not least, all of the authors.

Bielefeld, Germany   Dieter Metzing
Mannheim, Germany   Andreas Witt
June 2009

Contents

Contributors

Maja Bärenfänger Justus-Liebig-Universität Gießen, Gießen, Germany

Scott Farrar Department of Linguistics, University of Washington, Seattle, WA, USA, farrar@u.washington.edu

Daniela Goecke Bielefeld University, Bielefeld, Germany, daniela.goecke@uni-bielefeld.de

Mirco Hilbert Justus-Liebig-Universität Gießen, Gießen, Germany

Stephan Kepser Theoretical Computational Linguistics Group, Linguistics Department, University of Tübingen, Germany, kepser@sfs.uni.tuebingen.de

Jin-Dong Kim University of Tokyo, Tokyo, Japan, jdkim@is.s.u-tokyo.ac.jp

D. Terence Langendoen Division of Information & Intelligent Systems, National Science Foundation, Arlington, VA, USA

Eva Anna Lenz Institut für Deutsche Sprache und Literatur, Universität Dortmund, Dortmund, Germany, lenz@hytex.info

Henning Lobin Justus-Liebig-Universität Gießen, Gießen, Germany

Harald Lüngen Justus-Liebig-Universität Gießen, Gießen, Germany, luengen@uni-giessen.de

Alexander Mehler Bielefeld University, Bielefeld, Germany, alexander.mehler@uni-bielefeld.de

Dieter Metzing Bielefeld University, Bielefeld, Germany, dieter.metzing@uni-bielefeld.de

Uwe Mönnich Theoretical Computational Linguistics Group, Linguistics Department, University of Tübingen, Germany

Frank Morawietz Theoretical Computational Linguistics Group, Linguistics Department, University of Tübingen, Germany

Tomoko Ohta University of Tokyo, Tokyo, Japan

Csilla Puskás Justus-Liebig-Universität Gießen, Gießen, Germany

Georg Rehm vionto GmbH, Berlin, Germany, georg.rehm@vionto.com

Felix Sasaki University of Applied Sciences Potsdam, Potsdam, Germany (Manager of the W3C Germany and Austria Office), felix.sasaki@fh-potsdam.de

Thomas Schmidt Special Research Centre (SFB 538) on Multilingualism, University of Hamburg, Hamburg, Germany, thomas.schmidt@uni-hamburg.de

Manfred Stede Universität Potsdam, Potsdam, Germany, stede@ling.uni-potsdam.de

Angelika Storrer Institut für Deutsche Sprache und Literatur, Universität Dortmund, Dortmund, Germany, storrer@hytex.info

Maik Stührenberg Bielefeld University, Bielefeld, Germany

Arthit Suriyawongkul Faculty of Sociology and Anthropology, Thammasat University and Opendream Labs, Bangkok, Thailand

Thorsten Trippel Fakultät für Linguistik und Literaturwissenschaft, Universität Bielefeld, Bielefeld, Germany, thorsten.trippel@unibielefeld.de

Jun'ichi Tsujii University of Tokyo, Tokyo, Japan; University of Manchester, Manchester, UK

Andreas Witt Institut für Deutsche Sprache Mannheim, Mannheim, Germany, witt@ids-mannheim.de

Chapter 1
Different Views on Markup

Distinguishing Levels and Layers

Daniela Goecke, Harald Lüngen, Dieter Metzing, Maik Stührenberg, and Andreas Witt

Abstract In this chapter, two different ways of grouping information represented in document markup are examined: *annotation levels*, referring to conceptual levels of description, and *annotation layers*, referring to the technical realisation of markup using e.g. document grammars. In many current XML annotation projects, multiple levels are integrated into one layer, often leading to the problem of having to deal with overlapping hierarchies. As a solution, we propose a framework for XML-based multiple, independent XML annotation layers for one text, based on an abstract representation of XML documents with logical predicates. Two realisations of the abstract representation are presented, a Prolog fact base format together with an application architecture, and a specification for XML native databases. We conclude with a discussion of projects that have currently adopted this framework.

Keywords Concurrent markup · XML · Annotations

1.1 Introduction

An annotated text document firstly contains the primary information, i.e. the text, and secondly, meta information, i.e. its annotation. Typically, the meta information structures the text according to a certain *view* on the text. Since language is a highly complex object of investigation, linguists often want to express more than a single view on a text. This chapter deals with problems that can arise when annotating multiple, different views on a text. We propose a practical and terminological distinction between aspects related to modelling issues and aspects related to the actual annotations. Such a distinction helps overcome problems that are often encountered when dealing with heterogeneously structured text.

This chapter is organised as follows: In Section 1.2, the terms *level* and *layer* are introduced, the relationship between levels, layers, and markup languages is

D. Goecke (✉)
Bielefeld University, Bielefeld, Germany
e-mail: daniela.goecke@uni-bielefeld.de

A. Witt, D. Metzing (eds.), *Linguistic Modeling of Information and Markup Languages*, Text, Speech and Language Technology 40,
DOI 10.1007/978-90-481-3331-4_1, © Springer Science+Business Media B.V. 2010

described in Section 1.3. In Section 1.4 approaches to XML-conformant annotation of multiple levels are presented. In Section 1.5 the need for an abstract representation of XML markup is motivated and two approaches are presented: In Section 1.5.1, inference tools for concurrent markup that have been developed during the first phase of the project *Sekimo – Secondary structuring of information*, are introduced. Here, an architecture for the integration of heterogeneous resources, which utilises the set of Sekimo tools, is described. In Section 1.5.2, it is demonstrated how text data with concurrent markup can be represented and stored in XML databases. The chapter concludes with a discussion of the relevance of the distinction between level and layer with references to selected publications.

1.2 Levels and Layers

Markup expresses additional information about text, e.g. authorship, or the part of speech of each word in it. Often it makes implicit information explicit, e.g. information encoded in the physical layout structure (such as paragraph and word boundaries).

The amount of information that is associated with text by means of markup has been constantly growing over the past few years. This development involved an organisation and structuring of the multitude of information. Structuring information by means of markup implies a conceptual process as well as a technical one. The conceptual and the technical process do not necessarily result in identical combinations of the pieces of information. We introduce the following terminology to clarify the two principally different ways of grouping units of information occurring in markup structures.

- *Annotation level* – referring to the conceptual level of information represented in markup
- *Annotation layer* – referring to the technical realisation of markup

For short, the term "level" refers to a model involving theoretical concepts e.g. of a research discipline. In linguistics, there are several subdisciplines which investigate different aspects and modalities of natural language and natural language description such as phonology, morphology, syntax, and semantics, which are often called the linguistic *levels of description*. Thus, an annotation unit (an XML element or attribute) will refer to one level while another annotation unit may refer to another level of linguistic description. In that sense, different *levels of markup* can be found in one annotated text. But even on one linguistic description level, different types of analyses can be represented which we still consider as different conceptual levels of markup. On the level of syntax, for example, alternative analyses according to different syntactic theories (e.g. Lexical Functional Grammar, Tree Adjoining Grammar, Categorial Grammar) may exist, and the annotation used to express any one of them refers to its own level of markup.

The term "layer", on the other hand, refers to the technical realisation of a modelling task. What it means exactly thus depends on the annotation system employed. In transcription systems based on the annotation graph framework (Bird and Liberman 2001), for example, a layer corresponds to a single labeled path which spans the transcribed text. Typically, an annotation graph consists of several such paths, thus multiple layers can be realised in one annotation graph. Another example of a technical realisation is the use of different XML documents to store annotations of one text (Witt 2005), each XML file then corresponds to one annotation layer.

Distinguishing between levels and layers calls for an explication of the possible relations between the two. Does one annotation layer always correspond to one annotation level and vice versa? A closer look at the theoretical conceptualisations of annotations and their practical realisations reveals that levels and layers can stand in an $1 : 1$, $1 : m$, $n : 1$, or an $n : m$ relation (where $n, m > 1$). Examples of these relations are shown in Fig. 1.1.

In an $1 : 1$ relation, one conceptual level is mirrored by exactly one annotation layer, and each technical layer realises exactly one annotation level. Given an $1 : 1$ relation, one layer can be easily removed or exchanged without changing other layers. In an $1 : m$ relation, units of one level are distributed over several layers, e.g. for the POS level, a different layer might be created for each word class. In an $n : 1$ relation, two or more descriptive levels are integrated into one annotation layer, e.g. syntax and morphology annotations are often encoded in one XML document. An $n : m$ relation involves both the splitting and the mixture of conceptual levels and is seldom found in annotated corpora.

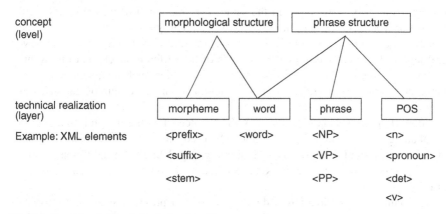

Fig. 1.1 Possible relations between level and layer

1.3 Levels, Layers, and Markup Languages

Markup Systems are formally defined. Consequently all markup languages are constrained. For SGML and XML, two restrictions are relevant when one aims at marking up information stemming from different linguistic levels of description:

- Firstly, they require that the elements used in a document instance must nest properly, i.e. the beginning and the end of a range of text annotated by one element must be contained in the same parent element.
- Secondly, one document instance can be associated with at most one document grammar.

The first restriction concerns the modelling aspect in a document instance and often results in the question of how to arrange different elements of a single layer in XML. Because a string annotated by one element must either be fully included in or totally separate from a string annotated by another element,[1] i.e. elements must not overlap, this problem is also called the *overlap problem*.

The second restriction often leads to difficulties when different levels are to be represented in one single XML document and thus addresses properties of markup systems. This problem concerns the use of document grammars, therefore we refer to it as the *document grammar problem*.

Ideally, an annotation level should be formally defined in one document grammar and a document grammar should only define one level of annotation in order to allow for a clear identification of the ontological status of the elements under consideration. Nevertheless, quite often a document grammar defines an annotation inventory for several levels. E. g., some versions of the DTDs for HTML allow for annotating both the text structure (paragraphs, headings, hypertext relations, etc.) and features that are intended to be used by the rendering engine when displaying the text (font-size, color, etc.). In the same way, one could try to merge different annotation vocabularies into one integrated document grammar. In order to define a common document grammar which permits the representation of units from several levels, the interrelation of the concepts of the different levels that one wants to express using markup has to be analysed. An integrated document grammar, however, is not recommended for a clear identification of the ontological status of elements.

Soon after the standardisation of XML the need for disentangling annotation vocabularies arose, since XML is not only used for annotating documents but also for as different purposes as programming (e.g. XSLT), the definition of document grammars (e.g. XSchema, Relax NG), and – through SVG – even for vector graphics.

The namespace standard was thus introduced to prefix element and attribute names for indicating the annotation level to which they belong. Hence, in principle, namespaces can be used to disentangle subsets of markup which belong to different linguistic levels of description. Other markup languages, e.g. LMNL (Cowan et al. 2005), provide a similar mechanism to refer to different levels. This approach is better suited than the construction of an integrated document grammar, since different annotation levels are associated with different namespace prefixes.

However, especially in XML, integrating different linguistic levels into one annotation often leads to the first problem, the overlap problem.

Despite the different nature of the two kinds of problems, the overlap problem and the document grammar problem, both often occur together. The reason for this is obvious: When different levels are annotated and their document grammars have been designed independently, overlaps are bound to occur frequently. Hence, it might be helpful to try and solve both problems at once.

A solution to both problems was provided by XML's predecessor SGML. When the additional SGML feature "concur" is enabled, it is possible to independently annotate a text according to different document grammars. In recent years, new proposals to introduce this feature in XML, too, have been put forward (Hilbert et al. 2005, Schonefeld and Witt 2006). In this context the development of techniques for the definition of document grammars for concurrent markup has been started (Sperberg-McQueen 2006, Schonefeld and Witt 2006, Tennison 2007).

Moreover, some non-SGML-based markup languages have been designed which allow for the annotation of overlapping elements as well as for the annotation on different levels, e.g. TexMECS (Huitfeld and Sperberg-McQueen 2001) and LMNL (Cowan et al. 2005).

1.4 XML-Conformant Annotation of Multiple Levels

Since there is often a need for annotating structures which would result in overlapping XML elements, several solutions have been proposed. The two most frequently employed techniques to avoid overlap are firstly the so-called *milestone elements* and secondly the *fragmentation* of elements.

- *Milestone elements:* This term describes the use of empty elements to mark only the boundaries of a text range which would otherwise be contained in a non-empty element.[2] Since elements with text content can in principle also be used as empty elements, there is a variant of the milestone technique in which it is recommended to use all elements which originally were not intended to be empty (e.g. the element `<line>`) as milestone elements. Special attributes then indicate the status of these elements. This approach is known under at least three different names: Trojan Milestones, Horse and CLIX (cf. DeRose 2004).
- *Fragmentation:* A text sequence included in an element which would otherwise be affected by overlap is artificially split into several text sequences. Each of the resulting strings is included in a fragment element. An element which marks up a fragment content (e.g. a part of a `<sentence>` has attributes that indicate its special status and point to the preceding and the following element fragment(s).

The second problem, caused by the single document grammar constraint, can also be tackled by different strategies:

- Find a new integrated document grammar. In order to define a common document grammar which permits the representation of units from several levels, the interrelation of the concepts on the different levels that one wants to express using markup has to be analysed.

- Use different markup vocabularies for an annotation according to different document grammars. The namespace technique can be used to point to the document grammar from which an element or attribute is taken.

Standoff annotation, introduced by Thompson and McKelvie (1997) as a technique to split annotations from the textual data, can be used both to separate multiple linguistic levels from each other and to avoid overlapping structures. Standoff annotation has been primarily intended to present a solution to read-only textual data, copyright issues and overlapping structures. Instead of embedding markup in the text, markup and text are separated. Technically, standoff annotations are realised by referencing textual data through character offsets, e.g. an element <s> begins at the 17th and ends at the 42nd character of the text in a given file "transcript.txt". More often than raw text data a primary annotation is used as the target of a reference, e.g. a primary annotation annotates all the tokens of a text and introduces identifiers which can be used as link targets by the standoff annotation.

Standoff markup is often regarded as appropriate markup technique when linguists have to deal with complex annotations (see Pianta and Bentivogli 2004). For real annotation tasks, however, standoff annotations easily become quite complex and therefore they are only editable and even human readable with specialised software (Dipper et al. 2007).

An alternative way to solve the problems is the simplest solution to represent multiple, possibly overlapping hierarchies: The same text is annotated several times, and for each level of description, a separate markup layer is introduced, resulting in an 1:1 relation between markup levels and layers. Obviously, the creation of redundant copies of the textual base might be conceived as a drawback, because if changes to the textual base have to made, they have to be repeated for each annotation layer. On the other hand, this approach offers a range of possibilities for working with multiple description levels, especially in the field of humanities computing where it is the rule that one text is associated with manifold analyses and interpretations.

In this solution, care has to be taken that all layers contain the same *primary data* (i.e. the text which is to be annotated): When editing multiply annotated text, the identity of the primary data has to be maintained. If the text base is changed in one of the XML layers but not in another one, identity conflicts may arise, and a connection between the different XML layers could be no longer established. However, several editors have been developed that facilitate the editing of multiply annotated text, see Witt (2005) for a detailed description of the tools that have been implemented in the Sekimo project. Further editors that support multi-layered annotations are described in Schmidt (2004), Dipper and Götze (2005) and Schonefeld and Witt (2006).

Despite the need to ensure the identity of the primary data, the proposed solution offers the advantage that representations of different description levels may be developed independently of each other. A distributed development of XML layers allows experts to create markup independently of categories and structures from different levels. Furthermore, markup for additional levels may be added at any time without changing already existing XML layers.

1.5 Modelling, Representation, Annotation

In the previous section we have reviewed multiple annotations as a way to represent multiple, possibly overlapping hierarchies. To obtain a common view on the textual data and their multiple annotations, all markup is separated from its textual base. In order to split markup and text, an *abstract representation* of XML markup in logical predicates has been developed. Making a distinction between the textual base (primary data) and (possibly) multiple markup has been proposed in Witt (2002a,b), and has been further developed in Bayerl et al. (2003).

In the NITE project, the *Nite Object Model* (*NOM*, Carletta et al. 2003) has been defined, which is similar to DOM, the standardised W3C Document Object Model, used for the representation of HTML and XML documents. The most important difference between DOM and NOM is that a DOM corresponds to a tree with a single root node for the outermost element in an XML document and the leaf nodes for the textual content of the elements. The underlying data structure of a NOM, however, is not one tree with a single root, but several interconnected trees. Since each of their roots (indirectly) spans the same leaves, i.e. the textual data, we use the term *multi-rooted tree* to refer to this data structure.

In the Sekimo project, two approaches to the realization of an abstract representation have been developed: In Section 1.5.1 Prolog-based inference tools for concurrent markup are introduced. Section 1.5.2 describes the *Sekimo Generic Format* (*SGF*), an abstract XML-based representation format. In contrast to NOM, SGF uses a single-rooted tree but allows for several annotation levels corresponding to the same primary data using the formal model of a multi-rooted tree.

1.5.1 Multi-Layered XML Documents and Prolog

In the following, both a realization of an abstract representation as well as an application of multiple annotations is presented. The realization is done in terms of a Prolog fact base, the application of the Prolog fact base focuses on the analysis and combination of different layers.

The Prolog fact base format is an extension of previous work by Sperberg-McQueen et al. (2000). In this approach, all XML markup is translated into Prolog predicates that describe both the textual data as well as XML markup in terms of elements or attributes. The original format of Sperberg-McQueen et al. (2000) (see also Sperberg-McQueen et al. 2002a), which we consider as an intra-layer approach, has been extended in order to allow both for intra-layer analyses as well as for inter-layer analyses (see Witt et al. 2005 for details). In the original format, each XML element is translated into a Prolog fact with two arguments, e. g.

```
node([1,5,2],element(p)).
```

Attributes are translated into facts with three arguments, e. g.

```
attr( [1,5,2], id, implied).
```
(examples taken from Sperberg-McQueen et al. (2000), p. 219).

When representing multiple annotations, it must be recorded for each element or attribute to which layer it belongs. The multiple annotations can be connected using the identical textual content as a link between the separate layers. Therefore the original `node` and `attr` facts have been extended with arguments including layer information as well as information on the start and end position of the elements under consideration. In addition, the PCDATA (i.e. the underlying textual data) is translated into separate facts with three arguments (start position, end position, and the character at that position). These facts have been included for the purpose of reconverting the Prolog fact base into an XML representation. Thus, there are three types of Prolog predicates with their argument positions:

- Predicates for XML elements:
  `node`(*Layer, StartPosition, EndPosition, PositionDocumentTree, ElementName*).
- Predicates for XML attributes:
  `attr`(*Layer, StartPosition, EndPosition, PositionDocumentTree, AttributeName, Attribute-Value*).
- Predicates for PCDATA:
  `pcdata_node`(*StartPosition, EndPosition, Character*).

A simple sentence like the one in Fig. 1.2 shall be used as an example to demonstrate the architecture of the application of multiple annotations. The textual content is represented character-wise by the multiple occurrence of the predicate `pcdata_node`, which has the arguments start position, end position and the character at that position as shown in Fig. 1.3. The offset of the character position is used on the one hand as a reference for different layers of markup and on the other hand in order to generate new XML output from the Prolog fact base.

```
00|01|02|03|04|05|06|07|08|09|10|11|12|13|14|15|16|17|18|19
   T  h  i  s     i  s     a     s  e  n  t  e  n  c  e  .
```

Fig. 1.2 A simple sentence

```
1   pcdata_node(0,   1,   'T').
2   pcdata_node(1,   2,   'h').
3   pcdata_node(2,   3,   'i').
4   pcdata_node(3,   4,   's').
5   pcdata_node(4,   5,   '⎵').
6   ...
7   pcdata_node(18,  19,  '.').
```

Fig. 1.3 PCDATA nodes in the Prolog fact base

```
1  <s xml:lang="en">
2    <np>
3      <pron>This</pron>
4    </np>
5    <vp>
6      <v>is</v>
7      <np>
8        <det>a</det>
9        <n>sentence</n>
10     </np>
11   </vp>.
12 </s>
```

```
1  <syll>
2    <s>This</s>
3    <s>is</s>
4    <s>a</s>
5    <s>sen</s>
6    <s>tence</s>.
7  </syll>
```

Fig. 1.4 Formatted markup of POS/syntactic (*above*) and syllable (*below*) level of the same text segment

For the example sentence we have created XML markup for the levels *Syllable Structure* (Layer syll) and *POS/syntactic Information* (Layer pos) (see Fig. 1.4). In Fig. 1.5, the Prolog fact base of all nodes representing element instances and attributes from the layers pos and syll is shown. The word *This* (character positions 0–4, see lines 1–4 in Fig. 1.3), for example, is annotated as a pronoun on the layer pos and as a syllable on the layer syll (Fig. 1.4, above on line 3, and below on line 2). In the Prolog representation in Fig. 1.5, these elements can be found on lines 3 and 10.

```
1  node('pos.xml', 0, 19, [1], element('s')).
2  node('pos.xml', 0, 4, [1, 1], element('np')).
3  node('pos.xml', 0, 4, [1, 1, 1], element('pron')).
4  node('pos.xml', 5, 18, [1, 2], element('vp')).
5  node('pos.xml', 5, 7, [1, 2, 1], element('v')).
6  node('pos.xml', 8, 18, [1, 2, 2], element('np')).
7  node('pos.xml', 8, 9, [1, 2, 2, 1], element('det')).
8  node('pos.xml', 10, 18, [1, 2, 2, 2], element('n')).
9  node('syll.xml', 0, 19, [1], element('syll')).
10 node('syll.xml', 0, 4, [1, 1], element('s')).
11 node('syll.xml', 5, 7, [1, 2], element('s')).
12 node('syll.xml', 8, 9, [1, 3], element('s')).
13 node('syll.xml', 10, 13, [1, 4], element('s')).
14 node('syll.xml', 13, 18, [1, 5], element('s')).
15
16 attr('pos.xml', 0, 19, [1], 'xml:lang', 'en').
```

Fig. 1.5 Element and Attribute information in the Prolog fact base

The Prolog representation of the XML markup can be used in order to query the corpus, e.g. for an analysis of the relation between elements from different layers. Taking the start and end positions of two (or more) elements from separate annotation layers into account, different relations between these elements can be identified, e.g. the element np from layer pos *includes* the element s from layer syll. The information on relations between elements from different layers is important in order to create an annotation *merger*, i.e. for a *markup unification* of different annotation layers. The process of markup unification is described in detail in Witt et al. (2005). Basically, the merger contains all markup from the input layers and the interrelationship of elements determines the hierarchical structure of the intended merger. Besides unifying different annotation layers by markup unification to *merge* different annotation layers it is also possible to *split* a single annotation layer into different partitions. However – unlike merging – splitting is already possible with standard XML tools (e.g. XSLT or XQuery). Thus, the Prolog fact base format has mainly been extended for the purpose of markup unification.

The Prolog fact base representing the merger of the facts in Fig. 1.5 is shown in Fig. 1.6; an XML output file generated from the merged fact base and the textual content is shown in Fig. 1.7. In order to avoid merging conflicts caused by identically named elements on different layers, each element name is provided with a prefix indicating its original layer.

An XML layer is the realisation of a data model, i.e. of a conceptual level. When having different layers that describe different aspects of the data, an analysis of the data should give answers to the question of how the different layers interact, i.e. which relations hold between the markup elements. The possible relationships between elements from two layers have been arranged and classified in Durusau and O'Donnell (2002). They are of central interest for the merging process as they give information as to what the hierarchical structure of the merged XML annotation should look like. In the overview given in Fig. 1.8, some of the relationships given in Durusau and O'Donnell (2002) have been collapsed and renamed for the illustration of our approach.

```
1   node('output', 0, 19, [1], element('pos.xml_s')).
2   attr('output', 0, 19, [1], 'xml:lang', 'en').
3   node('output', 0, 19, [1, 1], element('syll.xml_syll')).
4   node('output', 0, 4, [1, 1, 1], element('pos.xml_np')).
5   node('output', 0, 4, [1, 1, 1, 1], element('pos.xml_pron')).
6   node('output', 0, 4, [1, 1, 1, 1, 1], element('syll.xml_s')).
7   node('output', 5, 18, [1, 1, 2], element('pos.xml_vp')).
8   node('output', 5, 7, [1, 1, 2, 1], element('pos.xml_v')).
9   node('output', 5, 7, [1, 1, 2, 1, 1], element('syll.xml_s')).
10  node('output', 8, 18, [1, 1, 2, 2], element('pos.xml_np')).
11  node('output', 8, 9, [1, 1, 2, 2, 1], element('pos.xml_det')).
12  node('output', 8, 9, [1, 1, 2, 2, 1, 1], element('syll.xml_s')).
13  node('output', 10, 18, [1, 1, 2, 2, 2], element('pos.xml_n')).
14  node('output', 10, 13, [1, 1, 2, 2, 2, 1], element('syll.xml_s')).
15  node('output', 13, 18, [1, 1, 2, 2, 2, 2], element('syll.xml_s')).
```

Fig. 1.6 The merged Prolog fact base

```
1    <pos_s xml:lang="en">
2     <syll_syll>
3      <pos_np>
4       <pos_pron>
5        <syll_s>This</syll_s>
6       </pos_pron>
7      </pos_np>
8      <pos_vp>
9       <pos_v>
10       <syll_s>is</syll_s>
11      </pos_v>
12      <pos_np>
13       <pos_det>
14        <syll_s>a</syll_s>
15       </pos_det>
16       <pos_n>
17        <syll_s>sen</syll_s>
18        <syll_s>tence</syll_s>
19       </pos_n>
20      </pos_np>
21     </pos_vp>.
22    </syll_syll>
23   </pos_s>
```

Fig. 1.7 The merged output XML file

Using the tools described in Witt et al. (2005) interrelationships between different annotation layers can be analysed, and also two layers can be merged into a single XML document via the process of markup unification. Bayerl et al. (2003) describe the inter-layer analysis for three XML layers: the text's document structure on the one hand and the XML markup of two kinds of semantic levels on the other hand (the thematic level, i.e. topics in the text world that the article is about, and

```
1    start point identity:   <a>.................................</a>
2                            <b>............</b>
3
4    end point identity:     <a>.................................</a>
5                                               <b>............</b>
6
7    inclusion:              <a>.................................</a>
8                                        <b>............</b>
9
10   identity:               <a>.................................</a>
11                           <b>.................................</b>
12
13   overlap:                <a>....................</a>
14                                       <b>....................</b>
15
16   independent elements:   <a>...........</a>
17                                               <b>............</b>
```

Fig. 1.8 Possible relations between pairs of element instances (cf. Durusau and O'Donnell 2002)

the functional or rhetorical level). Goecke and Witt (2006) describe the inter-layer analysis of a text's document structure and the anaphoric relations that hold within the text. Apart from analysing elements from different layers, elements within one layer (intra-layer analysis) may be compared, too. In case of an n:1 relation between n levels and one layer, for example, an analysis of the relations between elements might help to split the layer into several layers, i.e. one for each level.

1.5.2 Multi-Layered Documents and XML-Databases

A different way of viewing and working with multi-layered documents is available when using an XML-based abstract representation format in connection with a native XML database. An XML-based format permits the application of several XML-related tools such as XPath, XSLT or XQuery. Dealing with multi-layered documents, however, bears the problem of overlapping structures which cannot be handled in plain XML (cf. Section 1.3). For this reason, we propose the abstract XML representation format *SGF (Sekimo Generic Format)* for multi-layered XML documents to be stored in a native XML database.[3] An overview of the architecture is shown in Fig. 1.9.

SGF is similar to the Prolog representation (cf. Section 1.5.1) in that the same mechanism for referencing characters and whitespaces is used: the offset position of each character. These are used to span sequences of character data over the text, which can be referred to in a second step as tokens in the annotation process. The root element corpus contains the element corpusData with its required attribute xml:id, the value of which is a unique identifier of the given input text, and a type attribute, determining the type of corpus data (textual or multimodal).

The different annotation layers appear in a structured fashion as child elements of the annotation element. Each layer belongs to a namespace indicating it. A mandatory primaryData element is used to store and structure the primary textual data. The abstract representation of the example sentence shown in Fig. 1.2 can be seen in Fig. 1.10.

The primary layer is flat in hierarchical terms. The primaryData element contains the complete whitespace-normalised textual input including whitespace and punctuation characters (for shorter texts) or a reference to a file in which the whitespace-normalised textual input is stored in (via the location element – not shown in the example). In the latter case an optional element checksum can be used to protect the integrity of the input data, providing both the computed checksum and the algorithm used. The element segments is used to store several segment elements, each of which contains an identifier, the segment type (in this case character) and the segment span (ranging from the start to the end attribute, referring to the offset of the first and last character of the string. Additional occurrences of the empty element segment can be used to define the position of whitespace character data, including a character reference. Relying on character offsets allows for dealing with different possible tokenisations (e.g. output from different text analysis tools).

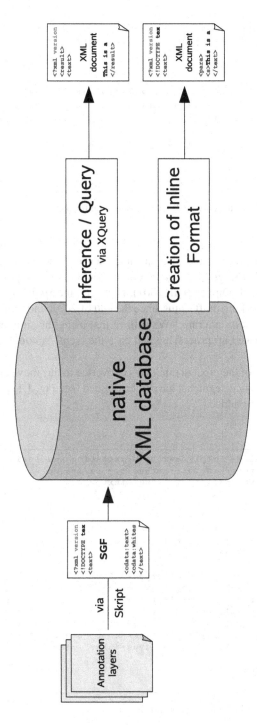

Fig. 1.9 An overview of the architecture

```
1   <base:corpus xmlns="http://www.text-technology.de/sekimo"
2   xmlns:base="http://www.text-technology.de/sekimo">
3     <base:corpusData xml:id="c1" type="text">
4       <base:meta>
5       <!-- [...] -->
6       </base:meta>
7       <base:primaryData start="0" end="19" xml:lang="en">
8         <base:textualContent>This is a sentence.</textualContent>
9       </base:primaryData>
10    </base:corpusData>
11    <base:corpusData xml:id="c2" type="text">
12    <!-- [...] -->
13    </base:corpusData>
14  </base:corpus>
```

Fig. 1.10 The root element of the abstract XML representation format

Instead of using the start and end attributes, a use of the XPointer *xpointer()* *Scheme* (and especially the *string-range* function) would have been possible (e.g. as in the PAULA format, cf. Dipper et al. 2007). However, the *xpointer() Scheme* has been pending in the working draft status since the end of 2002, and implementations of the string-range function are rare.[4] We believe that using the simpler concept of two attributes could speed up processing and ease the (semi-)automatic annotation process.

The textual content of the input document is converted to the above described primary layer. In the next step segments have to be defined (see Fig. 1.11). Afterwards, annotation layers can be added.

```
1   <base:corpus xmlns="http://www.text-technology.de/sekimo"
2   xmlns:base="http://www.text-technology.de/sekimo">
3     <base:corpusData xml:id="c1" type="text">
4       <base:meta>
5       <!-- [...] -->
6       </base:meta>
7       <base:primaryData start="0" end="19" xml:lang="en">
8         <base:textualContent>This is a sentence.</textualContent>
9       </base:primaryData>
10      <base:segments>
11        <base:segment xml:id="seg1" type="char" start="0" end="19"/>
12        <base:segment xml:id="seg2" type="char" start="0" end="4"/>
13        <base:segment xml:id="seg4" type="char" start="5" end="18"/>
14        <base:segment xml:id="seg5" type="char" start="5" end="7"/>
15        <base:segment xml:id="seg7" type="char" start="8" end="18"/>
16        <base:segment xml:id="seg8" type="char" start="8" end="9"/>
17        <base:segment xml:id="seg10" type="char" start="10" end="18"/>
18      </base:segments>
19    </base:corpusData>
20  </base:corpus>
```

Fig. 1.11 Adding segments in the instance document

In case that already existing inline annotation layers shall be used, the following steps have to be done for conversion:

1. A namespace referring to a converted representation of the schema of the annotation level is also added, following the notation http://www.text-technology. de/sekimo/[layer], and all elements of the imported layer are prefixed with the corresponding namespace prefix. If there are multiple annotations referring to the same schema (e.g. in case of an analysis of intra-layer relations), different namespace prefixes for the same namespace shall be used.[5] For this reason we refer to the prefix as *annotation layer prefix* rather than *namespace prefix*.
2. An optional `meta` element can be used to describe the annotation layer (e.g. its origin, the annotator, etc.). Apart from the `description` element, other elements derived from different namespaces are allowed as children of the *meta* element.
3. The attribute `segment` of the primary layer is added to each element.
4. Elements with a `PCDATA` content model are converted to empty elements, mixed content elements are converted to container elements. This is possible because all character content is already stored in the `primaryData` element of the primary layer or in another file.

A conversion of the annotation layers that were given in Fig. 1.4 would result in the representation shown in Fig. 1.12. Each annotation layer is stored in a `layer` element which is a child of the `annotation` element of the primary layer. Note, that only two more segments have been defined in order to represent the additional syllables layer.

The annotation levels can be prioritised by means of the optional attribute `priority` to allow for correct nesting in case of overlapping structures.

Keeping the explicit structural information of the non-terminal elements is a benefit provided by the XML-based representation format in contrast with other possible representation formats, allowing validation of annotation layers with only slightly changed version of the original document grammars (including cross-layer validation). As a second advantage, the XML-based representation format allows for storing meta-data such as the language of a sentence. Nontextual elements like images and figures can be embedded in special elements (e.g. `<nontext type="image" src="image.jpg"/>`). Since the scope of this work is the annotation of *textual* documents, the treatment of non-textual elements is not pursued further here. However, this framework can be used for the annotation of multi-modal corpora, too, by using timecode or frame positions as values for the `start` and `end` attributes and using `multimodal` as value for the `type` attribute of the `corpusData` element. In addition, it should be mentioned that constructing larger segments by referencing to other segments is possible as well (including disjoint segments). In this case the value of the `type` attribute of the `segment` element is set to `seg` and instead of `start` and `end` attributes a `segments` attribute is used (containing the identity references of the corresponding segments).

```
1    <base:corpus xmlns="http://www.text-technology.de/sekimo"
2     xmlns:base="http://www.text-technology.de/sekimo">
3      <base:corpusData xml:id="c1" type="text">
4       <base:primaryData start="0" end="19" xml:lang="en">
5        <base:textualContent>This is a sentence.</textualContent>
6       </base:primaryData>
7       <base:segments>
8        <base:segment xml:id="seg1" type="char" start="0" end="19"/>
9        <base:segment xml:id="seg2" type="char" start="0" end="4"/>
10       <base:segment xml:id="seg4" type="char" start="5" end="18"/>
11       <base:segment xml:id="seg5" type="char" start="5" end="7"/>
12       <base:segment xml:id="seg7" type="char" start="8" end="18"/>
13       <base:segment xml:id="seg8" type="char" start="8" end="9"/>
14       <base:segment xml:id="seg10" type="char" start="10" end="18"/>
15       <base:segment xml:id="seg11" type="char" start="10" end="13"/>
16       <base:segment xml:id="seg12" type="char" start="13" end="18"/>
17      </base:segments>
18      <base:annotation>
19       <base:level xml:id="pos" priority="0">
20        <base:layer xmlns:pos="http://www.text-technology.de/pos"
            xsi:schemaLocation="http://www.text-technology.de/pos⎵p.xsd">
21         <pos:s base:segment="seg1">
22          <pos:np base:segment="seg2">
23           <pos:pron base:segment="seg2"/>
24          </pos:np>
25          <pos:vp base:segment="seg4">
26           <pos:v base:segment="seg5"/>
27           <pos:np base:segment="seg7">
28            <pos:det base:segment="seg8"/>
29            <pos:n base:segment="seg10"/>
30           </pos:np>
31          </pos:vp>
32         </pos:s>
33        </base:layer>
34       </base:level>
35      </base:annotation>
36      <base:annotation>
37       <base:level xml:id="syll" priority="0">
38        <base:layer xmlns:syll="http://www.text-technology.de/syll"
            xsi:schemaLocation="http://www.text-technology.de/syll⎵s.xsd">
39         <syll:syll base:segment="seg1">
40          <syll:s base:segment="seg2"/>
41          <syll:s base:segment="seg5"/>
42          <syll:s base:segment="seg8"/>
43          <syll:s base:segment="seg11"/>
44          <syll:s base:segment="seg12"/>
45         </syll:syll>
46        </base:layer>
47       </base:level>
48      </base:annotation>
49     </base:corpusData>
50    </base:corpus>
```

Fig. 1.12 The converted SGF representation of the two annotation layers

A successor of SGF, called XStandoff, is already available as development release (Stührenberg and Jettka 2009). For sustainability reasons, the current version of the Sekimo Generic Format has undergone a feature-freeze in that way that the format and its corresponding tools are considered as stable.

Storing the multi-layered documents in a native XML database allows for using query and analysis mechanisms which are similar to those provided for the Prolog fact base. Most native XML database systems support XPath and at least a subset of XQuery and some sort of update mechanism (e.g. XUpdate as defined by the XML:DB Initiative[6]) or the upcoming XQuery Update Facility which is capable of processing and updating instances of the XQuery/XPath Data Model (XDM) (Chamberlin et al. 2008). The W3C is working on the extension of XQuery 1.0 with full-text search capabilities (Amer-Yahia et al. 2006).

Tests with the Open Source native XML databases eXist,[7] the Berkeley DB XML[8] and the commercial but freely available IBM DB2 Express-C[9] showed a good performance. Mechanisms like the above mentioned XUpdate or the upcoming XQuery Update Facility allow for updating the instance files. By now the use of a native XML database allows for easy intra- and inter-layer analysis. Having a powerful query language like XQuery allows for quite complex analyses. For a more detailed description of the Sekimo Generic Format and performance measures on a per-file basis in a real-world application (cf. Stührenberg and Goecke 2008).

1.6 Conclusions

Information contained in textual markup can be grouped according to two distinct principles: On the one hand, (annotation) *level* refers to a conceptual level of information such as the phonological, syntactic and semantic levels of description familiar from linguistics. (Annotation) *layer*, on the other hand, refers to the technical realisation of markup, e.g. one document grammar or one labelled path in an annotation graph defines one annotation layer. The ideal case in text-technological information modelling is that of a 1:1 correspondence between levels and layers. However, due to the single document grammar restriction for SGML-based markup languages, linguistic levels are often integrated into one annotation layer, resulting in a need to solve the so-called overlap problem. We showed that previous solutions to the overlap problem exhibit some drawbacks, so that we vote for a framework of XML-based multi-layer annotation where the same text is annotated several times, and a separate markup layer is introduced for each description level. That way, experts can create and maintain markup for their description levels independently of the structures defined for the same text by the experts for a different description level. Markup for additional levels can be added without having to make changes to existing markup layers. The use of special editors guarantees the identity of the primary data of each layer. An abstract representation in terms of logical predicates defines a common view on multiply annotated layers of one text. We presented two realisations of such abstract representations, firstly a Prolog fact base format, and secondly, a realisation that makes use of existing XML database facilities. For the Prolog fact base, we presented an application architecture in which multiply XML-annotated documents can be unified, and relations between element types in annotation layers can be inferred. We also showed that utilising XML databases for a realisation of the abstract representation format SGF, XML standards and tools such as XPath, XQuery and XUpdate can be used conveniently for retrieving and updating annotations within this framework.

Our framework of XML-based multiple annotations is currently applied in several text-technological projects for the automatic linguistic analysis of XML-annotated texts.

The annotations of the different levels of discourse structure described in Lüngen et al. (in this volume), for example, have been annotated separately in a corpus of scientific journal articles. The discourse parser described is realised in Prolog and takes the Prolog fact base derived from the multiple annotations of one document as its input and adds the independent annotation layer of rhetorical structure as its output.

Stührenberg et al. (2006) apply the framework within the context of anaphora resolution. Necessary resources for the resolution process (e.g. morphology, syntax, logical document structure, ontological knowledge) have been annotated separately and the resulting annotation layers are combined in the representation format. On the basis of the combined XML data, feature vectors have been extracted that serve as input for corpus analyses and the resolution process.

Both, the Sekimo Generic Format and its currently developed successor, XStandoff, are freely available under the LGPL 3 license including the accompanied tools, other interested parties and projects are invited to use and enhance this framework.[10]

For a broader discussion of the issue of sustainability of multiply structured linguistic data see Stührenberg et al. (2008), Rehm et al. (2009), and Witt et al. (2009).

Notes

1. This is the reason for stating that SGML or XML documents form an "ordered hierarchy of content objects" (OHCO).
2. E.g. instead of using the element `<line>` such that it contains the text of a single print line, two empty elements `<lb/>` could be employed to annotate the line breaks before and after a line.
3. Storing on a per-file basis or in a relational database is possible as well.
4. Cf. http://www.w3.org/XML/2000/09/LinkingImplementations.html
5. It would also be possible to declare multiple namespaces as an ad hoc solution, but this would be against the intention of the XML namespace standard.
6. Cf. http://xmldb-org.sourceforge.net/xupdate/
7. Cf. http://www.exist-db.org
8. Cf. http://www.sleepycat.com/products/bdbxml.html
9. Cf. http://www.ibm.com/software/data/db2/express/
10. Cf. http://www.xstandoff.net for further details.

References

Amer-Yahia, S., Botev, C., Buxton, S., Case, P., Doerre, J., Holstege, M., McBeath, D., Rys, M., and Shanmugasundaram, J. (eds.) (2006). *XQuery 1.0 and XPath 2.0 Full-Text.* W3C Candidate Recommendation 16 May 2008 http://www.w3.org/TR/2008/CR-xpath-full-text-10-20080516/

Barnard, D., Burnard, L., Gaspart, J., Price, L. A., Sperberg-McQueen, C. M., and Varile, G. B. (1995). *Hierarchical encoding of text: technical problems and SGML solutions.* In: Computers and the Humanities. 29:211–231.

Bayerl, P. S., Goecke, D., Lüngen, H., and Witt, A. (2003). *Methods for the semantic analysis of document markup.* In: Roisin, C., E. Munson and C. Vanoirbeek (eds.). Proceedings of the 3rd ACM Symposium on Document Engineering (DocEng), Grenoble: 161–170.

Bird, S. and Liberman, M. (2001). *A formal framework for linguistic annotation.* In: Speech Communication 33(1,2):23–60.

Carletta, J., Kilgour, J., O'Donnnell, T., Evert, S., and Voormann, H. (2003). *The NITE Object Model Library for Handling Structured Linguistic Annotation on Multimodal Data Sets.* In: Proceedings of the EACL Workshop on Language Technology and the Semantic Web (3rd Workshop on NLP and XML, NLPXML-2003). Budapest.

Chamberlin, D., Florescu, D., and Robie, J. (eds.) (2008). *XQuery Update Facility.* W3C Candidate Recommendation 1 August 2008 http://www.w3.org/TR/2008/CR-xquery-update-10-20080801/

Clark, H. (1977) *Bridging.* In: Johnson-Laird P.C. and P.N. Wason (eds.), Thinking: Readings in Cognitive Science, Cambridge University Press, Cambridge: 411–420.

Cowan, J., Tennison, J., and Piez, W. *LMNL update.* In: Proceedings of Extreme Markup Languages 2006, Montreal.

Czmiel, Al. (2004) *XML for Overlapping Structures (XfOS) Using a Non XML Data Model.* In: Proceedings of the Joint Conference of the ALLC and ACH, Göteborg, Sweden.

DeRose, S. *Markup overlap: a review and a horse.* In: Proceedings of Extreme Markup Languages 2004, Montreal.

DeRose, S. J., Durand, D. G., Mylonas, E., and Renear, A. (1990). *What is text, really?* Journal of Computing in Higher Education, ACM Press, 1:3–26.

Dipper, S. and Götze, M. (2005). *Accessing heterogeneous linguistic data – generic XML-based representation and flexible visualization.* In: Proceedings of the 2nd Language & Technology Conference: Human Language Technologies as a Challenge for Computer Science and Linguistics, Poznan:206–210.

Dipper, S., Götze, M., Küssner, U., and Stede, M. (2007). *Representing and querying standoff XML.* In: G. Rehm, A. Witt, and L. Lemnitzer (eds.), Data Structures for Linguistic Resources and Applications. Proceedings of the Biennial GLDV Conference 2007, Gunter Narr Verlag, Tübingen:337–346.

Durusau, P. and O'Donnell, M. B. (2002). *Concurrent markup for XML documents.* In: Proceedings of XML Europe 2002.

Goecke, D. and Witt, A. (2006). *Exploiting logical document structure for anaphora resolution.* In: Proceedings of the 5th International Conference on Language Resources and Evaluation (LREC 2006). Genoa, Italy.

Hilbert, M., Schonefeld, O., and Witt, A. *Making CONCUR work.* In: Proceedings of Extreme Markup Languages 2005, Montreal.

Huitfeld, C. and Sperberg-McQueen, C. M. (2001). *TexMECS: An experimental markup metalanguage for complex documents.* http://xml.coverpages.org/MLCD-texmecs20010510.html.

Karttunen, L. (1976). *Discourse referents.* In: Syntax and Semantics: Notes from the Linguistic Underground, 7:363–385.

Mitkov, R. (2002). *Anaphora resolution.* Longman, London.

Pianta, E. and Bentivogli, L. (2004). *Annotating discontinuous structures in XML: the multiword case.* In: Proceedings of the LREC-Satellite Workshop on XML-based Richly Annotated Corpora. Lisbon 2004.

Piez, W. (2004) *Half-steps toward LMNL*. In: Proceedings of Extreme Markup Languages 2004, Montreal.

Rehm, G., Schonefeld, O., Witt, A., Hinrichs, E., and Reis, M. (2009). *Sustainability of annotated resources in linguistics: a web-platform for exploring, querying and distributing linguistic corpora and other resources*. In: Literary and Linguistic Computing 2009 24(2):193–210.

Renear, A., Mylonas, E., and Durand, D. (1996). *Refining our notion of what text really is: The problem of overlapping hierarchies*. In: N. Ide and S. Hockey (eds.) Research in Humanities Computing. Selected Papers from the ALLC/ACH Conference, Christ Church, Oxford, April 1992, 4:263–280.

Schonefeld, O. and Witt, A. *Towards validation of concurrent markup*. In: Proceedings of Extreme Markup Languages 2006, Montreal.

Schmidt, T. (2004). *EXMARaLDA – ein System zur computergestützten Diskurstranskription*. In: Mehler, A. and Lobin, H. (eds.) Automatische Textanalyse: Systeme und Methoden zur Annotation und Analyse natürlichsprachlicher Texte. Wiesbaden: VS Verlag:203–218.

Simons, G., Lewis, W., Farrar, S., Langendoen, T., Fitzsimons, B., and Gonzalez, H. (2004). *The semantics of markup: mapping legacy markup schemas to a common semantics*. In: Proceedings of the ACL 2004 Workshop on RDF/RDFS and OWL in Language Technology (NLP XML-2004), Barcelona.

Sperberg-McQueen, C. M., Huitfeldt, C., and Renear, A. (2002). *Meaning and interpretation of markup*. In: Markup Languages: Theory & Practice 2.3 (2000):215–234.

Sperberg-McQueen, C. M., Dubin, D., Huitfeldt, C., and Renear, A. (2002). *Drawing inferences on the basis of markup*. In: Proceedings of Extreme Markup Languages 2002, Montreal.

Sperberg-McQueen, C. M. and Burnard, L. (eds.) (2002). *TEI P4: guidelines for electronic text encoding and interchange*. Text Encoding Initiative Consortium. XML Version: Oxford, Providence, Charlottesville, Bergen.

Sperberg-McQueen, C. M. (2006). *Rabbit/duck grammars: a validation method for overlapping structures*. In: Proceedings of Extreme Markup Languages 2006, Montreal.

Stührenberg, M., Witt, A., Goecke, D., Metzing, D., and Schonefeld, O. (2006). *Multidimensional markup and heterogeneous linguistic resources*. In: Proceedings of the 5th Workshop on NLP and XML (NLPXML-2006): Multi-Dimensional Markup in Natural Language Processing. April 4, 2006. Trento, Italy.

Stührenberg, M. and Goecke, D. (2008). *SGF – an integrated model for multiple annotations and its application in a linguistic domain*. In: Proceedings of Balisage: The Markup Conference 2008, Montreal.

Stührenberg, M., Kühnberger, K.-U., Lüngen, H., Mehler, A., Metzing, D., and Mönnich, U. (2008) *Sustainability of text-technological resources*. In: Proceedings of the LREC 2008 Workshop Sustainability of Language Resources and Tools for Natural Language Processing, Marrakech, Morocco:33–40.

Stührenberg, M. and Jettka, D. (2009). *A toolkit for multi-dimensional markup – the development of SGF to XStandoff*. In: Proceedings of Balisage: The Markup Conference 2009, Montreal.

Strube, M. and Müller, C. (2003). *A machine learning approach to pronoun resolution in spoken dialogue*. ACL 03.

Tennison, J. (2007). *Creole: validating overlapping markup*. In: Proceedings of XTech 2007, Paris.

Thompson, H. S. and McKelvie, D. (1997). *Hyperlink semantics for standoff markup of read-only documents*. In: Proceedings of SGML Europe '97, Barcelona.

Trippel, T. Sasaki, F., Hell, B., and Gibbon, D. (2003). *Acquiring lexical information from multilevel temporal annotations*. 8th European Conference on Speech Communication and Technology.

Vieira, R. and Teufel, S. (1997). *Towards resolution of bridging descriptions*. In: Proceedings of ACL/EACL, Madrid.

Webber, B. L. (1988) *Discourse deixis: reference to discourse segments*. In: Proceedings of the ACL:113–122.

Witt, A. (2002). *Meaning and interpretation of concurrent markup*. In: Proceedings of the Joint Conference of the ALLC and ACH, Tübingen, Germany.

Witt, A. (2002). *Multiple Informationsstrukturierung mit Auszeichnungssprachen. XML-basierte Methoden und deren Nutzen für die Sprachtechnologie.* Phd Thesis, Universität Bielefeld.

Witt, A. (2005). *Multiple hierarchies: new aspects of an old solution.* Re-published in: Dipper, S., M. Götze, and M. Stede (eds.) Heterogeneity in Focus: Creating and Using Linguistic Databases. Volume 2 of Interdisciplinary Studies on Information Structure (ISIS), Working Papers of the SFB 632. Universitätsverlag Potsdam, Germany.

Witt, A., Goecke, D., Sasaki, F., and Lüngen, H. (2005). *Unification of XML documents with concurrent markup.* Literary and Linguistic Computing 2005 20(1):103–116.

Witt, A., Rehm, G., Hinrichs, E., Lehmberg, T., and Stegmann, J. (2009). *SusTEInability of Linguistic Resources through Feature Structures.* In: Literary and Linguistic Computing 2009; doi: 10.1093/llc/fqp024.

Chapter 2
Another Extension of the Stylesheet Metaphor

Visualising Multi-Layer Annotations as Musical Scores

Thomas Schmidt

Abstract This paper proposes a method for deriving visualisations of linguistic documents from an encoding of their logical structure. The method is based on an extension of the stylesheet processing metaphor as applied, for instance, in XSLT transformations of XML documents. The paper discusses the method using a piece of discourse transcription in musical score notation as an example for a visualisation and AG and NITE type data models as examples of logical representations of linguistic data. It is argued that this can be generalised to other visualisation types and other data models.

Keywords Transcription · Multilayer annotation · Visualisation · Linguistic annotation

2.1 Introduction

The separation of the logical from the graphical structure of data is a fundamental principle in all application of markup languages. The original reason for this separation lies in the observation that a written document can be more easily and flexibly processed by a computer when the digital representation abstracts over its physical appearance and instead encodes the logical distinctions that motivate this appearance. Various graphical displays can then be derived automatically from the encoding of the logical structure.

The same principle is applied when it comes to digital representations of linguistic data in general. In fact, it seems that not only is it a commonplace that the logical and graphical structures of linguistic data have to be separated, but also that text technological approaches usually consider the former the more important

T. Schmidt (✉)
Special Research Centre (SFB 538) on Multilingualism, University of Hamburg,
Hamburg, Germany
e-mail: thomas.schmidt@uni-hamburg.de

A. Witt, D. Metzing (eds.), *Linguistic Modeling of Information and Markup Languages*, Text, Speech and Language Technology 40,
DOI 10.1007/978-90-481-3331-4_2, © Springer Science+Business Media B.V. 2010

aspect. Thus, for instance, Johannson (1995) states that the approach of the Text Encoding Initiative's Guidelines "focuses on an underlying representation, while acknowledging that this can be transformed for particular processing purposes and display", and Bird and Liberman (2001) also emphasize that their annotation graph framework "focus[es] on the logical structure of linguistic annotations".

As a practical outcome of this one-sided focus, there exist now different elaborate approaches to the encoding of the logical structure of multi-level annotated data, and these approaches greatly facilitate the exchange and the computer-assisted query of linguistic corpora. At the same time, however, the question of how this logical structure can be transformed into a graphical visualisation for the human user has been often neglected. Carletta et al. (2002) allude to this problem:

> Perhaps the toughest and most overlooked requirement is the need for flexible display and interface mechanisms.

It is crucial to note that these display and interface mechanisms have an equally important place in the work with corpora: firstly, good data visualisations are needed for many kinds of *qualitative analyses*. The methodologies of conversation and discourse analysis, for example, rely heavily on the manual study of printed transcripts in which various levels of linguistic analysis are graphically condensed into a single representation (see the example in Section 2.3). Secondly, a human-readable display is perhaps even more indispensable in the process of *data creation*. Wherever manual annotation is required in this process (i.e. almost everywhere except for some simple steps like tokenization and POS tagging), the speed and quality of the result strongly depend on the appropriateness of visualisations in software user interfaces. In the long run, the elaborate frameworks for the encoding of the logical structure of linguistic data will therefore have to be supplemented with equally elaborate frameworks for the display of such data. Carletta et al. (2002) make some detailed suggestions about the properties such a framework should have. In ongoing work in the NITE project, these suggestions have been partly implemented in NXT – "a java program which processes an xml meta-data input file and produces a user interface display" (Kilgour 2003). This approach is closely linked to the NITE Object Model (Evert et al. 2003), and it focuses on display techniques for data creation and annotation.

By backgrounding the concrete underlying data model and focussing on display for data *analysis* rather than data creation, this paper explores the same subject matter from a slightly different angle: it departs from a typical visualisation of a multi-level annotated data set, as it is commonly used in qualitative discourse or conversation analysis. After showing that the underlying logical structure of this graphical display can be represented within different existing text-technological frameworks, the mechanisms by which logical structure is mapped onto graphical structure are analysed. Based on this analysis, an extension of the stylesheet processing metaphor (explained in Section 2.2) is outlined which minimises the programming work for the user and is applicable across different data models and technological environments.

2.2 The Stylesheet Processing Metaphor

In discussing their data model for the encoding of the logical structure of multi-level annotations, Carletta et al. (2002) use the term "stylesheet processing metaphor" to characterize what they see as the best approach for supporting complex linguistic annotation:

> If all we needed were simple display for flat or rigidly hierarchical codes, XML and XSLT would already provide a basic engine for processing linguistic annotation [...] Therefore our proposal is to support the remaining linguistic annotation needs by extension of the stylesheet processing metaphor. [...] For this approach to work, further development is required in two areas: data modelling, and display and interface techniques.

Before exploring in the following sections some of the details of such an extension, the stylesheet processing metaphor itself shall be briefly sketched here. The term refers to the method by which an XML document can be transformed into another document for (among other things[1]) the purpose of displaying it on a computer screen. As Fig. 2.1 illustrates, this process involves five distinct components:

1. In the *input document* (an XML document) the logical structure of the data is encoded;
2. in the *transformation document* (an XSLT document) rules are specified for mapping the elements of the input document (and other documents that conform to the same document structure) onto elements of the output document;
3. the *transformer* (an XSL processor) is a piece of software which is able to interpret the transformation rules and, by applying them to the input document, produces the output document;
4. in the *output document* (often an HTML document) the graphical structure of the data is encoded; and
5. a *viewer* (often a web browser) is a piece of software which is able to interpret the encoding of the graphical structure in the output document and to display it on a screen or on paper.

One convenient feature of the way this is implemented lies in the relation between input document, output document and transformer – the transformation rules are formulated in a declarative way by simply stating which patterns in the input document are to be mapped onto which output elements. The stylesheet writer does not have to concern himself with the way these patterns are found and processed in the input document because this "knowledge" is built into the transformer. Another – often overlooked – convenient feature lies in the relation between output document and viewer. Somebody writing a stylesheet for transforming an XML into an HTML document, for example, need not be concerned with every detail of the physical appearance of the document – for instance, he will usually not have to calculate the precise coordinates of symbols in the visualisation. Instead, he can simply declare the symbol to be a part of (e.g.) a <p> element, and the viewer application (the web browser), using its "knowledge" about font metrics, line-wrapping methods, etc.,

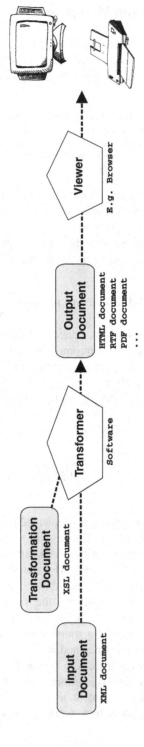

Fig. 2.1 Stylesheet metaphor: processing chain

will take care of computing the horizontal and vertical position where this symbol appears on the screen.

"Extending the stylesheet metaphor" then will mean extending the capabilities of one or several of these components or replacing one or several of them with components that better suit the needs of the task in question. The following sections will explore this in more detail.

2.3 An Example

Figure 2.2 is a typical example of a transcript used in discourse analysis. A researcher familiar with the HIAT transcription system (Rehbein et al. 2004) will be able to read this transcript as a representation of a conversational exchange between two speakers in which several levels of linguistic analysis are contained:

- the temporal structure of the speakers' verbal and non-verbal behaviour is represented in the arrangement of the corresponding descriptions in a "musical score";
- speaker turns are segmented into utterances, words, pauses (represented by two bold dots) and non-phonological material (the "cough" of speaker X);
- utterances are qualified with respect to their speech act qualities,[2] and interrupted utterances are marked as such;
- within utterances, speech act augments (like "well") and repair sequences consisting of a reparandum, an intervention and a reparans (like "I th/" – "ehm" – "I mean") are identified;
- stressed syllables (like "how") are marked;
- for some of the utterances a translation into German is provided.

In text technological terms, then, this is an example of a multi-level annotation, and it is possible to express the logical structure of this excerpt within text-technological frameworks intended for that purpose. Figure 2.3[3] depicts a representation of the data as a set of interwoven hierarchies where some elements in the hierarchy have timestamps. This conforms to the NITE Object Model approach suggested in Evert et al. (2003).

Alternatively, the data set can be thought of as a directed acyclic graph whose nodes represent an abstract timeline and whose arc labels carry the non-temporal information, as shown in Fig. 2.4. Hierarchical structures can then be derived via an inclusion relation between arcs. This conforms to the annotation graph approach suggested in Bird and Liberman (2001).[4]

X [nv]	*left hand up*		
X [v]	Yes, • • sure. But ((cough)) <u>how</u> exactly?		Oh, well!
X [de]	Ja, • • klar.	Aber ((hustet)) wie genau?	
Y [nv]			*Eyebrows raised*
Y [v]		Well, I th/ ehm I mean…I don't know.	

Fig. 2.2 Example of a musical score transcription

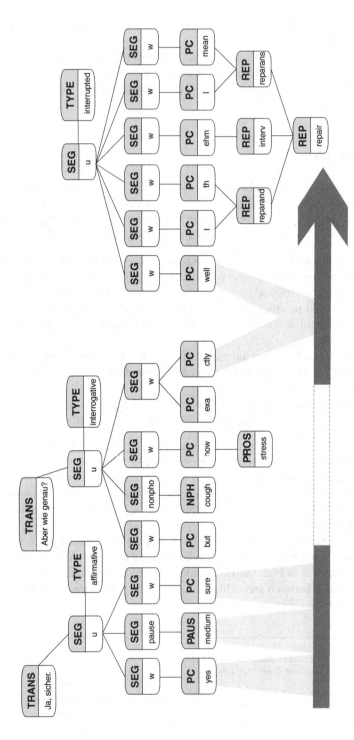

Fig. 2.3 NITE representation of the example

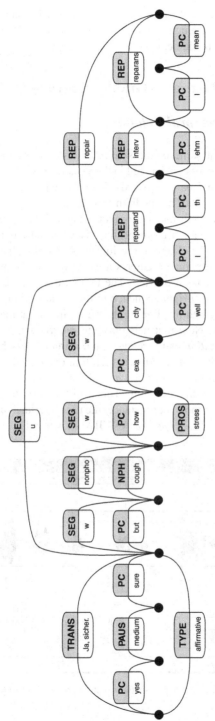

Fig. 2.4 AG representation of the example

With either representation, the question that this paper is concerned with can be reformulated as "How are elements in such a representation of the logical structure of the data set mapped onto elements of the visualisation?"

2.4 Mapping from Logical to Graphical Structure

2.4.1 Mapping of Temporal Relations

A first observation is that some of the symbolic descriptions used in the logical structure reappear more or less unchanged in the visualisation (e.g. the orthographic transcriptions of words and parts of words or the translation string "Ja, sicher.") while others (e.g. the description "medium" for a pause, the prosody description "stress" or the description "affirmative" for an utterance type) do not.

Leaving the latter aside for a moment, the visualisation has a straightforward way of mapping temporal relations in the logical structure to spatial relations in the graphical structure: individual elements are first organised into tiers where no two elements within a tier must overlap. The temporal sequence of two elements is then mapped onto a left-to-right sequence in the visualisation, and simultaneity of two elements is represented by aligning their descriptions at the same horizontal position in different tiers. Note that it is only the *relative* temporal *ordering*, not the *absolute* temporal *duration* that is relevant in this mapping – the actual absolute position of a symbol in the visualisation is therefore calculated only as a function of the typographic extent of its description, not of the absolute temporal duration of the corresponding stretch in the recording. This is different in the user interfaces of many tier-based annotation tools. For instance, the user interface of Praat (like those of the TASX annotator, of ELAN and of ANVIL), shown in Fig. 2.5, uses absolute

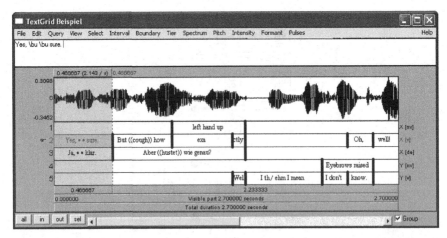

Fig. 2.5 The example in a Praat TextGrid: spatial extent is proportional to temporal duration of described entities

temporal duration to determine the size and position of individual elements in the visualisation.

While this is generally an advantage in the transcription process because it provides the user with an intuitive way of selecting portions of a waveform representation of the signal and assigning symbolic descriptions to them, it may be perceived as a disadvantage in analysis because it makes a continuous reading of connected strings within a tier more difficult.

2.4.2 Mapping of Entity/Feature and Hierarchical Relations

Regarding those symbols from the logical description of the data that do *not* reappear unchanged in the visualisation, the easiest case is that of *iconification*. The medium-length pause in the above example is mapped onto two consecutive bold dots in the visualisation, but otherwise integrates itself into the same logic by which the descriptions of words, etc. find their way into the display (see Fig. 2.6).

From the point of view of computer processing, this is a simple one-to-one mapping of one chain of symbols to another chain of symbols and thus seems to have no effect on the informational or structural properties of the data set. However, there are two reasons why it is an advantage in terms of readability for the human user: firstly, these dots are more easily visually separated from the orthographic transcription of words than a symbol chain like "pause/medium" would be, and the fact that these entities are qualitatively different is thus more easily perceived by the reader.[5] Secondly, by using one dot for a short pause, two dots for a medium pause and three dots for a long pause, HIAT makes the duration of the pause correspond to the length of the symbol chain in the visualisation. Hence, the value of this mapping lies in the fact that it increases *iconicity* – a feature that is irrelevant for computer processing, but important for human processing of the data.

For other entities from the logical description of the data structure, however, the mapping to the visualisation involves something different from a simple iconification. These cases can be subsumed under the notion of *intralinearisation*, distinguishing two subcases: The first is *intralinearisation through formatting* and is applied in the above example for the stress annotated on the phoneme chain "how". In the logical structure of the data, this is an entity/feature relation. In the visualisation, it is mapped onto a linear sequence of symbols (hence: intralinearisation) with a certain formatting property (here: underlining). This is illustrated in Fig. 2.7.

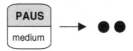

Fig. 2.6 Iconification of an annotation

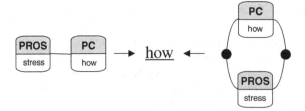

Fig. 2.7 Intralinearistaion through formatting

The other subcase is *intralinearisation through symbol insertion*. This is applied, for instance for the utterance type "affirmative" annotated on the first utterance of speaker X. Again, this is an entity/feature relation in the logical structure of the data which, in this case, is mirrored in the visualisation by appending a symbol (here: a period) to the linear sequence of symbols that describe the annotated entity (here: the phoneme chain "sure"). Figure 2.8 illustrates this.

As Fig. 2.9 illustrates, the same process is applied in the mapping of hierarchical relations: the hierarchical embedding of words and non-phonological segments into utterances, for instance, is represented by marking word boundaries with spaces, putting non-phonological segments into a pair of double brackets (each an intra-linearisation through symbol insertion) and by marking utterance beginnings[6] with capital letters (intralinearisation through formatting) in the visualisation. The same principle is applied in the well-known method of intralinearising phrase structure trees as bracketed symbol sequences (see Fig. 2.10).[7]

Finally, it has to be noted that some entities and relations that can be found in the logical description of the data do not have any correspondent at all in the visu-alisation. For instance, the repair structure, which, in the logical description, is hier-archically decomposed into a reparandum, an intervention and a reparans, is only partially mapped onto the graphical display: only the reparandum is intralinearised through the insertion of a forward slash, the other two elements are not represented at all.[8]

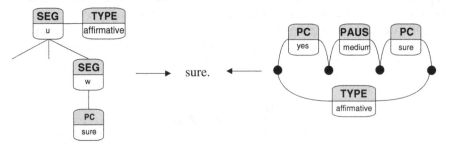

Fig. 2.8 Intralinearistaion through symbol insertion

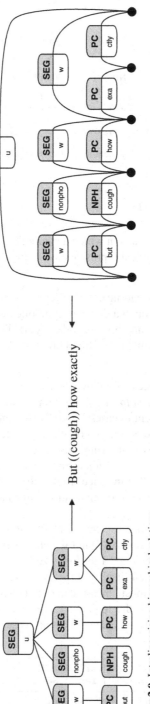

Fig. 2.9 Intralinearising hierarchical relations

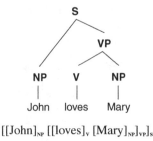

$$[[\text{John}]_{\text{NP}} \, [[\text{loves}]_{\text{V}} \, [\text{Mary}]_{\text{NP}}]_{\text{VP}}]_{\text{S}}$$

Fig. 2.10 Phrase structure tree and equivalent intralinearised symbol sequence

2.5 Transformation Rules

Thus, there are five different ways in which a symbolic description can find its way from the logical into the graphical representation of the data:

1. not at all,
2. unchanged (except for formatting),
3. iconified, i.e. replaced through a different symbolic description,
4. intralinearised through formatting of another symbolic description,
5. intralinearised through symbol insertion before and/or behind another symbolic description.

More generally, these processes all involve a *source element* to be mapped from logical to graphical structure, a *target element* onto which this mapping is applied (identical to the source element in cases 2 and 3, different from it in cases 4 and 5), and an *operation* that is to be performed on the target element (inserting, replacing and/or formatting). I suggest capturing this in declarative transformation rules whose left side specifies the source element and whose right side specifies the target element and the operations. For instance, in the above example, a transformation rule for visualising the utterance-type annotation "affirmative" could be formulated as in Listing 2.1.

This states that for each source element TYPE whose value is "assertive", the "rightmost" target element has to be found which is a PC, a PAUS or a NPH, and that a period (formatted in Serif and 12pt font size – because this happens to be the formatting of the target element itself, see below) is to be appended to this target element. What exactly "rightmost" means can only be specified with respect to the concrete framework by which the logical structure of the data is expressed. The target element to be found in the example, in any case, is the PC whose value is

```
TYPE(assertive)    >    find_right[PC|PAUS|NPH]
                        append['.'] format[Serif; 12 pt]
```

Listing 2.1 Transformation rule for affirmative utterance "sure". Finding this element in a NITE-like system of intersecting hierarchies will involve going up a tree from the source element TYPE to the nearest node that has a PC (or a PAUS or a NPH) as a child and then going down that tree and finding the rightmost of such children. In an AG-like representation, it will mean finding the minimal arc spanning *both* the source element *and* one or more PC, PAUS or NPH arcs and again selecting the rightmost of such arcs.[9] Similar rules can be formulated for the remaining entities and their corresponding visualisations (see Listing 2.2).

Note that in the cases where symbols are iconified or mapped unchanged, the "find" statement is also used, but simply formulated in such a way that the target element will be identical to the source element[10] of the transformation rule.

By applying these rules for each source element onto the corresponding target elements and keeping typing and timing information[11] on the latter, the building blocks of the visualisation given in Fig. 2.11 can be derived (again, considering only a part of the data set for the sake of brevity).

Together with a timeline which linearly orders the start and end tags for the building blocks, this information is almost sufficient for calculating the above visualisation. What remains to be specified is which of these building blocks are to be grouped within a tier. This could be done with a set of rules of the kind given in Listing 2.3 by which the set of visual entities is partitioned into distinct layers.

The actual musical score visualisation can then be conceived of as a two-dimensional coordinate system whose vertical axis contains these layers in a given order and whose horizontal axis corresponds to the ordered timeline. As Fig. 2.12 shows, each building block from the above table is assigned its place in that coordinate system by virtue of its timing and layering information.

```
PC                    >    find_right[PC]
                           format[Serif; 12pt]
TRANS                 >    find_right[TRANS]
                           format[Serif; 10 pt]
PAUS(medium)          >    find[PAUS(medium)]
                           replace['o o'] format[Serif; 12 pt]
TYPE(assertive)       >    find_right[PC|PAUS|NPH]
                           append['.'] format[Serif; 12 pt]
TYPE(interrogative)   >    find_right[PC|PAUS|NPH]
                           append['?'] format[Serif; 12 pt]
TYPE(interrupted)     >    find_right[PC|PAUS|NPH]
                           append['...'] format[Serif; 12 pt]
PROS(stress)          >    find_right[PC]
                           format[underline]
REP(reparand)         >    find_right[PC]
                           append['/'] format[Serif; 12 pt]
SEG (non-pho)         >    find_right[NPH]
                           prepend['(('] append[')) '] format[Serif;      12pt]
SEG(w)                >    find_right[PC]
                           append[' ']
SEG(u)                >    find_left[PC]
                           format[capitalize_initial]
```

Listing 2.2 Transformation rules

Type	Start	End	Symbols	Formatting
PC	T0	T1	Yes_	Serif, 12pt
PAUS	T1	T2	• •	Serif, 12pt
PC	T2	T3	sure._	Serif, 12pt
PC	T3	T4	But_	Serif, 12pt
NPH	T4	T5	((cough))_	Serif, 12pt
PC	T5	T6	how_	Serif, 12pt, underline
PC	T6	T7	exa	Serif, 12pt
PC	T7	T8	ctly?_	Serif, 12pt
TRANS	T0	T3	Ja, sicher.	Serif, 10pt
TRANS	T3	T8	Aber ((hustet)) wie genau?	Serif, 10pt
PC	T7	T8	Well_	Serif, 12pt
PC	T8	T9	I_	Serif, 12pt
PC	T9	T10	th/	Serif, 12pt
...	...	...	...	...

Fig. 2.11 Building blocks for the visualisation

```
Layer[PC,PAUS,NPH](speaker=X)
Layer[TRANS](speaker=X)
Layer[PC, PAUS,NPH](speaker=Y)
```

Listing 2.3 Layering rules

	T0	T1	T2	T3	T4	T5	T6	T7	T8	T9	T10	T11
Group 1												
Group 2												
Group 3												

Fig. 2.12 Building blocks arranged in a musical score coordinate system

2.6 Other Data Sets, Other Visualisations

Although the above rules have only been developed on and illustrated for a specific multi-level annotation set and a specific visualisation, it should be obvious that they are applicable across a wider range of data. Applying the same rules onto a different or larger annotation set in which the same categories are used requires no change in the transformation rules because these rules refer to abstract regularities of the annotation scheme and the display method, rather than to concrete instances of each. Conversely, similar rules could be formulated that produce a different visualisation for the same piece of data. This could be done by using other formatting attributes (e.g. bold or italic font face, different font colours), by inserting different symbols (possibly at other positions), by a different layering (e.g. putting pauses and non-phonological segments onto a separate layer) or simply by making different choices as to which elements are to be included in the visualisation at all.

X:	Yes, • • sure.
	{left hand up} But ((cough)) how exa[ctly]?
Y:	[Well], I th/ ehm I mean…
	{Eyebrows raised} I don't know

Fig. 2.13 Line notation visualisation

However, the suggested visualisation method does not cater for visualisations that use a completely different layout principle for their data, i.e. visualisations that do not use musical score notation, but, for instance, a line notation of type illustrated in Fig. 2.13.[12]

While it is certainly non-trivial to adapt the suggested method to this purpose,[13] the necessary modifications should only concern its second part while the mechanisms for iconification and intralinearisation of symbolic descriptions, and hence the basic transformation rules, should basically remain the same. It is plausible that this also holds for other layout principles.

2.7 Extending the Stylesheet Processing Metaphor

On the basis of a visualisation method like the one depicted here, a first characterisation of a possible "extension of the stylesheet metaphor" (see above) can be attempted. As in the preceding sections, I will regard the structure of the input document as a given, i.e. I will assume that the input document is formulated either as a NITE-like system of intersecting hierarchies or as an AG-like directed acyclic graph. The following sections therefore focus on the remaining four components of the stylesheet transformation process.

2.7.1 Transformation Rules

In introducing their proposal for an extension of the stylesheet metaphor, Carletta et al. (2002) claim that "[…] in [their] experience even people who would consider themselves novice programmers are able to write stylesheets that transform XML into the HTML representation of their choice". In my own experience from ongoing work on EXMARaLDA as well as from introductory student courses in linguistics, this observation is not always confirmed, at least not for every type of stylesheet: while formatting an XML document with a list of CSS[14] statements does indeed seem to be manageable for almost every user, XSL transformations overtax the majority of linguists who do not have a programming background. CSS, of course, owes its comparative simplicity to a very limited expressive power, whereas XSLT offers transformation capabilities like a full-grown programming language at the cost of ease of use. As with data models for the encoding of the logical structure, one challenge in constructing frameworks for display is therefore to find a reasonable compromise between simplicity and expressive power.[15]

The transformation rules in Section 2.5 can be regarded as such a compromise – they are sufficiently expressive to allow for a flexible visualisation of the data, but they do not require the user to know more about programming and data transformations than what the task in question immediately demands, namely to formulate a systematic mapping of entities in the logical structure of the data set to entities in its graphical display. Moreover, the transformation rules as formulated here require no detailed knowledge of the way the logical structure is encoded – while the rules are certainly not completely independent of a specific multi-level annotation framework, it has been argued that they can at least be applied across two different such frameworks. Finally, and in a further contrast to an XML to HTML transformation via XSLT, these transformation rules do not require the user to actually *construct* an output document by completely specifying which output entity of the transformation process is to be placed at which position in the output document's structure.[16] Rather, the user only provides the necessary instructions as to how the building blocks of the visualisation can be derived from the input document and how they are then to be assembled in a general layout structure. As will be shown below, the task of constructing an actual (HTML, PDF, RTF or SVG, etc.) document out of that information is then deferred to later stages of the processing.

2.7.2 Transformer

The simplicity gained by having such easy-to-use transformation rules must be paid for in part with more complex transformer software. Because the transformation rules abstract over the concrete way that the input document is encoded and because they describe a declarative mapping rather than a step-by-step procedure for finding source and building target entities of that mapping, mechanisms for translating these abstract declarative rules into a concrete algorithm for traversing and transforming the input must be built into the transformer. More specifically, this involves:

1. compiling the expression on the left part of a rule as well as the "find left" and "find right" statements on its right side into a query expression suitable for the data model in question;
2. implementing an algorithm that applies this query expression to an input document;
3. implementing an algorithm that applies the replacing, formatting and insertion operations on the target elements;
4. devising a way of calculating and storing intermediate results and the final building blocks of the visualisation; and
5. constructing an output document from these building blocks

Carletta et al. (2002) suggest building a technology for working with complex annotation data on top of existing XML processing mechanisms rather than implementing it from scratch. Similarly, the components of the stylesheet processor outlined here could be realised as an additional layer on top of such an extended XML technology. For instance, the target of the compilation in step (1) could be an expression in the NITE Query language and steps (2) and (3) would then simply consist in using appropriate components of the NITE API with these compiled transformation rules. Likewise, the intermediate and final results of the transformation can be conceived of as additional "formatting" annotations on the input data, expressed by the same means as the "regular" annotations (e.g. as standoff XML elements pointing to their corresponding target elements). The remaining step (5) – the construction of the output document – will be described in the following section.

2.7.3 Output Document and Viewer

One reason for not making the entire construction of the output document a task of the first part of the stylesheet transformation has already been given above – it allows for simpler and hence more user-friendly transformation rules. Another, more technically fundamental reason is, that an appropriate candidate language for describing the graphical structure of a musical score transcript does simply not exist. The salient information – the "building blocks" given at the end of Section 2.5 – for constructing such a visualisation is calculated in the application of transformation rules to the input. Ideally, the resulting output document would then consist of descriptions like the one given in Listing 2.4 in which these building blocks are made part of a <score> element.[17]

Like in the description of a paragraph as a <p> element (see Section 2.2), the viewer software would then take care of calculating the exact coordinates of each of the symbols contained in that description, using its "knowledge" of font metrics and of mechanisms for wrapping musical score transcripts. Unfortunately, neither HTML nor any other widely-used document description language (e.g. RTF, PDF) provide a suitable component for describing such a layout, and, consequently, no viewer is capable of displaying it in the intended way. One possibility to remedy this would be to extend one such language accordingly and to develop a viewer that can process the original language as well as its extension. However this would not only mean that one would have to duplicate many capabilities that are already

```
<score>
<alignmentPoints>
<ap id="T0"/> <ap id="T1"/> <ap id="T2"/> [...]
</alignmentPoints>
   <tier>
      <entity align-start="T0" align-end="T1">Yes, </entity>
      <entity align-start="T1" align-end="T2"> o o </entity>
      <entity align-start="T2" align-end="T3">sure. </entity>
   </tier>
   <tier>
      <entity align-start="T0" align-end="T3">Ja, o o  sicher. </entity>
   </tier>
</score>
```

Listing 2.4 XML representation of a musical score

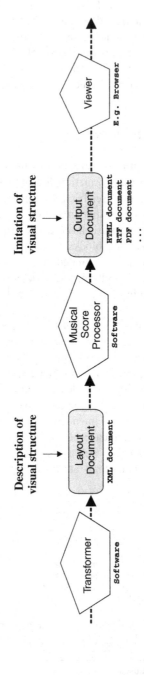

Fig. 2.14 Stylesheet metaphor: Processing chain with an additional step

part of mature commercial applications (like formatting and displaying characters, printing, page numbering), it would also require the user to handle his linguistic data visualisations with a separate tool from his standard (office) applications. In EXMARaLDA (Schmidt 2003, 2004) where the possibility of displaying musical score transcripts has been a basic requirement from the beginning, a different solution has therefore been developed. The result of the transformation from logical to graphical structure is first stored as an XML tree similar to the one in Listing 2.4. After that, an "Interlinear Text processor" software takes this XML tree as an input, calculates absolute coordinates of strings on the basis of their font metrics, performs a wrapping of musical scores where necessary and produces an output document (see Schmidt 2003 for a detailed description of that process). The output document can either be an HTML or RTF document in which the visual structure of the musical score is expressed with the help of blind (i.e. cell-border-less) tables with appropriately spanned cells, or an SVG document in which strings are positioned directly through their absolute coordinates. In either case, the problem of the missing "musical score" element in the output document description language is circumvented by *imitating* a description of the visual structure with the help of existing elements. Standard viewer software (Web-Browsers, MS Word or SVG viewers) can then be used to display or print the resulting document. In terms of the stylesheet metaphor, this can be conceived of as an additional step between transformer and output document, as Fig. 2.14 illustrates.

2.8 Conclusion

The three main points of this paper can be summarized as follows:

Firstly, the relation between a multi-level discourse annotation and its visualisation as a musical score transcript can be thought of as a two step process: The first step consists of a mapping of elements in the logical description of the data onto elements of the visualisation involving three simple operations – iconification, intralinearisation through formatting and intralinearisation through symbol insertion. The second step consists in an arrangement of the resulting building blocks of the visualisation in an abstract layout system. It has been argued that this process can be applied across different approaches to the encoding of the logical structure (NITE and AG), and that its first step will be usable in an identical fashion also for other layout types (like line notation).

Secondly, formulating the rules for such a process can be much simpler than a general XSL-like stylesheet transformation. Ideally, a user defining a visualisation for a given set of data could be largely exempted from thinking about details of the structure of the input document and of the technical specifics of the output document. In that way, the task of writing stylesheets for a given set of data could become manageable for a much wider group of users.

Thirdly, this improved user-friendliness must be achieved by changing or extending the capabilities of different components of the stylesheet transformation process.

This extension can, for instance, consist in building more knowledge of the structure of input documents and of mapping operations into the transformer software, or in putting an additional automated processing step between the transformer output and the display in a viewer application.

Obviously, the relatively specific and restricted procedure outlined here can only act as a supplement, not as a replacement of a more general and powerful approach like the one suggested in Carletta et al. (2002). It is perhaps best thought of as an additional layer of abstraction on top of a framework like NXT. However, from the point of view of user-friendliness – and hence, ultimately, for the way linguists create and work with data – such an additional layer of abstraction might prove important.

Notes

1. As mentioned above, in NITE, the stylesheet metaphor is not restricted to the purpose of *displaying* a document, but also applied for generating interactive annotation interfaces.
2. According to HIAT, standard punctuation symbols (period, question mark, exclamation mark) are used to mark the end point of utterances. The choice of the symbol depends primarily on the utterance mood (assertive, interrogative, exclamative, etc.).
3. Because of spatial limitations, this is only a schematic representation: it leaves out some of the entities contained in the visualisation, e.g. the descriptions of non-verbal behaviour, speaker X's third and speaker Y's second utterance, and it does not assign entities to speakers. The NITE framework, however, would allow for such a complete representation, and the simplifications in this figure are of no consequence for the ideas developed in the remainder of this paper. The following abbreviations are used: PC = "Phoneme Chain", PAUS = "Pause", NPH = "Non-Phonological Segment", SEG = "Segmentation", PROS = "Prosodic annotation", TYPE = "Utterance Type", TRANS = "Utterance-based translation", REP = "Repair sequence". The terms these abbreviations stand for are all defined and discussed in the HIAT transcription convention (Rehbein et al. 2004).
4. Again, this is a schematic representation which does not cover the complete structure of the example. Here too, the missing information could be added by using the same means as the ones illustrated.
5. Conversely, using the dots in the description of the logical structure of the data would usually not be considered a good choice because it is less explicit than using a verbal description.
6. Utterance ends are already marked by the symbol describing their type, see above.
7. Of course, the linear representation of the phrase structure is significantly more detailed and explicit than the linear representation of the utterance-word/nph hierarchy, because it not only marks the boundaries of hierarchy elements, but also includes their labels. The basic principle of mapping the tree onto a linear sequence of symbols, however, is identical in both cases.
8. It would, however, be possible in principal to represent also the other components through an insertion of appropriate symbols. The fact that this is not done is a choice of the transcription system designers and may be based on the assumption that a human reader is able to reconstruct the intervention and the reparans if the end of the reparandum is indicated. Explicitly marking the intervention and the reparans would therefore only mean an unnecessary burden for the reader.
9. In both cases, speaker assignments of nodes and arcs respectively may have to be taken into account. For the sake of brevity, this is disregarded here.
10. Assuming that each node in a NITE representation dominates itself and that each arc in an AG representation spans itself, this is conformant with the above specification of the "find" command.

11. In an AG-like representation, this timing information is a part of any element in the logical description of the data. In NITE-like representations, not all nodes in the hierarchy need have timestamps and it may therefore be necessary to propagate this information through the trees onto the building blocks in question. This propagation mechanism is already a part of the NITE Object Model (see Evert et al. 2003). In both cases, problems may arise when two entities in the annotation cannot be brought into an unequivocal order, i.e. if the resulting timeline is not fully ordered. In Schmidt (2005), I make a detailed suggestion for handling such cases in an AG-like data models, using a mapping of unordered time points onto an ordered predecessor and combining the corresponding symbolic descriptions. Since, however, the problem does not arise for the example used here, I will ignore it for the present discussion.

12. This kind of notation is used in many conversation analytical transcription systems associated with the Sacks / Schegloff / Jefferson school (e.g. GAT – Selting et al. 1998, DT – DuBois et al. 1993). Compared to HIAT's musical score notation transcripts, these transcripts put less emphasis on a precise representation of temporal structure and instead foreground the sequential structure of speakers' utterances or intonational units. For a detailed discussion of the differences in visualisation and the modelling decisions by which they are motivated, see Schmidt (2005).

13. In Schmidt (2005), I suggest an additional step of *grouping* which is similar to the layering described above in that it partitions the smallest entities of the visualisation into distinct groups. In the same way that each tier of a musical score corresponds to a layer, each of these groups then corresponds to a line in the line notation transcript.

14. Cascading Stylesheets – a simple way of assigning formatting to elements in a markup document.

15. Compare this to what Carletta et al. (2002) say about their standoff-annotation approach when opposing it to the AG approach: "The question, then, is whether there is any data model which suffices for most or all linguistic annotation and is less complex than supporting general graph operations." The question discussed here is whether there is a method that is sufficient for most or all visualisation of linguistic annotation, but is less complex than general XSL transformations.

16. Likewise, writing a CSS stylesheet for an XML document does not require the user to think about the resulting HTML document's structure, because this structure will be identical to that of the input document.

17. Once more, this is a schematized depiction. In order to fully represent the result of the transformation process, the character data of each `<entity>` element would have to be given appropriate formatting attributes. This however, could be done with standard HTML means and is therefore not taken into account here.

References

Bird, Steven and Liberman, Mark (2001). A formal framework for linguistic annotation. *Speech Communication*, 33(1,2):23–60.

Carletta, Jean, Isard, Amy, and McKelvie, David (2002). Supporting linguistic annotation using XML and stylesheets. In Sampson, Geoffrey and McCarthy, Diana, editors, *Readings in Corpus Linguistics*. Continuum International, London, New York.

DuBois, John, Schuetze-Coburn, Stephan, Cumming, Susanne, and Paolino, Danae (1993). Outline of discourse transcription. In Edwards, Jane A. and Lampert, Martin D., editors, *Talking Data: Transcription and Coding in Discourse Research*, pages 45–89. Erlbaum, Hillsdale, NJ.

Evert, Stefan, Carletta, Jean, O'Donnell, Timothy, Kilgour, Jonathan, Vögele, Andreas, and Voormann, Holger (2003). The NXT object model. Technical report Version 2.1., IMS, University of Stuttgart.

Johannson, Stig (1995). The approach of the text encoding initiative to the encoding of spoken discourse. In Leech, Geoffrey, Myers, Gregg, and Thomas, Jenny, editors, *Spoken English on Computer: Transcription, Markup and Application*, pages 82–98. Longman, London.

Kilgour, Jonathan (2003). Guide to stylesheet writing in NXT. Technical report, LTG, University of Edinburgh.

Rehbein, Jochen, Schmidt, Thomas, Meyer, Bernd, Watzke, Franziska, and Herkenrath, Annette (2004)Handbuch für das computergestützte transkribieren nach HIAT. *Arbeiten zur Mehrsprachigkeit, Folge B*, 56.

Schmidt, Thomas (2003).Visualising linguistic annotation as interlinear text. *Arbeiten zur Mehrsprachigkeit, Folge B*, 46.

Schmidt, Thomas (2004). Transcribing and annotating spoken language with EXMARaLDA. In *Proceedings of the LREC-Workshop on XML based richly annotated corpora, Lisbon 2004*, Paris. ELRA.

Schmidt, Thomas (2005). *Computergestützte Transkription – Modellierung und Visualisierung gesprochener Sprache mit texttechnologischen Mitteln*, volume 7 of *Sprache, Sprechen und Computerand Computer Studies in Language and Speech*. Peter Lang, Frankfurt a. M.

Selting, Margret, Auer, Peter, Barden, Birgit, Bergmann, Jörg, Couper-Kuhlen, Elizabeth, Günthner, Susanne, Meier, Christoph, Quasthoff, Uta, Schlobinski, Peter, and Uhmann, Susanne (1998). Gesprächsanalytisches transkriptionssystem (GAT). *Linguistische Berichte*, 173:91–122.

Chapter 3
An OWL-DL Implementation of Gold

An Ontology for the Semantic Web

Scott Farrar and D. Terence Langendoen

Abstract An OWL-DL implementation of the General Ontology for Linguistic Description (GOLD) is presented with relevant examples of axioms given throughout. As background, an introduction to Description Logic is presented using examples from linguistics and with particular attention to $\mathcal{SHOIN}(\mathbf{D})$, the logic which most closely relates to OWL-DL. The types of axioms used to develop an ontology in OWL-DL are explained. In addition, a domain independent methodology is given for creating description-logic based ontologies of any kind, not just those for linguistics. Using the $\mathcal{SHOIN}(\mathbf{D})$ notation, the methodology is demonstrated for the linguistics domain with particular attention given to illustrating the use of each type of axiom. Finally, the relevant issues and limitations to linguistic modeling in OWL-DL are discussed.

Keywords OWL-DL · Description logic · Ontology · Language description

3.1 Introduction

The General Ontology for Linguistic Description (GOLD) is an ontological theory for the domain of linguistics. Motivations for an ontological theory for linguistics, including GOLD, have been given elsewhere (e.g. Farrar and Langendoen 2003, Farrar 2007). Minimally, an ontological theory specifies the entities of interest in a given domain. Those entities include classes and their instances along with the relations that hold among those instances. Lightweight ontologies stop there, by providing an enumeration of the classes and a limited number of relations, usually enough to arrange the classes in a taxonomy. A more comprehensive ontology – some do not refer to light-weight ontologies as ontologies at all – places many

S. Farrar (✉)
Department of Linguistics, University of Washington, Seattle, WA, USA
e-mail: farrar@u.washington.edu

This material is based in part upon work supported while Langendoen was serving at the National Science Foundation. Any opinion and conclusions are those of the authors and do not necessarily reflect the views of the National Science Foundation.

A. Witt, D. Metzing (eds.), *Linguistic Modeling of Information and Markup Languages*, Text, Speech and Language Technology 40,
DOI 10.1007/978-90-481-3331-4_3, © Springer Science+Business Media B.V. 2010

more restrictions on the entities in the domain and can serve to facilitate automated reasoning. The logical sentences used to make explicit assertions about the base entities are referred to as **axioms**. That axioms play a crucial role in the design of formal ontologies is well known in the knowledge engineering literature (Niles and Pease 2001, Masolo et al. 2003, among others).

The goal of the current work, then, is to demonstrate how to axiomatize one such ontology, GOLD.[1] The point of the current chapter is not only to present a particular aspect of an ontology for linguistics, but also to explore the limitations of OWL-DL (Smith et al. 2004) with respect to ontological modeling of the linguistics domain. This chapter could be written for any particular domain of inquiry, not just linguistics, to which an ontological theory is applied. However, it is the hope that this chapter, through its use of linguistic examples, will be particularly relevant for linguists who are interested in modeling one aspect of language or another.

As background for this task, Section 3.2 includes an introduction to knowledge engineering and ontologies. This section details the class of logical formalisms known as **description logic** (DL) that has led to the creation of OWL-DL (Horrocks et al. 2003). Included is a discussion of the standard notation for generic DLs and an in-depth look at $\mathcal{SHOIN}(\mathbf{D})$, the description logic which most closely relates to the final OWL-DL implementation. The use of DL notation in this chapter is justified for reasons of brevity, as the XML syntax for OWL-DL is too verbose to present in running text. In addition, a step-by-step methodology for creating an ontological theory is given in Section 3.3. Next in Section 3.4, the methodology for ontology creation is demonstrated using $\mathcal{SHOIN}(\mathbf{D})$ axioms. Finally in Section 3.5, the limitation to ontological modeling in OWL-DL are presented with a discussion on why OWL-DL is a suitable modeling language for certain reasoning tasks.

3.2 Background

In order to understand how GOLD is to be axiomatized, this section presents the relevant background. After a brief introduction to knowledge engineering and ontologies, we give a detailed discussion of the main formalism to be used throughout the paper, namely that of description logic. After an introduction to description logic in general, we give an overview of $\mathcal{SHOIN}(\mathbf{D})$, the description logic which most closely resembles that of OWL-DL. We then present a methodology whereby a knowledge base can be instantiated by using a description logic.

3.2.1 Knowledge Engineering and Ontologies

Knowledge engineering is the task of representing the knowledge of a particular domain in a machine readable format. For a particular knowledge engineering task, the formal language used to represent the knowledge often has far-reaching effects as to what kinds of domain knowledge can be captured by the representation.

Furthermore, the product of knowledge engineering, the knowledge base, can be used in conjunction with automated reasoning tools to produce new knowledge, to prove the consistency of existing knowledge, and to enhance search within the knowledge base. The central assumptions in a knowledge base are captured in the **ontological theory**, or the set of statements that make up the essential knowledge of the domain, in other words, the knowledge that must always hold if the theory is to be coherent. We refer to such sets of statements as simply the *ontology*.

The statements included in the ontology hold according to a particular **conceptualization** of the domain. A conceptualization is an abstract, simplified view of the world (Gruber 1993). Due to the complexity of any real-world domain, a conceptualization is necessarily a simplified approximation of reality. Still, that the conceptualization is approximate does not preclude it from being useful. A major issue in the modeling of the linguistics domain is that various linguistic theories adopt different and often incompatible conceptualizations. In fact, from the standpoint of the ontologist, the aim of science may be cast as the search for the ideal conceptualization. But admittedly, what is meant by "ideal" can vary according to the task at hand. For our task, achieving interoperability over a broad spectrum of language descriptions, we require only that our conceptualization be rich enough to account for differences in various linguistic descriptions. The nature of this task relaxes some of the requirements on the ontological theory. An ontology for all of linguistics is, at this point, unachievable and would require deep consensus as to how language is conceptualized. Still, we will undoubtedly come across descriptions that are incompatible with one another due to different theoretical assumptions, in other words, disparate conceptualizations.

3.2.2 Description Logic

The task of ontology building requires the use of logic as a means of axiomatization. First-order logic (FOL), for instance, is one well understood language for this task and is often employed, in one form or another, for this purpose; see the ontologies of SUMO (Niles and Pease 2001) and DOLCE (Masolo et al. 2003). An alternative to FOL in the design of knowledge-based systems is the class of logics known collectively as **Description Logics** (DLs) (Baader et al. 2003). A DL is a less expressive, but highly structured fragment of first-order logic. Using a DL buys improved computational tractability but at the cost of expressivity. This means that algorithms for working with DLs will be fast, but that expressing certain concepts in a DL might not be possible. This section gives an introduction to this class of logics by discussing some of the key properties of DLs illustrated by examples in typical DL notation. Furthermore, we limit our discussion here to the linguistics domain.

3.2.2.1 Basic Notions and Terminology

A description logic is a formal logic in the strict sense. That is, it has a formal syntax which specifies how to construct well-formed sentences and a formal semantics which relates those sentences to a model. A description logic, as with all formal logics, has an associated proof theory, or a system of how certain entailments follow from a set of sentences. The focus of this section is mainly on the syntactic operations of description logic, but supplemented with an informal discussion of semantics. For a full account of the semantics of description logic, see Baader et al. (2003).

Whereas the predicates in FOL have equal ontological status, those in a DL come in two sorts: **concepts** and **roles**. Concepts in a DL correspond to unary predicates, while DL roles are used in place of binary predicates. What are referred to as constants in a first-order logic are referred to as **individuals** in DL. Intuitively a concept represents a category or kind in the domain being modeled. A concept is a universal notion and can be instantiated by individuals. The relation of **instantiation** holds between concepts and individuals, making an individual an instance of some concept (Nardi and Brachman 2003). Individuals are disjoint from concepts and cannot be instantiated or related by the subsumption relation. A role is a binary relation between individuals. Description logic by definition has only binary relations and, thus, relations of higher arity (e.g. ternary relations) are disallowed. The terms *concept* and *role* show that the origins of description logic lie in the early work on knowledge representation, particularly on **frame-based** languages (Baader et al. 2003). In such languages, information is gathered together into structures called *frames* (structured objects), each particular type of which admits a specified set of possible attributes related by slots (roles).

The terms *concept*, *individual*, and *role* are particular to the body of literature concerning description logics. More general works in ontology and knowledge engineering use *class*, *instance*, and (binary) *predicate*, instead of the DL-specific terms. In the language of OWL-DL, *property* is – confusingly – used in place of binary relation. Though the current work is meant to guide the reader in constructing OWL ontologies, we use DL terminology throughout, mainly for the sake of consistency since logical formulas are given in DL notation.

Within a description logic system, concepts and roles are separated from individuals by partitioning the **knowledge base** into a **TBox** (short for *terminology box*) and an **ABox** (short for *assertion box*, in the sense that assertions are made about a given terminology.). The TBox consists of axioms about the domain in general in the form of logical sentences, while the ABox consists of facts about individuals. A description logic knowledge base KB may be defined minimally as the tuple consisting of a TBox T and an ABox A, i.e. $KB = \langle T, A \rangle$, where T is the union of the set of concepts with the set of roles in the domain, and A is the set of individuals in the domain; furthermore, the TBox also contains axioms relating to concepts and roles, while the ABox contains axioms relating to individuals.

Description logic can be used to represent much more than just basic concepts and individuals. Complex, non-atomic concepts can be specified through logical statements. Statements in a DL differ considerably from those in standard FOL. Moreover, statements in a DL are expressed at the level of predicates, i.e., there are no variables. Thus, axiom (3.1) gives an expression in a DL.

$$\text{InflectedUnit} \equiv \text{GrammarUnit} \sqcap \exists \text{ hasConstituent.InflectionalUnit} \qquad (3.1)$$

This can be glossed as: "The class InflectedUnit is defined as the intersection of the class of GrammarUnit and any class having at least one hasConstituent role whose value is restricted to the class InflectionalUnit." (See Section 3.4.1.2 for a further explanation of this axiom.) Statements in a description logic are therefore formulas containing predicates, technically with one free-variable, but omitted in the syntax. Predicates in a DL represent concepts and roles. Concepts are either **atomic**, i.e. those identified by name and may or may not be defined,[2] or **complex**, i.e. those derived from atomic concepts using a set of **constructors**. The supported concept and role constructors in a particular DL determine its expressive power (Horrocks et al. 2003, p. 6). Thus, the constructors are used to derive well-formed formulas. In the following we have listed some examples of very common constructors in DLs with notes about their respective semantics and how they could be used in an ontology for linguistics. Furthermore, these constructors and others are used to create right-hand side expressions that define anonymous concepts. Any of the expressions below could be placed with a named concept on the left and related with either $\equiv$ or $\sqsubseteq$ (see Section 3.2.2.2 for definition of these symbols).

Conjunction ($\sqcap$)

$$\text{AfricanLanguage} \sqcap \text{EndangeredLanguage} \qquad (3.2)$$

Expression (3.2) can be glossed as "those individuals which are shared between the concepts AfricanLanguage and EndangeredLanguage". Conjunction is interpreted as the intersection of sets of individuals.

Disjunction ($\sqcup$)

$$\text{TenseFeature} \sqcup \text{AspectFeature} \qquad (3.3)$$

Expression (3.3) can be glossed as "the individuals that either belong to the concept TenseFeature or AspectFeature". Disjunction is interpreted as union of sets of individuals.

Negation ($\neg$)

$$\neg \text{PhonologicalUnit} \qquad (3.4)$$

Expression (3.4) can be glossed as "the set of all individuals that are not instances of PhonologicalUnit". Negation is interpreted as the complement of a set of individuals with respect to the universal set of the domain.

Existential quantifier ($\exists$)

$$\exists \text{ hasPart.GrammarUnit} \qquad (3.5)$$

Expression (3.5) can be glossed as "the set of individuals each of which has some member of GrammarUnit as its part." The expression does not limit things other than members of GrammarUnit from being parts. The fact that other entities could be members of GrammarUnit is because of the open-world assumption built into the DL, namely that the domain is not assumed to be complete unless explicitly stated. To make the above description of quantification clear, the following serves to compare a simple DL formula (3.6) with the equivalent in standard FOL (3.7).

$$\exists R.C \tag{3.6}$$

$$\{x \mid \exists y \, R(x, y) \wedge C(y)\} \tag{3.7}$$

Universal quantification ($\forall$)

$$\forall \, \text{hasFeature.MorphosyntacticFeature} \tag{3.8}$$

Expression (3.8) can be glossed as "the set of individuals whose features are *only* individuals of MorphosyntacticFeature". Universal quantification restricts all roles of some concept to be value-restricted by concepts of a certain type. Universal quantification does not ensure that there will be a role that satisfies the condition, but if there are such roles, their ranges have to be restricted to the given type. Again, the following serves to compare a simple DL formula (3.9) with the equivalent in standard FOL (3.10).

$$\forall R.C \tag{3.9}$$

$$\{x \mid \forall y \, R(x, y) \rightarrow C(y)\} \tag{3.10}$$

3.2.2.2 Beyond the Basics

With a brief introduction to description logic out of the way, we now focus on a variety of description logic that is the most useful in constructing an ontology using OWL-DL, namely a description logic called $\mathcal{SHOIN}(\mathbf{D})$. First off, $\mathcal{SHOIN}(\mathbf{D})$ is a notational variant of the OWL-DL language and is derived from a family of description logics referred to as the $\mathcal{SHOIN}(\mathbf{D})$ family. As in the naming of other DLs, the expressive power of $\mathcal{SHOIN}(\mathbf{D})$ is reflected in its name. For example, the S is due to the family's relationship to the modal logic S4 (Horrocks et al. 1999). The other components of the name are to be described as follows: H means that role hierarchies are included; O means that individuals are included; I means that inverse roles are allowed; N means that number restrictions are allowed; and (D) means the optional inclusion of concrete data types. In order to encode knowledge in $\mathcal{SHOIN}(\mathbf{D})$, and eventually in OWL-DL, an understanding of the allowed constructors for $\mathcal{SHOIN}(\mathbf{D})$ is necessary. These, along with the corresponding OWL-DL constructors, are listed in Table 3.1.[3]

An in-depth analysis of OWL-DL in relation to other description logics is given by Horrocks et al. (2003). Also, Horridge et al. (2004) is a very helpful and practical guide to building OWL ontologies in the Protégé environment.

Table 3.1 A comparison of $\mathcal{SHOIN}(\mathbf{D})$ and OWL-DL constructors

Constructor	$\mathcal{SHOIN}(\mathbf{D})$	OWL-DL
conjunction	$C_1 \sqcap C_2$	unionOf(C_1, C_2)
disjunction	$C_1 \sqcup C_2$	intersectionOf(C_1, C_2)
negation	$\neg C_1$	complementOf(C)
oneOf	$\{o_1, \ldots, o_n\}$	oneOf($o_1, \ldots, o_n$)
exists restriction	$\exists R.C$	someValuesFrom(C); onProperty(R)
value restriction	$\forall R.C$	allValuesFrom(C); onProperty(R)
atleast restriction	$\geqslant n R$	minCardinality(n); onProperty(R)
atmost restriction	$\leqslant n R$	maxCardinality(n); onProperty(R)
datatype exists	$\exists R.D$	someValuesFrom(D); onProperty(R)
datatype value	$\forall R.D$	allValuesFrom(D); onProperty(R)
datatype atleast	$\geqslant n R$	minCardinality(n); onProperty(R)
datatype atmost	$\leqslant n R$	maxCardinality(n); onProperty(R)
datatype oneOf	$\{v_1, \ldots, v_n\}$	oneOf($v_1, \ldots, v_n$)

The basic constructors of a DL such as $\mathcal{SHOIN}(\mathbf{D})$ can be used on the right side of either the $\sqsubseteq$ or $\equiv$ symbol to create logical statements of various kinds (see below). The resulting logical statements are the axioms of a DL. A DL axiom may be defined as some restriction on a concept or role. It is an assertion of knowledge using the entities in the ontology; that is, an axiom holds a priori of any knowledge that is later generated using the ontology, at least in a monotonic knowledge system. Which kinds of axioms to include in an ontology is, of course, a major focus of ontological engineering. Axioms in a DL knowledge-based system can be classified according to what objects they describe (TBox or ABox entities) and according to whether or not they are definitional (necessary and sufficient). Based on these criteria, a taxonomy of the various sorts of DL axioms is given in Fig. 3.1, and the remainder of this section explores each sort in turn.

Terminological axioms make statements about entities in the TBox, i.e., concepts and roles, not individuals. Terminological axioms for a given concept can be classified as either necessary or as necessary *and* sufficient conditions to be included in that concept. Terminological axioms that give the necessary conditions for some

- Terminological (TBox) axioms
  - inclusions (necessary)
    * concept inclusions
    * specializations
  - equalities (necessary and sufficient)
    * concept equations
    * concept definitions
- Assertional (ABox) axioms
  - concept assertions
  - role assertions

Fig. 3.1 A taxonomy of DL axioms sorts

concept to be included (subclassed) in another are called **inclusion** axioms. There are two types of inclusions.

The first type of inclusion is simply a **concept inclusion**. A concept inclusion has the abstract form $C \sqsubseteq D$. A concept inclusion states a necessary, but not sufficient, condition for membership in some concept. It can be read as "having property D is necessary for a TBox entity to be included in concept C, but this condition alone is not sufficient to conclude that the object is in concept C". Both C and D can be arbitrary concept expressions. An example of this kind of axiom is given in (3.11).

$$\text{Head} \sqcap \text{Verb} \sqsubseteq \text{MainVerb} \qquad (3.11)$$

The second type of inclusion axiom is a **specialization**, which has the abstract form $A \sqsubseteq C$. This is very similar to that of the inclusion axioms, but specializations are different from concept inclusions because the left-hand side of a specialization must be atomic (hence A). The abstract form can be read as "having properties of concept C is necessary for an entity in order to be included in concept A". Axiom (3.12) is an example of a specialization.

$$\text{SemanticUnit} \sqsubseteq \text{Abstract} \qquad (3.12)$$

A specialization axiom is useful when some concept cannot be defined completely (Baader and Nutt 2003, p. 58). Both sorts of inclusion axioms in a TBox can be viewed as a limited kind of logical implication (Nardi and Brachman 2003, p. 18). Concept inclusion axioms are very important in the structure of the knowledge base as they are used to generate a taxonomy from a set of assertions in a TBox.

Another type of terminological axiom, those concerning concepts and roles, are equalities. A **concept equation** has the general form of $C \equiv D$ as in (3.13):

$$\text{ContentBearingPhysical} \equiv \exists \, \text{expresses.LinguisticSign} \qquad (3.13)$$

This axiom simply states that a ContentBearingPhysical is defined as anything that realizes a LinguisticSign. A special kind of equation is a **concept definition** of the form $A \equiv C$ where the left-hand side is an atomic concept. A concept definition states the necessary and sufficient conditions that must hold in order for a TBox entity to be included in some other concept. Having property C is necessary and sufficient for a TBox entity to be included in concept A. Axiom (3.14) is an example of a concept definition:

$$\text{Language} \equiv \text{SpokenLanguage} \sqcup \text{WrittenLanguage} \sqcup \text{SignLanguage} \qquad (3.14)$$

This can be glossed as "a language is either spoken, written, or signed; there is no other type of language". Axiom (3.14) is furthermore a **covering axiom**, as it guarantees that Language will only have 3 subclasses. Furthermore, a concept definition has the effect of introducing a symbolic name for some constructed concept into the TBox (Baader and Nutt 2003, p. 55).

Finally, axioms that pertain only to individuals are called **assertional axioms**, hence the label ABox. Assertions can either pertain to concepts or roles. A concept assertion is of the form C(I), where C is some concept from the TBox and I is an individual. C(I) means that I is an instance of C. A linguistic example would be (3.15):[4]

$$\text{Noun}(\text{NOUN}123) \qquad\qquad (3.15)$$

A **role assertion** is of the form R(A, B), where R is some role from the TBox and A and B are individuals. R(A, B) means that B is a filler of A for role R. An example of an assertional axiom is given in 3.16.

$$\text{precedes}(\text{NOUN}123, \text{VERB}456) \qquad\qquad (3.16)$$

3.3 Methodology

The development of a knowledge base, including an ontology, is essentially a two-stage process. Figure 3.2 lists these steps specifically for a knowledge base for linguistics that incorporates GOLD as well as linguistic data. The following

1. Design the TBox for the knowledge base.
   (a) Classify entities as concept, role, or individual.
   (b) Add concepts to TBox.
      i. Declare atomic concepts.
      ii. Define non-atomic (constructed) concepts.
      iii. Create concept taxonomy.
      iv. Partition the concept taxonomy.
   (c) Add roles to TBox.
      i. Declare transitive and symmetric roles.
      ii. Declare inverse roles.
      iii. Declare functional roles.
      iv. Add domain and range restrictions to roles.
      v. Add cardinality restrictions to roles.
   (d) Add other axioms to further refine concepts and roles.
2. Populate the ABox with individuals.
   (a) Enumerate and classify each individual according to available concepts.
   (b) Relate individuals via available roles in ontology.
3. Relate TBox and ABox.
   (a) Create enumerated concepts.
   (b) Relate individuals to concepts via roles.

Fig. 3.2 The steps in creating a knowledge base in DL

enumeration is in part adapted from Borgida and Brachman (2003, p. 379). The methodology given here supersedes an earlier version given in Farrar (2007). The steps in the methodology are discussed in detail in the next section.

3.4 Linguistic Modeling in OWL-DL

In this section we discuss the steps in creating a DL knowledge base for the descriptive linguistics domain. We use DL notation as introduced in Section 3.2.2, though the ultimate aim of this section is to act as a guide to creating such a knowledge base in OWL-DL. At issue are the specific kinds of axioms needed to express a wide variety of linguistic knowledge found in the domain. The structure of the current section mirrors the steps in methodology for creating a DL knowledge base listed in Fig. 3.2.

3.4.1 Design the TBox for the Knowledge Base

This step includes developing the basic structure of the ontology. The most important task in creating any ontology is to properly enumerate the entities found in the domain. If the inventory is *ad hoc* or incomplete, then the resulting ontology will not be an accurate conceptualization. The key is to establish a rigid foundation such that later additions will not create problems for the overall theory. We refer to such a foundation as the **upper ontology**. For descriptive linguistics such an upper ontology contains the fundamental knowledge of structure, form, and meaning, that which is usually possessed by a well trained linguist. This, ideally, would include general knowledge that applies to any language or theoretical framework. Examples of general knowledge of this sort are given below:

- A verb is a part of speech.
- A verb can assign case.
- Gender can be semantically grounded.
- Linguistic expressions realize morphemes.

This kind of knowledge is typical of that represented in an ontology in knowledge based systems. The ontology provides the means of formalizing such expressions and defining them in a larger conceptual framework. For example, it provides the means of specifying how a spoken linguistic expression is related to the printed form of a writing system, or how Tense is defined in terms of a temporal calculus.

Of the most fundamental entities that occur in the linguistics domain are the linguistic expressions themselves. The basic entities here are orthographic expressions, spoken expressions, and signed expressions. Other than such concepts that are physical in nature, those occupying time and space, there are the abstract concepts such as the units of grammatical structure, and meaning. As presented in Farrar (2007), these three types of entities are unified under the concept of Sign via a set of relations. From these three fundamental types, the basic units of linguistic analysis can be derived, including concepts such as Glyph, Phoneme, SyntacticCategory, SemanticUnit, etc.

Next, there are the entities that relate the fundamental units to one another. For instance, two expressions can be related via precedence in time and/or space, but also via dominance relations as in grammatical structure. The mereology of such units is a necessary component in the ontology, that is, how units are composed of other units. Consider the example of sound structure. There are the basic phonological entities, in general, PhonologicalUnit, including the concept of Phoneme. Larger phonological units include the PhonologicalWord. Parts of the phonological unit include the Mora. Each level of linguistic analysis with have its own unit types, relations, and theory, in short, its own mereology.

Next, there are more specific entities that may be considered as part of the overall upper ontology, for instance, the various *features* associated with the fundamental units. Features can be phonological, morphosyntactic, syntactic or semantic: MorphosyntacticFeature, SyntacticFeature, PhonologicalFeature, and Semantic Feature. Depending on the level of granularity, the various kinds of features may be divided into subgroups. For instance, TenseFeature and NumberFeature are both kinds of MorphosyntacticFeature.

Finally, there are the various structuring devices used in linguistic analysis. In general, we refer to these as **linguistic data types**. There are several fundamental types, including Lexicon, GlossedText, PhonologicalParadigm, FeatureStructure, StructuralDescription, etc. Each of these data types has its own mereology, e.g. FeatureStructure which is the pairing of a feature name and a feature value.

3.4.1.1 Classify Entities as Concept, Role, or Individual

As discussed in Section 3.2.2.1, a concept in DL represents a category or kind in the domain being modeled. A concept is a universal notion and can be instantiated by individuals. Concepts in a DL, then, are classes of individuals. The binary relations that hold among various individuals are known as roles. The next crucial task in creating the ontology is to decide to which sort each entity in the domain belongs.

In any DL, the most basic distinction is between concepts and roles. Such a decision is perhaps the most intuitive of all modeling decision. This is reflected in how entities are named. That is, it is often possible to simply assign entities to either concept or role based on whether they are named using nouns or verbs respectively, at least in English. For instance, consider the notion feature and the relating of a feature to its value. We may refer to feature simply as Feature, a noun in English and hence a concept. We may refer its having a value as hasValue, as in the DL literature, in which there is a strong tendency to name roles using the word *has* combined with the concept that acts as the range, thus, hasValue, hasPart, hasHead, etc. There are of course problematic cases pertaining to the distinction between concepts and roles. Consider the example where a verb is said to assign case. On the one hand, one could posit the role of assignsCase and include Verb as the domain of the role.

On the other hand, one could use the concept of CaseAssigner, say that pertained to verbs, determiners, etc. to create the complex concept of CaseAssigningVerb. On the one hand "things" have an unchanging essence. A stone is a still a stone even when it is used as a doorstop or a weapon. On the other hand, roles that things play can change depending on the context. At one moment, John may be student of guitar, while at another, he may be a professor of philosophy. In a DL system, it is preferable to limit the number of concepts when possible by using roles that help to extend concepts to form others. For instance, we may enumerate several atomic syntactic categories, e.g. Noun, Verb, Determiner, and then use the role assignsCase to compose complex concepts when needed, such as CaseAssigningVerb, a particular type of case assigner that happens to be a verb. It would be even simpler and more advantageous in a DL to simply use the role assigns. In this way, one could enumerate various categories such as Case, Gender, and Number and use assigns to derive concepts such as GenderAssigningNoun and CaseAssigningVerb.

Next, there is the issue of whether an entity is a concept or an individual. In some cases, the distinction is quite clear. Consider the notions of *Germanic* versus *standard German*. Since we know that there is more than one type of Germanic language, we can feel assured that Germanic is a concept. Likewise, since we know that there is usually only one variety referred to as standard German, we might propose HOCHDEUTSCH as that individual, that is, an instance of Germanic, as in (3.17):

$$\text{Germanic(HOCHDEUTSCH)} \tag{3.17}$$

Problems arise when the domain is conceptualized differently, for instance, when entities such as *Germanic* are treated as individuals, for instance, when reasoning about specific groups of languages is needed. As shown in (3.18), one could introduce the concept of LanguageFamily such that its instances included the individuals such as GERMANIC, TIBETAN, BANTU, etc.

$$\text{LanguageFamily(GERMANIC), LanguageFamily(TIBETAN), \ldots} \tag{3.18}$$

How then does the individual HOCHDEUTSCH relate to individual GERMANIC? Statement (3.17) is no longer allowed. In OWL-DL it is not possible for a concept to be both a class and an instance. One solution to the problem is to introduce another type of role, for instance inFamily, such that LanguageFamily is a concept with GERMANIC as an instance, and HOCHDEUTSCH relates to GERMAN via the inFamily role, summed up in axioms (3.19–3.21):

$$\text{LanguageFamily(GERMANIC)} \tag{3.19}$$
$$\text{LanguageVariety(HOCHDEUTSCH)} \tag{3.20}$$
$$\text{inFamily(HOCHDEUTSCH, GERMANIC)} \tag{3.21}$$

This solution favors the treatment of Germanic as an individual. Note that with this particular conceptualization, there is no need for the concept GermanicLanguage as a subclass of LanguageVariety. Germanic takes its place. Our treatment easily allows for competing classifications of languages since different ABoxes (corresponding to different classification schemes) could be developed from the same TBox (corresponding to the non-controversial knowledge of the field, namely that there are families and varieties, with no specific classification implied).

3.4.1.2 Add Concepts to TBox

Once entities have been classified as concepts, they can now be added to the TBox. There are (potentially) two kinds of concepts and each is treated differently. First, there are concepts that are assumed to exist in the absence of any definitional axioms. These are known as **atomic concepts** and are entered into the TBox using unique names. Next, there may be concepts that are defined in terms of other concepts, referred to as **non-atomic**. For instance, equation (3.22) shows an example of a defined concept.

$$\text{InflectedUnit} \equiv \text{GrammarUnit} \sqcap \exists \, \text{hasConstituent.InflectionalUnit} \qquad (3.22)$$

Thus, an inflected unit is defined in terms of grammar unit and inflectional unit. Specifically, the axiom states that it is not possible for some individual to be an inflected unit with having some inflectional unit as one of its constituents.

With the entities enumerated and classified as one of the three DL sorts, it is now possible to add structure to the ontology by classifying them according to the subsumption relation. Recall that subsumption is a built-in partial-ordering relation – it is reflexive, transitive and anti-symmetric – and is used to form concept and role taxonomies. In a DL, subsumption is a type of inclusion axiom in the form of $A \sqsubseteq B$, where A is subsumed by B. The crucial point at this step is not to misinterpret the intended meaning of subsumption. One common mistake is to interpret subsumption as the part-whole relation. For instance, consider the various phonological concepts: PhonologicalWord, Syllable, Foot and Mora. These can be related via the part-whole relation to form a mereology, such that a Foot is part of a PhonologicalWord, a Syllable is part of a Foot (of course by transitivity, a Syllable is also part of a PhonologicalWord), and a Mora is part of a Syllable (or more precisely a part of a Coda, which is part of a Syllable). It would be a mistake to use subsumption in this manner. Instead, there is some concept, call it PhonologicalUnit, that subsumes all the aforementioned phonological concepts:

$$\text{PhonologicalWord} \sqsubseteq \text{PhonologicalUnit} \qquad (3.23)$$
$$\text{Syllable} \sqsubseteq \text{PhonologicalUnit} \qquad (3.24)$$
$$\text{Foot} \sqsubseteq \text{PhonologicalUnit} \qquad (3.25)$$
$$\text{Mora} \sqsubseteq \text{PhonologicalUnit} \qquad (3.26)$$

The mistake arises from the fact that "is part of", like "is subsumed by", is a partial ordering, but is not reducible to it. Every PhonologicalWord has parts, each of which is a MetricalFoot, as expressed in (3.27).

$$\text{PhonologicalWord} \sqsubseteq \exists \text{hasPart.MetricalFoot} \qquad (3.27)$$

This is distinct from saying that PhonologicalWord subsumes MetricalFoot. If every MetricalFoot is a PhonologicalWord, then it is correct to say that PhonologicalWord subsumes MetricalFoot, but that is very different from saying that every PhonologicalWord is made up of at least one MetricalFoot.

Partition the Concept Taxonomy

The next step is to create partitions in the concept taxonomy. A partition ensures that two or more concepts never share individuals; such concepts are referred to as **disjoint**. If A and B are disjoint, then $A \sqcap B \equiv \bot$ must be true. In other words, the set formed by the intersection of two or more disjoint concepts will always be empty. Partitioning the domain is one way to speed up certain reasoning tasks, since in a DL concepts are assumed to overlap unless stated otherwise. As a linguistic example, consider the case of WrittenExpression versus SpokenExpression versus SignedExpression. These three concepts may never share individuals since a given linguistic expression can never exist in more than one physical form at the same time. The spoken word "dog", the written word *dog*, and the sign for *dog* are all different entities. The three forms may be related in a regular way – the word *dog* definitely relates to its spoken counterpart – but no conceptualization allows for more than one simultaneous mode of being such as this. Thus, axioms (3.28), (3.29) and (3.30) are necessary to handle the linguistic example:

$$\text{SpokenExpression} \sqcap \text{WrittenExpression} \equiv \bot \qquad (3.28)$$
$$\text{SpokenExpression} \sqcap \text{SignedExpression} \equiv \bot \qquad (3.29)$$
$$\text{SignedExpression} \sqcap \text{WrittenExpression} \equiv \bot \qquad (3.30)$$

And finally, to ensure that there can be no other kind of Expression, we include the covering axiom (3.31):

$$\text{Expression} \equiv \text{SpokenExpression} \sqcup \text{WrittenExpression} \sqcup \text{SignedExpression} \quad (3.31)$$

3.4.1.3 Add Roles to TBox

The next step is to add roles to the TBox. At this step, there are several issues to be addressed in order to properly characterize a role. First, roles in a DL can be classified as transitive. An example of a transitive role from the linguistics domain is the hasConstituent, holding among syntactic units. If *A* has constituent *B* and *B* has constituent *C*, then *A* also has constituent *C*.

It is also possible to declare roles as symmetric, as in translationOf since if A is a translation of B, presumably B is a translation of A. Likewise, many lexical relations are also symmetric: antonymOf, synonymOf, etc. The relation of agreement, denoted by agrees, is another example of a symmetric relation. An example of a role that is neither transitive nor symmetric would be the hasValue role that relates a feature to its value.

With a number of roles in place, the inverses of roles should now be declared. Inverse roles simply serve to express the opposite relation between two individuals. For instance, consider the relationship between two forms, one with inflection and one without. The role inflectedForm could be used to relate the base form to the inflected form, while baseForm could be used for the inverse. There is no need to state further axioms for the inverse, since inflectedForm is already defined. Other examples include linear ordering relations in morphology such as follows and precedes.

It is possible to add domain and range restrictions to roles thereby restricting a given role to taking particular concepts as its domain and particular concepts as its range. Axiom (3.32), for instance, limits the range of hasHead to only individuals of type SyntacticWord.

$$\top \sqsubseteq \forall \, \text{hasHead.SyntacticWord} \qquad (3.32)$$

Note the use of $\top$. This symbol means that for anything in the knowledge base, the range of hasHead must be filled with a SyntacticWord. However, leaving the domain and range values open is often advantageous. Consider the part-whole relations with respect to morphosyntactic structure. It would be useful to have a single relation hasConstituent that could hold between any complex structure and its constituent. We might want this relation to pertain to both syntactic units and morphological units. If we declared strict domain and range constraints then we would need a different relation in each case, something like hasMorphConstituent and hasSynConstituent. But by leaving the domain and range constraints open, we can get by with using hasConstituent. Other axioms such as (3.33) may be added to constrain its use:

$$\text{Phrase} \sqsubseteq \exists \, \text{hasConstituent.SyntacticWord} \qquad (3.33)$$

Cardinality restrictions place restrictions on the number of particular kinds of relationships a concept may participate in. For instance, language endangerment could be defined (albeit simplistically) as any language that has no more than 2,000 speakers.

$$\text{EndangeredLanguage} \equiv \text{Language} \sqcap \, \leqslant 2000 \, \text{hasSpeaker} \qquad (3.34)$$

Roles may also be arranged into a taxonomy to add structure to the TBox. This is useful when there are several roles, for example, that share the same range. Consider the various kinds of syntactic roles that hold between constituents and the main clause: hasPredicate, hasSubject, hasObject, etc. We might say that there is a single role, say syntacticRole, that subsumes all of these:

$$\text{hasPredicate} \sqsubseteq \text{syntacticRole} \tag{3.35}$$

$$\text{hasSubject} \sqsubseteq \text{syntacticRole} \tag{3.36}$$

$$\text{hasObject} \sqsubseteq \text{syntacticRole} \tag{3.37}$$

The result of adding the above axioms is a role taxonomy, much like the concept taxonomy discussed earlier. In practice, role taxonomies will not be as detailed as those for concepts.

3.4.1.4 Add Other Axioms to Further Refine Concepts and Roles

The next step is to establish role restrictions on concepts, that is, to assert how individuals of particular concepts are related via roles. Such relations can be asserted using either the existential or the universal role restriction. An example using the existential is that any morphosyntactic feature must have at least one value that is a morphosyntactic value.

$$\text{MorphosyntacticFeature} \sqsubseteq \exists \, \text{hasValue.MorphosyntacticValue} \tag{3.38}$$

In order to ensure that some feature does not have any other type as its value, then the right-hand side of (3.38) must be augmented as in (3.39):

$$\text{MorphosyntacticFeature} \sqsubseteq \ldots \sqcap \forall \, \text{hasValue.MorphosyntacticValue} \tag{3.39}$$

Thus, equation (3.39) combines the existential with the universal to achieve a tighter restriction and can be glossed as "a morphosyntactic feature must have at least one morphosyntactic value as its value (the existential) and only morphosyntactic values can be related to morphosyntactic feature via the hasValue role (the universal)". If the universal were used by itself, then it would be possible for a feature *not* to have a value. The existential-universal combination, then, is a common design pattern used in ontology engineering with OWL-DL (Horridge et al. 2004).

The part-whole relationship has already been introduced with reference to mereology. Part-whole relationships apply in a straight-forward manner to phonological and morphosyntactic structure. For instance, constituency structure can be spelled out by using axioms such as (3.40):

$$\text{SyntacticPhrase} \sqsubseteq \exists \, \text{hasContituent.SyntacticWord} \tag{3.40}$$

This axiom states simply that syntactic phrases must have at least one syntactic word as a constituent.

3.4.2 Populate the ABox with Individuals

The next step is to instantiate the various concepts and thereby populate the knowledge base, in fact the ABox, with individuals. This step includes enumerating the individuals, sorting them, and finally asserting knowledge about each individual.

3.4.2.1 Enumerate and Classify Each Individual According to Available Concepts

This step concerns adding concrete data to the schema knowledge contained in the knowledge base. An obvious example is to add all the known language varieties to the concept of LanguageVariety. A single statement such as (3.41) is required for each introduction and classification of an individual.

$$\text{LanguageVariety}(\text{OLDENGLISH}) \tag{3.41}$$

The task of determining exactly what are the language varieties that exists is of course contentious. In general, the TBox should contain universal (or widely accepted) knowledge, while the ABox should be dedicated to that which may be contested. In general, the TBox/ABox separation represents the split between general linguistic knowledge and that pertaining to individual languages, the latter of which is usually more contested. For example, although the fact that Hopi has an ImperfectiveAspect and that English and Greek both have a PastTense constitute linguistic knowledge (perhaps widely held, general knowledge), this kind of knowledge can be differentiated, as it only pertains to specific languages and, thus, is better placed in the ABox as individuals. The drawback is that this would lead to an explosion in the number of individuals required for even an ontology that included a relatively small number of languages: HOPIPASTTENSE, ENGLISHPASTTENSE, GREEKPASTTENSE, . . .

3.4.2.2 Relate Individuals via Available Roles in Ontology

With the axiomatization in the TBox in place, it is a relatively straightforward procedure to assert knowledge about individuals, for instance to relate each individual language to the country where it is spoken:

$$\text{spokenIn}(\text{MANDARIN}, \text{CHINA}) \tag{3.42}$$

$$\text{spokenIn}(\text{MANDARIN}, \text{CANADA}) \tag{3.43}$$

3.4.3 Relate TBox and ABox

The final step in the methodology is to relate the TBox to the ABox by introducing mixed axioms that contain all three logical sorts: concepts, roles and individuals.

Mixed axioms can be formed in a number of ways, for instance by relating a concept with the enumerated set of its individuals or by relating specific individuals to concepts using roles.

3.4.3.1 Create Enumerated Concepts

Enumerating a concept's individuals is useful when there is a need to tie a concept absolutely to a specific set of individuals, meaning that the set is not likely to change. For instance, when enumerating the values of some morphosyntactic system for a given language and these values are well-agreed upon, an enumerated concept could be used as follows:

$$\text{TenseSystem} \equiv \{\text{DISTANTPAST, HODIERNALPAST, PRESENT}\} \qquad (3.44)$$

This axiom fully defines TenseSystem by stating its necessary and sufficient conditions, namely, an enumeration of its individuals. Put another way, TenseSystem is equivalent to the set of the three given individuals.

3.4.3.2 Relate Individuals to Concepts via Roles

Finally, it is possible to use an individual to place a narrow restriction on a given class. Assuming that the individual NULL represents the absence of phonetic material, a linguistic expression with no phonetic component, a zero morpheme could be defined as any morpheme that is expressed by the null element.

$$\text{ZeroMorpheme} \equiv \exists \, \text{expressedBy}.\{\text{NULL}\} \sqcap \text{Morpheme} \qquad (3.45)$$

Secondly, individuals can be defined by relating them to concepts via roles.

$$\{\text{VERB123}\} \sqsubseteq \exists \, \text{hasSyntRole.Agent} \qquad (3.46)$$

The above axiom states that the specific verb VERB123 must have an agent as one of its syntactic roles.

3.5 Limitations and Tool-Related Issues

3.5.1 The Fundamental Types

The first issue to be discussed is whether or not the fundamental predicate types – concepts (classes), roles (properties), and individuals – are adequate for linguistic modeling.[5] For concepts, there is little difference between a language such as OWL-DL and first-order ontology modeling languages like SUO-KIF. Concepts within an OWL-DL taxonomy behave in the expected way, structured by the partial-ordering relation of subclassOf, the most common built-in relation among concepts in OWL-DL. This causes little issue and even multiple inheritance is allowed. When a concept is subsumed by two or more other concepts, then all of the individuals of the subsumed concept are members of each parent concept. But what does it mean to be a member of a concept?

OWL-DL interprets an individual as being a member of a particular concept. Here, concepts are interpreted as sets. Set theory is a powerful modeling device used extensively in mathematics and formal concept analysis. In basic set theory, the fundamental notions of union, intersection, and subset play a key role. Furthermore, the mathematical notion of set membership should not be confused with instantiation. Gangemi et al. 2001 use the following example to illustrate the difference between set membership and instantiation. Consider two possible interpretations of "Socrates is a man":

1. Socrates belongs to the class of all human beings;
2. Socrates exhibits the property of *being a man*;

Then:

> Usually, in mathematics, the two views are assumed to be equivalent, and a predicate is taken as coinciding with the set of entities that satisfy it. This view is however too simplistic, since in Tarskian semantics set membership is taken as a basis to decide the *truth value* of property instantiation, so the former notion is independent from the latter. The existence of a mapping between the two relations does not justify their identification: one thing is a set, another thing is a property common to the elements of a set. (Gangemi et al. 2001, p. 3)

As noted, a concept may simply be declared, be defined using other concepts and constructors, or be defined by an enumeration of its members. It is worth mentioning that the last method is not found, for example, in SUO-KIF.

Turning to individuals, these are, as expected, instantiations of concepts and can be used in ABox and mixed axioms, much in the same way as in FOL ontologies. The main difference is the presence of the TBox and ABox which places concepts and individuals in separate parts of the knowledge base. It would seem that individuals are not really a part of the ontology. In general, however, it should be noted that ontologies may include not only concepts and relations, but also individuals. Therefore, in the design of a knowledge base, its ontology will, technically speaking, contain statements of the TBox and of the ABox variety. Some description logic literature uses the term *ontology* to refer only to the TBox itself. In the modeling of linguistics, individuals such as GERMAN or SWAHILI are undeniably part of the ontological landscape. To sum up, even though description logics refer to the TBox as the ontology, the ontology of a given domain can and should include individuals as well.

Turning to the last DL sort, roles, it is clear that OWL-DL places the restriction on its relations in that only binary relations are allowed. Thus, it is impossible to express a fact summarized as, "feature F carries value V in feature system S," in a ternary predicate such as:

$$carries(F, V, S) \tag{3.47}$$

Instead, one possibility would be to say that the feature has some value and that the pairing of a the feature with the value belongs to a feature system. Thus, it is the pairing itself, the predication, that is included in the feature system. However, it is not possible to predicate over relations using binary roles. A statement cannot itself be related to another entity via a role relation. This is not surprising considering that OWL-DL is a subset of FOL which itself does not permit such reification of predications. Otherwise, it would not be "first order". The closest that one could hope in a DL account of such a statement would be to include axioms summarized as "feature F has value V and that F is related to system S.

$$hasValue(F, V) \tag{3.48}$$
$$inSpec(F, S) \tag{3.49}$$

This issue is that pairings of features and values cannot be related within feature systems, at least not directly. Such statements about which features can bear which values are crucial, however, to many linguistic theories and should be dealt with.

Before leaving the discussion of the three basic sorts, it should be noted that roles can be grouped into hierarchies. In practical ontology building, such hierarchies are of little use and may only complicate the modeling process.

3.5.2 *Justification for Using OWL-DL*

OWL is actually a family of languages: OWL-Lite, OWL-DL, and OWL-Full. OWL-DL is a compromise of expressive power and tractability. The expressive power of OWL-Lite is low, e.g. it does not include the possibility of using quantification, and is not adequate for the complexities of a knowledge-based system for linguistics. On the other hand OWL-Full is known to be undecidable and not practical for currently available reasoning systems, in part due to the possibility of predicating over concepts, not just individuals. This means that OWL-DL is compatible with a number of inferencing engines, including the RACER (Haarslev and Möller 2001) or Pellet (Sirin et al. 2007) reasoning system. In fact, "OWL-DL was carefully crafted to remain decidable" just for that purpose: implementation (Horrocks et al. 2003, p. 18).

In addition, due to the recent interest in description logic formalisms triggered by their intended application within the Semantic Web, there are now an increasing number of authoring and other related utilities available. One very popular ontology editor and visualization tool is *Protégé* (Noy et al. 2001, Knublauch et al. 2004).[6] Protégé is particularly useful as it has the ability to create and store ontologies in various formats, including OWL, DAML+OIL, UML, and other XML-based formats. Although not initially intended as a reasoner front-end, Protégé now comes packaged with the FaCT++ and Pellet reasoners. The most important function of these reasoners is that of consistency checking.

Finally, OWL now has a number of different serialization formats, including XML/RDF, OWL/XML, OWL Functionaly Syntax, and the Manchester OWL Syntax. These serializations are endowed with a fixed set of data types inherited from XML Schema and RDF (Smith et al. 2004). Especially in the context of creating an infrastructure for linked linguistic data Berners-Lee 2006, XML/RDF syntax of OWL conforms to best-practice recommendations for data portability (Bird and Simons 2003). That is, the XML/RDF version of OWL is good candidate for interoperability, at least in terms of the format, with linguistic data also in XML/RDF.

Notes

1. All references to GOLD are based on the version found at http://www.linguistics-ontology.org/
2. Concepts that are never defined are referred to as *primitive* concepts.
3. In the table D is assumed to be a built-in data type and not a declared concept.
4. As a convention, individuals are given in small-caps and sometimes with an arbitrary number, e.g. NOUN123.
5. Recall the OWL-DL terminology for concept and role, given here in parenthesis.
6. The latest version of the Protégé tool is available for free at http://protege.stanford.edu/

References

Baader, Franz, Calvanese, Diego, McGuinness, Debora L., Nardi, Daniele, and Patel-Schneider, Peter (2003). *The Description Logic Handbook*. Cambridge University Press, Cambridge.

Baader, Franz and Nutt, Werner (2003). Basic description logics. In Baader, F., Calvanese, D., McGuinness, D.L., Nardi, D., and Patel-Schneider, P.F., editors, *The Description Logic Handbook*, chapter 2, pages 47–100. Cambridge University Press, Cambridge.

Berners-Lee, Tim (2006). Linked data. Published electronically at: http://www.w3.org/DesignIssues/LinkedData.html.

Bird, Steven and Simons, Gary F. (2003). Seven dimensions of portability for language documentation and description. *Language*, 79:557–582.

Borgida, Alex and Brachman, Ronald J. (2003). Conceptual modeling with description logics. In Baader, F., Calvanese, D., McGuinness, D.L., Nardi, D., and Patel-Schneider, P.F., editors, *The Description Logic Handbook*, chapter 10, pages 349–372. Cambridge University Press, Cambridge.

Farrar, Scott (2007). Using 'Ontolinguistics' for language description. In Schalley, Andrea and Zaefferer, Dietmar, editors, *Ontolinguistics: How ontological status shapes the linguistic coding of concepts*, pages 175–191. Mouton de Gruyter, Berlin.

Farrar, Scott and Langendoen, D. Terence (2003). A linguistic ontology for the Semantic Web. *GLOT International*, 7(3):97–100.

Gangemi, Aldo, Guarino, Nicola, Masolo, Claudio, and Oltramari, Alessandro (2001). Understanding top-level ontological distinctions. In *Proceedings of IJCAI 2001 workshop on Ontologies and Information Sharing*.

Gruber, Thomas R. (1993). A translation approach to portable ontology specifications. *Knowledge Acquisition*, 5(2):199–220.

Haarslev, Volker and Möller, Ralf (2001). RACER system description. In *International Joint Conference on Automated Reasoning (IJCAR'2001)*, number 2083 in Lecture Notes in Computer Science, pages 701–712, Springer-Verlag, Berlin.

Horridge, Matthew, Knublauch, Holger, Rector, Alan, Stevens, Robert, and Wroe, Chris (2004).
   A practical guide ot building owl ontologies using the protégé owl plugin and CO-ODE tools,
   edition 1.0. Technical report, The University of Manchester and Stanford University.

Horrocks, Ian, Patel-Schneider, Peter F., and van Harmelen, Frank (2003). From SHIQ and RDF
   to OWL: The making of a web ontology language. *Journal of Web Semantics*, 1(1):7–26.

Horrocks, Ian, Sattler, Ulrike, and Tobies, Stephan (1999). Practical reasoning for expressive
   description logics. In Ganzinger, H., McAllester, D., and Voronkov, A., editors, *Proceedings
   of the 6th. International Conference on Logic for Programming and Automated Reasoning
   (LPAR'99)*, number 1705 in Lecture Notes in Artificial Intelligence, pages 161–180, Springer-
   Verlag, Berlin.

Knublauch, Holger, Musen, Mark A., and Rector, Alan L. (2004). Editing description logic ontologies with the Protégé OWL Plugin. In *Proceedings of Description Logics 2004*.

Masolo, Claudio, Borgo, Stefano, Gangemi, Aldo, Guarino, Nicola, and Oltramari, Alessandro
   (2003). Ontologies library (final). WonderWeb Deliverable D18, ISTC-CNR, Padova, Italy.

Nardi, Daniele and Brachman, Ronald J. (2003). An introduction to description logics. In Baader,
   F., Calvanese, D., McGuinness, D.L., Nardi, D., and Patel-Schneider, P.F., editors, *The Description Logic Handbook*, chapter 1, pages 1–40. Cambridge University Press, Cambridge.

Niles, Ian and Pease, Adam (2001). Toward a standard upper ontology. In Welty, C. and Smith, B.,
   editors, *Proceedings of the 2nd International Conference on Formal Ontology in Information
   Systems (FOIS-2001)*, Ogunquit, Maine. Association for Computing Machinery.

Noy, Natalya F., Sintek, Michael, Decker, Stefan, Crubezy, Monica, Fergerson, Ray W., and Musen,
   Mark A. (2001). Creating Semantic Web contents with protege-2000. *IEEE Intelligent Systems*,
   16(2):60–71.

Sirin, Evren, Parsia, Bijan, Grau, Bernardo Cuenca, Kalyanpur, Aditya, and Katz, Yarden (2007).
   Pellet: A practical owl-dl reasoner. *Journal of Web Semantics*, 5(2):51–53.

Smith, Michael K., Welty, Chris, and McGuinness, Deborah L. (2004). Owl web ontology language
   guide. W3C Recommendation 20040210, W3C. http://www.w3.org/TR/owl-guide/.

Chapter 4
Markup Languages and Internationalization

Felix Sasaki

Abstract The success of the markup language XML is partly due to its internationalization capabilities. "internationalization" means the readiness of a product or a technology for an international market and users with different languages, cultures and cultural preferences. The aim of the paper is threefold. First, it introduces aspects of internationalization found within the XML standard itself, like the support of the Unicode character encoding. Second, it demonstrates specific benefits of XML-related technologies for users with internationalization and localization needs. That includes technologies like ITS and XLIFF which are used within the localization industry. Third, the paper discusses current and future topics of Web internationalization, with XML as the backbone of a yet to come truly multilingual web. These three aspects are presented in relation to other areas of information modeling which are part of this volume.

Keywords Internationalization · Localization · Standardization · ITS

4.1 Introduction: What Is Internationalization?

A common definition of "internationalization" (see Ishida and Miller 2006) is the process of preparing a product or its underlying technology ready for applications in various languages, cultures and regions. The acronym of Internationalization is used as "i18n" because there are 18 characters between the first character "i" and the last character "n".

Closely related to internationalization is "localization", which is the process of adapting a product and technology to a specific language, region or market. Sometimes in software localization, this target of localization is referred to as a "locale". The acronym "l10n" is used because there are ten characters between the first character "l" and the last character "n".

F. Sasaki (✉)
University of Applied Sciences Potsdam, Potsdam, Germany
e-mail: felix.sasaki@fh-potsdam.de

A. Witt, D. Metzing (eds.), *Linguistic Modeling of Information and Markup Languages*, Text, Speech and Language Technology 40,
DOI 10.1007/978-90-481-3331-4_4, © Springer Science+Business Media B.V. 2010

An example for the relation between internationalization and localization, from the world of programming languages, is the Java class "resourceBundle". It allows for gathering locale specific information like calendars or currencies. The fact that Java provides "resourceBundle" means that the programming language has been "internationalized". Localization then means to use a "resourceBundle", for example to adapt a user interface to a locale. For proper localization, it is important that aspects of internationalization are taken into account as soon as possible in the process of product or technology design. Otherwise expensive reverse engineering might be necessary.

Sasaki (2005) and Phillips (2006) demonstrate that internationalization is not a specific feature, but a requirement for software design in general. "Software" can be a text processor, a web service – or a linguistic corpus and its processing tools. For each design target, there are different internationalization requirements.

For linguistic corpus data, issues of "internationalization" are rarely discussed. This is due to the fact that aspects of internationalization are often hidden underneath technologies which are the basis of linguistic research and applications development. The currently most prominent example of such a technology is XML (eXtensible Markup Language). Today XML is *the* standardized representation format for a great variety of linguistic data, encompassing textual corpora or lexica, but also multimodal annotations or speech corpora. The contributions to this volume give more details on aspects of these kinds of linguistic resources.

In the design of monolingual "linguistic corpora", the internationalization features of XML and related standards are often used just "as is", without further reflection. If then an existing corpus design is to be reused for languages not foreseen, or a multilingual corpus has to be created, the reverse engineering mentioned above might become necessary.

Taking this "hidden status" of internationalization issues in linguistic corpora into account, the purpose of this article is twofold:

- it explains how to avoid problems related to internationalization in the design of XML-based, linguistic corpora, and
- it shows what benefit linguistic research can gain from existing and new internationalization related standards.

In the center of interest are internationalization issues of the markup language XML and related technologies. There is a variety of internationalization related issues which are relevant for processing marked-up, textual data. This paper will discuss them in a "bottom up" view on marked-up documents, starting with the textual data itself:

- Characters: issues of encoding, visualization and processing (Section 4.2)
- Language identification (Section 4.3)
- Markup for internationalization and localization purposes (Section 4.4)

It will be assumed that the design target is a "multilingual, XML based textual corpus". The corpus should contain existing and yet to be created data in various languages.

A conclusion will be given in Section 4.5.

4.2 Character Related Issues

4.2.1 Creating a Corpus: Character Encoding Issues

In the past, multilingual corpora like the Japanese, English and German data in Verbmobil (Wahlster 2000) have been created relying only on the ASCII character repertoire. Today the usage of the *Unicode* (Aliprand et al. 2005) character repertoire is common sense, for corpus and many other kinds of textual data. The Basic Multilingual Plane of Unicode encompasses characters from many widely used scripts, which solves basic problems of multilingual corpus design.

Quite often, the names *ISO/IEC 10646* and Unicode are used in similar contexts. The former standard is developed and published jointly by the organisations ISO and IEC, the latter by the Unicode Consortium. ISO/IEC and the Unicode Consortium define the same character repertoire and encoding form. In addition, the Unicode Standard adds information which partly will be explained below, like character properties, character equivalence and normalization specifications, a normative algorithm for bidirectional text and various other implementation information.

Using Unicode does not solve all problems. Still various decisions have to be made for corpus creation: what encoding form is suitable, how characters not in Unicode are handled, or how to deal with "glyph" variants.

The encoding form is the serialization of characters into a given base data type. The Unicode standard provides three encoding forms for its character repertoire: UTF-8, UTF-16 and UTF-32.[1] The most widely used encoding form is UTF-8. If the multilingual corpus contains only Latin based textual data, UTF-8 will lead to a small corpus size, since this data can be represented mostly with sequences of single bytes. If corpus size and bandwidth are no issues, UTF-32 can be used. However, especially for web based corpora, UTF-32 will slow down data access. UTF-16 is for environments which need both efficient access to characters and economical use of storage. Finally, the aspect that an XML processor must be able to process "only" UTF-8 and UTF-16, and not necessarily other encoding forms, should be taken into account when deciding about the appropriate encoding form.

Unicode encodes widely used scripts and unifies regional and historic differences. Such differences are described as *glyphs*. Unicode unifies many glyphs into singular characters. The most prominent example for the unification of glyphs is the *Han unification*, which maps multiple glyph variants of Korean, Chinese and Japanese into a single character repertoire.

For a multilingual corpus, glyphs characteristics might be quite important. Diachronic glyph variants and rarely used scripts have nearly no chance of becoming a part of the Unicode character repertoire. As one solution to the problem, Unicode provides "variation selectors" which follow a graphic character to identify a (glyph related) restriction on the graphic character.[2] However, it is impossible to have one collection of variation sequences which satisfies all user communities' needs.

A different solution would be the encoding of variants as characters. However, Unicode is an industrial consortium, and minority scripts and historical scripts have a small lobby. This makes it difficult for corpus data in such scripts to be represented in Unicode. Fortunately, the *Script Encoding Initiative*[3] has been founded to support proposals to the Unicode consortium for the encoding of rarely used scripts and script elements.

For those who want to use new characters without waiting for standardization, the *Text Encoding Initiative* (TEI) provides a means to represent non-standard characters and glyphs with markup. The following figure exemplifies the definition of two variants which are similar to the character *r*. For each glyph variant there is a `glyph` element with information about the name, character properties and a graphical representation. These elements can be referenced by their `xml:id` attributes, as is demonstrated in the text passage below.

The example demonstrates only a simple application of the TEI for dealing with non-standard characters and glyphs. The interested reader may be referred to Chapter 5 of the TEI guidelines.[4]

```
1   <charDecl>
2    <glyph xml:id="r1">
3     <glyphName>LATIN SMALL LETTER R WITH ONE FUNNY STROKE</glyphName>
4     <charProp>
5      <localName>entity</localName>
6      <value>r1</value>
7     </charProp>
8     <graphic url="r1img.png"/>
9    </glyph>
10   <glyph xml:id="r2">
11    <glyphName>LATIN SMALL LETTER R WITH TWO FUNNY STROKES</glyphName
       >
12    <charProp>
13     <localName>entity</localName>
14     <value>r2</value>
15    </charProp>
16    <graphic url="r2img.png"/>
17   </glyph>
18  </charDecl>
19
20  <p>Wo<g ref="#r1">r</g>ds in this
21  manusc<g ref="#r2">r</g>ipt are sometimes
22  written in a funny way.</p>
```

4.2.2 Visualizing a Corpus: Bidirectional Text

In this section, the scope of multilingual corpus design is narrowed to corpora with scripts written from right to left, like Arabic and Hebrew. For each character, Unicode has a property called "directionality" in its repertoire. This property is used by the bidirectional algorithm (Davis 2005) to support appropriate order in text visualization. If a corpus contains only one script, the bidirectional algorithm assures proper visualization. As an example, HTML (Raggett et al. 1999) uses Unicode as the document character encoding and the HTML visualization order of the source code "HEBREW" (if written in the Hebrew script) will be "WERBEH".

However, the Unicode bidirectional algorithm needs help in certain cases of mixed scripts sequences:

```
1  Source code:
2    engl1 ''HEBREW2 engl3 HEBREW4'' engl5
3  Visualization a):
4    engl1 ''2WERBEH'' engl3 ''4WERBEH'' engl5
5  Visualization b):
6    engl1 ''4WERBEH engl3 2WERBEH'' engl5
```

In the example, the source code can be visualized as (a), an English text with two Hebrew citations, or (b), an English text with a Hebrew citation, which itself contains an English citation. Without further information, the Unicode bidirectional algorithm will create visualization (a). The reason is that the algorithm works with *embedding levels* of mixed script texts. It works best if there is just one level, and that leads to visualization (a), that is Hebrew text embedded in English text. To achieve visualization (b), we need to indicate that there is another embedding level: English text contains Hebrew text which contains English text.

For indicating the borders of a new embedding level, there are two methods. First, Unicode control characters can be used. They are inserted as shown below to indicate the borders of the new embedding level needed for visualization (b).

```
1    engl1 ''*U+202B*HEBREW2 engl3 HEBREW4*U+202C*'' engl5
```

In texts with markup, an attribute like @dir (for "directionality") in HTML can produce the same effect. The value rtl indicates the new directionality level right-to-left.

```
1    engl1 ''<span dir=''RTL''>HEBREW2 engl3 HEBREW4</span>'' engl5
```

The source code with plain text encompasses 27 characters. The source code with markup encompasses 25 characters. To avoid such influence of directionality indicators on e.g. word length queries, using markup is highly recommended.

Such directionality issues are only one example of the relation between Unicode and markup languages: markup often provides features similar to those provided by Unicode characters in plain text. Another example of such overlap is the relation between *interlinear annotation characters* versus Ruby markup (see for more information about Ruby Section 4.4.1 and Sawicki et al. 2001). The interlinear annotation characters should not be used if Ruby markup is available, since that markup provides additional formatting information. Another example of overlapping functionalities is the indication of line breaks via characters versus e.g. the HTML br element. Using characters for this purpose is not recommended since it would lead to a duplication of information.

Dürst and Freytag (2003) discuss such topics in detail and provide guidelines for other kinds of characters which conflict or sometimes do not conflict with markup.

In the area of mixed scripts sequences, the guideline for processors, e.g. a browser visualizing mixed scripts sequences, is to ignore the Unicode characters and to enhance the bidirectional algorithm only with information provided via markup. The guideline for encoders, e.g. an editing tool or human editors of such sequences, is to replace the characters with markup.

4.2.3 Processing Textual Corpus Data

As the corpus is created and can be visualized, the next step is processing of character data. The following processes will be discussed in this section: Counting, normalization and collation sensitive ordering.

The notion of "counting characters" varies across technologies. In the Java programming language, regular expressions in Java count character borders: Java takes the beginning of an input sequence into account, even if it is empty. In contrast, XML Schema (Biron and Malhotra 2004) counts "only" characters. Hence, given the empty input sequence " " and the regular expression "a?", there will be a match in Java, but not in XML Schema.

For comparison of character sequences, there are two prerequisites. First, the strings have to be in the same encoding. This is not a trivial requirement if massive corpus data is gathered from the Web. Emerson (2006) describes character encoding detection issues for such tasks.

Second, characters have to be in the same *normalization form*. Normalization is the process of bringing two strings to a canonical form before they are processed. This is necessary because some character encodings allow multiple representations for the same string. An example: The character "LATIN SMALL LETTER C WITH CEDILLA" can be represented in Unicode as a single character with the code point "U+00E7" or as a sequence "U+0063 U+0327". It is obvious that for example a search will provide unforeseen results, if normalization is not assured.

It is not possible to guarantee that all strings in all XML documents are, in fact, normalized, or that they are normalized in the same manner. There may be implementations of processes like comparisons that operate on not normalized strings and others that implicitly normalize strings before processing them. The XML Query language XQuery (Boag et al. 2005) provides at least a function `normalize-unicode`, which a user can apply "manually" to assure a normalization form.

Normalization of text and string identify matching for XML and related technologies is not fully standardized yet. Current proposals are described in detail in the "Character Model for the World Wide Web 1.0: Normalization"(Yergeau et al. 2005).

The last process discussed for characters is ordering based on *collations*. A collation is a specification of the manner in which character strings are compared and ordered. A simple collation is a code point based collation. It is used for example as the default collation in XPath 2.0 functions (Berglund et al. 2005), which is also applied in XQuery. "Code point based" means that strings are compared relying on the order given by the numeric identifiers of code points. More enhanced collations take *locale* specific information into account.

An example for locale specific collations are the ordering defined for German lexicons, versus German phone books. In the lexicon the *Umlaut characters* ä, ö and ü are sorted together with "a", "o" and "u" respectively. In the phone book the Umlaut characters are sorted as if they were spelled "ae", "oe" and "ue".

4.3 Language and Locale Identification

The topics of comparisons and collations naturally lead to language and locale identification. In the example above, the same language is given (German), but two different collations need to be applied (phone book versus lexicon).

It is crucial to have proper language identification within corpus meta data standards like IMDI (Wittenburg et al. 2000) or OLAC (Simons and Bird 2003). But language identification is also useful for glyph identification mentioned above, i.e. to separate language and region specific differences for a HAN character.

Corpora being created with XML can make use of the attribute *xml:lang*. It supplies language values in the format described by RFC 3066 (Alvestrand 2001) or its successor.[5] "RFC 3066 or its successor" can (and should) also be referenced in a different way, as BCP 47 (Phillips and Davis 2006b). BCP 47 (the "Best Current Practice 47") is always represented by the most recent RFC for language identification. Currently, these are RFC 4646 (Phillips and Davis 2006c) and RFC 4647 (Phillips and Davis 2006a).[6] These will be described in the following section.

4.3.1 Structure of the Language Tags

RFC 4646 and RFC 4647 are compatible with RFC 3066:[7] an RFC 4646 language tag has constraints defined in RFC 4646 to differentiate between various types of subtags: script, region, variant, extension and privateuse.

The various subtags have the following meaning.

The primary language subtag (2 or 3 letters, 4 letters or 5–8 letters) indicates the language in accordance with ISO 639-1 (two letter) or ISO 639-2 (three letter). Three letter subtags immediately following the primary subtag are called "extlang". These are reserved for values from ISO 639 part 3. An example of a language subtag with an ISO 639-1 value is "de", meaning "German". An example of an ISO 639-2 value is "alt", meaning "Southern Altai". An example of an ISO 639-3 value is "ain", meaning "Ainu (a language in Japan)".

```
1   langtag = (language
2     ["-" script]
3     ["-" region]
4     *("-" variant)
5     *("-" extension)
6     ["-" privateuse])
```

The differences between these three parts of ISO 639 (there are three more parts not yet integrated into BCP 47) is the number of codes and the application area. ISO 693-1 encompasses around 180 codes and was developed for applications in linguistics, terminology and lexicography. ISO 639-2 encompasses around 480 codes and is used for terminology but also for libraries. ISO 639-3 is intended for a comprehensive identification of languages and provides by far the largest list of language codes, currently more than 6900 languages. That includes for example also codes for dialects like Kölsch "ksh".

The script subtag (4 letters) indicates script or writing system variations, in accordance with ISO 15924. An example of a language tag including a script subtag is "ja-latn", meaning "Japanese written with the Latin script".

The region subtag (2 letters or 3 digits): 2 letters indicate country, territory, or region, in accordance with ISO 3166, part 1. This subtag fulfills the same role as the 2-letter second subtags in RFC 3066. 3 digits indicate region information in accordance to UN "Standard Country or Area Codes for Statistical Use" within the region subtag. An example of a subtag is "de-DE", meaning "German in Germany".

The variant subtag (starting with a letter: at least 5 characters; starting with a digit: at least 4 character) indicate variations not associated with an external standard. These must be registered in the IANA subtag registry (see below). An example is "de-DE-1996", meaning "German written in Germany, using the German orthography introduced in 1996)".

The extension subtag (introduced by a single character subtag) indicates an extension to RFC 4646. RFC 4646 defines mechanisms how such extensions must be registered, which encompasses e. g. the creation of an RFC document about the extension. An example is an extension introduced by "r": "en-Latn-GB-r-extended-sequence-x-private".

Finally, the privateuse subtag (introduced by "x") indicates a private agreement.

RFC 4646 defines also a registry called "IANA language subtag registry". It contains not whole language tags, but subtags. All language tags defined already for RFC 3066, and all subtags currently (and in the future) available in the underlying ISO standards are part of this registry. RFC 4646 introduces two conformance criteria for language tags: "well formed" versus "valid". The former checks the syntax defined above, the latter checks in addition conformance to the language subtag registry.

As an addition to the structure of language tags and a registry for subtags defined in RFC 4646, RFC 4647 supplies mechanisms for matching values. These encompass the matching types "filtering" (zero or more least specific language tags match) versus "lookup" (exactly one, i.e. the most specific language tags match).

4.3.2 Language Tags and XML Based Corpora

RFC 4646 has been designed carefully to fulfill both the needs of the linguistic corpus design and other application areas. The main means for language identification of linguistic corpora is ISO 639 part 3.[8] Its aim is the creation of identifiers for all human languages. As said above, this is in contrast to ISO 639 part 1, which focuses on identifiers necessary for terminology and lexicography, and part 2, which focuses on identifiers for terminology and bibliography. Part 3 allows for distinguishing extinct, ancient, historic and constructed languages. RFC 4646 is currently being updated, and the new RFC will take ISO 639 part 3 into account.

The W3C Internationalization Activity is working on a document about language and locale identifiers in internet based scenarios.[9] It has two purposes. First, it will provide a common set of identifier (values), which is necessary for any reliable processing of distributed (language) resources. Here the document will mainly rely on RFC 4646.

Second, the document will provide "best practices" for the distinction of language versus locale. These concepts are closely related, but still different. A locale is important for processing e. g. of dates, times, numbers, or currencies. It is also relevant for linguistic related processing, like the mentioned sort-order (collation). An example of the difference between language and locale was given above for German ordering conventions (telephone book versus lexicon): Both are conventions for the German language, but with different ordering preferences. Linguistic processing may also rely on the script. It is for example necessary to differentiate Romanized, transliterated Japanese from Japanese in its mainly used version which combines four scripts. Locale definitions can also effect text boundaries (character, word, line, and sentence), or text transformation definitions (including transliterations).

The reason that only "best practices" are being created is that a normative differentiation between language and locale seems to be impossible. Sometimes language is in the core of locale, as in the collation examples above. But sometimes language is not present at all, for example if the time zone or currency are mostly relevant. Hence, the best practices describe only a more or less stable set of user preferences which are commonly encompassed by a locale.

4.4 Internationalization Tag Set

The purpose of the "Internationalization Tag Set" (ITS 1.0, see Lieske et al. 2007) is to provide a set of elements and attributes for common needs of XML internationalization and localization. Various examples of such needs have been described in the previous sections: For example, HTML defines an attribute for directionality, or the working draft for language and locale identifiers defines locale specific information. ITS gathers these state of the art definitions, to enable their application in existing or emerging XML vocabularies.

4.4.1 ITS: General Approach

ITS encompasses various *data categories* for internationalization and localization and their implementation in XML. The separation of data categories versus their implementation is made to allow for a great variety of usage scenarios, which will be described below. ITS is currently a working draft. A first version of ITS will be finalized in the near future.

The following data categories are covered in the ITS specification:

- "Translate" conveys information about whether a piece of textual content in a document should be translated or not.
- "Directionality" conveys the directionality information which is beneficial for visualization of text with mixed directionality.
- "Terminology" indicates terms and is used to add reference information to external resources like terminology data bases.
- "Localization Note" provides a means to add information necessary for the localization process to the localizer.
- "Ruby" is used to provide pronunciation or further information, in compliance with the W3C Ruby specification (Sawicki et al. 2001).
- "Language Information" is used to specify that a piece of content is of a language, as defined by RFC 4646.
- "Elements Within Text" describes the relation of elements to the textual flow and is necessary for example to provide basic text segmentation hints for tools such as translation memory systems.

More and more textual data is being created in XML based formats. Hence, many of these data categories have direct relevance for the language resource community which deals with such formats. For example, Senellart and Senellart (2005) describe a methodology to pass information to machine translation tools on the translatability of textual content in XML document. ITS can be used to define such information.

4.4.2 Local Implementation of ITS Data Categories

The simple, so-called "local" implementation of the data category "Translate" is an attribute its:translate with the values yes or no. It can be attached to any element in an XML document:

```
1  <text its:translate="no" ...> ... <p its:translate="yes">..."</p>
2  </text>
```

The attribute expresses information about elements, including child elements and textual content, but excluding attributes. The value of this definition is to have a common agreement on the scope and the values of the data category "Translate", and a unique attribute in a unique XML namespace.

4.4.3 Global Implementation of ITS Data Categories

The "local" implementation of ITS data categories is used locally in XML documents. In contrast, there is a "global" usage of data categories, which is independent of a specific position:

```
1  <its:rules>
2    <its:translateRule selector="//p" its:translate="yes"/>
3    <its:termRule selector="//qterm"/>
4  </its:rules>
```

In the rules element, there is an element `translateRule` for the "Translate" data category. It contains an attribute `selector`. Its value is an XPath expression which selects in the example all `p` elements. The second attribute `translate='yes'` expresses that these attributes are translatable.

For XML-based, linguistic corpora, global usage of ITS is important for the preparation of a variety of processes. For example, the application of a term data base can make use of global rules which define that a specific name in an XML vocabulary is used to mark up terms. Or the "Translate" data category can be used to differentiate translatable and non-translatable text as input for (semi-)automatic machine translation, as described above.

There is an additional usage of global rules which is important for the combined reuse of a variety of markup schemes.

```
1  <its:rules>
2    <its:langRule selector="//*" langPointer="@someAttribute"/>
3  </its:rules>
```

In the example, it is assumed that a document contains attributes with language information. The `selector` attribute again selects nodes, as in the examples before. The "pointer" attribute at the "langRule" element is used to specify the element or attribute on which the information is available.

```
1  <text someAttribute="en-US"> ... </text>
```

Given these global rules and the example document above, the value of the `someAttribute` attribute are interpreted as language values. The value of ITS global rules here is that they specify a common semantics for markup: In the ITS specification, it is defined that the `someAttribute` attribute value has the meaning of RFC 4646. The benefit is that there is no need to change existing markup to specify this semantics. This is identical to the aim of Simons et al. (2004), see also the contribution of Farrar and Langendoen in this volume. The difference is that Simons et al. (2004) rely on an RDF representation of markup semantics, while the ITS approach uses an XML representation.

4.4.4 Relation to Other Standardization Efforts

ITS is related to various existing standards and standardization efforts. This concerns especially TMX (Savourel 2005) and XLIFF (Savourel and Reid 2003). TMX is used to allow easier exchange of translation memory data. The goal of XLIFF is to align data from source and target language(s).

Both of these formats are important *during* the localization process. In contrast, ITS is necessary to assure "localizability" itself: Its aim is to provide proper internationalization, as a requirement for successful localization. From the perspective of XML-based linguistic corpora, ITS is not meant as a part of a corpus processing scenario. It is rather a means to prepare (large sets of) documents, e. g. to be able to use the same processes of language values for heterogeneous markup schemes.

4.5 Conclusion and Outlook

This paper demonstrated that markup languages have internationalization related aspects on various levels, starting from character encoding, going through character processing and language information, to markup for internationalization and localization purposes. These aspects are of relevance for XML based, multilingual linguistic corpora, but also for XML applications in general.

From the perspective of other contributions to this volume, the aspects of internationalization presented in this paper can be reviewed as follows:

- Aspects related to characters (encoding, visualization, processing) are often characterized as "low level issues". Nevertheless they need to be taken into account for representation and processing of textual corpora as presented e.g. by Kim et al., or for visualization. Visualization is a topic for Schmidt, who discusses this for musical scores in multi-layer annotations. An interesting question would be what requirements are to be fulfiled for visualization of multi-layer annotations with mixed scripts text.
- Aspects related to language identification are of importance for markup projects on a "higher level". The reason is that results and the underlying algorithms for many approaches in the areas of information extraction (see again Kim et al.) or document and discourse relation analysis (see Stede et al. and Lobin et al.) may differ depending on the language of the data in question. For modeling linguistic resources like lexicons, see Trippel in this volume, a proper implementation of language information provided by the standards described in Section 4.3.1 is helpful in multilingual application scenarios.

- Finally, the topic area of markup for internationalization and localization purposes is important for the contributions to this volume mentioned above under the aspect of "data reuse". Here, the approach of ITS 1.0 to map existing markup to new interpretations could be the basis of data reuse. Hypertext Conversion related projects as in the contributions of Lenz and of Storrer may also benefit from these techniques, since ITS 1.0 provides a layer of indirection between markup in various formats and a pivot format for the conversion.

To put this differently, often internationalization issues are important for basic issues of the *representation* of markup and (mostly textual) data. However, it can be expected that the aspects of *data modeling, data reuse* and *data integration* will play a more and more important role in internationalization in the future. Often the projects presented in this volume can provide answers to questions imposed by multilingual data. But maybe in some cases the "application domain" of multilingual data can formulate requirements and provide solutions which contribute to general aspects of linguistic modeling of information and markup languages.

Notes

1. UTF-8 encodes characters as sequences of a variable length: one, two, three or four bytes. UTF-16 uses variable sequences of one or two double bytes. UTF-32 is a character serialization with a fixed length of four bytes.
2. See the Ideographic Variation Database http://unicode.org/reports/tr37/ as an application of these selectors.
3. See http://www.linguistics.berkeley.edu/sei/ for further information.
4. See http://www.tei-c.org/release/doc/tei-p5-doc/html/WD.html for further information.
5. There is no means in XML for validating that this attribute contains RFC 3066 compliant values. However, many applications built on top of XML rely on these values and execute the necessary processing.
6. Currently, a successor of RFC 4646 is under preparation, see http://tools.ietf.org/html/draft-ietf-ltru-4646bis for further information.
7. Since the XML specification defines language values in terms of RFC 3066 or its successor, RFC 4646 values are also covered by xml:lang.
8. See http://www.sil.org/iso639-3/ for further information.
9. A draft document can be found at http://www.w3.org/International/core/langtags/

References

Aliprand, J., Allen, J., et al., editors (2005). *The Unicode Standard. Version 4.0.* Addison-Wesley, Boston.

Alvestrand, H. (2001). Tags for the Identification of Languages. Technical report, IETF. http://www.ietf.org/rfc/rfc3066.txt.

Berglund, A., Boag, S., et al. (2005). XML Path Language (XPath) 2.0. W3C Canidate Recommendation. Technical report, W3C. http://www.w3.org/TR/xpath20/.

Biron, P. V. and Malhotra, A. (2004). XML Schema Part 2: Datatypes Second Edition. W3C Recommendation. Technical report, W3C. http://www.w3.org/TR/xmlschema-2/.

Boag, S., Chamberlin, D., et al. (2005). XQuery 1.0: An XML Query Language. W3C Candidate Recommendation. Technical report, W3C. http://www.w3.org/TR/xquery/.

Davis, M. (2005). The Bidirectional Algorithm. Unicode Standard Annex #9. Technical report, Unicode Consortium. http://www.unicode.org/reports/tr9/.

Dürst, M. and Freytag, A. (2003). Unicode in XML and other Markup Languages. Technical report, W3C and Unicode Consortium. http://www.w3.org/TR/unicode-xml/.

Emerson, T. (2006). Large Corpus Construction for Chinese Lexicon Development. In *Proceedings of the 29th Internationalization and Unicode Conference*, San Francisco.

Ishida, R. and Miller, S. (2006). Localization vs. Internationalization. Article of the W3C i18n Activity. http://www.w3.org/International/questions/qa-i18n.

Lieske, C. and F. Sasaki (2007). Internationalization Tag Set (ITS) 1.0. W3C Recommendation. Technical report, W3C. http://www.w3.org/TR/its/.

Phillips, A. (2006). Internationalization: An Introduction. In *Proceedings of the 29th Internationalization and Unicode Conference*, San Francisco.

Phillips, A. and Davis, M. (2006a). Matching of Language Tags. Technical report, IETF. http://www.ietf.org/rfc/rfc4647.txt.

Phillips, A. and Davis, M. (2006b). Tags for Identifying Languages. Technical report, IETF. http://www.ietf.org/rfc/rfc4647.txt.

Phillips, A. and Davis, M. (2006c). Tags for Identifying Languages. Technical report, IETF. http://www.ietf.org/rfc/rfc4646.txt.

Raggett, D., Hors, A. Le, and Jacobs, I. (1999). HTML 4.01 Specification. W3C Recommendation. Technical report, W3C. http://www.w3.org/TR/html401.

Sasaki, F. (2005). Internationalization is everywhere. *ACM Ubiquity*, 6. http://www.acm.org/ubiquity/issues6.html.

Savourel, Y. (2005). TMX 1.4b Specification. Technical report, Localisation Industry Standards Association (LISA). TMX 1.4b Specification.

Savourel, Y. and Reid, J. (2003). XLIFF 1.1 Specification. Technical report, OASIS. http://www.oasis-open.org/committees/xliff/documents/xliff-specification.htm.

Sawicki, M., Suignard, M., et al. (2001). Ruby Annotation. W3C Recommendation. Technical report, W3C. http://www.w3.org/TR/ruby/.

Senellart, P. and Senellart, J. (2005). SYSTRAN Translation Stylesheets: Machine Translation driven by XSLT. In *Proceedings of XML Conference 2005*, Atlanta.

Simons, G. and Bird, S. (2003). OLAC Metadata. Technical report, SIL International and others. http://www.language-archives.org/OLAC/metadata.html.

Simons, G. F., Lewis, W. D., et al. (2004). The Semantics of Markup: Mapping Legacy Markup Schemas to a Common Semantics. In *Proceedings of Coling 2004*, Geneva.

Wahlster, W., editor (2000). *Verbmobil: Foundations of Speech-to-Speech Translation*. Springer, Berlin.

Wittenburg, P., Broeder, D., and Sloman, B. (2000). EAGLES/ISLE: A Proposal for a Meta Description Standard for Language Resources. In *Proceedings of LREC 2000*, Athens.

Yergeau, F., Dürst, M., et al. (2005). Character Model for the World Wide Web 1.0: Normalization. W3C Working Draft. Technical report, W3C. http://www.w3.org/TR/charmod-norm/.

Chapter 5
Identifying Logical Structure and Content Structure in Loosely-Structured Documents

Manfred Stede and Arthit Suriyawongkul

Abstract Text documents are structured on (at least) two separate levels: The "logical" structure is largely reflected in the layout (headlines, paragraphs, etc.), and the "content" structure specifies the functional zones that serve a part of the text's overall communicative purpose. The latter is clearly genre-specific, whereas the former is independent of the particular text genre. In this chapter, we describe an approach to identifying both structural levels automatically. For content structure, we focus on the genre "film review": Based on a corpus study, we propose an inventory of zone labels, and describe our method for identifying these zones, using a hybrid approach that makes use of both symbolic rules and statistical (bag-of-words) classification.

Keywords Document structure · Genre-specific content structure · Discourse parsing

5.1 Introduction

A basic problem for many text-technological applications is analyzing the structure of text documents: What are the individual portions of the text, how do they relate to one another, and how do they collectively form a coherent and, in some sense, complete document? It is useful to split this task in two parts, the analysis of the "logical" structure, and that of the "content" structure. Logical structure captures the (possibly partial) hierarchy of (sub-) divisions of the document as it is reflected in the layout; it can be derived by surface-oriented methods without knowledge of the domain or the text genre.[1] Content structure, on the other hand, is much more difficult to grasp. Human readers can employ their domain and world knowledge for assessing the function of the sequence of text portions, but the machine cannot. Thus, the challenging question is: To what extent can content structure, too, be

---

M. Stede (✉)
Universität Potsdam, Potsdam, Germany
e-mail: stede@ling.uni-potsdam.de

The work reported in this chapter originated when one of the authors (A. Suriyawongkul) was a researcher at Potsdam University.

analyzed by surface-oriented methods? In our work, we combine shallow analysis techniques with pre-stored knowledge about *text genres* in order to hypothesize the content structure of texts. The genre knowledge specifies the typical shape (to be clarified in Section 5.5) of documents belonging to the same genre, which can be matched against a document instance with the help of shallow analysis.

While classification of complete texts has been an active area of research for a long time, uncovering the internal structure has only been pursued by a few approaches, concentrating on the genre of scientific papers (Teufel and Moens 2002, Langer et al. 2004). For such documents, the interesting challenge is to exploit the rigid hierarchical structure in assigning content labels to segments (e.g., introduction, experiment, evaluation, conclusion, references, etc.). In contrast, our goal is to explore methods for dealing with text of less hierarchical, looser and more varied structure. In this paper, we consider the case of film reviews. As we shall see, such texts have certain elements in common, but there is a lot of variation with respect to optional elements and the overall ordering within the text. We propose a hybrid approach of rule-based and statistical methods to uncover the content structure of such reviews, which are taken from online newspapers and other web sites.

Our work is situated in the context of a text summarization project, which we briefly describe in the following section. Afterwards, we describe our corpus of film reviews and give some observations on text structures encountered there. We then turn to our specific analysis framework, split into analysis of logical structure (Section 5.4) and of content structure (Section 5.5), which involves representational issues and the procedure for content analysis.

5.2 Framework: Text Summarization in SUMMAR

The prevalent approach to text summarization is that of *sentence extraction*: Based on statistical calculations of sentence relevance, the n highest-ranked sentences are taken out of the text and collectively constitute the summary, with n being dependent on the desired compression rate. Sentence relevance is usually determined by counting the number of relevant terms (either word forms, word stems, or character n-grams), whose relevance in turn derives from their relative frequency in the text as compared to a reference corpus: Those terms that occur more often than expected in the text are supposed to be indicative of the text's topic, and thus the sentences containing these words are deemed most relevant. Notice that these terms are always content words, because the ubiquitous function words will be sorted out automatically, since they will usually be equally frequent in the reference corpus. Additional factors for sentence relevance that can be added to the calculation are the sentence's position in the text and the presence of particular cue words indicating "importance".

There are several well-known problems with these purely statistical, surface-oriented approaches to text summarization. For one thing, the sentence relevance calculation schema invites *redundancy* in the summary: When a relevant sentence is repeated more or less identically later in the text, the second version will by definition also be extracted. Conversely, "important" sentences are not always recognizable by topic-indicating content words, viz. the second sentence in "Smith and Wilson proposed a new algorithm for the travelling salesman problem. Unfortunately it does not work." Finally, text extracts are in danger of lacking both *cohesion* and *coherence*. As for cohesion, a sentence in the extract might contain some anaphoric devices (pronoun, connective, comparative, etc.), but the portion of the original text that contains the antecedent expression might not be part of the extract. Coherence, on the other hand, is lacking when the contents of the sentences in the extracted sequence do not sufficiently related to one another – this can happen easily, even if all sentences contain terms indicating the text's overall topic.

To some extent, all these problems can be tackled with additional surface-oriented methods. One can try to detect redundancy by computing term similarity between sentences (including measures such as WordNet path distance). Important sentences lacking topic-indicating content words can possibly be determined by a more sophisticated version of the cue word method, extended by genre-specific terms; in our example given above, this seems rather difficult, though. The cohesion problem is sometimes fought by simply removing sentences from the extract when they contain one of the aforementioned anaphoric devices. Finally, the coherence of adjacent sentences might be measured by calculations akin to the sentence similarity scores mentioned above – a sentence following another should not repeat the same information but attach to the contents of the predecessor, for instance by holding one or more (but probably not all) discourse referents constant.

Not surprisingly, such measures can help in certain cases but on the whole are not able to lead to "good" summaries. The opposite end of the methodological spectrum is knowledge-intensive, deep analysis of sentence and text meaning. It has been explored in the 1980s for instance in the TOPIC project (Hahn and Reimer 1986), which on the basis of a domain knowledge base constructed frame-based semantic representations for sentences and their combinations, i.e. for texts; a set of condensation rules would then operate on the complex text representation and reduce it to a kernel representation, which the user could browse interactively. As with other AI-inspired approaches of the time, the basic problems were brittleness and lack of scalability: As soon as the text leaves the domain concepts that have been coded in the knowledge base, the whole procedure essentially breaks down. This, of course, was a main reason for the rise of the robust, statistical, surface-oriented methods in language processing.

The goal of the SUMMAR project at Potsdam University is to extend the surface-oriented methods towards linguistic methods, but without sacrificing robustness and domain-independence. Accordingly, we do not aim at deep-semantic analyses of text content. Instead, we try to supplement the statistical sentence relevance calculations on the one hand with robust syntactic parsing and subsequent coreference analysis, and on the other hand with knowledge about the genre, which informs the summarizer about probable locations of "important" sentences and of genre-specific cues indicating relevant sentences. The idea is that genre knowledge is independent of the content domain – for instance, a *review article* will have a range of characteristic features regardless of what is being reviewed, and likewise a user instruction manual is characterized by certain layout and linguistic conventions that are independent of the technical device under discussion.

Knowledge of genres can itself be organized in a hierarchical way, since, e.g., different classes of reviews in turn share certain features: Literature and film reviews can be distinguished from reviews of technical products; at the same time, reviews in newspapers differ in several respects from reviews published on websites.[2] For the purposes of this paper, however, we focus on one individual genre: reviews of films. The goal here is to make the summarizer sensitive to the functions that the various portions of the text fulfill.[3] A film review typically provides a description of the story, evaluates various aspects of the film, provides an overall judgement, and gives some "technical" data (cast, credits, MPAA rating, etc.). A good summary should not lump these different kinds of information arbitrarily together but keep them as distinct as they are in the original text. Furthermore, the summary should (possibly depending on the user's desires) contain pieces from all these content zones. To put it another way: Suppose statistical sentence relevance calculation incidentally leads to an extract that contains only sentences describing the story, but no author's opinion; in this case, clearly something went wrong.

5.3 Defining the Tagset: Corpus Study

A thorough analysis of the genre *film review* was undertaken by Stegert (1993). He broadly distinguishes between *formal* and *functional* elements of reviews, with the former being "constituents" whose presence is characteristic for the genre, and the latter making contributions to the communicative goals of the author. Stegert provides a particularly detailed classification of the functional elements, which he breaks down to the level of individual speech acts. Here are examples from the five groups he distinguishes:

- Inform: list, report, present, ...
- Illustrate: give-example, describe, narrate, ...
- Orientate: compare, categorize, explain, ...
- Argue: claim, deny, prove, ...
- Evaluate: criticize, recommend, defend, ...

For our purposes, we are interested in the functions of paragraph-size units of text, and thus the speech-act based classification appears too fine-grained. At the same time, Stegert's list of the formal elements does not include a few elements that we noticed on film reviews on websites. We therefore opted for a data-oriented approach and developed our own tagset "bottom-up" from studying sample texts and selecting tags to cover the phenomena encountered; later, we made a few changes to the set in accordance with Stegert's terminology.

Several websites nowadays provide a collection of links to film reviews coming from general newspapers or from other websites dedicated to the genre, such as the *Internet Movie Database*.[4] For our corpus study, we started from the *Movie Review Query Engine*[5] to select 45 reviews of 20 different films from 10 different sources (a mixture of online newspapers such as *The New York Times* and *The Washington*

Post, and various websites such as the *BBC* film pages). See Fig. 5.1 for a sample text.[6] Later, we added 100 reviews in German to our corpus and verified that they can also be adequately covered by our tagset.

The goal of the corpus study was to discern the composition of the reviews in terms of their content "zones", similar to the analyses of the argumentation in scientific papers in the SEMDOK project (Langer et al. 2004), which in turn builds on earlier work by Teufel and Moens (2002). To this end, all reviews were converted to plain text files, with paragraph breaks mirroring a break in the original layout structure.

One of the important decisions to be made in devising the tagset is the *granularity*: Assume, for example, one author spending a paragraph assessing the particular foreign accent of the lead actor. Should one then introduce a tag "comment-accent-leadactor", or subsume it under a general "comment"? Halfway between these extremes, we decided to introduce a specific tag only if it was applicable several times in the corpus, and otherwise use a generic tag like "comment-specific" (author assesses *any* specific aspect that is not included in the tagset) – to be distinguished from "comment-general" (author assesses the film on the whole) and "comment-overall" (author sums up his judgement).

Following Stegert, we split the tagset in two groups for formal and functional tags, as shown in Fig. 5.2: Formal zones have to be provided by the author so that the document agrees with the conventions (of the publication and/or of the genre) – they cannot be controlled by her or him. The one tag that seems ambivalent with respect to the groups is "lead": The short lead text that often introduces

The Draughtsman's Contract

by James Mackenzie

James Mackenzie is currently finishing a Bachelor of Arts at Adelaide University, majoring in philosophy.

The Draughtman's Contract (1982 UK 108 mins)

Source: CAC/NLA **Prod Co:** BFI/Channel 4 **Prod:** David Payne **Dir, Scr:** Peter Greenaway **Ph:** Curtis Clark **Ed:** John Wilson **Art Dir:** Bob Ringwood **Mus:** Michael Nyman

Cast: Anthony Higgins, Janet Suzman, Anne Louise Lambert, Hugh Fraser, Suzanne Crowley, Neil Cunningham

In 1981, Peter Greenaway spent a warm summer drawing his house on the Welsh Border. So that the house was in the same light every time he sketched it, eight set views were drawn at eight set times of the day. The carefulness of the plan balanced the chaos of its enactment: cows, neighbours and children were equally constant, if pleasurable, interruptions. Anybody who has seen *The Draughtsman's Contract* may find this scenario familiar. It was the basis of the film. But the relevance of any biographical detail stops there.

Like all of Greenaway's work, *The Draughtsman's Contract* addresses issues of representation: between mediums (drawn and photographic representation); between art and nature (the inbreeding between landscape art and ornamental garden design); and the value of classical naturalism in art.

Though he is described snidely as a materialist, the Draughtsman, Neville (played by Anthony Higgins), is an idealist. He prides himself on being able to draw something exactly as it appears. Just like a camera, his drawings supposedly re-create what exists, without interpretation or expression. His understanding of drawing techniques and systems makes him confident of this.

Yet in Greenaway's world, systems or codes of any kind are treated as inadequate, hopelessly subjective fantasies that deserve contempt.

Fig. 5.1 Excerpt from webpage of our film review corpus

I.Formal units

audience-restriction	director	show_loc_date
author	format	tagline
author+place	genre	title
author+rating	language	
cast	legal-notice	DATA
country+year	note	structure
credits	rating	src
date	runtime	

II.Functional units

comment-actors+roles	comment-story	describe-background
comment-character	comment-technology	describe-character
comment-director		describe-content
comment-general	interpretation	describe-story
comment-overall	lead	describe+comment-story
comment-specific	quote	

Fig. 5.2 Tagset for film reviews

a review (especially those from the newspaper sites) may well contain evaluative phrasings that already contribute to the author's intentions; at the same time, the lead is clearly bound to a fixed position in the document and has quite strict length regulations, so that we include it in the "formal" group. On the "functional" side, our corpus demonstrates a fairly clean separation of "description" and "comment" zones – authors mix these two functions only rarely; our annotators assigned the tag "describe+comment-story" to just 2% of the 560 zones in the English corpus (compare to 23% for all description zones and 39% for all comment zones).

Since we chose to annotate only full paragraphs and not break them up (because paragraphs are the units we eventually want to tag automatically – see Section 5.5), we occasionally need tags for combinations of zones, such as "title+author". Furthermore, for the cases where a multitude of different formal zones are combined in the same paragraph, we use the – rather uninformative – "DATA" tag; it appears in upper case letters to distinguish it as a non-standard tag.

Each tag has been documented briefly, and the resulting annotation guidelines were used by annotators during the final phase of revisions; the guidelines have not yet been formally evaluated for inter-annotator agreement. For illustration, the beginning of the annotated text for the *Draughtsman's Contract* review (from Fig. 5.1) is shown in Fig. 5.3.

Reflecting on the role of such genre-specific tagsets and their relationship to other endeavours (which ultimately should turn into a standardization process, cf. Sasaki (this volume)), we would suggest that the formal units (cf. Fig. 5.2) indeed are highly specific to the particular genre, as they serve, in Stegert's terms, to "constitute" that particular genre. This corresponds to the MEDLINE-specific tagset used by Kim et al. (this volume). Our functional tags, on the other hand, can be expected to relate to tag sets for other genres belonging to the type "review"; here, a hierarchical organisation of tag sets should be possible in correspondence to a hierarchy of

```
<title>
The Draughtsman's Contract
</title>

<author>
by James Mackenzie
James Mackenzie is currently finishing a Bachelor of Arts at Adelaide
 University, majoring in philosophy.
</author>

<title+data>
The Draughtman's Contract (1982 UK 108 mins)
</title>

<data>
Source: CAC/NLA Prod Co: BFI/Channel 4 Prod: David Payne Dir, Scr: Peter
 Greenaway Ph: Curtis Clark Ed: John Wilson Art Dir: Bob Ringwood Mus:
 Michael Nyman
</data>

<cast>
Cast: Anthony Higgins, Janet Suzman, Anne Louise Lambert, Hugh Fraser,
 Suzanne Crowley, Neil Cunningham
</cast>

<describe-background>
In 1981, Peter Greenaway spent a warm summer drawing his house on the Welsh
 Border. So that the house was in the same light every time he sketched it,
 eight set views were drawn at eight set times of the [...]
</describe-background>

<describe-content>
Like all of Greenaway's work, The Draughtsman's Contract addresses issues of
  representation: between mediums (drawn and photographic representation);
 between art and nature (the inbreeding between [...]
</describe-content>

[...]
```

Fig. 5.3 Portion of annotated text from our corpus

genres, as we had suggested at the end of Section 5.2. A recent initiative for defining a tag set more generally pertaining to "review" is the hReview microformat.[7]

5.4 Deriving Logical Document Structure

Turning now to the task of automatically identifying the document structure, we begin with the *logical* structure, i.e., with the mapping between layout and an XML representation of distinguishable units, which for convenience we abbreviate here as *ldoc*.

5.4.1 The ldoc Schema

The logical structure of a document has been characterized by Summers 1998 as "a hierarchy of visually observable organizational components of a document, such as paragraphs, lists, sections, etc." It is independent of the particular domain and of content and in the case of web pages can to a good extent be derived from the

HTML markup. In the SUMMAR project, we process documents of various types (XML, HTML, plain text) and therefore have defined a pre-processing step that maps all input formats first to our *ldoc* format, which is thus the only format that the summarization engine needs to know. Since sophisticated HTML conversion, worrying about tables, images, etc., is not a goal of the project, a main objective in the design of the *ldoc* XML representation was simplicity. We borrowed tags from *XHTML*[8] and ideas from *Cascading Style Sheets (CSS)*,[9] and simplified them into our small set of tags and attributes (the tags are from XHTML and the attributes are mostly from CSS) that are sufficient to describe the types of documents used in SUMMAR (*inter alia*, the film reviews we discuss in this paper).

An *ldoc* document consists mainly of *div* and *span*, for text blocks and inline text regions, respectively, along with their attributes for additional information (like division type or font face). For the document head (metadata), tags are borrowed or inspired from *Dublin Core*[10] and *TEI*:[11] Information such as document source, language, encoding, and publication information is stored in this part.

The ldoc schema (which at present is still open to further extensions) is formulated in *RELAX NG Compact Syntax*,[12] which is a schema definition language comparable to conventional DTD. An excerpt from our schema definition is given in Fig. 5.4.

```
datatypes xsd = "http://www.w3.org/2001/XMLSchema-datatypes"

start = Ldoc
Ldoc = element ldoc { Id.attrib, Head, Body }

Body = element body { Div* }

Inline = ( text | Span )*

Div = element div {
  Id.attrib, Lang.attrib,
  attribute textIndent { xsd:integer }?,
  attribute type { "division" | "paragraph" | "heading" | "list" | "
  listitem" },
  (Inline | Div)+
}

Span = element span {
  Id.attrib?, Lang.attrib?, Style.attrib,
    Inline
}

Id.attrib = attribute id { xsd:ID }
Lang.attrib = attribute lang { xsd:language }
Style.attrib = (
  attribute face { xsd:string }?,
  attribute style { "normal" | "italic" }?,
  attribute variant { "normal"|"small-caps" }?,
  attribute weight { "normal"|"bold"|"lighter" }?,
  attribute size { "small"|"medium"|"large"}?,
  attribute underline { xsd:boolean }?,
  attribute lineThrough { xsd:boolean }?
)
```

Fig. 5.4 Portion of our *ldoc* schema in RELAX NG compact syntax

5.4.2 Layout Identification Procedure

As mentioned above, we produce *ldoc* from documents in different kinds of XML formats, in plain text, and to some extent in HTML. The latter are processed with help from *HTML Tidy*,[13] a tool that produces well-formed XHTML from possibly-malformed HTML. The current implementation of our logical structure extractor is written in Python, with optional assistance from an XSL transformation engine for XML inputs. Along with the layout structure, the extractor also tries to extract metadata of the document.

For plain text documents, the only layout information is the use of spacing, vertically and horizontally, and some creative typography like surrounding words with asterisks for **emphasis**. A central task is the interpretation of CR/LF, which might or might not represent a paragraph boundary. As a heuristic, beforehand we determine the longest line in the document and from its length guess whether subsequent lines of equal length in the document are likely to be intended as one continuous paragraph or not. Here are some example mapping rules from the program:

Paragraph: If lines are very long, they are regarded as a single paragraph *(div)*, and a linebreak as a paragraph boundary. Otherwise, adjacent lines are grouped into one paragraph, and paragraph boundaries are recognized from double linebreaks (i.e. blank lines).

Heading: If a line consists of capital letters only, or begins with indicative numerals, and if the last character is not a punctuation sign (other than "?" and "!"), it is taken to be a *heading*. If a paragraph boundary has been identified as a linebreak, a heading boundary is preceded by two linebreaks and followed by one.

Heading: A line followed by a line of same length, consisting of "-" or "=", is interpreted as a *heading*.

Emphasis: A character sequence surrounded by asterisks (with no intervening blanks) is mapped to *italic*; one surrounded by "_" is mapped to *underline*.

For "familiar" XML documents, we use a library of *XSL* sheets and have the transformation engine extract all layout structure as well as the metadata from the document. In the case of "unfamiliar" XML and HTML documents, heuristics are used for extracting a generic *ldoc* by selectively inspecting a set of elements and attributes. Some examples are given below. The result *ldoc* representation for our sample text is shown in Fig. 5.5.

Title: *title* element or element with *class* attribute = "title"

Heading: *h1, h2, h3, h4, h5, h6, header, heading* element or *class* attribute = "head", "subhead"

Heading: short line that is completely in emphasis

```
<?xml version="1.0"n encoding="utf-8"?>
<ldoc>
<head>
  <contentDesc>
    <lang>de</lang>
    <title>The Draughtsman's Contract</title>
  </contentDesc>
</head>

<body>
<div type="heading"><span size="+3" style="italic" weight="bold">The
Draughtsman's Contract</span></div>

<div type="paragraph"><span size="+2">by James Mackenzie</span></div>

<div type="paragraph"><span size="-1">James Mackenzie is currently
finishing a Bachelor of Arts at Adelaide University, majoring in philosophy
.
</span></div>

<div type="paragraph"><span size="-1"><span style="italic" weight="bold">
The Draughtman's Contract</span> (1982 UK 108 mins)</span></div>

<div type="paragraph"><span size="-1">
<span weight="bold">Source</span>: CAC/NLA
<span weight="bold">Prod Co</span>: BFI/Channel 4
<span weight="bold">Prod</span>: David Payne
<span weight="bold">Dir, Scr</span>: Peter Greenaway
<span weight="bold">Ph</span>: Curtis Clark
<span weight="bold">Ed</span>: John Wilson
<span weight="bold">Art Dir</span>: Bob Ringwood
<span weight="bold">Mus</span>: Michael Nyman</span></div>

<div type="paragraph"><span size="-1"><span weight="bold">Cast</span>:
Anthony Higgins, Janet Suzman, Anne Louise Lambert, Hugh Fraser, Suzanne
Crowley, Neil Cunningham</span></div>

<div type="paragraph">In 1981, Peter Greenaway spent a warm summer drawing
his house on the Welsh Border. So that the house was in the same light
every time he sketched it, eight set views were drawn at eight set times of
the [...]</div>

<div type="paragraph">Like all of Greenaway's work, <span style="italic">
The Draughtsman's Contract</span> addresses issues of representation·
between mediums (drawn and photographic representation); between art and
nature (the inbreeding between [...]</div>

[...]
```

Fig. 5.5 Portions of *ldoc* representation for review from Fig. 5.1

Paragraph: text in *p*, *para*, *paragraph*, *div* element
Emphasis: *strong, em, b, i, u, big* element
Emphasis: *size* attribute = "+n"; (*n* a small integer)

5.5 Genre Knowledge and Content Structure Analysis

For human readers, some kinds of texts can be identified as belonging to their *kind* at first glance: Cooking recipes or user's instructions, for instance, are likely to be categorized correctly without the categorizing eye actually having read much of the text. The layout conventions alone are often sufficient to trigger identification of the text genre (e.g., recipes contain general description, list of ingredients, clearly delineated – often numbered – individual actions, and closing material). With other genres, such as the film reviews, layout is much less standardized, but there are typical patterns of content structure, which leads to what we label "loosely-structured documents". At the opposite end of the spectrum are genres like essays, for which it is almost impossible to state any conventionalized patterns of overall structure.

In this section, we first describe our approach to representing such knowledge about the content structure of genres and then proceed to the task of analyzing the content structure of documents automatically.

5.5.1 Knowledge of Content Structure: The Case of Film Reviews

Typical moves for the communication form "review a film" consist in giving the name of the film and of the director, introducing the main protagonists, summarizing the plot, describing the images, and assessing the drama. (Stegert 1993, p. 14; our translation from German)

The occasional reader of a film review will probably agree that these are indeed the main "ingredients". In order to operationalize this intuition, we peruse the data collected in the corpus study described in Section 5.3. In order to see the "constituent structure" of reviews, we can simply extract the XML tags from the annotated text; doing this for all the reviews results in all the observed sequences of content zones. It is now easy to determine, e.g., how obligatory or optional zones are; for instance, "title" occurs in 100% of the reviews, "describe-background" only in 23%. Another way to interpret these sequences is to induce a bigram language model that reflects the local neighbourhoods of the content zones. For this step, we used the *Ngram statistics package* (Banerjee and Pedersen 2003). With this data at hand, information like the following can be derived:

- Reviews have a strong tendency to start with the zone "title" or "title+X" (85%); other beginnings are "rating" and "date".
- A legal notice occurs, if at all, at the very end.
- The author of the review is mentioned either toward the beginning (before the narrative material starts) or close to the end.
- Similarly, the overall rating (if any) is given either at the beginning or at the end.
- The story of the film is usually told continuously (if it is interrupted at all, then by a comment, not by anything else).
- Credits and cast list have a tendency to collocate: 45% of "credit" zones are followed by "cast", and 20% of "cast" are followed by "credit".

In addition to zone occurrence probabilities and ordering information, we are interested in internal features of the individual zones: their average length, and the possible presence of any specific cues that make the zone identifiable. Evaluating the corpus in these directions reveals, for instance, that most titles are no longer than three words, that lists of actors are reliably marked by the heading "Cast", that the

MPAA rating always includes one of the terms "G", "PG", "PG-13", "R", "NC-17" and is often but not always headed by the word "Rating", etc.

In summary, we found that the characteristic features of the content structure of "loosely-structured" texts are

- the set of all *possible* content zones (here: our tagset),
- the set of all *obligatory* zones, i.e., those that have to be present in a text (here: author, title, describe-X, comment-X),
- for each zone
    - its probability for showing up in a text ("degree of optionality")
    - position information: its probabilities for occurring in the neighbourhood of other zones, including the pseudo-zones "start" and "end"
    - the average length of material in the zone
    - necessary, sufficient, or indicative features such as cue words, enumerative style (rather than sentences), etc.
    - specifically for the purpose of text summarization: cue words indicating "important" sentences for this zone[14]

5.5.2 Automatic Content Structure Analysis

Following the assumption that content structure is built on the same elementary units as logical structure, we represent the content structure as attributes to the `<div>` tags of the logical structure document. Thus, our task now is to supplement each `<div>` of the logical structure, which we derive as described in Section 5.4, with one `contentzone` attribute, whose value is to be taken from the tagset shown in Fig. 5.2.

5.5.2.1 Formal Zones

Since the formal zones have quite reliable properties that often are easy to identify, we opted for writing a set of symbolic recognition rules. They encode three different kinds of information: "Sufficient" feature combinations allow for reliably assigning a zone in the event of matching; "necessary" feature combinations are required to match for a zone to be assigned; "indicative" feature combinations do not warrant a clear decision but render a certain zone to be a likely candidate. Again, we give some examples of recognition rules; the text-region relations (e.g., *starts-with, contains*) are taken from Miller and Myers 1999.

author: doc-position != middle AND short-division AND (starts-with "by" OR "reviewed by" OR "a review by")

legal-notice: (starts-with "copyright" OR (contains "(c)" OR "all right reserved")) AND doc-position == bottom OR end

cast: (starts-with "cast:" OR "starring") OR (just-after heading with content == "cast")

audience-restriction: short division AND (starts-with "rated" OR "mpaa")
audience-restriction: short division AND (contains "G" or "PG(-..?)?" or "NC-..?"
or "R" or "M" ... or "Uc?" pattern)
runtime: short division AND (starts-with "running time" or "running length" or
"length")
runtime: short division AND (ends-with OR starts-with "[time] (m|mins|minutes)"
or "[time] (h|hr|hrs|hours)" or "[time] (h|hr|hrs|hours) [time] (m|mins
|minutes)" pattern)

Our symbolic rules perform very well on the zones *rating*, *author+rating*,
audience-restriction and *format* (all with 100% prec. and recall). The average performance for the other zones is 70% precision and 63% recall.

5.5.2.2 Functional Zones

For the functional zones, the situation is quite different – enumerating surface features for reliably identifying them is not realistic. Instead, we built a statistical classifier for this task. The interesting aspect here is the distinction between "comment"
and "describe" zones, which corresponds to the question whether a piece of text
contains subjective *opinion* or not. Automatic identification of opinion is a research
area that has attracted much interest in recent years (see, e.g., the collection Qu
et al. 2004), and a variety of raw and annotated corpora have become available. For
film reviews, Pang and Lee 2004 made datasets of balanced positive and negative
reviews available, which we used for our first experiments with training classifiers.
Thereafter, we began to work with German data, for which we collected twice the
amount of data (see above). Rather than trying to discriminate between the various
kinds of *describe* and *comment* (see Fig. 5.2), we joined them into two general
classes. Thus, our training material consists of the *describe* and *comment* paragraphs
from 100 German reviews. They consist of 2–29 sentences each, with the average
length being 6.25 sentences (there is no significant difference in length between
the two classes). The classifier uses a bag-of-words model, where a "word" is a
character 5-g. All 5-g occurring in a paragraph are weighted according to the tf*idf
measure, where idf is the inverse paragraph frequency according to a reference
corpus of film reviews. Also, we added a feature UNKNOWN, which records the
number of 5-g that are unknown to the reference corpus and, hence, not part of the
feature set.

Pang et al. (2002) compared different machine learning methods for distinguishing opinion from description in English film reviews. They achieved accuracies
between 72.8 and 82.9%, depending on the training features and the method. In their
evaluation, Support Vector Machines perform best for many of the feature combinations. In our approach with the German data, we also use SVM, but our features
are 5-g, as pointed out above. We used the SVMlight tool (Joachims 1999) and
divided the film reviews in a set of training (66%) and test data (33%). The results
are: *Comment* zones – prec. 81.6%; rec. 79.7%. *Describe* zones – prec. 76.8%; rec.
78.9%.

5.5.2.3 Overall Parsing Strategy

Given a film review in the *ldoc* format, we first apply the rule set for the formal zones to each paragraph (i.e., *div*). Since the rules encode necessary, sufficient, or merely indicative features of zones, the result after processing the document is that some formal zones have been identified (on the basis of sufficient features), for some paragraphs many formal zones have been ruled out (on the basis of necessary features), and for some paragraphs it seems "likely" that a certain zone is the right one.

For the paragraphs that remain unidentified, we determine contiguous spans that could be *describe* and *comment* zones, and apply the opinion-classifier to them; it thus adds information about those two zones.

After these steps, the document can be viewed as a landscape with "peaks" (in-zones) and "valleys" (out-zones) – which is a situation that in speech recognition has occasionally been handled with the "island parsing" approach. Stock et al. (1988), for instance, have extended the standard chart parsing algorithm to maintaining bidirectional charts. Likelihoods of category membership are abstracted to three discrete classes, and then parsing rules are applied, not from left to right, but starting from "islands of certainty" in both directions. The parser thus tries to extend each island step by step until the entire utterance is covered. The underlying intuition is that uncertainty should not unnecessarily be based on other uncertainty; instead, the various spots of confidently recognized words, scattered over the utterance, serve as anchors to supply reliable context information for the more difficult areas.

We borrow this basic idea, but unlike Stock et al. do not parse with a CFG; instead we use the bigram probabilities to assign zones to the remaining unlabelled paragraphs in the neighbourhood of already-labelled islands. Since the bigrams offer fairly strong tendencies for the beginning and end of documents, we add artificial START and END islands to the process.

5.6 Conclusions

Film reviews, we argued, belong to a class of "loosely-structured documents" that do not obey very rigid formal rules but are not entirely unrestricted, either. The range of formal and functional elements that take place in reviews is quite restricted, as our tagset demonstrates, and there are a number of rules and tendencies as to the linear ordering of the elements. Thus we started from the hypothesis that the automatic derivation of the content structure of film reviews is not an impossible endeavour; applications that can profit from such structural knowledge include information extraction, question answering, and – as we have emphasized – text summarization.

As a result of a corpus study, we proposed a tagset of content zones for film reviews, and made observations on attributes of the zones: mandatory or indicative lexical elements, length, linear position in the review and with respect to other elements. We see this as the "content structure knowledge" pertaining to the particular genre of film reviews.

Our procedure for identifying the structure of a review first maps the plain text or HTML to an XML format representing the logical document structure – this part is independent of the genre, insofar as the tags make no reference to the *contents* of the text. In the second step, we enrich the logical structure tags with attributes for the content zones, using a hybrid approach that combines symbolic rules with statistical classification. The pipeline of layout identification and subsequent content identification rests on the assumption that different content zones tend to be separated from one another in the layout of the text; our corpus study indicated that the assumption can be made for the film reviews.

Our work shares a lot of motivation with that of the SEMDOK project (Langer et al. 2004, Lüngen et al. this volume). Their concern is with scientific papers, and they employ sophisticated XML processing techniques to deal with hierarchical structures in documents; content zones are identified with statistical classifiers. With our texts being much more "flat", our focus is on different aspects, though. In future work we intend to investigate more thoroughly the prospects of representing text genre knowledge for different purposes. A key step will be to explore related genres, in particular different kinds of reviews (of different products and from different media), and to devise representations that allow for sharing the elements that the genres have in common. The term "genre" has received a great deal of attention in text linguistics, but this has not lead to particularly precise definitions. Making progress on this issue, with computational means, is one of the goals worth pursuing.

Acknowledgments The work reported in this chapter was funded by the German Federal Ministry of Education and Research, grant 03WKH22. We thank Heike Bieler and Stefanie Dipper for their contributions to the SUMMaR project, and Annika Neumann and Andreas Peldszus for their help with defining tag sets and performing annotations.

Notes

1. Strictly speaking, one could make an additional distinction here between a "physical" structure that describes solely the layout, and a logical structure that captures the hierarchical information "below" the surface. However, as we directly derive our logical structure with the help of the layout, we do not distinguish between these two levels. Note that we use "level" in the sense that is being characterized by Goecke et al. (this volume).
2. On the task of classifying related genres, see also Rehm (this volume).
3. For the case of technical support websites, the role of the document structure for producing high-quality summaries was emphasized in a study by Wolf et al. (2004).
4. http://www.imdb.com
5. http://www.mrqe.com
6. Source: http://www.sensesofcinema.com
7. http://microformats.org/wiki/hreview
8. http://www.w3.org/MarkUp/
9. http://www.w3.org/Style/CSS/
10. http://www.dublincore.org
11. http://www.tei-c.org

12. http://www.relaxng.org
13. http://tidy.sourceforge.net
14. The sentence relevance assignment of the extraction procedure can then prefer such sentences. Conditioning the cue words on the zones can be a useful extension to the (well-known) generic use of "boostwords" such as *importantly, I should emphasize, ...*

References

S. Banerjee, T. Pedersen. "The Design, Implementation, and Use of the Ngram Statistics Package." In: Proc. of the Fourth International Conference on Intelligent Text Processing and Computational Linguistics, Mexico City, 2003.

U. Hahn, U. Reimer. "Topic Essentials." In: Proc. of COLING 1986, S. 497–503, 1986.

T. Joachims. "Making large-scale SVM learning practical." In: B. Schñolkopf, C. Burges, A. Smola (eds.): *Advances in Kernel Methods – Support Vector Learning.* MIT Press, Cambridge, 1999.

H. Langer, H. Lüngen, P. Bayerl. "Text Type Structure and Logical Document Structure." In: Proceedings of the ACL 2004 Workshop on Discourse Annotation. pp. 49–56. Barcelona, 2004.

R. Miller, B. Myers. "Lightweight Structured Text Processing." In: Proc. of the USENIX Annual Technical Conference, Monterey, CA, June 1999, pp. 131–144.

B. Pang, L. Lee, S. Vaithyanathan. "Thumbs up? Sentiment classification using machine learning techniques." In. Proceedings of the Conference on Empirical Methods in Natural Language Processing (EMNLP), 2002.

B. Pang, L. Lee: "A Sentimental Education: Sentiment Analysis Using Subjectivity Summarization Based on Minimum Cuts." In: Proceedings of the Annual Meeting of the Assoc. for Computational Linguistics (ACL), Barcelona, 2004.

Y. Qu, J. Shanahan, J. Wiebe (eds.): "Exploring Attitude and Affect in Text: Theories and Applications." (Papers from the 2004 AAAI Spring Symposium) Technical report SS-04-07. AAAI Press, Menlo Park, CA, 2004.

G. Stegert. *Filme Rezensieren in Presse, Radio und Fernsehen.* TR-Verlagsunion, München, 1993.

O. Stock, R. Falcone, P. Insinnamo: "Island parsing and bidirectional charts." In: Proc. of the Int'l Conference on Computational Linguistics (Coling), 1988.

K.M. Summers. "Automatic Discovery of Logical Document Structure." Ph.D. Thesis, Cornell University, 1998.

S. Teufel, M. Moens. "Summarizing scientific articles: Experiments with relevance and rhetorical status." *Computational Linguistics* 28(4):409–445, 2002.

C.G. Wolf, S.R. Alpert, J.G. Vergo, L. Kozakov, Y. Doganata. "Summarizing technical support documents for search: Expert and user studies." *IBM Systems Journal* 43(3):564–586, 2004.

Chapter 6
Discourse Relations and Document Structure

Harald Lüngen, Maja Bärenfänger, Mirco Hilbert, Henning Lobin, and Csilla Puskás

Abstract This chapter addresses the requirements and linguistic foundations of automatic relational discourse analysis of complex text types such as scientific journal articles. It is argued that besides lexical and grammatical discourse markers, which have traditionally been employed in discourse parsing, cues derived from the logical and generical document structure and the thematic structure of a text must be taken into account. An approach to modelling such types of linguistic information in terms of XML-based multi-layer annotations and to a text-technological representation of additional knowledge sources is presented. By means of quantitative and qualitative corpus analyses, cues and constraints for automatic discourse analysis can be derived. Furthermore, the proposed representations are used as the input sources for discourse parsing. A short overview of the projected parsing architecture is given.

Keywords Discourse parsing · Discourse relations · Document structure · Text technology · Linguistic annotations · XML

6.1 Introduction

In the past, several approaches to automatic discourse analysis have been developed as applications of relational discourse theories which describe the semantics of discourse. These approaches are often based on the analysis of discourse connectives as well as morphological and syntactic features. Such surface-oriented strategies are adequate and have yielded good results when applied to the analysis of simple text types like newspaper articles, which are characterised by a limited size and a relatively simple document and syntactic structure. When dealing with more complex text types, however, an analysis of lexis and grammar is not sufficient. Sources of knowledge about discourse and document semantics have to be considered as well.

H. Lüngen (✉)
Justus-Liebig-Universität Gießen, Gießen, Germany
e-mail: luengen@uni-giessen.de

A. Witt, D. Metzing (eds.), *Linguistic Modeling of Information and Markup Languages*, Text, Speech and Language Technology 40,
DOI 10.1007/978-90-481-3331-4_6, © Springer Science+Business Media B.V. 2010

This chapter deals with the linguistic foundations of discourse analysis for a complex text type by the example of scientific journal articles. Its focus is on the contribution of logical document structure, generic document structure and thematic structure to discourse parsing. The modelling and representation of linguistic structures and knowledge sources based on text-technological (XML-based) formalisms and methods is addressed. The representations are used in investigating correlations and interactions between different types of linguistic information and serve as an input to a discourse parsing system.

In the project *SemDok*, which is part of the Research Group *Text-technological modelling of information* funded by the German Research Foundation DFG and scheduled to run in its second phase for three years 2005–2008, a discourse parser for the complex text type "scientific research article" is being developed. Scientific articles exhibit a highly complex document structure (both logical document structures and relational discourse structures are deeply nested) and a relatively large average size in terms of word count. The discourse parser is envisaged in a specific application scenario: It shall be part of an explorative reading system which supports novice students in learning to adopt adequate strategies for reading scientific articles. The system shall have two dimensions: Firstly, it shall provide a tool to support selective and explorative reading and, secondly, it shall function as a learning environment where students can acquire knowledge about the genre "scientific article", its generic text type structure (with categories such as *introduction, method, results* and *discussion*) and possible argumentative strategies and thematic structures. Support for explorative and selective reading shall be based on two mechanisms: highlighting text structures and providing automatically generated link lists to different structural nodes as navigation elements. Highlighting and linking both serve as starting points for the exploration of an article. By offering link lists or by directing attention to highlighted passages, readers are guided to thematically or rhetorically significant parts of a text. Additionally, access to the different structural levels of the text is simplified, as the building plan of the text is made explicit.

Highlighting and linking requires the preprocessing of articles. They must be automatically analysed and annotated on the levels of document structure, text type structure, rhetorical and thematic structure. The automatisation of analysis and annotation is necessary to enable users of the system to upload articles that they themselves consider relevant. The discourse parser developed in the *SemDok* project will automatically add discourse structure annotations and thus allow students a personalised use of the system.

The present chapter is structured as follows: Section 6.2 gives a theoretical overview of the different linguistic levels relevant for the analysis of the relational discourse structure of a scientific article: logical document structure, thematic structure (referential structure, lexical cohesion), and generic document structure. Furthermore, our notion of relational discourse structure, which refers to Rhetorical Structure Theory (RST, Mann and Thompson 1988), is introduced. In Sections 6.3.1

and 6.3.2, the corpus and the layers of annotations that we employ in developing and evaluating the parser, are characterised. Section 6.3.3 addresses additional resources such as the discourse marker lexicon and the inventory of rhetorical relations and describes their representation in XML. The chapter is concluded by a short overview of the architecture of the projected discourse parser and an outlook on future work.

6.2 Linguistic Foundations

6.2.1 Document Structure

The research described in this chapter is based on the assumption that documents can be regarded as complex signs. As complex signs they are built up from smaller units in which these units themselves and their connections are constituted by linguistic and visual mechanisms. These units of a document are complex and elementary segments. Elementary segments are usually rectangular areas, which can be delimited clearly according to certain features and are not put together from segments (e.g. paragraphs or headings). Complex segments are adjacent combinations of segments to which a common document function can be assigned (e.g. sections).

Documents can be regarded as signs with respect to their syntagmatic, their semantic and their pragmatic dimensions. In a syntagmatic perspective, documents can be described by grammars which define the way in which segments can be combined to yield valid documents of a certain type. In a semantic perspective, the meaning of a document is a function of the meanings of its parts and its document type. The combination of elementary segments to form complex segments follows compositional principles. These, however, are activated by the document type assumptions and expectations, which complete the compositionally formed document meaning.

Constitutive units of documents are 2D objects, segments. Segments can almost always be geometrically described as rectangles which cover parts of the document area. Segments are e.g. text blocks, tables, headings, address fields, but also graphics and illustrations, i.e. flat objects which have a recognisable coherent structure and can be described not by linguistic means alone. Tables and lists contain on the one hand linguistically definable structures (e.g. lists can be interpreted as coordination), however, on the other hand, they are specified by geometric and graphic properties at the same time.

Only text blocks, which do not show any further geometric properties apart from the line break, represent purely linguistic objects. Text blocks form the transition between the one-dimensionality of the language and the two-dimensionality of the document by being split up mechanically into lines which fill the segment from top to bottom.

Segments are aggregated in the document area in which semantic connections between the segments are encoded by topology and graphic design. The document area is restricted, though; it is defined by the restrictions of the medium (size of the printable paper, screen or window etc.). If this does not suffice, document parts are formed so that they can be read in a temporal order one after the other (successive pages of a book, window content which can be scrolled, or window content which is replaced by the activation of a link). In this respect, many documents also have a temporal dimension besides the two spatial ones so that one can talk about documents as of a 2.5-dimensionality.

The syntagmatic structure of text segments has been examined quite extensively in text linguistics. Dependencies between the sentences are established by means of cohesion of different types. The linguistic properties of the syntagmatic level of text segments can be described by rules which permit the sentence syntax to continue above the sentence boundaries. The syntagmatic structure of segments with graphic elements, such as tables, is given by the iconic properties of lines, columns and boxes. These relations can also be described by rules that are based primarily on the cognitive processes of perception. Complex segments and whole documents are formed by the aggregation of segments. Typical is the aggregation of several text segments (paragraphs) to form a text body that is provided with a heading to yield a section. The formation of a complex segment is defined by the adjacent aggregation of the segments in the text area. These syntagmatic properties of documents can be described by rules which resemble those for the formation of sentences; they can be collected in a document grammar. In document grammars, the media-specific conditions of a document are omitted systematically. The necessary page breaks are included in a document grammar no more than line breaks are in the descriptions of segments in a text grammar.

Grammatical dependencies indicate semantic relations. The syntactic structure of a sentence licenses the construction or representation of its meaning in a suitable formalism. There are different approaches to text semantics which presuppose the availability of meaning representations for the individual sentences as well as cohesive means for the representation of the meaning of segments. An example of this is the logical text representation in terms of (S)DRT (Asher and Lascarides 2003). The meaning of a document arises from the composite meanings of the segments contained in it in connection with predefined meaning structures which are activated by document type and text type. To combine the meaning of segments it has to be decided which semantic relations are encoded by a certain configuration of segments (e.g. the semantic relationship between heading and text body). By the document type, a text type is activated which specifies a semantic structure which is valid for all instances of this type, regardless of the meanings specified by the segments. So it is clear from the start, e.g. for a scientific article, that the state of the art, methodological questions or results are represented in certain sections of the document.

Based on speech act theory, different expansions have been suggested on the textual level. Motsch and Viewweger (1991) describe the construction of complex illocutions in texts, Schröder (2003) examines the action structure of texts with the same aim. Following this line of research, document functions can be described in a similar way as complex illocutions.

6.2.2 Relational Discourse Structure

Current text-type independent linguistic discourse theories such as the Unified Linguistic Discourse Model (ULDM, Polanyi et al. 2004a, b), Segmented Discourse Representation Theory (SDRT, Asher and Lascarides 2003, Asher and Vieu 2005), and Rhetorical Structure Theory (RST, Mann and Thompson 1988, Marcu 2000) describe *discourse structures* as a system of discourse coherence relations that hold between adjacent discourse constituents (spans). Discourse constituents can be either elementary discourse segments or complex discourse segments, the latter are relationally structured themselves. It seems to be generally acknowledged that discourse is structured hierarchically, but it is controversial whether the basic information structure for discourse representation should be a tree or a graph. While SDRT employs graph structures, in ULDM and RST, discourse *trees* with labelled nodes and edges are constructed. Recently, Wolf and Gibson (2005) have put forward linguistic arguments for a graph representation of discourse structures.

In the present project, we adopt the view that a discourse representation is basically a tree structure, which may be enhanced to include re-entrant edges in certain well-defined cases (cf. Lüngen et al. 2006a).

It is also generally accepted that there are two main structural types of discourse relations under which all other relations can be subsumed, namely *subordinating* vs. *coordinating* relations. In RST, these types are called *mononuclear* (or sometimes *hypotactic*) and *multinuclear* (*paratactic*) relations. In a mononuclear relation, one of the elements (text spans) involved has the status of being the *nucleus*, the "more salient, essential piece of information" (Carlson et al. 2001) of the relation. The other ones are labelled the *satellites*, which contain "supporting or background information" (Carlson et al. 2001). Like many authors (e.g. Corston-Oliver 1998, Marcu 2000, Egg and Redeker 2005), we restrict the representation of mononuclear relations to binary trees, i.e. with exactly one nucleus and one satellite. In multinuclear relations, all elements (possibly more than two) are labelled as nuclei.

While in ULDM subordinating and coordinating relations are the only types of relations, the original RST is actually a theory about the nature and diversity of mono- and multinuclear discourse relations, thus a set of 26 so-called *rhetorical* relations and their definitions are introduced in Mann and Thompson (1988).

The fact that all rhetorical relations are either mononuclear or multinuclear and that some (such as EVALUATION and INTERPRETATION) are rhetorically similar, and furthermore that some relations are special cases of other relations (e.g. NON-VOLITIONAL-CAUSE and CAUSE), can be accounted for by grouping relations into *classes* and constructing *taxonomies* over these classes. This has previously been done e.g. by Hovy and Maier (1995) and Carlson and Marcu (2001); see also Goecke et al. (2005). On the one hand, Mann and Thompson (1988) have provided a relation set which is supposed to be text type- and application-independent, on the other hand they stress that the set is open to extension. In practice, depending on a text type and application (e.g. discourse analysis vs. generation), specific subsets or extended sets of relations have been chosen (cf. Hovy and Maier 1995). Many of the RST rhetorical relation types examined in the literature, such as EVIDENCE or INTERPRETATION, are immediately relevant for our text type, which was one factor that led us to opt for RST-based text parsing. Based on relation sets previously described in the literature as well as on corpus investigations, we have defined an extended relation taxonomy for the *SemDok* project, see Section 6.3.3.2.

Discourse theories also differ in their strategies of *discourse interpretation*, that is, the question of how discourse analysis and the construction of a formal representation of a specific discourse is achieved. In a theory like SDRT, a full-fledged semantic representation of discourse segments is required to perform discourse analysis. Its output then is a logical form, too. In the original conception of RST, text spans comprise plain text, not logical forms. Relational analysis as designed in Mann and Thompson (1988), however, also presupposes knowledge about the meaning of discourse segments as well as goals and beliefs of authors and readers about these meanings. Since a complete and robust automatic semantic analysis of input segments seems not feasible, computational analysis of discourse has often relied on linguistic properties that are more easily obtainable, such as *discourse connectives* and syntactic and morphological features derived from (deep or shallow) grammatical analysis, see the projects described in Corston-Oliver (1998), Marcu (2000), Reitter (2003b), Polanyi et al. (2004a), and cf. also the argumentation in Egg and Redeker (2005). This is also the path that is taken in the *SemDok* project. But since we are dealing with a complex text type, we are also investigating cues for the more global (or macro) discourse structure such as thematic structure and lexical cohesion (lexical chains and anaphoric structure, see Section 6.2.3), logical document structure, and text type structure (Section 6.2.4).

In the extract from our corpus in Listing 6.1,[1] the adverbial discourse connective *z.B.* introduces a mononuclear ELABORATION-EXAMPLE relation where the segment that contains the connective is the satellite. This relation defines a complex discourse segment which is related to the previous segment, which contains the discourse marking conjunction *und*, introducing a multinuclear LIST-COORDINATION relation. The corresponding RST tree is shown in Fig. 6.1.[2] An equivalent discourse dependency tree representation according to Danlos (2005), which better

```
<cds type="block" docIdref="i1161">
  <sds id="s260">
    <eds id="e465">In der Schrift hat die Sprachpflege einen etwas besseren Erfolg
        als im Gespräch gehabt.
    </eds>
  </sds>
  <sds id="s261">
    <eds id="e466">In öffentlichen Dokumenten ist man <dm id="i322" lexid="c6"
        lemma="z.b." pos="ADV">z.B.</dm> darauf bedacht, dass die Termini
        dem Gebrauch in Schweden entsprechen,
    </eds>
    <eds id="e468"><dm id="i325" lexid="c89" lemma="und" pos="CC">und</dm>
        man vermeidet auch typisch finnlandschwedische Wendungen.
    </eds>
  </sds>
  ...
</cds>
```

Listing 6.1 Discourse segments and discourse markers

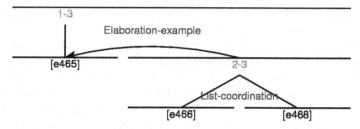

Fig. 6.1 RST tree

corresponds to data structures preferred in computational linguistics, is shown in Fig. 6.2. The involved segments are represented by IDs that refer to the textual content of elementary discourse segments as shown in Listing 6.1.

Elementary discourse segments (EDSs) in our project are based on syntax (syntactic tagging), punctuation and logical document structure. The basic idea is that elementary discourse segments correspond to clauses as in most theories, but may also correspond to other kinds of phrases () when they are especially marked by punctuation (e.g. bracketing) or logical document structure (e.g. a <doc:title> element). Moreover, a minimal unit of discourse is supposed to be part of a discourse relation where the nucleus is semantically independent enough so that the satellite can potentially be omitted. This means that e.g. complement clauses, conditional clauses, and restricting relative clauses cannot be EDSs in our scheme. Since in these respects we deviate from the definition of English *elementary discourse units* in Marcu (1999), we did not adopt his technical term *edu* for our minimal segments.

We developed a discourse segmenter that is able to perform EDS segmentation automatically based on the input of the syntactic and logical document structure annotations (annotation layers CNX and DOC, cf. Section 6.3.2) of an input text. It outputs a new annotation layer called SEG, where besides EDSs, also SDSs (sentential discourse segments, i.e. sentences) from the text, and CDSs (complex discourse segments, which correspond to DOC elements) are marked, as can be seen

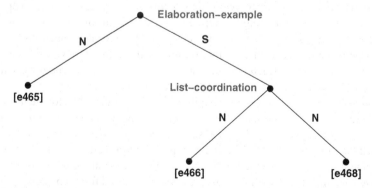

Fig. 6.2 Discourse dependency tree according to Danlos (2005)

in Listing 6.1. The criteria for EDSs as well as the discourse segmenter algorithm are described in Lüngen et al. (2006b).

Among CDSs, we further distinguish three types (cf. Bärenfänger et al. 2006): First, CDS type="block" corresponds to paragraphs and 2D objects that are on a par with paragraphs, such as titles, captions, and images, i.e. the elementary element types from the document structure that contain only text or non-textual 2D objects like images or diagrams, cf. Section 6.2.1. Second, CDS type="division" corresponds to the lowest section level or elements that are on a par with it in terms of DOC markup, e.g. titles and paragraphs that are sisters of section elements. Finally, CDS type="document" comprises all residual section elements, i.e. those which are on a higher level than CDS type="division". In our approach to discourse parsing, these segment types serve to constrain the extent to which discourse segment can be relationally combined, e.g. a CDS type="block" can only be related to another CDS type="block", but not a CDS type="division". In practice this means that the core parser module is called several times in a cascade architecture, starting out with EDSs, and leach time using the next higher one of the above sketched segments types as its base segment type.

6.2.3 Thematic Structure

The thematic structure of a text constitutes its thematic coherence in that it is responsible for the thematic connections between micro- and macrosegments of the text, and for their connection to an overall discourse topic, which serves as a frame for integrating the subtopics with regard to content. These connections between discourse topics and subtopics (and the thematically homogeneous macrosegments of the text, respectively) can be either semantic or functional or schema-based/associative. They constitute global thematic coherence.

Apart from thematic coherence on the global level, coherence can also be manifested by a relationship between adjacent sentences or clauses (i.e. elementary discourse segments). Such local relations are often signalled by explicit grammatical connections, which are formally realised by recurrence (e.g. coreference, anaphora) or by means of connectivity (e.g. conjunctions). These forms of connections are also called cohesion. Existing frameworks which model these local connections between elementary discourse segments operate on one of the different levels of discourse structure, i.e. referential structure (anaphoric relations), thematic structure (thematic development) and relational discourse structure (rhetorical relations).

The best known model for the description of local thematic development (i.e. the thematic relations between elementary discourse segments) is the *model of thematic progression* by Danes (1970). Another, similar, *model of thematic organisation* was proposed by Zifonun et al. (1997). Their proposed major patterns of local thematic development can be summarised as follows: 1. Continuation (of theme or rheme[3]) 2. Derived Theme (a. derived from a hypertheme, b. derived from a preceding theme or rheme), 3. Associated Theme. Apart from associated theme, all connections between two adjacent topics are based on semantic relations like *part-of* or *identity* and are often explicitly signalled by means of coreference. But such connections are not sufficient to describe all possible thematic relations. As Brinker (1997) points out, models like the one by Danes (1970) do not cover anything that cannot be covered by an analysis of the referential structure alone.

Research investigating functional and associative connections between topics is therefore important to overcome limitations of models which solely focus on semantic or referential ties between sentences to describe patterns of thematic development. Examples of more functionally oriented research are Lötscher (1987), Brinker (1997) and Schröder (2003), who propose functional relations like *reason, justify*, or *exemplification* to model thematic connections. The integration of functional relations in the analysis of the thematic structure seems quite natural, because an elaboration of a topic not only comprises the elaboration of its parts (which could be modelled by semantic relations like hyperonymy) but also the specification of functionally connected aspects of the topic, which could be modelled by RST relations.

To be able to model both kinds of relations (semantic and functional) in one discourse representation framework, we interpret the RST relation ELABORATION to represent coherence relations between discourse segments that are induced by the semantically motivated relations between discourse referents contained in them. For a detailed modeling of patterns as described in Danes (1970) or Zifonun et al. (1997), an extension of the ELABORATION relation with different subtypes was necessary. Figure 6.3 shows the subtypes that we defined for discourse annotation in the project *SemDok*.[4]

ELABORATION-DERIVATION comprises all relations between a nucleus and a satellite which are based on topic derivation, or ontological subordination. The subtypes of this relation are all mentioned in various publications but have not been grouped together before (cf. Mann and Thompson 1988, Hovy and Maier 1995, Carlson and Marcu 2001). ELABORATION-IDENTITY holds between a nucleus and a satellite that share a referential identity, that are about the same discourse referent. On the one hand we distinguish between forms of *theme-theme-* or *rheme-theme-* chaining (cf. Polanyi et al. 2003), on the other hand between *assignment* (of a technical term or an abbreviation) and other forms of *specification* where the meaning of the topic in the nucleus is expanded, restricted or specified by a syntactically incomplete satellite.

With this extension of the set of rhetorical relations we can capture all patterns of thematic development by means of RST (Table 6.1). It must be emphasised that ELABORATION has some special characteristics compared with other discourse relations: First, it is a relation that potentially holds between all thematically connected discourse segments. It is therefore one of the "most prevalent forms of modification of a nucleus" and "extremely common at all levels of the discourse structure" (Carlson et al. 2001) – in our corpus, ELABORATION is the second most frequent relation (about 25% of all relation instances in the presently annotated subcorpus). In an annotation process ELABORATION can be overridden by more specific discourse relations, i.e. whenever there are signals for a more specific discourse

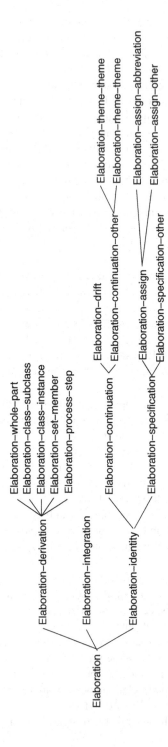

Fig. 6.3 SemDok hierarchy of ELABORATION relations

Table 6.1 Thematic relations

Patterns of thematic development	Thematic connections	
	Semantic relations	Rhetorical relations
(Referential) Continuation	synonymy, identity, paraphrase	ELABORATION-IDENTITY ELABORATION-CONTINUATION ELABORATION-SPECIFICATION ELABORATION-RESTATEMENT ELABORATION-EXAMPLE ELABORATION-DEFINITION
(Ontological) Derivation	hyponymy, hyperonymy, partonymy, meronymy	ELABORATION-DERIVATION ELABORATION-SET-MEMBER ELABORATION-PROCESS-STEP ELABORATION-CLASS-SUBCLASS ELABORATION-CLASS-INSTANCE ELABORATION-WHOLE-PART ELABORATION-INTEGRATION
(Functional) Supplementation/ Association		BACKGROUND, CIRCUMSTANCE CAUSE, RESULT, CONSEQUENCE PURPOSE, CONDITION, CONTRAST INTERPRETATION, EVALUATION,...

relation to hold between two discourse segments, this more specific relation is annotated. Second, ELABORATION is seldom signalled by syntactic or lexical discourse markers. Instead, ELABORATION may be identified by means of those linguistic features that signal thematic development: lexical-semantic and referential (anaphoric) relations between the central discourse entities of two discourse segments as well as lexical chains (Morris and Hirst 1991). As shown in Table 6.1, ELABORATION-DERIVATION and the converse relation ELABORATION-INTEGRATION are theoretically signalled by semantic relations like *hyponymy, hyperonymy, holonymy* etc., ELABORATION-IDENTITY by relations like *synonymy, identity* etc. Figure 6.4 and 6.5 show two examples where *holonymy* induces ELABORATION-DERIVATION, and *pertonymy* ELABORATION-DRIFT.[5]

These semantic relations (and the corresponding ELABORATION subtypes) can in principle be identified by consulting a lexico-semantic resource like *GermaNet* (cf. Kunze 2001) – only the coverage of GermaNet 5.0 is not sufficient for our corpus of scientific articles: only 69.3% of all noun tokens and 41.8% of all noun types in our corpus can be found in it (cf. Bärenfänger et al. 2007). We therefore primarily focus on the identification of ELABORATION and its subtypes by means of (annotations of) anaphoric relations and lexical chains as supplied by our project partners.

In various studies it has been pointed out that thematic development is closely connected with referential continuity, and that anaphoric relations may be used as signals for thematic continuity (cf. Danes 1970, Givon 1983, Zifonun et al. 1997). For the utilisation of anaphoric relations as cues for ELABORATION we cooperate with the *Sekimo* project where our corpus was annotated according to a schema for anaphoric relations (CHS, cf. Holler 2004). Two types of intra-textual anaphoric

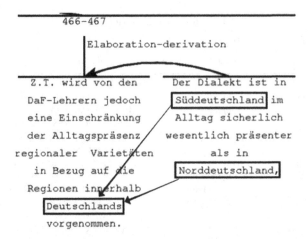

Fig. 6.4 Holonymy as a cue for ELABORATION-DERIVATION

relations are distinguished: *bridging* and *cospecification* relations. In cospecification relations (COSPEC), anaphora and antecedent are referentially identical, while bridging relations (BRIDGING) are based on semantic relations like meronymy, set-membership, and associative relations between anaphor and antecedent which have to be inferred from context.

Analyses of our corpus have shown that the presence of an anaphoric relation between discourse entities in two discourse segments is (approximately) a necessary condition for ELABORATION to hold between them. Yet, it is not a sufficient condition – this is amongst other things due to the status of ELABORATION as a default relation. However, correlations between certain subtypes of ELABORATION and specific anaphoric relations could be found as well, e.g. in 66.7% of all

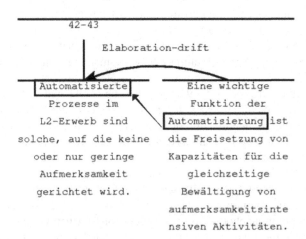

Fig. 6.5 Pertonymy as a cue for ELABORATION-DRIFT

```
<relationInstance rtype="elaboration-continuation-other">
    <segment1>Im folgenden Abschnitt werden wir zunächst einige terminologische Klärungen
             vornehmen .
    </segment1>
    <segment2>Diese betreffen einerseits unser Verständnis von regionalen Varietäten
             ( 2.1 ), andererseits das Spracheinstellungskonzept ( 2.2 ).
    </segment2>

    <anaphora atype="cospec:ident">
            <antecedent>einige terminologische Klärungen</antecedent>
            <anaphor>Diese</anaphor>
    </anaphora>
</relationInstance>
```

Listing 6.2 Correspondence of COSPEC:IDENTITY and ELABORATION-CONTINUATION

occurrences of *bridging:has-member*, ELABORATION-INTEGRATION holds, and in 82% of all ELABORATION-CONTINUATION occurrences, *cospec:ident* holds. An example of the latter is shown in Listing 6.2.[6]

Another approach to identifying thematically connected discourse segments is based on lexical cohesion, or, more specifically, the presence of lexical chains between discourse segments. "Lexical chains tend to indicate the topicality of segments" (Morris and Hirst 1991). This suggests that lexical chains can be employed to identify pairs of thematically homogeneous segments and, conversely, thematic breaks within logically defined segments. Lexical chains could thus also be used to revise the segment boundaries defined by the logical document structure. Incidents where discourse or thematic structure deviates from the logical document structure defined by the author of a text have sometimes been observed (cf. Stein 2003, Sporleder and Lapata 2004). In the two partner projects *HyTex* (see Storrer in this volume; Lenz in this volume) and *IndoGram* (Mehler in this volume), algorithms for the automatic construction of lexical chains have been implemented.

As emphasised above, thematic structure can be split into a local and a global level. Using RST, it is possible to analyse and represent both levels, the local level by annotating the relations between adjacent elementary discourse segments and the global level by relating complex discourse segments. Particularly for the analysis of the latter relations across larger spans of text, the relation ELABORATION and its subtypes are beneficial (cf. also Carlson et al. 2001). The goal of our approach to thematic structure is thus not to identify and label discourse topics, but to integrate semantic and functional thematic relations in one discourse representation model.

6.2.4 Generic Document Structure

Genre-specific *superstructure* or *text type structure* (van Dijk 1980, Swales 1990) is an aspect of global discourse structure. An analysis of our corpus showed that most scientific articles are sequentially structured along the text type-specific categories *problem, evidence, answers*, although deviations are possible, and commonly found (cf. Bärenfänger et al. 2006). These text type-specific functional categories (also e.g. *method, results,* and *discussion*) can be hierarchically organised in a text type

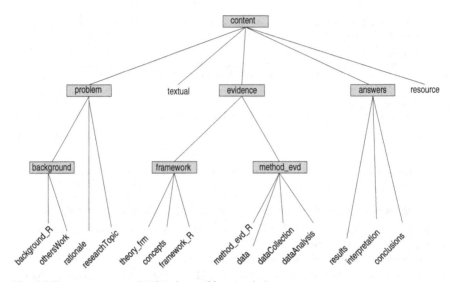

Fig. 6.6 Text type structure (TTS) schema (23 categories)

structure schema. One such schema (cf. Fig. 6.6) was designed in the first phase of the present project and is used for the *text type structure* corpus annotation level (TTS) described in Section 6.3.2. Previous approaches to text parsing of scientific articles have focussed on automatically assigning text type-specific functional categories (or *zones*, after Teufel 1999) from the text type structure to text segments using automatic text categorisation methods (Kando 1999, Teufel and Moens 2002, Langer et al. 2004a).

One aim of the present project, however, is to formulate a method to integrate text type structure and overall relational discourse structure. Text structural categories are functions of text parts within the whole text, i.e. they represent a mapping between pairs of one text span and the whole text into the set of textual category labels. RST analyses can be viewed as functions that map pairs of text spans onto a rhetorical relation label. Several of the category names used in previously proposed text type schemas (Kando 1999, Teufel and Moens 2002, Langer et al. 2004a) such as *problem, results, conclusion* suggest that text type structure and rhetorical structure can actually be interleaved (cf. Gruber and Muntigl 2005). This hypothesis

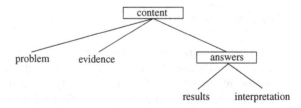

Fig. 6.7 Possible instantiation of text structural categories

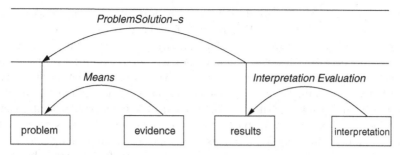

Fig. 6.8 Relational structuring of the categories in Fig. 6.7

is supported by the results of an empirical analysis of our corpus which showed significant correlations between generic and rhetorical structure. An *interpretation* constituent in a text type structure schema instantiation of an article (Fig. 6.7) can, for example, very often be characterised as an RST satellite to a nucleus which are related through INTERPRETATION (Fig. 6.8). The distribution of RST relations over the different TTS categories shows clear deviations from a normal distribution – some TTS and RST pairings are much more likely to occur than other pairings, e.g. the TTS category *OthersWork* significantly correlates with the RST relation BACKGROUND, *ResearchTopic* with ELABORATION. The overall findings of the corpus study are described in full length in Bärenfänger et al. (2006).

6.3 Resources

6.3.1 Corpus

For the development of the knowledge sources and the preprocessing components of the discourse parser, we work with a corpus that was compiled and annotated during the first project phase (2001–2004). The corpus comprises 120 scientific articles from two different disciplines (psychology and linguistics), languages (English and German) and sub-genres (experimental and review). English psychological and linguistic documents were taken from electronically available journals which were ranked highly in the listings of the Institute for Scientific Information (ISI) and published in the years 2000–2002. German linguistic articles were compiled from the online-journal "Linguistik Online" (volumes 2000–2003).

6.3.2 Annotation Levels

Our approach to corpus annotation was based on the assumption of four annotation levels that play a role in discourse analysis. (a) logical document structure (as e.g. encoded in DocBook, cf. Walsh and Muellner 1999, or *ldoc*, cf. Stede and

Suriyawongkul in this volume), (b) genre-specific text type structure (as described in van Dijk 1980, Swales 1990, Kando 1999, Teufel and Moens 2002), (c) rhetorical structure (Mann and Thompson 1988), and (d) syntactic structure. To examine dependencies between these levels, the corpus was analysed on all of them, and the analyses themselves were represented as XML-based multi-layer-annotations (Witt et al. 2005). In the multi-layer annotation approach, each information level is realised as an independent XML annotation layer and stored in a separate file. Thus, we distinguish between annotation *levels* (abstract information levels such as the syntax and morphology level of a linguistic grammar) and annotation *layers* (their realisations in XML) (cf. Goecke et al. in this volume). In the following, the levels and XML layers of logical document structure, text type structure, and rhetorical structure are described in more detail.

Logical document structure (DOC): The logical document structure is an abstraction of the physical layout structure. The annotation of the logical document structure (abbreviated DOC) – i.e. the hierarchical division of the text in sections, titles, paragraphs, footnotes, lists etc. – was provided using a subset of the DocBook DTD, extended by 13 elements relevant for the corpus (such as <footnoteSect>).

Text type structure (TTS): To represent the canonical text type structure of a scientific article (see Section 6.2.4), an XML schema was created which contains 135 functional categories such as *framework, method*, or *dataCollection*. The creation of the text type schema was based on an empirical analysis of the corpus and on an evaluation of similar approaches regarding so-called rhetorical zones (Teufel and Moens 2002) and text-level constituents (Kando 1999). The categories are arranged hierarchically in the schema. The resulting tree structure was also used to generate a reduced schema with 23 categories, which is more suitable for an efficient and consistent annotation. Besides, as linguistic articles show a variety of orders of functional categories, a flat schema version was derived from the hierarchical one by means of an XSLT style sheet. Articles annotated according to the flat schema still contain information about the original hierarchical structure encoded using the ID/IDREF-mechanism of XML (cf. Bayerl et al. 2003a, Langer et al. 2004a).

Rhetorical structure (RST): The rhetorical structure describes functional-argumentative relations (e.g. CONCESSION, or EVIDENCE) between discourse segments, cf. Section 6.2.2. The set of rhetorical relations used for the annotation of the corpus is basically the one proposed by Mann and Thompson (1988) in the framework of Rhetorical Structure Theory (RST). We employed the RSTTool developed by O'Donnell (2000) to manually annotate the rhetorical structure. By means of a Perl program, we can convert the flat XML output of the RSTTool to our hierarchical *RST-HP-format*, which, together with some extensions will be the format of the target structure of our discourse parser, cf. Lüngen et al. (2006a). From the English psychological articles, 15 sections (2–3 pages each) were annotated starting from elementary discourse segments, and 10 German linguistic articles were annotated completely but starting from paragraphs as smallest units. Currently, the rhetorical annotations are being extended using the more scenario-specific relation set RRSET described in Section 6.3.3.2. The RST annotations serve as training and evaluation material for the discourse parser.

Syntactic structure (CNX): The morphology/syntax layer was created automatically using the commercial *Machinese Syntax* tagger software from Connexor Oy.

During the annotation process, the quality of the manual annotations was supervised in two ways: Inter-rater reliability and intra-individual consistency (coder drift) were checked for the manually created annotations (cf. Bayerl et al. 2003b) using κ as a measure of agreement (Cohen 1960). The results of the tests for inter-rater reliability show that the quality of the TTS annotation was "substantial" (average $\kappa = .64$). κ for the RST annotations was .77 for the intra-sentential relations. The quality of the DOC annotation ($\kappa = .98$) is "nearly perfect" (cf. Landis and Koch 1977).

Table 6.2 Corpus annotations

	TTS (135)	TTS (23)	DOC	RST	CNX
English psychological articles	73	73 (automatically generated)	73	15 (several sections)	73
German linguistic articles		47	47	3 + 10 CDS-block	47

The extensive XML-based multi-layer-annotated corpus gives us the possibility to examine interrelations between these levels and to identify cues for rhetorical relations, e.g. cues on the level of document structure (such as an occurrence of the element <itemizedList>) or syntactic or topical cues (e.g. the occurrence of the text type-category *dataCollection*). Moreover, cues from different annotation levels can be combined to form complex conditions for the assignment of a specific rhetorical relation.

6.3.3 Additional Resources

6.3.3.1 Discourse Marker Lexicon

Discourse markers are functional elements that can be regarded as signals for a rhetorical relation (coherence relation) between two text segments. As we have indicated above, there are different types of discourse markers: Firstly, there are lexical discourse markers, or *connectives*. These are syntactically mostly adverbs or conjunctions. They may consist of one word (*weil*, "because"), multiple adjacent parts (*so dass*, "so that") or multiple discontinuous parts (*wenn . . . dann . . . sonst . . .*, "if . . . then . . . else . . ."). Secondly, configurations of grammatical and/or document type-related features can function as (more abstract) discourse markers. An occurrence of a <doc:itemizedlist>-environment on the logical document structure level would indicate one nucleus of a multinuclear LIST or SEQUENCE relation, <doc:glossterm> would induce the nucleus of an ELABORATION-DEFINITION relation, <doc:glossdef> its satellite, and <doc:title> the satellite of a PREPARATION relation. In the present stage of the project, the lexicon comprises lexical discourse markers, other discourse markers are currently treated in the rule component of the parser.

Many lexical discourse connectives are highly ambiguous. Frequently they do not clearly denote an individual rhetorical relation, but on the contrary the same markers signal different relations depending on their context. Our intention was to provide an XML-encoded inventory of German discourse connectives which resolves these ambiguities.

First, we extracted a list of discourse connectives from our corpus and developed a suitable representational format in XML. The definition and validation of the XML data was implemented in XML-Schema. The dictionary contains orthographic and syntactic characteristics of the respective discourse markers. The syntactic information included is based on the annotation generated by the *Machinese Syntax* Tagger from *Connexor Oy*, the descriptions in the *Handbuch der deutschen Konnektoren* of the *IDS Mannheim* (Pasch et al. 2003) and the grammar by Helbig and Buscha (1998). The encoding the topological fields resembles the format employed in DiMLex (Stede and Umbach 1998).

```
<dm id="c63" typ="lexical">
  <cue>
    <text>wenn</text>
    <lemma pos="CS">wenn</lemma>
    <position>
      <sub>+</sub>
    </position>
  </cue>
  <kommentar>"wenn auch X" is always Concession.</kommentar>
  <kommentar>"wenn X auch" is an alternative - not yet considered here</kommentar>
  <filter>
    <!-- obligatory conditions -->
    <hypothese relname="Concession">
      <word fenster="9" richtung="r">
        <text>auch</text>
        <lemma pos="ADV">auch</lemma>
      </word>
    </hypothese>
  </filter>
  <rels default="Circumstance">
    <relation score="0.5" relname="Circumstance" skopus="eds+" typ="s" beds-richtung="lr"/>
    <relation score="0.5" relname="Concession"  skopus="eds+" typ="s" beds-richtung="lr">
    <!-- optional conditions -->
    </relation>
  </rels>
</dm>
```

Listing 6.3 Entry for "wenn" in the discourse marker lexicon

Each entry in the dictionary is represented by a <dm>-element (see Listing 6.3 for a sample entry). A <dm>-entry generally consists of three main parts: an identification unit, a filter unit, and an allocation unit. The identification unit identifies a lexical discourse marker (word or phrase) by its form (<text>), by the word stem (<lemma>) and its part of speech (@pos). The optional filter unit allows for disambiguation of discourse markers by providing hypotheses about possible contexts and their associated specific rhetorical relations. Obligatory combinations of features (of the current segment and the reference segment) are combined to form hypotheses. Its attributes are supposed to override the general attribute values given in the allocation unit with their specific values in the current context. In the allocation unit all relations expressed by the discourse marker are specified. The @score attribute contains the conditional score for the relation given the discourse marker. It is presently based on an assumption of equal distribution but will eventually be estimated from our corpus. The attributes @beds-richtung and @skopus determine the position of the segment in comparison to the reference segment and the scope of the segment. If a segment offers several competing relations signalled by different discourse markers, a hierarchy of relations can be expressed on the basis of the attribute @skopus, so that the discourse parsing engine has criteria for a decision about the order in which the individual relations are applied and promoted (cf. Corston-Oliver 1998). The allocation unit can contain additional conditions for the segment and the reference segment, which provide the discourse parsing engine with further indicators to confirm a relation or to find the corresponding reference segment.

The discourse marker lexicon currently contains 92 <dm> entries. A perl program for tagging lexical discourse markers in texts based on a CNX annotation of the text (see Section 6.3.2) and the discourse marker lexicon exists.

6.3.3.2 Set of Rhetorical Relations

One goal of the present project was to develop a set of rhetorical relations suitable for analysing scientific articles in our explorative reading scenario, cf. Section 6.1. Our strategy was as follows: We took the extended classical MT (Mann/Thompson) relation set of 34 relation types as a starting point (cf. Mann and Taboada 2005); additionally we reviewed the comprehensive relation taxonomies previously suggested for English by Carlson et al. (2001) (96 relation types, 78 of which are at the base level of the taxonomy, which were employed in the rhetorical analysis of newspaper articles) and Hovy and Maier (1995) (65 relation types, 43 of which at base level, which were designed mostly from the perspective of natural language generation and are not RST-specific) and chose candidate relations for extending the MT relation set. We then evaluated the RST annotations that were available from the first project phrase (see Section 6.3.1) for determining the relevance of each relation in our corpus. Subsequently, we designed our relation set (called the RRSET) along the following criteria:

- we introduced subrelations when we found strong associations with certain discourse markers that seemed highly scenario-relevant; for instance we wanted to

distinguish between LIST-COORDINATION relations that come about by syntactic
coordination vs. LIST-DM_OTHER relations that come about through discourse
markers on the logical document structure level such as the `<listitem>` elements.
Similarly, we introduced PREPARATION-TITLE, PREPARATION-QUESTION,
Preparation-other, CITATION-EVIDENCE, and CITATION-ATTRIBUTION;

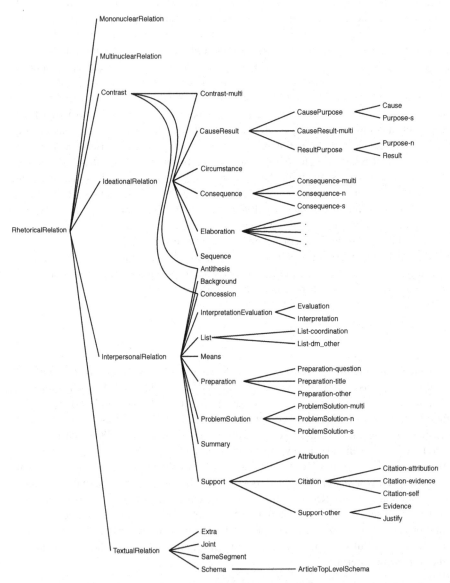

Fig. 6.9 SemDok RRSET ontology (save the subclasses of ELABORATION) (edges from
MONONUCLEARRELATION and MULTINUCLEARRELATION are not shown)

- we introduced the comprehensive sub-taxonomy of ELABORATION relations described in Section 6.2.3;
- we omitted two relations from Mann and Thompson (1988), which had proved to be irrelevant in our text type (MOTIVATION and ENABLEMENT);
- we introduced new superordinate relation classes for relations that were hardly distinguished by discourse markers and that were also often confused by human annotators when trying to apply semantically oriented definitions (SUPPORT-OTHER, CONTRAST, LISTSEQUENCE, and INTERPRETATIONEVALUATION);
- we introduced relation types that denote heavily underspecified relations (MONO-NUCLEARRELATION, MULTINUCLEARRELATION, IDEATIONALRELATION, INTERPERSONALRELATION, and TEXTUALRELATION).
- we introduced certain subrelations based on alternative nuclearity assignments as in Carlson et al. (2001) (CONSEQUENCE-MULTI, CAUSERESULT-MULTI, and PROBLEMSOLUTION-MULTI);

The resulting *SemDok* RRSET taxonomy consists of 70 relation types (44 at base level) and is encoded in the semantic web ontology language OWL (cf. Bechhofer et al. 2004 and see also Farrar and Langendoen in this volume). OWL consists of the three sublanguages OWL Lite, OWL DL and OWL Full, which differ in expressivity. We chose OWL DL (based on *description logics*) to encode our RRSET ontology because current reasoning software such as RacerPro,[7] which can be used for consistency checking and drawing inferences, is designed for the decidable sublanguage OWL DL. Since we wanted to declare disjointness between certain rhetorical relation types and to encode properties of rhetorical relations that are to be inherited by their subrelations, we modelled RST relations as OWL classes. All RRSET relations are cross-classified along the two dimensions *nuclearity* and *metafunction*, giving rise to multiple inheritance. SUPPORT, for instance, is both a subclass of INTERPERSONALRELATION and of MONONUCLEARRELATION. Figure 6.9 shows the hierarchy of relations as induced by the <rdfs:subClassOf> specifications of the OWL representation (the complete ELABORATION subhierarchy is shown in Fig. 6.3) (cf. Bärenfänger et al. 2007).

6.4 Discourse Parsing Architecture

This section shortly describes the architecture and algorithm of the discourse parser that is developed in the *SemDok* project based on the theoretical assumptions and resources described so far. In Fig. 6.10, the architecture of the discourse parsing system is shown.

The declarative knowledge sources are used in several preprocessing steps by auxiliary components to analyse an input text[8] and to provide it with multiple annotation layers. The discourse parser itself takes these different annotation layers as its input to guide its decisions for selecting and applying rules to build up a set of possible annotations of the rhetorical discourse structure.

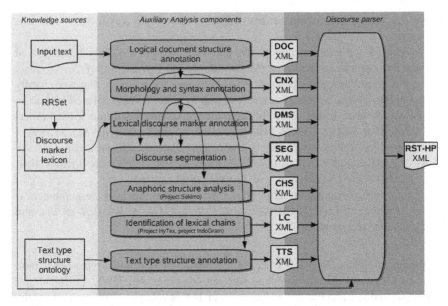

Fig. 6.10 Discourse parser architecture

The base annotation layer controlling the parsing cycles is the discourse segmentation layer (SEG, cf. Section 6.2.2). The parser strategy follows the segmentation bottom-up, firstly combining adjacent elementary discourse segments (EDS) recursively to sentential ones (SDS), secondly combining sentential discourse segments to complex discourse segments (CDS) of type block, then combining the block level segments to division level segments (i. e. sections) and finally division level segments up to the level of the complete document. Each one of these phases is called a *cascade step*.

The remaining annotation layers – i. e. the logical document structure (DOC), the morphological and syntactic tagging (CNX, cf. Section 6.3.2), the lexical discourse marker annotation (DMS, cf. Section 6.3.3.1) and the anaphoric structure (CHS, cf. Section 6.2.3) – provide linguistic cues and constraints for rhetorical relations and are referenced in the rule component of the parser. These cues and constraints describe correlations between different discourse markers represented as configurations of XML elements and attributes on the different annotation layers and yield hypotheses of rhetorical relations that hold between the discourse segments of the input text.

The output of the parser is a set of well-formed RST trees in the extended RST-HP format described in Lüngen et al. (2006a).

The parsing strategy used in each cascade step is a bottom-up passive chart parser. Each time a tuple of adjacent spans matches all cues and constraints specified in a rule, a new edge is inserted into the chart, labelled with a rhetorical relation and a nuclearity setting, and representing a new discourse-coherent span over the input segments.

To evaluate competing rhetorical relation hypotheses, each edge of the chart is assigned a score expressing its adequacy in a resulting discourse structure. The score of an edge depends on the context in which it is inserted into the chart, i. e. it is a function of the scores of its child edges and the score of the rule which is applied to insert the edge (cf. Le Thanh et al. 2004). The rule score is composed of the a priori probability of the rhetorical relation that is induced by the rule, i. e. the probability with which the relation occurs in the corpus, combined with the conditional probability of the relation given the discourse marker that is mentioned in the rule. The probabilities are estimated by calculating percentages of occurrences of relation instances and discourse markers in the development corpus.

To reduce the search space, a list of *applied discourse marker identifiers* is also associated with each edge in the chart. They form a control structure that ensures that one discourse marker cannot be applied twice during the construction of a rhetorical tree. Thus, they partly replace the promotion sets as proposed by Marcu (2000).

In forthcoming versions of the parser, the processing of additional linguistic resources shall be incorporated. These are annotations of lexical chains (cf. Section 6.2.3) and genre-specific text type structure (cf. Section 6.2.4).

6.5 Conclusion

In this chapter, we discussed the theoretical foundations of discourse analysis of texts of a complex genre from the perspectives of document engineering, discourse theory, and text linguistics. We identified those aspects of discourse and discourse analysis that are relevant for our text type and application scenario, especially the prominent role of logical document structure, thematic structure and text type structure when analysing a complex genre. We argued that for discourse analysis, an augmented version of RST (Rhetorical Structure Theory) should be adopted. One of the proposed augmentations is the accomodation of thematic structure by differentiating various subtypes of the familiar ELABORATION relation based on semantic relations between the themes of the discourse.

Subsequently, the resources and methods based on XML technologies that we use in developing the discourse parser were introduced in more detail. We sketched the structure of the discourse marker lexicon which contains mostly lexical discourse markers (connectives). We introduced a set of 44 rhetorical relation labels based on the original RST relation set but adapted to our project scenario and text type. The rhetorical relation labels are hierarchically ordered in a relation taxonomy.

One future focus of the project will be on evaluation. The output of the system will be compared to manually created annotations of our corpus, which will serve as a gold standard, using standard methods and measures. Besides, system performance will be compared with a baseline provided by trivial algorithms such as random relation assignment or exclusive assignment of the most frequent relation according to our corpus annotations. Moreover, it will be interesting to compare the system with other existing RST parsers, such as the one for German newspaper commentaries developed at Potsdam University (cf. Reitter 2003a, b).

Traditionally, the external evaluation of a discourse parser is done by assessing its contribution to automatic text summarisation systems (cf. Marcu 2000, Rehm 1998, Polanyi et al. 2004a). In the context of the DFG-Forschergruppe *Texttechnologische Informationsmodellierung*, however, it will be possible to examine whether and how the analyses provided by the discourse parser can improve the performance of the automatic hypertextualisation system developed in the *HyTex* project (Lenz in this volume, Storrer in this volume).

Notes

1. Text extract from Saari, Mirja (2000). Schwedisch als die zweite Nationalsprache Finnlands: Soziolinguistische Aspekte. *Linguistik Online,* 7, http://www.linguistik-online.de.
2. We employ the tool described in O'Donnell (2000) for drawing RST trees.
3. *Rheme* as in the theory of *Functional Sentence Perspective*.
4. Apart from the subtypes of elaboration shown in Fig. 6.3, we distinguish ELABORATION-EXAMPLE, ELABORATION-DEFINITION and ELABORATION-RESTATEMENT.
5. Text extract from Baßler, Harald and Helmut Spiekermann (2001). Dialekt und Standardsprache im DaF-Unterricht. Wie Schüler urteilen – wie Lehrer urteilen. *Linguistik Online* 9, http://www.linguistik-online.de.
6. Extract from Baßler and Spiekermann (2001) (see Footnote 5).
7. http://www.racer-systems.com
8. The test corpus consists of a suite of German linguistic journal articles.

References

Asher, Nichoas and Vieu, Laure (2005). Subordinating and coordinating discourse relations. *Lingua,* 115(4):591–610.

Asher, Nicholas and Lascarides, Alex (2003). *Logics of Conversation.* Cambridge University Press, Cambridge, UK.

Bärenfänger, Maja, Lüngen, Harald, Hilbert, Mirco, and Lobin, Henning (in press). The role of logical and generic document structure in relational discourse analysis. In Benz, Anton, Kühnlein, Peter, and Sidner, Candy, editors, *Constraints in Discourse 2.* Series Pragmatics & Beyond. John Benjamins, Amsterdam.

Bärenfänger, Maja, Lobin, Henning, Lüngen, Harald, and Hilbert, Mirco (2008). OWL ontologies in discourse parsing. *LDV-Forum. GLDV-Journal for Computational Linguistics and language Technololgy* 23(1):7–26.

Bayerl, Petra Saskia, Lüngen, H., Gut, U., and Paul, K.I. (2003a). Methodology for reliable schema development and evaluation of manual annotations. In *Workshop Notes for the Workshop on Knowledge Markup and Semantic Annotation, Second International Conference on Knowledge Capture (K-CAP 2003),* pages 17–23, Sanibel, Florida.

Bayerl, Petra Saskia, Lüngen, Harald, Goecke, Daniela, Witt, Andreas, and Naber, Daniel (2003b). Methods for the semantic analysis of document markup. In *Proceedings of the ACM Symposium on Document Engineering (DocEng 2003),* pages 161–170, Grenoble.

Bechhofer, Sean, van Harmelen, Frank, Hendler, Jim, Horrocks, Ian, McGuiness, Deborah L., Patel-Schneider, Peter F., and Stein, Andrea Lynn (2004). OWL Web Ontology Language – Reference. Technical report, W3C (World Wide Web) Consortium. http://www.w3.org/TR/2004/REC-owl-ref-20040210/.

Brinker, Klaus (1997). *Linguistische Textanalyse. Eine Einführung in Grundbegriffe und Methoden.* 4th edition, Erich Schmidt, Berlin.

Carlson, Lynn and Marcu, Daniel (2001). Discourse tagging reference manual. Technical report, Information Science Institute, Marina del Rey, CA. ISI-TR-545.

Carlson, Lynn, Marcu, Daniel, and Okurowski, Mary Ellen (2001). Building a discourse-tagged corpus in the framework of rhetorical structure theory. In *Proceedings of the 2nd SIGDIAL Workshop on Discourse and Dialogue*, Eurospeech 2001, Denmark.

Cohen, J. (1960). A coefficient of agreement for nominal scales. *Educational and Psychological Measurements*, 20:37–46.

Corston-Oliver, Simon (1998). *Computing of Representations of the Structure of Written Discourse.* PhD thesis, University of California, Santa Barbara.

Daneš, Frantisek (1970). Zur linguistischen Analyse der Textstruktur. *Folia Linguistica*, 4:72–78.

Danlos, Laurence (2005). Comparing RST and SDRT discourse structures through dependency graphs. In Sassen, Claudia, Benz, Anton, and Kühnlein, Peter, editors, *Proceedings of Constraints in Discourse*, pages 55–62, Dortmund.

Egg, Markus and Redeker, Gisela (2005). Underspecified discourse representation. In Sassen, Claudia, Benz, Anton, and Kühnlein, Peter, editors, *Proceedings of Constraints in Discourse*, pages 46–53, Dortmund.

Givon, Talmy (1983). Topic Continuity in Discourse: An Introduction. In Givon, Talmy, editor, *Topic Continuity in Discourse: A Quantitative Cross-Language Study*, pages 5–41. John Benjamins, Amsterdam, Philadelphia.

Goecke, Daniela, Lüngen, Harald, Sasaki, Felix, Witt, Andreas, and Farrar, Scott (2005). GOLD and discourse: Domain- and community-specific extensions. In *Proceedings of the 2005 E-MELD-Workshop*, Boston, MA.

Gruber, H. and Muntigl, P. (2005). Generic and rhetorical structures of texts: Two sides of the same coin? *Folia Linguistica. Special Issue: Approaches to Genre*, XXXIX(1–2):75–114.

Helbig, Gerhard and Buscha, Joachim (1998). *Deutsche Grammatik: Ein Handbuch für den Ausländerunterricht.* 18th edition, Langenscheidt, Leipzig.

Holler, Anke und Jan Frederik Maas und Angelika Storrer (2004). Exploiting coreference annotations for text-to-hypertext conversion. In *Proceedings of LREC*, volume II, pages 651–654, Lisboa.

Hovy, Eduard and Maier, Elisabeth (1995). Parsimonious or profligate: How many and which discourse structure relations? Unpublished paper, http://www.isi.edu/natural-language/people/hovy/publications.html.

Kando, Noriko (1999). Text structure analysis as a tool to make retrieved documents usable. In *Proceedings of the 4th International Workshop on Information Retrieval with Asian Languages*, pages 126–135, Taipei, Taiwan.

Kunze, Claudia (2001). Lexikalisch-semantische Wortnetze. In Carstensen, Kai-Uwe et al., editor, *Computerlinguistik und Sprachtechnologie: eine Einführung*, pages 386–393. Spektrum Verlag, Heidelberg.

Landis, J.R. and Koch, G. G. (1977). The measurement of observer agreement for categorical data. *Biometrics*, 33:159–174.

Langer, Hagen, Lüngen, Harald, and Bayerl, Petra Saskia (2004a). Text type structure and logical document structure. In *Proceedings of the ACL 2004 Workshop on Discourse Annotation*, pages 49–56, Barcelona.

Le Thanh, Huong, Abeysinghe, Geetha, and Huyck, Christian (2004). Generating discourse structures for written texts. In *Proceedings of COLING'04*, Geneva, Switzerland.

Lötscher, Andreas (1987). *Text und Thema. Studien zur thematischen Konstituenz von Texten.* Reihe Germanistische Linguistik, 81. Niemeyer, Tübingen.

Lüngen, Harald, Lobin, Henning, Bärenfänger, Maja, Hilbert, Mirco, and Puskàs, Csilla (2006a). Text parsing of a complex genre. In *Proceedings of the Conference on Electronic Publishing (ELPUB)*, pages 247–256, Bansko, Bulgaria.

Lüngen, Harald, Puskàs, Csilla, Bärenfänger, Maja, Hilbert, Mirco, and Lobin, Henning (2006b). Discourse segmentation of German written text. In *Proceedings of the 5th International Conference on Natural Language Processing (FinTAL 2006)*, pages 245–256, Åbo, Finland. Springer.

Mann, William C. and Taboada, Maite (2005). RST – Rhetorical Structure Theory. W3C page. http://www.sfu.ca/rst.

Mann, William C. and Thompson, Sandra A. (1988). Rhetorical Structure Theory: Toward a functional theory of text organisation. *Text*, 8(3):243–281.

Marcu, Daniel (1999). A decision-based approach to rhetorical parsing. In *Proceedings of the 37th annual meeting of the ACL*, pages 365–372, Maryland. Association for Computational Linguistics.

Marcu, Daniel (2000). *The Theory and Practice of Discourse Parsing and Summarization*. MIT Press, Cambridge, MA.

Morris, Jane and Hirst, Graeme (1991). Lexical cohesion computed by thesaural relations as an indicator of the structure of text. *Computational Linguistics*, 17(1):21–48.

Motsch, Wolfgang and Viehweger, Dieter (1991). Illokutionsstruktur als Komponente einer modularen Textanalyse. In Brinker, Klaus, editor, *Aspekte der Textlinguistik*, volume 106/107 of *Germanistische Linguistik*, pages 107–132. Olms, Hildesheim/Zürich/New York.

O'Donnell, Michael (2000). RSTTool 2.4 – A markup tool for Rhetorical Structure Theory. In *Proceedings of the International Natural Language Generation Conference (INLG'2000)*, pages 253 – 256, Mitzpe Ramon, Israel.

Pasch, Renate, Brauße, Ursula, Breindl, Eva, and Waßner, Ulrich Hermann, editors (2003). *Handbuch der deutschen Konnektoren. Linguistische Grundlagen der Beschreibung und syntaktische Merkmale der deutschen Satzverknüpfer (Konjunktionen, Satzadverbien und Partikeln)*. Schriften des Instituts für Deutsche Sprache. de Gruyter, Berlin.

Polanyi, Livia, Culy, Chris, van den Berg, Martin, Thione, Gian Lorenzo, and Ahn, David (2004a). A rule based approach to discourse parsing. In *Proceedings of the 5th Workshop in Discourse and Dialogue*, pages 108–117, Cambridge, MA. 2004.

Polanyi, Livia, Culy, Chris, van den Berg, Martin, Thione, Gian Lorenzo, and Ahn, David (2004b). Sentential structure and discourse parsing. In *Proceedings of the ACL 2004 Workshop on Discourse Annotation*, pages 49–56, Barcelona.

Polanyi, Livia, van den Berg, Martin, and Ahn, David (2003). Discourse structure and sentential information structure. *Journal of Logic, Language and Information*, 12:337–350.

Rehm, Georg (1998). Vorüberlegungen zur automatischen Zusammenfassung deutschsprachiger Texte mittels einer SGML- und DSSSL-basierten Repräsentation von RST-Relationen. Master's thesis, Universität Osnabrück.

Reitter, David (2003a). Rhetorical analysis with rich-feature support vector models. Master's thesis, University of Potsdam.

Reitter, David (2003b). Simple signals for complex rhetorics: On rhetorical analysis with rich-feature support vector models. In Seewald-Heeg, Uta, editor, *Sprachtechnologie für die multilinguale Kommunikation. Textproduktion, Recherche, Übersetzung, Lokalisierung. Beiträge der GLDV-Frühjahrstagung 2003*, volume 18 of *LDV-Forum*, pages 38–52, Köthen.

Schröder, Thomas (2003). *Die Handlungsstruktur von Texten. Ein integrativer Beitrag zur Texttheorie*. Gunter Narr, Tübingen.

Sporleder, Caroline and Lapata, Mirella (2004). Automatic paragraph identification: A study across languages and domains. In *Proceedings of the 2004 Conference on Empirical Methods in Natural Language Processing (EMNLP-04)*, pages 72–79, Barcelona.

Stede, Manfred and Umbach, Carla (1998). DiMLex: A lexicon of discourse markers for text generation and understanding. In *Proceedings of the 17th international conference on Computational Linguistics (COLING-98)*, pages 1238–1242, Montreal, Canada.

Stein, Stephan (2003). *Textgliederung. Einheitenbildung im geschriebenen und gesprochenen Deutsch: Theorie und Empirie*, volume 69 of *Studia Linguistica Germanica*. de Gruyter, Berlin.

Swales, John M. (1990). *Genre Analysis. English in academic and research settings*. Cambridge University Press, Cambridge, UK.

Teufel, Simone (1999). *Argumentative Zoning: Information Extraction from Scientific Text*. PhD thesis, University of Edinburgh.

Teufel, Simone and Moens, Marc (2002). Summarizing scientfic articles: Experiments with relevance and rhetorical status. *Computational Linguistics*, 28(4):409–445.

van Dijk, Teun A. (1980). *Macrostructures: An interdisciplinary study of global structures in discourse, interaction, and cognition*. Lawrence Erlbaum Associates, Hillsdale, NJ.

Walsh, Norman and Muellner, Leonard (1999). *DocBook: The Definitive Guide*. O'Reilly, Sebastopol, CA.

Witt, Andreas, Lüngen, Harald, Goecke, Daniela, and Sasaki, Felix (2005). Unification of XML documents with concurrent markup. *Literary and Linguistic Computing*, 20(1):103–116.

Wolf, Florian and Gibson, Edward (2005). Representing discourse coherence: A corpus-based study. *Computational Linguistics*, 31(2):249–288.

Zifonun, Gisela, Hoffmann, Ludger, and Strecker, Bruno (1997). *Grammatik der deutschen Sprache*, volume 7 of *Schriften des Instituts für deutsche Sprache*, chapter C6 "Thematische Organisation von Text und Diskurs", pages 535–591. de Gruyter, Berlin/New York.

Chapter 7
Multilevel Annotation for Information Extraction

Introduction to the GENIA Annotation

Jin-Dong Kim, Tomoko Ohta, and Jun'ichi Tsujii

Abstract Information Extraction (IE) is the broad task of detecting and extracting specific structured information from unstructured natural language text. IE typically requires analysis to determine the linguistic structure of text and semantic processing to map linguistic structures to semantic ones. For real-world applications, this processing often needs to be performed at various levels, determining e.g. the parts-of-speech, syntactic structure, named entities, and events. Multilevel annotations made to a corpus are a necessary resource for the development of multilevel text processing tools and eventually automatic IE systems, providing both reference and training material for method development and benchmark data sets. This chapter introduces the GENIA corpus and various annotations made to it as an example of multilevel annotation made for IE, and discusses general issues in multilevel annotation.

Keywords Natural language processing · Corpus annotation · Information extraction · Text mining

7.1 Introduction

Recent progress in natural language processing (NLP) research promotes the integration of various NLP techniques to effectively exploit the information to be obtained from multiple levels of text analysis. Multilevel annotation has emerged to support the development of NLP software, particularly in integrated ways. Efforts to facilitate multilevel annotation include the development of annotation tools, e.g. MATE (Carletta and Isard 1999), MMAX (Müller and Strube 2006), and encoding

J.-D. Kim (✉)
University of Tokyo, Tokyo, Japan
e-mail: jdkim@is.s.u-tokyo.ac.jp

A. Witt, D. Metzing (eds.), *Linguistic Modeling of Information and Markup Languages*, Text, Speech and Language Technology 40,
DOI 10.1007/978-90-481-3331-4_7, © Springer Science+Business Media B.V. 2010

standards, e.g. CES/XCES (Ide et al. 2000), LAF/GrAF (Ide and Romary 2007). Some corpus annotation projects explicitly aim at multilevel annotation, e.g. ANC (Ide and Suderman 2006), Ontonotes (Hovy et al. 2006). For the molecular biology domain, which is a recently emerging target domain of NLP, also several corpora have been developed with multilevel annotation, e.g. GENIA (Kim et al. 2008), PennBioIE (Kulick et al., 2004a), BioInfer(Pyysalo et al. 2007).

While the standardization efforts for corpus encoding are under progress, currently available resources to support them are limited. Since the corpus annotation itself is usually an expensive task, the encoding scheme is often minimized to reduce the cost for the preparation of software tools and also the burden on annotators.

This chapter discusses fundamental techniques for multilevel annotation to help the principled decisions for design and implementation of multilevel annotation. In the end, the GENIA corpus and annotations made to it are introduced as an example of multilevel annotation.

7.2 Inline vs. Standoff Annotation

In the context of NLP or Computational Linguistics (CL), the target of annotation is often natural language text which is stored as a sequence of characters on computers. Corpus annotation is a task to find linguistic structures in the text and to create metadata describing them to allow computers direct access to the structures. It is therefore a fundamental step of corpus annotation to identify specific spans of text which exhibit linguistic structures. Metadata is then created to associate relevant spans and descriptions to represent useful information underlying the text.

There are two contrasting methods of modeling spans and storing metadata: inline vs. standoff annotation. With inline annotation, delimiters are inserted in text to indicate the spans to be annotated, and metadata is put around the span to represent the annotated information. For example, suppose that we have a text which begins with

The stability of c-Fos was decreased when the protein was dimerized with c-Jun.

and we are to annotate it for linguistic structures, e.g. words, phrases, etc. In Penn Treebank, parentheses are inserted around phrases and clauses to indicate their boundary, and the labels indicating their syntactic class are put right after the opening parenthesis, e.g.

(NP (NP The stability) (PP of (NP c-fos))) $\cdots$

For part-of-speech tagging, it is assumed that words are delimited by space characters, and the POS label for each word is put right next to the word with slash ("/") as the delimiter between a word and its POS label.

The/DT stability/NN of/PP c-fos/NN $\cdots$

Recently, XML is widely adopted for the encoding of corpora and annotation as it is a de facto standard framework of document encoding. In XML, a pair of opening and end markups are inserted around a span to be annotated. Additional information is stored as valuated attributes of the markups.

```
<word POS="DT"> The </word> <word POS="DT"> stability </word>
<word POS="DT"> of </word> <word POS="DT"> c-fos </word> ···
```

Advantage of inline annotation mostly comes from its simplicity. Since the annotation is stored in the same file as the target document and metadata are put around corresponding text spans, inline annotation is easy to maintain and its processing for creation, searching, transformation and browsing is relatively simple. Especially, when it is encoded in XML, which has a large community of users and software developers, there are a huge number of software tools available for handling XML documents, and annotation practitioners do not need to reinvent the whole wheel.

Standoff annotation has emerged with emphasis on the separation of documents and annotation (Thompson and McKelvie 1997). With standoff annotation, documents are kept unchanged during and after the annotation, and metadata are stored in separate files. It is a common practice to represent a specific span by its beginning and end position in the text, to establish a connection between the metadata stored in a separate file with corresponding spans of the target document.

```
Id:W1, Structure:Word, Span:0..3,   POS:DT  # The
Id:W2, Structure:Word, Span:4..13,  POS:NN  # stability
Id:W3, Structure:Word, Span:14..16, POS:IN  # of
Id:W4, Structure:Word, Span:17..22, POS:NN  # c-fos
```

For the span representation, the character offset model and the caret (or cursor) offset model are often used. The difference of the two offset models is illustrated in the Fig. 7.1. With the character offset model, the position of each character is expressed by its offset from the beginning of the text. For example, the span "The" in the above example is expressed as (1..3) indicating the first through the third characters constitute the span. In the caret offset model, it is assumed that there is a caret position between every two neighboring characters, and a span is expressed by the caret positions before and after the span, e.g. (0..3) for the span "The". Throughout this chapter, we will use the caret offset model when we show examples of standoff annotation, but the conversion between the two models is trivial.

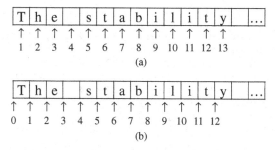

Fig. 7.1 (a) character offset model, (b) caret offset model

Standoff annotation is particularly emphasized when the annotation practitioners do not have the permission to modify the target documents, which is often the case with web documents. It is however a responsibility of annotation practitioners to check the validness of the span references, i.e. the validness of span references is subject to the change of the target document. Another advantage of standoff annotation is that spans with crossed boundary can be stored in the same annotation file, which is usually impossible with inline annotation due to its nature of representing things in a tree structure.

7.3 Type of Annotated Information

In corpus annotation, the most fundamental task is to find structures of interest in the two-dimensional text data. The structures then become elements of further annotation which may be attributional or relational.

Structural annotation sometimes involves finding hierarchical structures. With inline annotation, the hierarchy is represented by inclusion of a span in another. For example, the following annotation identifies structures at word and phrase levels:

```
<phrase id="p4">
  <phrase id="p1">
    <word id="w1">The</word>
    <word id="w2">stability</word>
  </phrase>
  <phrase id="p3">
    <word id="w3">of</word>
    <phrase id="p2">
      <word id="w4">c-Fos</word>
    </phrase>
  </phrase>
</phrase>

  ...
```

With standoff annotation, the hierarchy can be represented implicitly or explicitly. In the following example, the hierarchy of the words and phrases is represented implicitly by the regional relation of the spans, e.g. inclusion of one in another:

```
Id:W1, Structure:Word,   Span:0..3     # The
Id:W2, Structure:Word,   Span:4..13    # stability
Id:W3, Structure:Word,   Span:14..16   # of
Id:W4, Structure:Word,   Span:17..22   # c-fos
Id:P1, Structure:Phrase, Span:0..13    # The stability
Id:P2, Structure:Phrase, Span:17..22   # c-fos
Id:P3, Structure:Phrase, Span:14..22   # of c-fos
Id:P4, Structure:Phrase, Span:0..22    # The stability of c-fos

  ...
```

Alternatively, the words constituting phrases can be explicitly expressed. In the following example, only the words, which are the most fundamental structures, are identified on the spans, and the phrases are identified by referring to the constituting words.

```
Id:P1, Structure:Phrase, Node:W1..W2
Id:P2, Structure:Phrase, Node:W4..W4
Id:P3, Structure:Phrase, Node:W3..W4
Id:P4, Structure:Phrase, Node:W1..W4
```

The following example represents even more hierarchy explicitly, expressing higher level structures by referring to directly dependent structures:

```
Id:P1, Structure:Phrase, Node:{W1,W2}
Id:P2, Structure:Phrase, Node:{W4}
Id:P3, Structure:Phrase, Node:{W3,P4}
Id:P4, Structure:Phrase, Node:{P1,P3}
```

Note that in the above example a set representation is used to refer to the constituting structures since there is no natural linear order between phrases and words. Generally, the more it encodes dependency, the less it becomes robust to the change to lower level structures.

Attributional annotation gives categorical information to the structures identified. In inline annotation, the markup enclosing each span is the place where attributional annotation is stored.

```
<phrase id="p4" cat="NP">
  <phrase id="p1" cat="NP">
    <word id="w1" pos="DT">The</word>
    <word id="w2" pos="NN">stability</word>
  </phrase>
  <phrase id="p3" cat="PP">
    <word id="w3" pos="IN">of</word>
    <phrase id="p2" cat="PP">
      <word id="w4" pos="NN">c-Fos</word>
    </phrase>
  </phrase>
</phrase>
```

...

In standoff annotation, the metadata for attributional annotation may be added to the already created record for structural annotation.

```
Id:W1, Structure:Word,   Span:0..3,    POS:DT
Id:W2, Structure:Word,   Span:4..13,   POS:NN
Id:W3, Structure:Word,   Span:14..16,  POS:IN
```

```
Id:W4,  Structure:Word,    Span:17..22,   POS:NN
Id:P1,  Structure:Phrase,  Node:W1..W2,   Cat:NP
Id:P2,  Structure:Phrase,  Node:W4..W4,   Cat:NP
Id:P3,  Structure:Phrase,  Node:W3..W4,   Cat:PP
Id:P3,  Structure:Phrase,  Node:W1..W4,   Cat:NP


    ...
```

Alternatively, separate records can be created to store the attributional annotation with links to corresponding structural annotations.

```
Id:A1,  Annotation:WCAT,  Object:W1,  POS:DT
Id:A2,  Annotation:WCAT,  Object:W2,  POS:NN
Id:A3,  Annotation:WCAT,  Object:W3,  POS:IN
Id:A4,  Annotation:WCAT,  Object:W4,  POS:NN
Id:A5,  Annotation:PCAT,  Object:P1,  Cat:NP
Id:A6,  Annotation:PCAT,  Object:P2,  Cat:PP
Id:A7,  Annotation:PCAT,  Object:P3,  Cat:NP


    ...
```

In the latter case, the new metadata can be created without modifying already existing ones, allowing an incremental way of annotation.

Relational annotation associates several structures to express relations between them. For example, coreferencing expressions can be annotated as related structures because they have the same referent. Relational information is either directed or undirected. With the undirected relationship, objects are associated without order, yielding a set. The undirected relationship is thus often expressed by the set-membership of each object to a certain set. For example, the following annotation expresses the coreference links between the span "c-Fos" (17..22) and "the protein" (46..53) an undirected relationship:

```
Id:W4,  Structure:Word,    Span:17..22,  POS:NN                # c-fos
Id:W8,  Structure:Word,    Span:42..45,  POS:DT                # the
Id:W9,  Structure:Word,    Span:46..53,  POS:NN                # protein
Id:P2,  Structure:Phrase,  Node:W4..W4,  Cat:NP, Coref:C1
Id:P9,  Structure:Phrase,  Node:W8..W9,  Cat:NP, Coref:C1
```

On the other hand, directed relations are usually expressed by designating destination objects in the source object. The following expresses the coreference relation as an undirected relation:

```
Id:P2,  Structure:Phrase,  Node:W4..W4,  Cat:NP
Id:P9,  Structure:Phrase,  Node:W8..W9,  Cat:NP, Coref:P1
```

7.4 Multilevel Corpus Annotation

Corpus annotation can be performed at various levels to account for different types of information. The following is an example of multilevel annotation made at five different levels: sentence, word, named entity, phrase (base noun phrases) and coreference.

```
[Sentence level]
  Id:S1,  Structure:Sentence, Span:0..79

[Word level]
  Id:W1,   Structure:Word, Span:0..3,   POS:DT
  Id:W2,   Structure:Word, Span:4..13,  POS:NN
  Id:W3,   Structure:Word, Span:14..16, POS:IN
  Id:W4,   Structure:Word, Span:17..22, POS:NN
  Id:W5,   Structure:Word, Span:23..26, POS:VBD
  Id:W6,   Structure:Word, Span:27..36, POS:VBN
  Id:W7,   Structure:Word, Span:37..41, POS:WRB
  Id:W8,   Structure:Word, Span:42..45, POS:DT
  Id:W9,   Structure:Word, Span:46..53, POS:NN
  Id:W10,  Structure:Word, Span:54..57, POS:VBD
  Id:W11,  Structure:Word, Span:58..67, POS:JJ
  Id:W12,  Structure:Word, Span:68..72, POS:IN
  Id:W13,  Structure:Word, Span:73..78, POS:NN
  Id:W14,  Structure:Word, Span:78..79, POS:PERIOD

[NE level]
  Id:T1,  Type:Protein, Span:17..22, Name:c-Fos
  Id:T2,  Type:Protein, Span:73..78, Name:c-Jun

[phrase level]
  Id:P1, Cat:NP, Node:W1..W2
  Id:P2, Cat:NP, Node:W4..W4
  Id:P3, Cat:NP, Node:W8..W9
  Id:P4, Cat:NP, Node:W13..W13

[Coreference level]
  Id:C1, Item:P2, Coref:CorefSet1
  Id:C2, Item:P3, Coref:CorefSet1
```

Note that the metadata for the different types of annotation are separated clearly in different levels. The separation of annotation is a core idea of multilevel annotation. By separately maintaining the annotated metadata from the original document, the original document is kept unchanged. Also, by separating the annotation into different levels, different annotation tasks can be distributed to annotators with different expertise.

After creation of multilevel annotation, we need to retrieve the information in an integrated way. To to that, we can first think about merging the multilevel annotation into one file. Following is an example of XML file which contains annotation at sentence and NE level together.

```
<sentence id="S1">The stability of <protein id="T1" name="c-Fos">c-
Fos</protein> was decreased when the protein was dimerized with <protein id="T2"
name="c-Jun">c-Jun</protein>.</sentence>
```

After multilevel annotation is merged in a XML file, it can be browsed or queried using XML tools. Following is a XQuery query which finds all the pairs of protein annotations appearing in the same sentences.

```
let $doc := .
for $pa in $doc//Protein,
    $pb in $doc//Protein
where $pa/@Id ne $pb/@Id
   and $pa/ancester::Sentence/@Span
        eq $pb/ancester::Sentence/@Span
return $pa/@Id, $pb/@Id
```

Currently, only a few software systems handle standoff annotation in a limited way. So the conversion of standoff annotation into a well-formed XML file in a inline style is adopted by several annotation projects, e.g. American National Corpus (ANC), LT XML, in order to benefit from the availability of many software systems.

MMAX (Müller and Strube 2006) is a software which supports standoff style multilevel annotation, and provides a query language for multilevel standoff annotation, MMAXQL. The following is an example MMAXQL query to find text spans which have annotations at two levels: the word level annotation tells it includes a determiner (DT) and the coreference level annotation tells its Coref attribute is not empty.

```
/Word.POS=DT in /!Coreference.Coref=empty
```

Sometimes, multilevel annotation is made with dependency between different annotation levels. For example, MMAX annotation model requires to model words first. Annotation at other levels then has to be dependent on the word level. Figures 7.2 and 7.3 show dependency of multilevel annotation made to the GENIA and Ontonotes corpora, respectively. In GENIA, the POS and term annotations are made independently of each other, but both are dependent on sentence segmentation. The syntactic tree and event annotations are made on top of the POS and term annotations respectively, so that there are other dependencies. In the case of Ontonotes, Treebank is the most fundamental level of annotation and other annotations are all dependent on the Treebank level.

There are pros and cons of annotations performed dependently on or independently of each other. If annotations are performed dependently on each other, the resulting set of annotations can be better integrated without incompatible annotation instances. One disadvantage of dependent annotation is that one type of annotation,

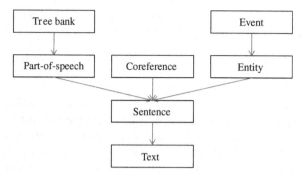

Fig. 7.2 Dependency of multilevel annotation in GENIA

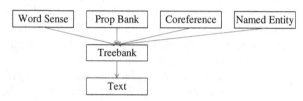

Fig. 7.3 Dependency of multilevel annotation in ontonotes

e.g. term annotation, can be affected by the quality of another type of annotation, e.g. POS annotation, which it depends on. Sometimes, it prevents a particular type of annotation to be made in its optimized shape. Another disadvantage is that all dependent annotations have to be performed in a sequential order following the order of dependencies, sometimes, making it impossible to make an optimal use of developing resources, e.g. human resources, time, and so on. The advantages and disadvantages of performing independent annotations are vice versa to the case of dependent annotations.

7.5 Discontinuous Spans

A well known problem with corpus annotation is how to express discontinuous spans as a single element. Suppose that we are to annotate the following example text to find protein references.

> The c- and v-Rel proteins supershifted or inhibited ⋯

There are two protein references in the text: "c-Rel" and "v-Rel". While the text span for the latter can be expressed by a single pair of beginning and end offsets, *(11..16)*, that for the former cannot as it is comprised of two discontinuous spans, *(4..6)* and *(13..16)*. Such discontinuous spans often appear in coordinated clauses.

A straightforward solution would be to generalize the span representation to accommodate sets of spans, which may yield the following annotation expression:

```
Id:NE1, Span:{4..6,13..16}, Structure:NE, Type:Protein, Name:c-Rel
Id:NE2, Span:11..16,        Structure:NE, Type:Protein, Name:v-Rel
```

Although such a set representation is effective to express discontinuous spans, it is not popularly used in actual practice. It is related to the fact that the NLP technology has been mostly developed without considering discontinuous structures, e.g. parsing based on tree structures, non-projectivity of dependency theory. While, currently a primary purpose of corpus annotation is to provide training and testing materials for the development of automatic NLP systems, there might be no strong reason to raise the complexity of formatting in order to encode information which will not be utilized. Another problem of the set representation is that it does not go well along with XML technology. It is well known that XML does not naturally accommodate discontinuous spans both in inline and standoff, e.g. XPointer, scheme. While XML is accepted as a de facto standard of text encoding, it would also cost high to attempt to express discontinuous spans.

In practice, therefore, it is much more popular to avoid expressing discontinuous spans, forcing to consider only continuous spans as corpus elements to be annotated. For example, the text span "c-" by itself can be regarded as the span which refers to the protein "c-Rel", yielding the following annotation:

```
Id:NE1, Span:4..6,    Structure:NE, Type:Protein, Name:c-Rel
```

A similar approach has been used for MUC Named Entity Recognition task (Chinchor and Robinson 1998). Alternatively, the minimal span including all discontinuous spans required for the protein reference can be identified and annotated.

```
Id:NE1, Span:4..16, Structure:NE, Type:Protein, Name:{c-Rel,v-Rel}
Id:NE2, Span:11..16, Structure:NE, Type:Protein, Name:v-Rel
```

In this case, although the span representation remains simple, the information associated with the span may become complex as the span encoding complex information is selected.

There is another approach for compromising the simplicity and the expressiveness, which is illustrated by the following annotation example:

```
Id:NE1, Span:4..6, Structure:NE, Type:Protein, Name:c-Rel, Chain:NE2
Id:NE2, Span:13..16, Structure:NE, Type:Protein
```

Here, each of the two discontinuous spans representing the protein 'c-Rel' is identified as an annotation element and annotated as protein. However, only one of them, the first or the most distinguishing one, is associated with the entity itself and the others are linked as a "chain" of spans. For simple processing without considering discontinuous spans, users can ignore the attribute for chaining and annotations without association with entities. A similar approach was used for the PennBioIE annotation project (Kulick et al. 2004b).

7.6 Case Study: GENIA Multilevel Annotation

This section introduces the GENIA corpus (Kim et al. 2008) and its annotations as an example of multilevel annotation. The GENIA corpus is a collection of journal article abstracts in molecular biology. The corpus has been annotated for a wide spectrum of information represented in the text. This has been done from two perspectives. The linguistic annotations of GENIA concern making the inherent structure of the natural language text explicit. It has been implemented at three levels: sentence segmentation, Part-of-Speech (POS) and syntactic tree annotation. The semantic annotation of GENIA links domain-specific knowledge pieces with the corresponding text expressions that convey the meaning. It has been implemented at two levels: entity identification and event identification. The GENIA corpus with its multilevel annotation is currently accepted a de facto standard resource for the development of software systems for bio-textmining (bioTM) (Kim et al. 2004, 2009).

In designing the encoding schemes for the GENIA corpus, a practical approach has been pursued and effort has been made to maximize the potential of utilizing currently available resources. All the annotations to the GENIA corpus have been made in inline style, encoding the annotated information directly into the text, which makes each annotated document a well-formed XML document. This approach enables writing annotation schemes in Document Type Definitions (DTD), and producing styled documents using Cascading Style Sheets (CSS). For another use case of CSS, see Schmidt (in this volume). Use of DTD and CSS is currently the most popular combination of XML technologies supported by many tools. This choice enables flexible design of annotation scheme, thus different annotation schemes for different annotation levels can be easily implemented with readily available software tools.

7.6.1 Sentence Segmentation

The GENIA corpus contains annotations for sentence segmentation, of which the example is shown in Fig. 7.4. As seen in the figure, sentence segmentation typically changes an input text into a flat (non-overlapping and non-recursive) sequence of sentences. It is the most simple type of structural annotation. After the sentence segmentation, every character except whitespace between sentences must belong to a sentence. It is also notable that the annotation involves only insertion of XML tags and does not involve any other modification of original text (including white spaces) so that the original text can be restored at any time by simply dropping the sentence segmentation tags.

⟨AbstractText⟩⟨sentence id="S2"⟩Mice transgenic for the human T cell leukemia virus (HTLV-I) Tax gene develop fibroblastic tumors that express NF-kappa B-inducible early genes.⟨/sentence⟩ ⟨sentence id="S3"⟩In vitro inhibition of NF-kappa B expression by antisense oligodeoxynucleotides (ODNs) inhibited growth of these culture-adapted Tax-transformed fibroblasts as well as an HTLV-I-transformed human lymphocyte line.⟨/sentence⟩ ⟨sentence id="S4"⟩In contrast, antisense inhibition of Tax itself had no apparent effect on cell growth.⟨/sentence⟩ ⟨sentence id="S5"⟩Mice treated with antisense to NF-kappa B ODNs showed rapid regression of transplanted fibrosarcomas.⟨/sentence⟩ ⟨sentence id="S6"⟩This suggests that NF-kappa B expression may be necessary for the maintenance of the malignant phenotype and provides a therapeutic approach for HTLV-I-associated disease.⟨/sentence⟩⟨/AbstractText⟩

Fig. 7.4 A GENIA corpus file with sentence segmentation tags inserted

7.6.2 Part-of-Speech Annotation

Part-of-speech (POS) annotation means the process of assigning POS labels or syntactic categories to each word of text. However, the concept "word" is often ambiguous when it is applied to real texts, and it does not usually cover the whole text, i.e. punctuations, which is the reason that the more concrete and precise concept "token" is introduced as the unit for POS labeling. Consequently, POS annotation is redefined as the process of assigning POS labels to each token of text, and it necessarily involves the tokenization process before the assigning process. Thus, the POS annotation is a mix of structural and attributional annotation. The token is often regarded not only as the unit of POS labeling but also as the atomic unit of language processing. The tokenization process changes a given text into a flat sequence of tokens. Like sentences, tokens are non-overlapping and non-recursive and they must cover the whole span of input text except whitespace between tokens. Figure 7.5 shows a sentence which has been tokenized into **w**(word) elements which have then been assigned correct POS labels.

⟨sentence id="S2"⟩⟨w c="NNS"⟩Mice⟨/w⟩ ⟨w c="JJ"⟩transgenic⟨/w⟩ ⟨w c="IN"⟩for⟨/w⟩ ⟨w c="DT"⟩the⟨/w⟩ ⟨w c="JJ"⟩human⟨/w⟩ ⟨w c="NN"⟩T⟨/w⟩ ⟨w c="NN"⟩cell⟨/w⟩ ⟨w c="NN"⟩leukemia⟨/w⟩ ⟨w c="NN"⟩virus⟨/w⟩ ⟨w c="LRB"⟩(⟨/w⟩⟨w c="NN"⟩HTLV-I⟨/w⟩⟨w c="RRB"⟩)⟨/w⟩ ⟨w c="NN"⟩Tax⟨/w⟩ ⟨w c="NN"⟩gene⟨/w⟩ ⟨w c="VBP"⟩develop⟨/w⟩ ⟨w c="JJ"⟩fibroblastic⟨/w⟩ ⟨w c="NNS"⟩tumors⟨/w⟩ ⟨w c="WDT"⟩that⟨/w⟩ ⟨w c="VBP"⟩express⟨/w⟩ ⟨w c="NN"⟩NF-kappa⟨/w⟩ ⟨w c="JJ"⟩B-inducible⟨/w⟩ ⟨w c="JJ"⟩early⟨/w⟩ ⟨w c="NNS"⟩genes⟨/w⟩⟨w c="PERIOD"⟩.⟨/w⟩⟨/sentence⟩

Fig. 7.5 A sentence with POS annotation

7.6.3 Syntactic Tree Annotation

Syntactic analysis reveals how words in a sentence are organized to form the meaning of the sentence. In a sentence, words may be grouped together into *phrases*. Again, phrases, with or without other words, may also be grouped to form larger phrases. This continues until eventually all the words are grouped together, yielding a tree structure of phrases with the root element covering the whole sentence, internal elements corresponding to phrases, and leaf elements corresponding to words. As such, linguistic structures can be naturally represented in tree structures in most cases.

It is, however, also true that there are linguistic phenomena which are not well represented in tree structures. An example is *wh-movement* which refers to the phenomena of moving a *wh-term* to the front of the sentence to form a *wh-question*. For example, in the sentence *What are you thinking about?*, the object of the preposition *about* (which is *what*) is moved to the front of the sentence, away from the place where the object of the preposition should usually be. This kind of movement involves breaking the normal order of arguments, and the resulting sentences can therefore not be annotated with the normal tree structures.

Parsing technology has been developed to represent all linguistic phenomena within the framework of tree structures, and special approaches have been devised to deal with these difficult cases. Examples include *empty nodes*, which can be inserted in the place of missing or moved argument. Figure 7.6 shows the use of an empty node to encode a sentence with wh-movement. This example is taken from the Penn Treebank (Marcus et al. 1994): After the preposition *about*, an empty node is inserted as a proxy object which has been moved out of the usual place. The empty node is then co-indexed with the true object to trace it later, forming a directed relational annotation.

```
(SBARQ
  (WHNP-1 what) (SQ are (NP-SBJ you) (VP thinking (PP-CLR about (NP *T*-1))))
  ?)
```

Fig. 7.6 Use of an empty node to represent the *wh*-movement

Figure 7.7 shows the GENIA encoding for the syntactic structure of a sentence, and Fig. 7.8 the same viewed by a CSS script. In GENIA, constituents are marked-up as **chunk** elements which have the **cat** attribute to specify the syntactic category of the phrase. An empty node is represented by the empty element, which has a **ref** attribute (of type **IDREF**) to reference back to the element representing the true argument that has been moved out of place. The insertion of the **chunk** markups represents a structural annotation, while the assigning of the **cat** and **ref** attribution represents an attributional and a directed relational annotation, respectively.

⟨sentence   id="S2"⟩⟨chunk   cat="S"⟩⟨chunk   cat="NP"
role="SBJ"⟩⟨chunk   cat="NP"⟩Mice⟨/chunk⟩   ⟨chunk
cat="ADJP"⟩transgenic ⟨chunk cat="PP"⟩for ⟨chunk cat="NP"⟩the
⟨chunk   cat="NP"⟩⟨chunk   cat="NP"⟩human   T   cell   leukemia
virus⟨/chunk⟩   ⟨chunk   cat="PRN"⟩(⟨chunk   cat="NP"⟩HTLV-
I⟨/chunk⟩)⟨/chunk⟩⟨/chunk⟩   Tax   gene⟨/chunk⟩⟨/chunk⟩⟨/chunk⟩⟨/chunk⟩
⟨chunk cat="VP"⟩develop ⟨chunk cat="NP"⟩⟨chunk cat="NP"⟩fibroblastic
tumors⟨/chunk⟩   ⟨chunk   cat="SBAR"⟩⟨chunk   cat="WHNP"
id="i1"⟩that⟨/chunk⟩   ⟨chunk   cat="S"⟩⟨chunk   cat="NP"
role="SBJ"   ref="i1"   null="T"/⟩⟨chunk   cat="VP"⟩express   ⟨chunk
cat="NP"⟩⟨chunk   cat="ADJP"⟩NF-kappa   B-inducible⟨/chunk⟩   early
genes⟨/chunk⟩⟨/chunk⟩⟨/chunk⟩⟨/chunk⟩⟨/chunk⟩⟨/chunk⟩.⟨/chunk⟩⟨/sentence⟩

Fig. 7.7 A tree-annotated sentence in XML encoding

(S ▷(NP ▷(NP ▷Mice◁) (ADJP ▷transgenic (PP ▷for (NP ▷the (NP ▷(NP
▷human T cell leukemia virus◁) (PRN ▷((NP ▷HTLV-I◁))◁) Tax gene◁)◁)◁)◁) (VP
▷develop (NP ▷(NP ▷fibroblastic tumors◁) (SBAR ▷(WHNP i1 ▷that◁) (S ▷(NP
▷◁)(VP ▷express (NP ▷(ADJP ▷NF-kappa B-inducible◁) early genes◁)◁)◁)◁)◁)◁).◁)

Fig. 7.8 A tree-annotated sentence in CSS-styled view

7.6.4 Entity Annotation

Recognition of the mention of bio-molecular entities, e.g. proteins or genes, in text
is one of the most fundamental tasks of bio-textmining. In GENIA, bio-molecular
entities are annotated in the scope of technical term annotation. The definition and
classification of such terms comes from the GENIA ontology (Kim et al. 2006).

Figure 7.9 shows the GENIA encoding for the terms that are mentioned in a
sentence and Fig. 7.10 shows the "styled" view using a CSS stylesheet. Text spans
referring to GENIA *terms* are marked up as **term** elements, representing a structural
annotation. Each term entity has the **sem** attribute to specify the *semantic* description
of the text span and the **lex** attribute to specify the *lexical* form of the term. For
example, the text span "Mice" is annotated as a multi cell organism (**Multi_cell**).
The term annotation may be recursive. For example, the three text spans, "human
T cell leukemia virus", "HTLV-1" and "Tax", are all annotated as terms inside a
bigger text span, "human T cell leukemia virus (HTLV-1) Tax gene", which is also
annotated as a term on its own.

7.6.5 Event Annotation

In GENIA, a biological event is defined as a temporal occurrence that happens to
one or more biological entities. Especially, a number of events which cause some
specific change on genes or gene products (proteins) are defined in the GENIA event
ontology, being the target of the GENIA event annotation.

⟨sentence id="S2"⟩⟨**term** id="T5" lex="mice" sem="Multi_cell"⟩Mice⟨/**term**⟩ transgenic for the ⟨**term** id="T6" lex="human_T_cell_leukemia_virus_(HTLV-I)_Tax_gene" sem="DNA_domain_or_region"⟩⟨**term** id="T7" lex="human_T_cell_leukemia_virus" sem="Virus"⟩human T cell leukemia virus⟨/**term**⟩ (⟨**term** id="T8" lex="HTLV-I" sem="Virus"⟩HTLV-I⟨/**term**⟩) ⟨**term** id="T9" lex="Tax" sem="Protein_molecule"⟩Tax⟨/**term**⟩ gene⟨/**term**⟩ develop ⟨**term** id="T10" lex="fibroblastic_tumor" sem="Tissue"⟩fibroblastic tumors⟨/**term**⟩ that express ⟨**term** id="T11" lex="NF-kappa_B-inducible_early_gene" sem="DNA_family_or_group"⟩NF-kappa B-inducible early genes⟨/**term**⟩.⟨/sentence⟩

Fig. 7.9 A sentence which has been annotated for terms. The XML encoding

▹Mice◃T5 transgenic for the ▹▹human T cell leukemia virus◃T7 (▹HTLV-I◃T8) ▹Tax◃T9 gene◃T6 develop ▹fibroblastic tumors◃T10 that express ▹NF-kappa B-inducible early genes◃T11.

Fig. 7.10 A sentence which has been annotated for terms. The CSS-styled view

Figure 7.11 shows the GENIA encoding for events mentioned in a sentence and Fig. 7.12 shows the styled view using CSS. In GENIA XML encoding, a sentence may be followed by one or more **event** elements, each of which encodes an event mentioned in the sentence. An event element encodes the type, themes and causes of an identified event. For the type of an event, a descriptor from the GENIA event ontology may be specified. For the themes and causes of an event, the IDs of pre-annotated terms or other events may be referenced.

Since the GENIA annotation seeks to link information pieces and language structures, the **clue** element has been introduced in the event element, to reveal the text

⟨sentence id="S2"⟩⟨term id="T5" lex="mice" sem="Multi_cell"⟩Mice⟨/term⟩ transgenic for the ⟨term id="T6" lex="human_T_cell_leukemia_virus_(HTLV-I)_Tax_gene" sem="DNA_domain_or_region"⟩⟨term id="T7" lex="human_T_cell_leukemia_virus" sem="Virus"⟩human T cell leukemia virus⟨/term⟩ (⟨term id="T8" lex="HTLV-I" sem="Virus"⟩HTLV-I⟨/term⟩) ⟨term id="T9" lex="Tax" sem="Protein_molecule"⟩Tax⟨/term⟩ gene⟨/term⟩ develop ⟨term id="T10" lex="fibroblastic_tumor" sem="Tissue"⟩fibroblastic tumors⟨/term⟩ that express ⟨term id="T11" lex="NF-kappa_B-inducible_early_gene" sem="DNA_family_or_group"⟩NF-kappa B-inducible early genes⟨/term⟩.⟨/sentence⟩⟨event id="E1"⟩⟨type class="Cell_differentiation"/⟩⟨theme idref="T10"/⟩⟨clue⟩Mice transgenic for the human T cell leukemia virus (HTLV-I) Tax gene ⟨clueType⟩develop⟨/clueType⟩ fibroblastic tumors that express NF-kappa B-inducible early genes.⟨/clue⟩⟨/event⟩⟨event id="E2"⟩⟨type class="Gene_expression"/⟩⟨theme idref="T11"/⟩⟨cause idref="T10"/⟩⟨clue⟩Mice transgenic for the human T cell leukemia virus (HTLV-I) Tax gene develop fibroblastic tumors ⟨linkCause⟩that⟨/linkCause⟩ ⟨clueType⟩express⟨/clueType⟩ NF-kappa B-inducible early genes.⟨/clue⟩⟨/event⟩

Fig. 7.11 A sentence has been annotated for events

▷Mice◁T5 transgenic for the ▷▷human T cell leukemia virus◁T7 (▷HTLV-I◁T8) ▷Tax◁T9 gene◁T6 develop ▷fibroblastic tumors◁T10 that express ▷NF-kappa B-inducible early genes◁T11.

EVENT E1
TYPE : Cell_differentiation
THEME : T10
CLUE : Mice transgenic for the human T cell leukemia virus (HTLV-I) Tax gene ▷develop◁ fibroblastic tumors that express NF-kappa B-inducible early genes.

EVENT E2
TYPE : Gene_expression
THEME : T11
CAUSE : T10
CLUE : Mice transgenic for the human T cell leukemia virus (HTLV-I) Tax gene develop fibroblastic tumors ▷that◁ ▷express◁ NF-kappa B-inducible early genes.

Fig. 7.12 A styled view of the XML encoding by CSS

parts which participate in mentioning the event. Inside the clue element, the text spans which are responsible for mentioning the type of the event, linking the event type to the themes and linking the event type to the causes are marked-up as **clueType**, **linkTheme** and **linkCause** elements respectively.

In Fig. 7.12, the event E1 identifies the event of tumor development, which has been classified as a **Cell_differentiation** event, of which the theme is denoted by the text span "fibroblastic tumors". The text span "develop" has been determined as a clue for the event classification. The event E2 identifies an event of **Gene_expression** whose theme is "NF-kappa B-inducible early genes" and the cause is "Mice". The word "express" is a key expression referring to the event type, while the word "that" links it with the cause of the event.

7.6.6 Integration of GENIA Multilevel Annotation

Although all the GENIA multilevel annotation is implemented in inline style, the text in each annotation file is carefully maintained to preserve the original text: if the XML markups in each corpus file are removed, the remaining text becomes the same as the original text. The only exception is event annotation which involves replication of original text. In the case of an event annotated file, to retrieve the original text, first everything in the <event> element is removed and then all the XML markups are removed.

For integrated annotation retrieval, a conversion tool from inline to standoff is provided. Although the annotation itself is performed in inline style, since the original text is preserved as it is in each annotation file, the standoff annotation produced by the converter becomes all valid with original text. This way, GENIA annotation supports multilevel annotation: inline XML annotation for annotation tasks, standoff conversion for retrieval.

7.7 Concluding Remarks

In this chapter, we discussed fundamental techniques of multilevel annotation, and studied the GENIA corpus as an example of multilevel annotation applied to the molecular biology domain. Although there are efforts for standardizing the framework of corpus annotation (Ide et al. 2000, Ide and Romary 2007), currently available resources, e.g. software tools, for the standards are limited. Since corpus annotation is in itself an expensive task in terms of labor and time, it is difficult for individual annotation projects to invest for the development of software tools. On the other hand, XML is rich of software tools. For that reason, despite of the many attractive features of standoff annotation dictated in the standardization efforts, the inline annotation conforming XML is a popular option for annotation projects. As the progress of standardization and development of supporting software, it is expected that more and more corpus and multilevel annotation will become conformant to the standards.

GENIA is a case which took a practical approach to minimize the cost for the preparation of supporting tools. GENIA multilevel annotation has been all developed in inline style by using XML technology. However, efforts were made to implement the important concepts of multilevel annotation, e.g. separability and comparability of annotation at different levels. Although the implementation is different from the standard, e.g. LAF/GrAF (Ide and Romary 2007), the conceptual design of GENIA annotation is conformant to the standard, e.g. structural, attributional and relational annotation. Thus, the GENIA annotation project pursues both practical annotation and support for standardization.

References

Carletta, Jean and Isard, Amy (1999). The mate annotation workbench: User requirements. In *Proceedings of the ACL Workshop: Towards Standards and Tools for Discourse Tagging*, pages 11–17.

Chinchor, Nancy and Robinson, Patty (1998). Muc-7 named entity task definition. In *Proceedings of the 7th Message Understanding Conference*.

Hovy, Eduard, Marcus, Mitchell, Palmer, Martha, Ramshaw, Lance, and Weischedel, Ralph (2006). Ontonotes: The 90% solution. In *Proceedings of the Human Language Technology Conference of the NAACL, Companion Volume: Short Papers*, pages 57–60, New York City, USA. Association for Computational Linguistics.

Ide, Nancy, Bonhomme, Patrice, and Romary, Laurent (2000). Xces: An xml-based standard for linguistic corpora. In *Proceedings of the Second Language Resources and Evaluation*.

Ide, Nancy and Romary, Laurent (2007). Towards international standards for language resources. In Dybkjær, Laila, Hemsen, Holmer, and Minker, Wolfgang, editors, *Evaluation of Text and Speech Systems*, pages 263–84. Springer, New York.

Ide, Nancy and Suderman, Keith (2006). Integrating linguistic resources: The american national corpus model. In *Proceedings of the Fifth Language Resources and Evaluation Conference (LREC)*.

Kim, Jin-Dong, Ohta, Tomoko, Pyysalo, Sampo, Kano, Yoshinobu, and Tsujii, Jun'ichi (2009). Overview of BioNLP'09 Shared Task on Event Extraction. In *Proceedings of Natural Language Processing in Biomedicine (BioNLP) NAACL 2009 Workshop*.

Kim, Jin-Dong, Ohta, Tomoko, Teteisi, Yuka, and Tsujii, Jun'ichi (2006). Genia ontology. Technical Report TR-NLP-UT-2006-2, Tsujii Laboratory, University of Tokyo.

Kim, Jin-Dong, Ohta, Tomoko, and Tsujii, Jun'ichi (2008). Corpus annotation for mining biomedical events from lterature. *BMC Bioinformatics*, 9(1):10.

Kim, Jin-Dong, Ohta, Tomoko, Tsuruoka, Yoshimasa, Tateisi, Yuka, and Collier, Nigel (2004). Introduction to the bio-entity recognition task at JNLPBA. In *Proceedings of the International Joint Workshop on Natural Language Processing in Biomedicine and its Applications (JNLPBA)*, pages 70–75.

Kulick, S., Bies, A., Liberman, M., Mandel, M., McDonald, R., Palmer, M., Schein, A., and Ungar, L. (2004a). Integrated annotation for biomedical information extraction. In *NAACL/HLT Workshop on Linking Biological Literature, Ontologies and Databases: Tools for Users*, pages 61–68.

Kulick, Seth, Bies, Ann, Liberman, Mark, Mandel, Mark, McDonald, Ryan, Palmer, Martha, Schein, Andrew, and Ungar, Lyle (2004b). Integrated annotation for biomedical information extraction. In *Proceedings of the NAACL/HLT Workshop on Linking Biological Literature, Ontologies and Databases: Tools for Users*, pages 61–68.

Marcus, Mitchell P., Santorini, Beatrice, and Marcinkiewicz, Mary Ann (1994). Building a large annotated corpus of english: The penn treebank. *Computational Linguistics*, 19(2):313–330.

Müller, Christoph and Strube, Michael (2006). Multi-level annotation of linguistic data with MMAX2. In Braun, Sabine, Kohn, Kurt, and Mukherjee, Joybrato, editors, *Corpus Technology and Language Pedagogy: New Resources, New Tools, New Methods*, pages 197–214. Peter Lang, Frankfurt a.M., Germany.

Pyysalo, Sampo, Ginter, Filip, Heimonen, Juho, Björne, Jari, Boberg, Jorma, Järvinen, Jouni, and Salakoski, Tapio (2007). BioInfer: A corpus for information extraction in the biomedical domain. *BMC Bioinformatics*, 8(50).

Thompson, Henry S. and McKelvie, David (1997). Hyperlink semantics for standoff markup of read-only documents. In *Proceedings of SGML Europe '97.*

Chapter 8
Hypertext Types and Markup Languages

The Relationship Between HTML and Web Genres

Georg Rehm

Abstract Text technological applications such as automatic summarisation or information extraction systems often process web documents. An important aspect of web documents that most systems ignore is the document type or document genre and the relationship the respective genre, as well as genres in general, have with regard to the Hypertext Markup Language. This chapter introduces the concept of hypertext types to highlight some of the most relevant aspects and applications. Hypertext types are very similar to traditional text types because hypertexts can be grouped into categories that share certain linguistic, textual, or pragmatic features such as communicative function, hypertextual structure, or content. Processing web documents based on their genres entails several advantages, the most prominent of which is the automatic identification of web genres for improved information retrieval aproaches.

Keywords Document genres · Hypertext · HTML · Hypertext types

8.1 Introduction

It is vital to take a closer look at the role of the Hypertext Markup Language (HTML, Raggett et al. 1999) with regard to text technological applications that aim at processing web documents (for example, automatic summarisation, information extraction, or text classification). This article introduces the concept of hypertext types to highlight some of the most relevant aspects and applications. Hypertext types are very similar to traditional text types, i. e., actual hypertexts can be grouped into categories that share certain linguistic, textual, or pragmatic features such as communicative function, hypertextual structure, or content. Nowadays, the term

G. Rehm (✉)
vionto GmbH, Berlin, Germany
e-mail: georg.rehm@vionto.com

A. Witt, D. Metzing (eds.), *Linguistic Modeling of Information and Markup Languages*, Text, Speech and Language Technology 40,
DOI 10.1007/978-90-481-3331-4_8, © Springer Science+Business Media B.V. 2010

hypertext (see, e. g., Kuhlen 1991, Hammwöhner 1997, Storrer 2004) is used almost synonymously with the World Wide Web (WWW). Therefore, the term *web genre* seems to be more appropriate to refer to different types of websites.

Categorising web documents into web genres potentially comprises several advantages. The automatic identification of web genres (Rehm 2002, 2007, Rehm and Santini 2007) is an intuitive application: summarisation techniques can be tailored to the instances of specific web genres, collecting corpus data within the "web as corpus" approach can be restricted to a certain set of web genres, or information extraction engines can be implemented that are specialised to web genres such as *C. V.* or *List of Publications*.

The remainder of this chapter is structured as follows: first, Section 8.2 describes the relationship between arbitrary markup languages and traditional text types. Section 8.3 details the concept of web genres and, among others, explains the evolutionary process that produces web genres. The contribution finishes with concluding remarks (Section 8.4).

8.2 HTML as a Markup Language

HTML (Raggett et al. 1999) and XHTML (Pemberton 2002) are applications of the metalanguages SGML (ISO 8879 1986) and XML (Bray et al. 2004) respectively. Therefore, both HTML and XHTML can be considered SGML / XML-based markup languages. Before we can examine the specifics of HTML more closely, we need to concentrate on the features of a typical, generic markup language (assuming such a thing exists; cf. Lobin 2001, p. 181).

Although markup languages can comprise more or less arbitrary pieces of information, a typical application scenario is to specify the structural patterns of a text type by means of a text grammar (or document type definition, DTD, in SGML/XML lingo) – popular examples often used in introductory classes or textbooks are the generic discourse structures of cooking recipes, poems, or books (Lobin et al. in this volume, Maler and Andaloussi 1996). In an abbreviated, rewrite-rule-like notation, a DTD for non-fiction books often comprises element declarations such as (i) book→contents, chapter+, index (ii) chapter→title, section+ (iii) section → title, paragraph+, subsection+ etc.

Neither HTML nor the nearly equivalent XHTML contain nested declarations of this depth or semantic specifity. HTML 4.01 (Raggett et al. 1999) comprises declarations for 91 elements and 119 attributes but only very few of these rules are related to structural or informational units that themselves can be related to the constituents of the structural patterns of specific text types. In other words, the informational units provided by HTML do not correspond to the parts or building blocks of one type of text or hypertext. Rather, HTML specifies a set of generic elements and attributes that serve, for example, presentational and typographic (i, b, font), structural (ol, ul), semantic or logical (em, strong), referential or hypertextual (a), and functional (`object`, `embed`) means (see Walker 1999 for a more detailed discussion).

HTML is not an ordinary, typical markup language. On the contrary: it is not aimed at one specific text type, it comprises several types of markup (see above) and must thus be considered a hybrid, heterogeneous markup language with a bias on presentational and functional aspects. Evidence for this can be found within HTML's sets of element and attribute names. Most of these are completely generic and universal and do not relate to text-structural or even genre-specific properties. In addition, there are almost no restrictions with regard to the nesting or the combination of specific block-level elements (lists, headlines, tables, quotations, etc.).[1] Further evidence can be found online: authors are constantly creating a multitude of different types of texts and hypertexts by employing only *one* single markup language – HTML.

8.3 Hypertext Types – Web Genres

The WWW comprises different types of hypertexts. Following the distinction of different types of texts as genres (*Textsorten* in German, cf. Brinker et al. 2000), these types can be conceptualised as individual web genres. In sharp contrast to the state of the art in traditional text linguistics, both theoretical and applied web genre-oriented research is, surprisingly, rather scarce (see, for example, Shepherd and Watters 1999, Crowston and Williams 2000, Rosso 2005).

8.3.1 Genres and Web Genres

According to the framework sometimes referred to as North American Genre Theory and established by the works of Miller (1984), Bazerman (1994), and Swales (1990), among others, a genre "comprises a class of communicative events, the members of which share some set of communicative purposes. These purposes [...] constitute the rationale for the genre. This rationale shapes the schematic structure of the discourse and influences and constrains choice of content and style" (Swales 1990, p. 58). Thus, genres are primarily function-oriented patterns of communication that aid in the realisation of specific communicative goals.

Yates and Orlikowski (1992, p. 299) apply genre theory in order to analyse genres of organisational communication and define genres as "typified communicative actions characterized by similar substance [social motives as well as content, G. R.] and form [the communicative action's physical manifestation, G. R.] and taken in response to recurrent situations." (see Erickson 2000). In a later article, Orlikowski and Yates (1994, p. 543) emphasise the influence of the discourse community and define genre as "a distinctive type of communicative action, characterized by a socially recognized communicative purpose and common aspects of form [...]. The communicative purpose of a genre is not rooted in a single individual's motive for communicating, but in a purpose that is constructed, recognized, and reinforced within a community". Yet another definition describes genres of organisational communication as "socially recognized types of communicative actions – such as memos, meetings, expense forms, training seminars – that are habitually enacted by members of a community to realize particular social purposes" (Orlikowski and Yates 1994, p. 542). Therefore, a genre structures communication processes by means of shared expectations that refer to both content and structure. At the same time, the cost of producing or interpreting the instance of an established genre is reduced.

All of the abovementioned properties of traditional genres can be and indeed have to be applied to digital genres as well. For example, electronic mail is employed millions of times each day to carry instances of hundreds of distinct digital genres that can be described and analysed in similar ways as paper-based genres. In principle, the same is true for web genres, but the World Wide Web, as a means of communication, exhibits characteristics that necessitate revising and extending the traditional approaches and categories. The most important aspect refers to the web's roots in hypertext (see Storrer in this volume): the foundation in the concept of hypertext is partly responsible for the often cited fragmented nature of HTML documents. Authors tend to bundle related informational units in lists of hyperlinks that connect individual nodes, therefore breaking up the traditional notion of a text as a coherent whole with an intrinsic beginning and end. Other aspects concern the influence of interactive features and the level of granularity that is needed for a proper analysis and description of web genres (see, for example, Shepherd and Watters 1998, 1999, Haas and Grams 1998, 2000, Rehm 2007, and Section 8.3.3).

8.3.2 The Evolution of Web Genres

It is necessary to have a closer look at the processes that are responsible for the gradual evolution of web genres in order to examine HTML's status as a markup language, especially with regard to operating on web pages by means of Natural Language Processing techniques. Generally speaking, we can distinguish between automatically converted and manually prepared HTML documents. Based on the respective tool or approach chosen by the author, additional stages with individual advantages and disadvantages can be identified (see Fig. 8.1).

The influence of the text type on the automatic conversion of existing documents is straightforward (see Fig. 8.2): a document created, for example, with a WYSI-WYG text processor, usually belongs to a certain text type or genre such as *Scientific Article*, *List of Publications*, or *Minutes*. The conversion process does not significantly alter the text type, so that we can assume that a document's original genre is directly transferred into the web. Whereas slight modifications are often carried out in the generated HTML document (e. g., removal of navigation bars or footers), extensive changes are applied only to the source document so that yet another pass through the converter generates an up-to-date HTML version of the document. While the source document underlies a document life cycle (Lobin 2000),

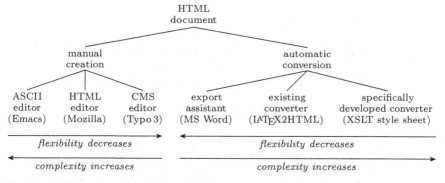

Fig. 8.1 Facilities of creating HTML documents

the converter itself is subject to a software life cycle: new editions of a conversion tool introduce new features that might result in, for example, new layout templates, or novel navigation approaches in the machine-generated HTML documents.

The evolutionary processes that shape and form web genres with regard to the manual creation of websites (i. e., HTML documents) are more complicated. Figure 8.3 depicts the most important influential factors, arranged in a cyclic and highly abstract model of web genre evolution that comprises four phases (Rehm 2007 provides a more detailed discussion). The two phases on the right hand side (*hypertext production, modification*) can be associated with a generic author who intends to build a website. The significant influential factors are, for example, the purpose and communicative function of the website, its designated content, the software used to build the site, and the author's personal history and experience browsing and using the web as well as traditional genres (see, e. g., Furuta and Marshall 1996, Eckkrammer 2001). The two phases on the left hand side (*change, reception*) represent the perpetual modification processes of other

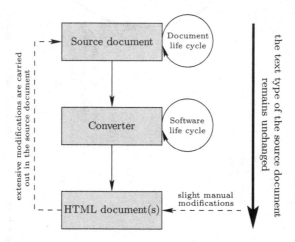

Fig. 8.2 The influence of the text type on the conversion of documents into HTML

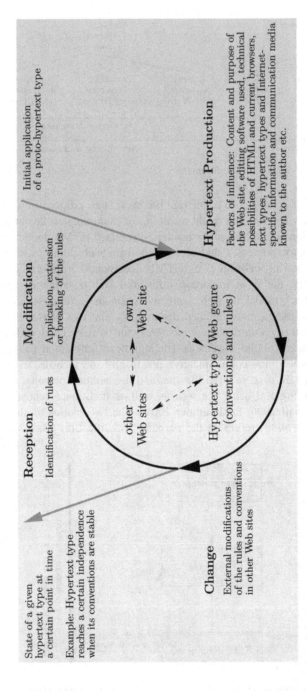

Fig. 8.3 The phases and influential factors of the evolution of hypertext types with regard to documents created manually

websites. These underlie rules and conventions whose spectrum ranges from very specific (e. g., obligatory functional elements that users expect to work the way they experienced on other sites) to very soft (rather optional features; see, e. g., Yates and Sumner 1997). The cycle's four phases describe the slow-going process of emerging rules and conventions for specific web genres: authors of HTML documents are always readers of HTML documents. If an author wants to build a site with a certain purpose and content (i. e., a site with a specific web genre), he or she incorporates – consciously or unconsciously – elements of related websites. Over a period of time, this process generates web genre-specific conventions and rules that authors choose to apply, to extend or to break (cf. Yoshioka et al. 2001): "When establishing a new site that serves a purpose similar to existing sites, the genre characteristics are copied and refined to reflect resemblance to an existing genre" (Eriksen and Ihlström 1999, p. 289). Empirical studies such as Ryan et al. (2003) or Emigh and Herring (2005), in which documents of specific web genres have been compared over long periods of time, yield further evidence for the cyclic model presented here.

The two abovementioned models complement and extend the taxonomy on the evolution of "cybergenres" (Shepherd and Watters 1998) that can be characterised by specific features with regard to content, form and functionality. Although (Shepherd and Watters 1998) do indeed use the term "taxonomy", this concept is misleading (see Rehm 2007 for critical remarks), as the model represents a kind of evolutionary continuum which comprises an "evolutionary path" that leads from "replicated genres" (*newspaper*) to "variant genres" (*electronic news*) and finally to "emerging genres" (*personalized news*). An additional node of the taxonomy is labeled "spontaneous cybergenres" (*homepage*).

8.3.3 The Web Genre Model

Though several specifics of digital genres and web genres have been addressed by previous research, an all-encompassing web genre theory is still missing. The model outlined in this section (see Fig. 8.4) aims to fill this gap, and is a revision and extension of the approach originally published in Rehm (2002). The roots of this model lie in text linguistics. It is primarily intended to aid linguistic analyses of websites as well as to guide approaches for their automatic processing. An exhaustive description can be found in Rehm (2007).

In principle, a web genre can be thought of as a generic text type, i. e., a conventionalised pattern of communication (see Section 8.3.1) used within the World Wide Web, or, in other words, it is a hypertext type. Probably the most important feature of a text type is its communicative function which authors intend to fulfill by means of instantiating the (hyper)text type (Jakobs 2003). Other features include contextual properties (such as the relationship between author and reader), specific hypertextual structuring conventions (for example, linear navigation from node to node used in online-payment sequences) or global web design features (decoration) that apply to all the nodes in a hypertext.

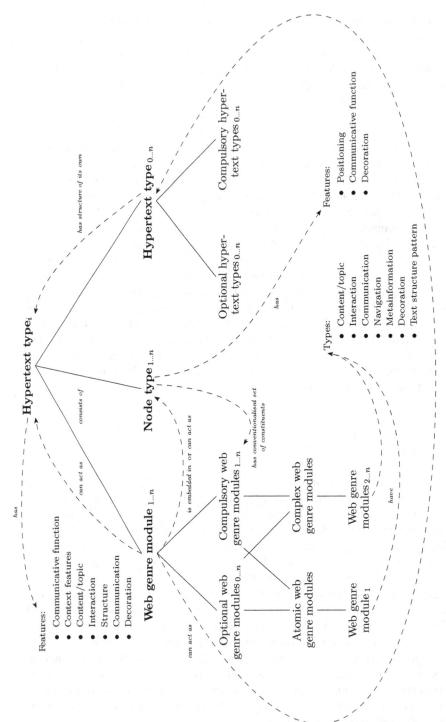

Fig. 8.4 The generic constituent structure of a hypertext type/web genre

The model consists of three levels of granularity that represent the constituents of a web genre: the most fundamental of these is the web genre module that serves as a basic building block. As web genres are not monolithic but instead rather flexible (Haas and Grams 1998), web genre modules act as basic logical-semantic entities that can be freely arranged in one or more HTML documents (see also Mehler in this volume). It is necessary to assume this conceptual level of text structural entities beneath the individual document as, for example, the entry page of an instance of the web genre *Academic's Personal Homepage* may comprise the web genre modules *List of Publications*, *Contact Information*, *Current Courses* and *Current Projects* (Santini 2007). While one author may arrange these web genre modules in a single HTML document, another author may choose to instantiate each of these web genre modules in HTML documents of their own. Based on their frequency, the fundamental constituents of a specific hypertext type can be divided into compulsory ($\geq 50\%$) and optional web genre modules ($< 50\%$), which form the peripheral boundaries of a web genre. Furthermore, we can distinguish between atomic and complex web genre modules with regard to their internal structure: for example, the atomic web genre modules *List of Publications*, *List of Presentations* and *Current Projects* constitute the complex web genre module *Scientific Profile* (with regard to the web genre *Academic's Personal Homepage*). In addition, every web genre module is reflected by at least one type: the *List of Publications* has a very significant *text structure pattern*, whereas the web genre module *E-Mail Address* is primarily reflected by the types *communication* and *interaction*.

The second group of constituents is called node type and relates to conventionalized configurations of web genre modules. In his information architecture handbook, Reiss (2000) mentions one such node type:

> More and more, [sic] companies are combining their site map, webmaster email address, disclaimer, and copyright information on a single page. Usually labeled "About this site", this combination page seems well on its way to becoming an established web convention. (Reiss 2000, p. 135)

What Reiss (2000) calls a "combination page" is, according to the web genre model, a conventionalised node type that consists of web genre modules such as "site map" and "disclaimer". The conceptual level represented by node types is needed in order to be able to capture conventions with regard to the internal structure of individual nodes (i. e., HTML documents). Node types have features that relate to the positioning of web genre modules and a node type's individual web design (that might differ from the web genre's global decoration feature).

Finally, the instance of a web genre such as *University Website* can embed instances of subordinate web genres such as *Website of a University Department* or *Computer Centre Website*. This process of embedding complex constituents is, again, nothing but another set of rules or conventions. As trivial as this example might seem: every university website contains sub sites (embedded hypertexts) for every department within a university. Usually, members of the departments are responsible for creating and maintaining these websites. This circumstance (two groups of authors who, with their texts, pursue different objectives, i. e., communicative functions) justifies the distinction between two different hypertext types in this example.

The boundaries between web genre modules, node types and hypertext types is not as clear-cut as it might initially seem (Mehler et al. 2004). As neither binding norms nor straightforward standards for web genres exist, authors are rather free to structure their content as they see fit. Based on the analyses described in Rehm (2007), it is safe to state that conventions with regard to specific sets of web genre modules exist in most web genres, but the way these web genre modules are structured and sequenced within one or more hypertexts is less conventionalised. This is why the model specifies that web genre modules can act as node types as well as hypertext types. Consider the web genre *List of Publication*. With regard to most instances of the web genre *Academic's Personal Homepage*, this web genre module is either embedded in a node together with other web genre modules, or it is the only web genre module in an HTML document (web genre module acts as node type). There are cases, however, in which authors chose to structure their lists of publications in more than one node, effectively creating a hypertext (for example, one node for monographs, another for refereed articles, etc.). Therefore, a minimal web genre (or hypertext type) instance comprises at least one compulsory web genre module that can act as a node type, resulting in a single node.

Finally it should be noted that descriptions of web genres and node types rely on empirical evidence. For example, if one wants to construct a profile for the web genre *Academic's Personal Homepage*, a sample of corresponding hypertexts needs to be gathered first. The sample analysis includes inductively generalising the web genre modules, node types and embedded web genres contained within the sample's hypertexts and integrating the data as a web genre profile (see Rehm 2007).

8.3.4 Analysing Web Genres

Analysing samples of HTML documents with regard to their web genres usually involves one of two goals. First, randomly collected instances of *one* web genre can be examined in order to construct empirically a web genre profile for this very web genre (see Section 8.3.3). Second, if a sample contains randomly collected documents of *arbitrary* web genres (i. e., arbitrary documents), the aim is to identify all web genres, node types and possibly web genre modules contained in the sample, in order to get an idea about the variety of web genres in use within a particular domain or discourse community. Furthermore, annotating a document sample with web genre information results in a data set that can be used as training and testing data in a machine learning scenario that aims at the automatic identification of web genres.

As initially suggested in Rehm (2002), it is crucial to select an analysis domain first (see, e. g., Rosso 2005), as the analysis of truly arbitrary documents such as the ones provided by randomly picking documents stored in the databases of search engines (an approach employed by Crowston and Williams 2000, Shepherd and

Watters 1999, Haas and Grams 2000), leads to results that are too broad and too vague to be of any actual use. Furthermore, a snapshot, i. e., a stable corpus of HTML documents is needed that comprises the documents to be analysed. For this purpose, web crawlers and additional components such as language identification tools can be used in order to filter and preprocess the documents to be integrated into the corpus (Rehm 2001).

A web-accessible corpus-database that assists the analysis of documents is described in Rehm (2007). Furthermore, the system provides an easy to handle interface for the generation and maintenance of document samples. The results of an analysis are automatically stored in a relational database. Several analyses have been carried out with the help of this tool. Gleim et al. (2007) present an integrated tool for the purpose of collecting, analysing, and annotating web corpora.

8.3.5 On the Variety of Web Genres

The analyses described in Rehm (2007) are based on a corpus of ca. four million HTML documents, written in German, that were crawled from the websites of 100 German universities. The domain of academia was chosen because it is assumed to be rather stable and highly structured, thus making it a prime candidate for a project related to the description and automatic identification of web genres. One of the analyses aimed to shed light on the number of web genres in use within the domain of academic websites. A random sample of 750 documents, generated by means of the corpus-database (see Section 8.3.4), was analysed with regard to the node types, web genres (i. e., the superordinate web genre to which an individual node belongs) and the organisational unit that published a document on their website.

Table 8.1 shows the web genres found in the sample and illustrates the enormous variety in the set of hypertext types instantiated in academic websites. Web genres such as, for example, *Website of an Organisational Unit, Conference Website, Course Materials, PhD Thesis, Diploma Thesis*, and *Examination Regulations* can be expected in the domain. Furthermore traditional genres, such as *Cook Book, Classifieds*, and *Lexicon*, as well as a small number of highly specialised genres of scientific communication (*Medical Diagnosis Procedure, Historical Building Data*) also occur. In addition, we find web genres primarily related to other internet services (*Mailing List Archive, FAQ Document*) or technical aspects of the World Wide Web (*Access Statistics*).

Table 8.2 shows the node types found in the sample of 750 randomly collected HTML documents. A rather salient example is *Page/paragraph* with occurrences in 119 documents. This category comprises 20 subtypes such as *Page/paragraph of a Software Documentation, Page/paragraph of a Handbook*, or *Page/paragraph of a Study Guide*. In printed manifestations of genres such as *Software Documentation, Handbook*, or *Study Guide*, logical constituents beneath the genre level or units corresponding to a physical page are usually not named (with the exception

Table 8.1 The 65 web genres found in a random sample of 750 documents

1. **Website of an organisational unit** (subtypes: 24) 28.4%; 2. **Website of an educational course** (subtypes: 4) 13.9%; 3. **Course program/directory** 6.0%; 4. **Software documentation** (subtypes: 4) 5.3%; 5. **Annual research report** 3.7%; 6. **Course materials (manuscript)** 3.7%; 7. **Photo gallery** (subtypes: 4) 3.5%; 8. **List of press releases** 3.2%; 9. **Organisational unit's publication** (subtypes: 8) 2.5%; 10. **Academic's personal homepage** 2.3%; 11. **Website of an organisation** (subtypes: 9) 1.9%; 12. **Student's homepage** 1.6%; 13. **School teaching materials** 1.5%; 14. **Study guide** 1.3%; 15. **Course of studies website**; 16. **Student presentations/theses** 1.2%; 17. **Employee directory**; 18. **Handbook** 1.1%; 19. **Virtual museum**; 20. **Instructions, manuals, documentations** 0.9%; 21. **Library catalogue** 0.8%; 22. **Textbook/textbook chapter**; 23. **Diploma thesis**; 24. **Digital library** 0.7%; 25. **Message/discussion board**; 26. **Student presentation/essay/thesis**; 27. **Conference website**; 28. **Medical diagnosis procedure** 0.5%; 29. **Lexicon**; 30. **Contest/event website**; 31. **Access statistics**; 32. **Tasks for student papers** 0.4%; 33. **Research projects of an organisational unit**; 34. **Medical diagnosis example**; 35. **Law, regulation, legal text**; 36. **Student statistics**; 37. **Final report (of a project)** 0.3%; 38. **Latest information, news**; 39. **Biography**; 40. **Digital map**; 41. **PhD thesis**; 42. **Subject-specific information portal**; 43. **FAQ document**; 44. **Graphical assistant for process development**; 45. **Internet journal (review forum)**; 46. **Mailing list archive**; 47. **Bibliography** 0.1%; 48. **Library classification scheme**; 49. **Historical building data**; 50. **Trip/excursion report**; 51. **Glossary**; 52. **Almanach**; 53. **Classifieds**; 54. **Cook book**; 55. **Art/cultural event**; 56. **Minutes archive**; 57. **Examination regulations**; 58. **Guidelines (for student papers)**; 59. **Materials on special reserve**; 60. **Study regulations**; 61. **Daily newspaper**; 62. **Betting game (on a sports event)**; 63. **Knowledge transfer catalogue**; 64. **Virtual library**; 65. **Scientific article**

of constituents such as *Table of Contents, Chapter, Section, List of References* etc.). Therefore, all the node types which correspond to superordinate genres but that do not possess an identifying label are subsumed under the category *Page/ paragraph*. As a natural consequence, the variety at the node level is greater than at the web genre level. The sample contains instances of node types as diverse as, for example, *Slide, Abstract, Press Release, Exercises, Announcement, Exhibit (of a Virtual Museum), Minutes, Consent Form, City Map, Invitation, Review, "under construction" Notice, Classified Ad, Price List, Travel Diary,* and *Riddle.*

When we return to the role of HTML as a markup language, the results of this analysis are highly relevant for two reasons. First, the study shows that hundreds of both traditional genres as well as novel web genres are used in the World Wide Web. Especially well-established genres, such as *Cook Book* and *Lexicon,* demonstrate that, in principle, one dedicated markup language is needed for every single genre to model the respective text structures' constituents. Second, the categories that have subtypes as well as closely related web genres reveal a problem that cannot be addressed with approaches such as DTDs or XML Schema descriptions. It is impossible formally to model typologies of genres, or, to be more precise, typologies of markup languages. Apart from representing identical parts of markup languages in DTD-fragments and importing these with the help of parameter entities, the family of XML standards does not provide a mechanism that is able adequately to represent a typology of document grammars (see Rehm 2007). As Fig. 8.5 illustrates, the relationships that hold between similar or related text types or markup languages respectively, cannot be modelled by a set of isolated DTDs alone.

Table 8.2 The 114 node types found in a random sample of 750 documents

1. **Page/paragraph** (subtypes: 20) 15.9%; 2. **Slide** (subtypes: 6) 10.7%; 3. **Organisational data (course)** (subtypes: 4) 6.1%; 4. **Abstract** (subtypes: 6) 5.6%; 5. **Photo** 3.9%; 6. **Entry page** 3.2%; 7. **Press release**; 8. **Employee's professional homepage** (subtypes: 2) 2.4%; 9. **Article (organisational unit's publication)** (subtypes: 6) 2.1%; 10. **Primary navigation bar** 1.7%; 11. **Description of a work group** 1.6%; 12. **Instruction, manual, documentation** 1.3%; 13. **Hotlist**; 14. **Academic's personal homepage**; 15. **Exercises**; 16. **Course program/directory** (subtypes: 3); 17. **Schedule/program (of a course)** 1.2%; 18. **List of publications** (subtypes: 2); 19. *Categorisation not possible*; 20. **Head line** 1.1%; 21. **Study guide** (subtypes: 3); 22. **School teaching materials**; 23. **Announcement** 0.9%; 24. **Photo gallery**; 25. **Exhibit (of a virtual museum)** 0.8%; 26. **Library catalogue (single record)**; 27. **E-mail**; 28. **Contact information**; 29. **Description of an organisational unit (functions and contact information)**; 30. **Description of technology transfer services** 0.7%; 31. **Lexicon entry**; 32. **Exercise solutions**; 33. **Employee directory**; 34. **Source code**; 35. **Student statistics**; 36. **Finished theses/possible topics for theses** 0.5%; 37. **Latest information, news**; 38. **Bibliography**; 39. **Invitation**; 40. **Table of contents** (subtypes: 3); 41. **Examination dates**; 42. **Medicial diagnosis procedure**; 43. **Statistical data (automatically generated)**; 44. **"under construction"**; 45. **Dispatcher**; 46. **Index (generated by web server)**; 47. **Possible topic for an essay/a thesis** 0.4%; 48. **Conference report**; 49. **Download list (multimedia resources)**; 50. **Course description**; 51. **Institution history**; 52. **Description of an organisational unit (profile/portrait)**; 53. **Minutes**; 54. **Question and answer**; 55. **Law, regulation, legal text**; 56. **Review**; 57. **Course of study description**; 58. **Study regulations**; 59. **Technical data/specification (hard-/software)**; 60. **Biography** 0.3%; 61. **Sports results**; 62. **Expose**; 63. **Footer**; 64. **Glossary entry**; 65. **Courses of studies list**; 66. **Medical diagnosis example**; 67. **Specification table**; 68. **Splash page**; 69. **Timetable**; 70. **Presentation manuscript**; 71. **Scientific article**; 72. **Newspaper article (scanned in)**; 73. **Access statistics**; 74. **Registration form** 0.1%; 75. **Directions**; 76. **Committee proposal**; 77. **Application form**; 78. **Medical information**; 79. **Library classification scheme (excerpt)**; 80. **Semester dates and deadlines**; 81. **Riddle**; 82. **Consent form**; 83. **Episode list (tv show)**; 84. **Errata**; 85. **Slides (thumbnails with interactive examples)**; 86. **Guestbook**; 87. **Calendar of memorial dates**; 88. **Glossary**; 89. **Image map**; 90. **City map**; 91. **Historical building data**; 92. **Plant data**; 93. **Cinema programme**; 94. **Test results**; 95. **Classified ad**; 96. **Recipe**; 97. **Club/society course directory**; 98. **Map/site plan**; 99. **List of course materials**; 100. **List of lexicon entries**; 101. **List of university projects**; 102. **List of doctoral projects within an organisational unit**; 103. **List of new or modified documents on a website**; 104. **Newsgroup (list of postings)**; 105. **Price list**; 106. **Press releases (list)**; 107. **Pupil's homepage**; 108. **Editors of a website**; 109. **Travel diary (single entry)**; 110. **Memo/circular**; 111. **Search form**; 112. **Participant list**; 113. **University newspaper (overview of one issue)**; 114. **Election results**

8.3.6 Modelling Web Genres with OWL

The two problems raised in Section 8.3.5 can be overcome only with the help of an additional representation layer that encapsulates the relations that hold between (the constituents of) related text types. We have shown (see Rehm 2007) that the Web Ontology Language (OWL) is an appropriate formalism for this text technological application (Rehm 2004c). Usually, OWL is used to model traditional ontologies for knowledge representation and Semantic Web purposes (see Farrar and Langendoen, in this volume). OWL possesses several advantages such as class hierarchies, multiple inheritance, and different types of properties (features of classes or instances respectively).

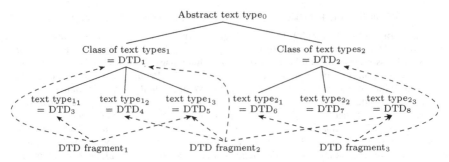

Fig. 8.5 Representing a typology of text types by means of individual XML document type definitions and imported DTD fragments

We developed a web genre ontology that is based as closely as possible on the internal structure of the web genre model (see Section 8.3.3).[2] The ontology contains three classes named `HypertextType`, `NodeType` and `WebGenreModule` that correspond to the model's three main components. Figure 8.6 shows this basic framework along with some of the core relations that, again, match the relations included in the model.

The web genre ontology comprises several hundred classes as well as relations and it is tightly intervowen with a domain ontology that models the generic structure of a German university. A very small excerpt from the web genre ontology is depicted in Fig. 8.7. This figure presents the framework of the web genre typology governed by the abstract class *Homepage of a Person*. The typology contains, among others, the web genres *Academic's Personal Homepage* and *Student's Private Homepage* as subgeneric variants. As the analyses have documented, all web genres of the personal or private homepage type share common properties that can be conceptualised as a prototypical core. Due to OWL's inheritance mechanism, these prototypical features are defined in the abstract class *Homepage of a Person* and automatically propagated to all subclasses, so that exceptions and extensions can be handled individually. Furthermore, Fig. 8.7 shows references to specific subclasses of `NodeType`. These subclasses themselves reference subclasses of `WebGenreModule` (not shown in the figure) that have been identified and collected in empirical sample analyses (i.e., the web genre ontology reflects empirical data with regard to a particular analysis domain). Whereas the definitions of

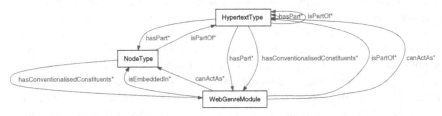

Fig. 8.6 The three basic classes of the web genre ontology (see Fig. 8.4)

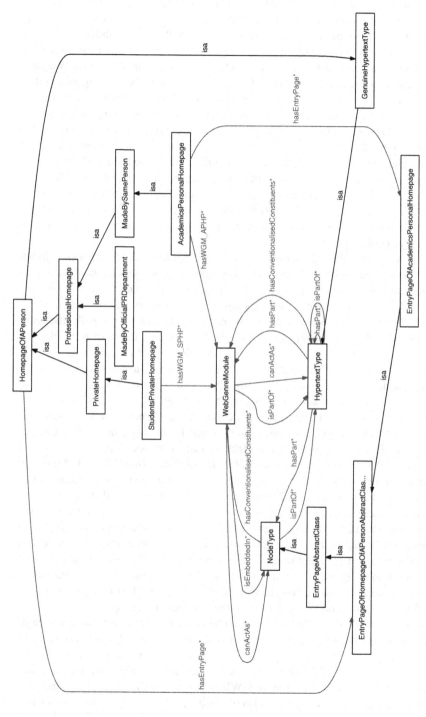

Fig. 8.7 The web genres of the abstract hypertext type *homepage of a person*

subclasses of NodeType mainly refer to specific configurations of web genre modules, the definitions of the subclasses of WebGenreModule can contain arbitrary information. The set of information associated with web genre modules can be comprised of, for example, DTD fragments, keywords, empirical data (e. g., word frequencies), comments or references to external resources. This flexibility is needed for the automatic processing of HTML documents, especially with regard to information extraction purposes or the categorization and identification of web genres. In addition, a lot of web genre modules are used in more than one web genre. To enable their re-use, definitions of web genre modules are simply referenced within the definitions of web genres and node types, so that the ontology itself is kept free of redundancies. Another challenge for the OWL-based modelling of web genres is the representation of conventions in hypertextual graph structures (see Mehler in this volume). Currently, these conventions are modelled as an additional layer of object properties, i. e., relations between the instances of web genre modules such as *Navigation Bar* (link anchors) and corresponding web genre modules as well as node types (link targets).

The web genre ontology has several potential application scenarios (see Rehm 2007 for a more detailed discussion). The automatic identification of web genres, for example, could be approached by categorising the macrostructural building blocks of HTML documents and mapping these objects onto web genre modules (Rehm 2004b, also see Stede and Suriyawongkul in this volume). Finally, the set of instantiated web genre modules could be used to compute the most probable web genre with the help of an inference engine. Another possible application involves the additional step of extracting information from instantiated web genre modules (Rehm 2004a): authors of web pages usually follow certain conventions that also apply to the basic informational units of web genre modules such as *Contact Information*. According to our analysis, this complex web genre module contains (in instances of the web genre *Academic's Personal Homepage*), the atomic components *E-Mail Address* (99%), *Street Address* (90%), *Phone Number* (86%), *Fax Number* (86%), *Room/Office Number* (30%), and *Office Hours* (27%). Assuming the majority of instances of a certain web genre module contains a specific set of information, it is possible to build specialised extraction engines that anticipate the presence of these sets of information and that represent the extracted data using tag sets such as EMailAddress, StreetAddress, PhoneNumber, etc. These tag names are reflected in the abovementioned DTD fragments that can be referenced in web genre module definitions. If we assume now that the most basic structural information of every web genre module of specific web genres can be extracted by automatic means, we had a web genre-driven HTML-to-XML conversion as well as an information extraction system for a certain number of web genres.

Genres in the World Wide Web must not be viewed as restrictive and as standardised as some traditional genres, because, especially with regard to non-commercial websites, no one enforces web genres (i. e., certain rules and conventions) and no author has to fear any negative consequences should he or she breach the rules. Defining web genres by means of an OWL ontology makes allowance for the flexibility inherent in the web genre concept. Web genres consist of compulsory and optional web genre modules so that it is possible to compile the corresponding DTD fragments into an overall document grammar for a markup language that can be used to represent instances of the entire web genre (see Erdmann 2001). Such a tool must be able to interpret the object properties employed to relate compulsory and optional web genre modules to a specific web genre and should be able to generate document grammars in several formats (DTD, XML Schema, Relax NG, etc.).

8.4 Concluding Remarks

With regard to the very close relationship between genres (i.e., text types) and markup languages, a peculiar situation exists in the World Wide Web. Usually, the generalised discourse structure of a genre or text type is modelled in the form of one specific document grammar or markup language that authors apply for the process of writing a document belonging to this very genre. In the World Wide Web, however, we have the situation that *one* markup language, HTML, is used to annotate and to design documents of hundreds of web genres. For this purpose, HTML and its companion standards (CSS, etc.) are bent as far as possible in order to produce innovative and appealing designs, generally by employing visual tools (for example, WYSIWYG editors) instead of traditional SGML / XML editors. Therefore, in practice, HTML is used more like a page description language, such as Postscript, than as a genuine markup language that is rooted in the SGML tradition.

Hypertext itself is neither a genre nor a text type. Instead, it is – in the incarnation of the World Wide Web – a well-established means of communication that has spawned dozens of novel web genres. Furthermore, hundreds, if not thousands, of traditional genres are used throughout the World Wide Web, primarily by automatically converting existing text documents into HTML or by copying and pasting existing content into the editors of content management systems (Rehm 2007). This observation has several consequences for current research trends in linguistics and computational linguistics. An important trend is the "web as corpus" approach (Kilgarriff 2001, Mehler et al. 2009). In their overview and introduction, Kilgarriff and Grefenstette (2003, p. 342) complain about a "lack of theory of text types". Later, the authors mention one of the most central problems:

> "Text type" is an area in which our understanding is, as yet, very limited. Although further work is required irrespective of the web, the use of the web forces the issue. Where researchers use established corpora, such as Brown, the BNC, or the Penn Treebank, researchers and readers are willing to accept the corpus name as a label for the type of text occurring in it without asking critical questions. Once we move to the web as a source of data, and our corpora have names like "April03-sample77", the issue of how the text type(s) can be characterized demands attention. (Kilgarriff and Grefenstette 2003, p. 343)

The situation can be approached from the opposite point of view as well: how can a web-based corpus of cook books, software manuals, guidelines for student papers or conference websites be constructed? These are but a tiny fraction of examples of established text types or genres in the World Wide Web. We need methods that enable us to identify genres automatically and to filter corpus collection processes based on that data. In other words: we do not want to label our corpus snapshot "April03-sample77" but, instead, we would like to use meaningful tags that, ideally, refer to a standardised inventory of web genre labels (Rehm 2009).

The automatic identification of web genres requires very sophisticated and robust methods. Lim et al. (2005), for example, present a supervised machine-learning approach that uses a total of 329 features to classify documents into 16 genres (e. g., "public homepages", "commercial homepages", "simple tables/lists", "input pages", "official materials", "informative materials" and "others"; the genres are based upon the inventory prepared by Dewe et al. (1998), also see Levering et al. (2008), Kim and Ross (2008)). Although the approach by Lim et al. (2005) does operate with a precision of about 75%, it fails to address the key aspects of web genres. All the existing approaches to genre identification treat HTML documents as monolithic instantiations of web genres, i. e., one document is the manifestation of exactly one web genre (but see Mehler et al. 2004). Both the level of web genre modules as well as the superordinate level of web genres that consist of specific node types are ignored completely. Furthermore, all existing approaches lack a theoretical foundation (for example, neither the concept of web genres, nor the inventory of genres used are thoroughly discussed or motivated). What is needed is an approach that goes beyond the individual HTML document and analyses the hypertextual structure of component documents (Eiron and McCurley 2003). In addition, the macrostructure of every HTML document needs to be processed in order to find instances of multiple web genre modules that might be used simultaneously in a single document. In Rehm (2005), the prototype of a parser for arbitrary HTML documents is presented. The system parses the HTML element tree and tries to identify the textual macrostructure's basic building blocks that can, in turn, be mapped onto web genre modules. First, the HTML document is converted to XHTML, so that it can be processed with XML tools (Myllymaki 2001). A DOM and XPath engine is used to analyse recursively the element tree based on the "visual semantics" of all HTML elements and attributes. Their visual effect rather than the elements themselves need to be taken into account due to the problem of tag abuse (Barnard et al. 1996). The results of the analysis (purely structure-oriented tags that encapsulate individual HTML element subtrees with information about lists, headlines, separators, paragraphs of running text, etc.) are stored within the scope of a new namespace directly in the converted XHTML document.

With regard to taking web genres into consideration from a theoretical as well as practical point of view, several important questions need to be addressed in the near future: genre rules and conventions stretch beyond the individual document, which is why approaches that treat single HTML documents fail in capturing the reality of everyday communication on the web. Furthermore, an extensible set of standardised web genre names needs to be established (see Rehm 2007 for an initial proposal) and, ideally, accompanied by a reference corpus (Rehm 2009, Rehm et al. 2008). An additional problem is introduced by the trend of bringing applications into the web. User interface programming paradigms such as Ajax enable truly dynamic applications and operate by replacing individual subtrees of the DOM structure by means of JavaScript's XMLHttpRequest object instead of refreshing the whole (X)HTML document each time the user initiates an action. This technique severely challenges the concept of HTML *documents*, so that a distinction between HTML documents and HTML-based *applications* will be needed in the future.

Notes

1. The declaration of the element `body` in the HTML 4.01 DTD (Raggett et al. 1999) contains *arbitrary* sequences of the elements `p`, `h1`, `h2`, `h3`, `h4`, `h5`, `h6`, `ul`, `dl`, `pre`, `dl`, `div`, `noscript`, `blockquote`, `form`, `hr`, `table`, `fieldset`, `address`, and `script`. A related problem concerns the phenomenon known as "tag abuse" (Barnard et al. 1996): authors often use specific elements for their presentational features only and completely ignore their original semantics.
2. The ontology was developed with the help of the Protégé-OWL ontology editor (see http://protege.stanford.edu). Figures 8.6 and 8.7 were generated using the Ontoviz plugin.

References

Barnard, David T., Burnard, Lou, DeRose, Steven J., Durand, David G., and Sperberg-McQueen, C.M. (1996). Lessons for the World Wide Web from the Text Encoding Initiative. *The World Wide Web Journal*, 1(1):349–357.

Bazerman, Charles (1994). Systems of Genres and the Enactment of Social Intentions. In Freedman, Aviva and Medway, Peter, editors, *Genre and the New Rhetoric*, pages 79–101. Taylor and Francis, London.

Bray, Tim, Paoli, Jean, Sperberg-McQueen, C. M., Maler, Eve, Yergeau, François, and Cowan, John (2004). Extensible Markup Language (XML) 1.1. Technical Specification, W3C. http://www.w3.org/TR/2004/REC-xml11-20040204/.

Brinker, Klaus, Antos, Gerd, Heinemann, Wolfgang, and Sager, Sven F., editors (2000). *Text- und Gesprächslinguistik*, volume 16.1 of *Handbücher zur Sprach- und Kommunikationswissenschaft (HSK)*. de Gruyter, Berlin, New York.

Crowston, Kevin and Williams, Marie (2000). Reproduced and Emergent Genres of Communication on the World Wide Web. *The Information Society*, 16(3):201–215.

Dewe, Johan, Karlgren, Jussi, and Bretan, Ivan (1998). Assembling a Balanced Corpus from the Internet. In *Proceedings of the 11th Nordic Conference of Computational Linguistics*, pages 100–107, Copenhagen.

Eckkrammer, Eva Martha (2001). Textsortenkonventionen im Medienwechsel. In Handler, Peter, editor, *E-Text: Strategien und Kompetenzen – Elektronische Kommunikation in Wissenschaft, Bildung und Beruf*, volume 7 of *Textproduktion und Medium*, pages 45–66. Peter Lang, Frankfurt/Main, Berlin, Bern etc.

Eiron, Nadav and McCurley, Kevin S. (2003). Untangling Compound Documents on the Web. In *Proceedings of the 14th ACM Conference on Hypertext and Hypermedia*, pages 85–94. Nottingham.

Emigh, William and Herring, Susan C. (2005). Collaborative Authoring on the Web: A Genre Analysis of Online Encyclopedias. In *Proceedings of the 38th Hawaii International Conference on Systems Sciences (HICSS-38)*, Big Island, Hawaii.

Erdmann, Michael (2001). *Ontologien zur konzeptuellen Modellierung der Semantik von XML*. Ph. d. thesis, University of Karlsruhe, Karlsruhe.

Erickson, Thomas (2000). Making Sense of Computer-Mediated Communication (CMC): Conversations as Genres, CMC Systems as Genre Ecologies. In *Proceedings of the 33rd Hawaii International Conference on Systems Sciences (HICSS-33)*.

Eriksen, Lars Bo and Ihlström, Carina (1999). In the Path of the Pioneers – Longitudinal Study of Web News Genre. In Käkölä, Timo K., editor, *Proceedings of the 22nd Information Systems Research Seminar in Scandinavia (IRIS 22): "Enterprise Architectures for Virtual Organizations"*, pages 289–304, Keuruu. University of Jyväskylä.

Furuta, Richard and Marshall, Catherine C. (1996). Genre as Reflection of Technology in the World-Wide Web. In Fraïssé, Sylvain, Garzotto, Franca, Isakowitz, Tomás, Nanard, Jocelyne, and Nanard, Marc, editors, *Hypermedia Design, Proceedings of the International Workshop on Hypermedia Design (IWHD 1995)*, Workshops in Computing, pages 182–195. Springer, Berlin, Heidelberg, New York etc.

Gleim, Rüdiger, Mehler, Alexander, Eikmeyer, Hans-Jürgen, and Rieser, Hannes (2007). Ein Ansatz zur Repräsentation und Verarbeitung großer Korpora. In Rehm, Georg, Witt, Andreas, and Lemnitzer, Lothar, editors, *Datenstrukturen für linguistische Ressourcen und ihre Anwendungen – Data Structures for Linguistic Resources and Applications: Proceedings of the Biennial GLDV Conference 2007*, pages 275–284. Gunter Narr, Tübingen.

Haas, Stephanie W. and Grams, Erika S. (1998). Page and Link Classifications: Connecting Diverse Resources. In Witten, I., Akscyn, R., and Shipman, F., editors, *Proceedings of Digital Libraries '98 – Third ACM Conference on Digital Libraries*, pages 99–107, Pittsburgh.

Haas, Stephanie W. and Grams, Erika S. (2000). Readers, Authors, and Page Structure – A Discussion of Four Questions Arising from a Content Analysis of Web Pages. *Journal of the American Society for Information Science*, 51(2):181–192.

Hammwöhner, Rainer (1997). *Offene Hypertextsysteme – Das Konstanzer Hypertextsystem (KHS) im wissenschaftlichen und technischen Kontext*. Number 32 in Schriften zur Informationswissenschaft. Universitätsverlag Konstanz, Konstanz.

ISO 8879 (1986). Information Processing – Text and Office Information Systems – Standard Generalized Markup Language. Internationaler Standard, International Organization for Standardization, Genf.

Jakobs, Eva-Maria (2003). Hypertextsorten. *Zeitschrift für germanistische Linguistik*, 31(2):232–252.

Kilgarriff, Adam (2001). Web as Corpus. In Rayson, Paul, Wilson, Andrew, McEnery, Tony, Hardie, Andrew, and Khoja, Shereen, editors, *Proceedings of the Corpus Linguistics 2001 Conference*, pages 342–344, Lancaster.

Kilgarriff, Adam and Grefenstette, Gregory (2003). Introduction to the Special Issue on the Web as Corpus. *Computational Linguistics*, 29(3): 333–348.

Kim, Yunhyong and Ross, Seamus (2008). Examining Variations of Prominent Features in Classification. In *Proceedings of the 41st Hawaii International Conference on Systems Sciences (HICSS-41)*, Big Island, Hawaii.

Kuhlen, Rainer (1991). *Hypertext – Ein nicht-lineares Medium zwischen Buch und Wissensbank*. Springer, Berlin, Heidelberg, New York etc.

Levering, Ryan, Cutler, Michal, and Yu, Lei (2008). Using Visual Features for Fine-Grained Genre Classification of Web Pages. In *Proceedings of the 41st Hawaii International Conference on Systems Sciences (HICSS-41)*, Big Island, Hawaii.

Lim, Chul Su, Lee, Kong Joo, and Kim, Gil Chang (2005). Multiple Sets of Features for Automatic Genre Classification of Web Documents. *Information Processing and Management*, 41(5):1263–1276.

Lobin, Henning (2000). Service-Handbücher – Linguistische Aspekte im Document Lifecycle. In Richter, Gerd, Riecke, Jörg, and Schuster, Britt-Marie, editors, *Raum, Zeit, Medium – Sprache und ihre Determinanten. Festschrift für Hans Ramge*, pages 791–808. Hessische Historische Kommission, Darmstadt.

Lobin, Henning (2001). *Informationsmodellierung in XML und SGML*. Springer, Berlin, Heidelberg, New York etc.

Maler, Eve and Andaloussi, Jeanne El (1996). *Developing SGML DTDs – From Text to Model to Markup*. Prentice Hall, Upper Saddle River.

Mehler, Alexander, Dehmer, Matthias, and Gleim, Rüdiger (2004). Towards Logical Hypertext Structure — A Graph-Theoretic Perspective. In Böhme, Thomas and Heyer, Gerhard, editors,

Proceedings of the Fourth International Workshop on Innovative Internet Computing Systems (I2CS '04), Lecture Notes in Computer Science, Berlin, New York. Springer.

Mehler, Alexander, Sharoff, Serge, Rehm, Georg, and Santini, Marina, editors (2009). *Genres on the Web: Computational Models and Empirical Studies*, Springer, New York.

Miller, Carolyn R. (1984). Genre as Social Action. *Quarterly Journal of Speech*, (70):151–167.

Myllymaki, Jussi (2001). Effective Web Data Extraction with Standard XML Technologies. In *Proceedings of the 10th International World Wide Web Conference (WWW-10)*, pages 689–696, Hong Kong.

Orlikowski, Wanda J. and Yates, JoAnne (1994). Genre Repertoire: The Structuring of Communicative Practices in Organizations. *Administrative Science Quarterly*, (39):541–574.

Pemberton, Steven (2002). XHTML 1.0: The Extensible Hypertext Markup Language (Second Edition). Technical Specification, W3C. http://www.w3.org/TR/xhtml1/.

Raggett, Dave, Hors, Arnaud Le, and Jacbos, Ian (1999). HTML 4.01 Specification. Technical Specification, W3C. http://www.w3.org/TR/html401/.

Rehm, Georg (2001). korpus.html – Zur Sammlung, Datenbank-basierten Erfassung, Annotation und Auswertung von HTML-Dokumenten. In Lobin, Henning, editor, *Proceedings of the GLDV Spring Meeting 2001*, pages 93–103, Giessen, Germany. Gesellschaft für linguistische Datenverarbeitung (Society for Computational Linguistics and Language Technology). http://www.uni-giessen.de/fb09/ascl/gldv2001/.

Rehm, Georg (2002). Towards Automatic Web Genre Identification – A Corpus-Based Approach in the Domain of Academia by Example of the Academic's Personal Homepage. In *Proceedings of the 35th Hawaii International Conference on System Sciences (HICSS-35)*, Big Island, Hawaii.

Rehm, Georg (2004a). Hypertextsorten-Klassifikation als Grundlage generischer Informationsextraktion. In Mehler, Alexander and Lobin, Henning, editors, *Automatische Textanalyse – Systeme und Methoden zur Annotation und Analyse natürlichsprachlicher Texte*, pages 219–233. Verlag für Sozialwissenschaften, Wiesbaden.

Rehm, Georg (2004b). Ontologie-basierte Hypertextsorten-Klassifikation. In Mehler, Alexander and Lobin, Henning, editors, *Automatische Textanalyse – Systeme und Methoden zur Annotation und Analyse natürlichsprachlicher Texte*, pages 121–137. Verlag für Sozialwissenschaften, Wiesbaden.

Rehm, Georg (2004c). Texttechnologische Grundlagen. In Carstensen, Kai-Uwe, Ebert, Christian, Endriss, Cornelia, Jekat, Susanne, Klabunde, Ralf, and Langer, Hagen, editors, *Computerlinguistik und Sprachtechnologie – Eine Einführung*, pages 138–147. Spektrum, Heidelberg, 2 edition.

Rehm, Georg (2005). Language-Independent Text Parsing of Arbitrary HTML-Documents – Towards A Foundation For Web Genre Identification. *LDV Forum*, 20(2):53–74.

Rehm, Georg (2007). *Hypertextsorten: Definition – Struktur – Klassifikation*. Books on Demand, Norderstedt. (Ph. D. thesis in Applied and Computational Linguistics, Giessen University, 2005).

Rehm, Georg (2009). A Comparative Analysis of Genre Category Sets as a Prerequisite for a Reference Corpus of Web Genres. In Mehler, Alexander, Sharoff, Serge, Rehm, Georg, and Santini, Marina, editors, *Genres on the Web: Computational Models and Empirical Studies*, Springer, New York.

Rehm, Georg and Santini, Marina, editors (2007). *Proceedings of the International Workshop Towards Genre-Enabled Search Engines: The Impact of Natural Language Processing*, Borovets, Bulgaria. Held in conjunction with RANLP 2007.

Rehm, Georg, Santini, Marina, Mehler, Alexander, Braslavski, Pavel, Gleim, Rüdiger, Stubbe, Andrea, Symonenko, Svetlana, Tavosanis, Mirko, and Vidulin, Vedrana (2008). Towards a Reference Corpus of Web Genres for the Evaluation of Genre Identification Systems. In *Proceedings of the 6th Language Resources and Evaluation Conference (LREC 2008)*, Marrakech, Morocco.

Reiss, Eric L. (2000). *Practical Information Architecture – A Hands-On Approach to Structuring Successful Websites*. Addison-Wesley, Harlow, London, New York etc.

Rosso, Mark A. (2005). *Using Genre to Improve Web Search*. Ph. D. thesis, School of Information and Library Science, University of North Carolina at Chapel Hill.

Ryan, Terry, Field, Richard H. G., and Olfman, Lorne (2003). The evolution of US state government home pages from 1997 to 2002. *International Journal of Human-Computer Studies*, 59(4):403–430.

Santini, Marina (2007). Characterizing Genres of Web Pages: Genre Hybridism and Individualization. In *Proceedings of the 40th Hawaii International Conference on Systems Sciences (HICSS-40)*, Big Island, Hawaii.

Shepherd, Michael and Watters, Carolyn (1998). The Evolution of Cybergenres. In *Proceedings of the 31st Hawaii International Conference on Systems Sciences (HICSS-31)*, volume 2, pages 97–109.

Shepherd, Michael and Watters, Carolyn (1999). The Functionality Attribute of Cybergenres. In *Proceedings of the 32nd Hawaii International Conference on Systems Sciences (HICSS-32)*.

Storrer, Angelika (2004). Text und Hypertext. In Lobin, Henning and Lemnitzer, Lothar, editors, *Texttechnologie – Anwendungen und Perspektiven*, Stauffenburg Handbücher, pages 13–49. Stauffenburg, Tübingen.

Swales, John M. (1990). *Genre Analysis – English in academic and research settings*. The Cambridge Applied Linguistics Series. Cambridge University Press, Cambridge.

Walker, Derek (1999). Taking Snapshots of the Web with a TEI Camera. *Computers and the Humanities*, 33(1–2):185–192.

Yates, Joanne and Orlikowski, Wanda J. (1992). Genres of Organizational Communication: A Structurational Approach to Studying Communication and Media. *Academy of Management Review*, 17(2):299–326.

Yates, Simeon J. and Sumner, Tamara R. (1997). Digital Genres and the New Burden of Fixity. In *Proceedings of the 30th Hawaii International Conference on Systems Sciences (HICSS-30)*, volume 6, pages 3–12.

Yoshioka, Takeshi, Herman, George, Yates, JoAnne, and Orlikowski, Wanda (2001). Genre Taxonomy. *ACM Transactions on Information Systems*, 19(4):431–456.

Chapter 9
Representation Formats and Models
for Lexicons

Thorsten Trippel

Abstract The chapter on formats and models for lexicons deals with different available data formats of lexical resources. It elaborates on their structure and possible uses. Motivated by the restrictions in merging different lexical resources based on widely spread formalisms and international standards, a formal lexicon model for lexical resources is developed which is related to graph structures in annotations. For lexicons this model is termed the Lexicon Graph. Within this model the concepts of lexicon entries and lexical structures frequently described in the literature are formally defined and examples are given. The article addresses the problem of ambiguity in those formal terms. An implementation based on XML and XML technology such as XQuery for the defined structures is given. The relation to international standards is included as well.

Keywords Lexicon model · Lexicon model formalism · Lexicon graph · Markup framework · Lexical markup framework · LMF · Term base eXchange format · TBX · Feature structure representation · FSR

9.1 Introduction

The term *lexicon* contains an ambiguity: first, it is used as a reference to one specific lexical resource, second, it is used synecdochically for all words and their distinguishing properties of a language. This chapter classifies lexical resources and shows that there are appropriate models for representing lexicons in a form that is interpretable and exchangeable according to best practice in text technology. It respects the ambiguity of the term *lexicon* by using the models for different specific lexicons and by allowing to combine different kinds of specific lexicons to one lexicon, which then potentially represents the body of all words of a language.

Figure 9.1 presents a simple hierarchy of lexicons. This article will not consider the mental lexicon but concentrate on lexical resources, hence the term lexicon will

T. Trippel (✉)
Fakultät für Linguistik und Literaturwissenschaft, Universität Bielefeld, Bielefeld, Germany
e-mail: thorsten.trippel@uni-bielefeld.de

A. Witt, D. Metzing (eds.), *Linguistic Modeling of Information and Markup Languages*, Text, Speech and Language Technology 40,
DOI 10.1007/978-90-481-3331-4_9, © Springer Science+Business Media B.V. 2010

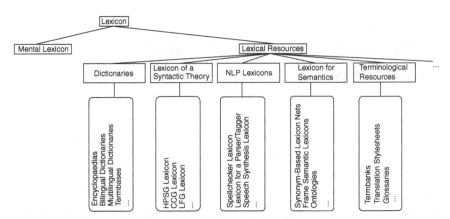

Fig. 9.1 Simple classification of types of lexicons

be used synonymously here for all resources of this kind. The further subclassification is by far not the only possible way of distinguishing resources from each other but indicates that there are fundamental differences even in the perception of what a lexicon is by researchers working with these kinds of resources. This implies that considering lexical resources in the further discussion will have representatives that can be seen as typical examples for a variety of other resources.

Each type of lexical resource is described by a different community, each using a specific terminology. For example, dictionaries are characterized in terms of their lexicon microstructure – the order, number and specification of the lexical data categories – and macrostructure – the ordering principle of lexicon entries. Some additional structures are defined such as the mesostructure, which describes the interrelation of lexicon articles with references to external resources, etc., and the lexicon megastructure that denotes the different parts of a print dictionary, which can for example include a user guide at the beginning of a dictionary. For a more detailed description of those structures see Hartmann (2001) and Gibbon (2005). Lexicons in syntactic theories could also be described in terms of lexical data categories involved, but they are usually given as a feature structure such as in HPSG (see for example Sag et al. 2003), where lexicon entries are divided up into terminal and nonterminal symbols as well. In contrast to that, resources from Natural Language Processing (NLP) contexts are usually tables with only few columns, such as the list of exceptional transcriptions in a grapheme-to-phoneme transducer. All of these resources share some data categories, though in detail they are quite different.

For the following chapter the fundamental assumptions are:

1. For each type of lexical resource there is at least one suitable representation format, which is designed for interchanging specifically this type of resource.
2. The interchange between different types of lexical resources is possible without losing information by applying a more abstract model, namely a graph. This implies that the interchange of lexical resources of different types is not necessarily possible by the specific representation formats. Lossless interchange is

defined as the combination of two different kinds of lexical resources which results in one resource that contains all pieces of information originally contained in both kinds of lexicons.

Example lexicon formats addressed here include lexicons for syntactic theories using an HPSG lexicon example. Other entries are taken from Combinatory Categorial Grammar. These lexicons are used in parallel to introduce possible implementations in XML based formalisms created for standardization purposes. Also included are dictionary and termbase articles.

9.2 Lexicons for Syntactic Theories and Representation Formalisms

A rather typical representation for lexical data is the hierarchical feature structure representation, as shown in Fig. 9.2. This lexicon entry is used as the lexicon basis for a syntactic theory with the data categories required by this theory, in this case HPSG (see Sag et al. 2003), but other formalisms use similar representations, such as the Generative Lexicon (Pustejovsky 1995). The hierarchy of data categories shows a dependency of syntactic and semantic categories and argument structures with references between them, indicated by the boxed symbols.

One possible way of encoding this type of structure in XML is the use of the Feature Structure Representation format (FSR, ISO 24610-1 2006), which is a standard issued by the International Organization for Standardization. Listing 9.1 shows an abbreviated implementation of the same feature structure in XML as Fig. 9.2.

It has to be noted that the hierarchical structure of data categories is made explicit by embedding the structures into each other. Shared features are introduced using the vLabel-element. The structure as such is not dependent on a syntactic theory, in practice the selection of data categories is predetermined by the theory. Even non-hierarchical lexicon articles can be represented by this structure, by listing the features, either as a set of attribute-value pairs or as an n-ary vector, though this use has not been intended originally.

Fig. 9.2 Feature structure representation of an HPSG lexicon entry for the English word *dog* showing hierarchical relations of lexical data categories, from Sag et al. (2003, p. 254)

$$
\left\langle \text{dog}, \begin{bmatrix} word \\ \text{SYN} \begin{bmatrix} \text{HEAD} \begin{bmatrix} noun \\ \text{AGR} \boxed{1} \begin{bmatrix} \text{PER 3rd} \\ \text{NUM sg} \end{bmatrix} \end{bmatrix} \\ \text{VAL} \begin{bmatrix} \text{SPR} \langle \boxed{2} [\text{AGR} \boxed{1}] \rangle \\ \text{COMPS} \langle \rangle \end{bmatrix} \end{bmatrix} \\ \text{SEM} \begin{bmatrix} \text{MODE ref} \\ \text{INDEX } i \\ \text{RESTR} \langle \begin{bmatrix} \text{RELN dog} \\ \text{INST } i \end{bmatrix} \rangle \end{bmatrix} \\ \text{ARG-ST} \langle \boxed{2} \begin{bmatrix} \text{DP} \\ \text{COUNT} + \end{bmatrix} \rangle \end{bmatrix} \right\rangle
$$

```
<f org="list" name="dog">
    <fs type="word">
        <f name="SYN">
            <fs>
                <f name="HEAD">
                    <fs type="noun">
                        <f name="AGR">
                            <vLabel name="n1">
                                <fs>
                                    <f name="PER">
                                        <symbol value="3rd"/>
                                    </f>
                                    <f name="NUM">
                                        <symbol value="sg"/>
                                    </f>
                                </fs>
                            </vLabel>
                        </f>
                    </fs>
                </f>
                <f name="VAL">
                    ...
                </f>
            </fs>
        </f>
        ...
    </fs>
</f>
```

Listing 9.1 Feature structure represented according to ISO 24610-1 (abbreviated)

Very similar is the approach taken in OpenCCG, an implementation of Combinatory Categorial Grammar. According to Bozsahin et al. (2005), the implementation uses a grammar which is a list of the grammar's components, a lexicon which is here a list of *lexical families*, a specification of words of the grammar and the rules. The wordlist is basically a list of words with part of speech information (see Listing 9.2) which additionally contains inflectional rules, called *macros*, not included here.

The main information is derived from the list of lexical families which consists of abstract classes of inheritance rules for the lexicon to be processed by the grammar. These use a kind of feature structure representation as seen before but in an idiosyncratic format.

```
<entry word="and" pos="Conj"/>
<entry word="or" pos="Conj"/>
<entry word="that" pos="RelPro"/>
```

Listing 9.2 OpenCCG wordlist from the implementation sample files

9.3 Dictionaries and XML Formats

Dictionaries are lexical resources with a long tradition of encoding information in typographical markup. Figure 9.3 shows an example of a lexicon entry. Usually this kind of article is included in typeset on multiple columns on one page. The bits of

unit /'juːnɪt/ *n* **1** a single thing, person or group that is complete in itself, although it can be part of sth larger: *a family unit* ○ *a course book with twenty units.* **2** a fixed amount or number used as a standard of measurement: *an unit of currency* ○ *The metre is a unit of length.* ○ *a bill for fifty units of electricity.* **3** ...

Fig. 9.3 Dictionary article, abbreviated version, adapted from Crowther (1995)

lexical information contained in this lexicon are the orthography of the keyword (printed in bold), a phonemic transcription in IPA characters, the syntactic annotation (part of speech in italics), and different definitions of polysemous words each with usage examples printed in italics again.

One possible way of making the typographical markup explicit can be seen in Listing 9.3, for simplicity the original IPA characters were replaced by the SAMPA rendering of the IPA, though IPA characters can be encoded with the same methods described in Sasaki (in this volume). The implementation is based on the recommendations of the Text Encoding Initiative (TEI P5 2008). This very verbose representation of a lexicon article, as abbreviated as it may be, contains no additional bits of information besides the TEI Header which was left out in the Listing. In comparison to previously mentioned lexicon formalisms this format is a rendering of the layout in as much as each structure receives a distinct typographical highlighting in print dictionaries, such as italics for examples, bold for the orthography, etc. The classification of the example as being of wordclass *n* (for noun) does not allow the easy inclusion of this lexicon entry in a formalism used in a syntactic theory. However, this kind of lexicon can easily be represented using among others XML and the TEI recommendations.

```
<TEI xmlns="http://www.tei-c.org/ns/1.0">
    <teiHeader>
        ...
    </teiHeader>
    <text>
        <body>
            <entry>
                <form>
                    <orth>unit</orth>
                    <pron>ju:nIt</pron>
                </form>
                <gramGrp>
                    <pos>n</pos>
                </gramGrp>
                <sense n="1">
                    <def>a single thing, person or group that ...</def>
                    <cit type="example"><quote>a family unit</quote></cit>
                    <cit type="example">..../cit>
                </sense>
                <sense n="2"> ...
                </sense>
            </entry>
        </body>
    </text>
</TEI>
```

Listing 9.3 Possible XML implementation of a dictionary article

9.4 Termbase Exchange Formats

Rather independent of linguistic research, the field of terminology has been introduced especially in the area of technical translation, i.e. translations of technical documents of various kinds. These industry-driven translation processes require a high degree of standardization of terminology, hence specialized methods for creating terminology databases have been introduced. Termbases as a special type of lexicon are usually not created by traditional lexicographers but by translators, engineers and terminology specialists. They are based on the concepts of a language, that is all synonyms, abbreviations, and translations of terms denoting the same concept are grouped together. Because the translation industry requires a lot of collaboration of different translators, the need for interchange of these resources led to the development of standards allowing interoperability. The most recent development is the Term Base eXchange format (TBX), currently a draft international standard (see ISO 30042:2008 2008).

The lexicon entries in a termbase in TBX format (see Listing 9.4) are based on a *termEntry* which is used for including all structured information belonging to one concept, which includes translations into other languages, abbreviations, synonyms, etc. Each language variant is embedded into a language section, which itself contains synonyms for the terms. The definition is seen to be language independent and belongs to the concept, though by tagging the language with a definition, multi-lingual definitions are possible as well.

```
<martif type="TBX" xml:lang="en">
 <martifHeader>...</martifHeader>
 <text>
  <body>
   <termEntry id="ubi_glos1">
    <descrip type="subjectField">study programme</descrip>
    <descrip type="definition" xml:lang="en">Credit points are ...</descrip>
    <langSet xml:lang="de">
     <tig>
      <term id="ubi_glos1LP">Leistungspunkt</term>
      <termNote type="termType">fullForm</termNote>
     </tig>
     ...
    </langSet>
    <langSet xml:lang="en">
     <tig>
      <term id="ubi_glos1CP">Credit point </term>
      <termNote type="termType">fullForm</termNote>
     </tig>
     <tig>
      <term id="ubi_glos1CPk">CP</term>
      <termNote type="termType">abbreviation</termNote>
     </tig>
    </langSet>
   </termEntry>
  </body>
 </text>
</martif>
```

Listing 9.4 Terminology databases implemented in TBX format, abbreviated

The Term Base eXchange format shows a very explicit modeling of involved data categories, which themselves are based on a data category repository, standardized by ISO 12620 (1999). Though this standardization is a side effect of interchange endeavors, the result contains many data categories also available in other lexical resources. Syntactic information is not intended to be in the primary focus.

9.5 The Lexical Markup Framework

The *Lexical Markup Framework* (LMF, ISO 24613:2008 2008) is a development in standardization to define an interchange format similar to the formats available in terminology. Its idea is to provide the means to model lexical resources from the human language technologies (HLT) and natural language processing (NLP), the first addressing machine readable dictionaries as previously modeled, for example, by Atkins et al. with the MILE lexicon, the latter addressing lexical resources used in NLP. In contrast to earlier work in these areas, with LMF a metamodel was created, i.e. a model for defining schemas of lexical resources. This metamodel consists of a core package and application specific extensions. The core package as such is built of a lexicon with various lexical entries including data on the form and meaning, called *sense* in LMF. At least one form property (such as orthography) is mandatory, the sense is optional. Listing 9.5 shows a sample of such a lexicon. Note that this is one way of implementing the LMF, but there is no fixed document grammar for LMF. In fact, the TEI encoding for lexicons as in Listing 9.3 is one possible implementation of LMF. On the other hand Listing 9.5 can easily be expressed by the TEI syntax.

The specification of a lexicon according to the LMF is given in form of UML diagrams that are mapped to document grammars in a concrete implementation. The major advantage of this form of implementation is that the intersection of different

```
<LexicalResource>
    <GlobalInformation>
        <feat att="languageCoding" val="ISO 639-3"/>
    </GlobalInformation>
    <Lexicon>
        <feat att="language" val="eng"/>
        <LexicalEntry>
            <feat att="partOfSpeech" val="commonNoun"/>
            <Lemma>
                <feat att="writtenForm" val="student"/>
            </Lemma>
            <WordForm>
                <feat att="writtenForm" val="student"/>
                <feat att="grammaticalNumber" val="singular"/>
            </WordForm>
            <WordForm>
                <feat att="writtenForm" val="students"/>
                <feat att="grammaticalNumber" val="plural"/>
            </WordForm>
        </LexicalEntry>
    </Lexicon>
</LexicalResource>
```

Listing 9.5 LMF sample

lexical resources in terms of document structure becomes readily available without detailed analysis, as long as the used data categories express the same thing. For that reason the LMF relies on a data category repository that is part of the revised standard ISO-FDIS 12620:2009 (2009).

9.6 Combining Lexical Resources: The Lexicon Graph Model

The previous sections showed that there are appropriate formalisms for lexicon encoding, and that these can be used for the interchange of lexical resources. Feature structures provide a very structured way of representing lexical data, the TEI allows the representation of dictionaries in a format that can be used as the source for print dictionaries, TBX allows the interchange of semantically rich termbases for translation applications. The LMF format works on the premises that a lexicon of a specified type has to be interchangeable with another application or system. FSR include in their definition the unification of feature structures, i.e. how to combine feature structures and under which conditions this is possible.

Though LMF and the corresponding standard in Terminology TMF (ISO 16642:2003 2003, see also Sasaki in this volume) are intended to allow the exchange and combination of lexical resources, they imply at least that they are similar, that is that they share data categories and structures. LMF for example differentiates between machine readable lexicons, NLP syntactic lexicons and morphological lexicons, providing extensions to the core for each, including distinct structures for them. In this sense LMF provides the container for combining such resources of different types, but does not merge them into one formalism. The umbrella standard, the Linguistic annotation framework (LAF, ISO-DIS 24612:2009 2009) is in the summer of 2009 in the process of being made available to the public as a draft standard.

By providing a container for different kinds of lexical resources or by specialization on specific types of resources, lexicon formats as described in the previous sections neglect something rather fundamental: large portions of lexical information are identical in a lot of lexicons. For example most of them contain some form of orthography, syntactic categories, phonemic representation, semantic information, etc. The details vary, but between most of them there are shared bits of information. The data models mentioned before do not show these common features of lexicons, instead the structures seem to be virtually exclusive. Common data categories would allow a combination of lexical resources even if their original purpose differs significantly and some details are different. To approach this problem a different basic model of the lexicon is introduced, the *Lexicon Graph*. The *Lexicon Graph* is a model that is a more abstract formalism that the one provided by LMF (ISO 24613:2008 2008) or TMF (ISO 16642:2003 2003) and operates for lexical resources on a level above LAF (ISO-DIS 24612:2009 2009) for annotations. However, it can be implemented in the Graph Annotation Format (GrAF), which is the serialization of LAF and defined in the standard. For other graph based approaches to texts, see for example Mehler (in this volume).

The *Lexicon Graph* (LG) parallels a formal model of linguistic annotation as defined by Bird and Liberman (2001). In this LG, every bit of lexical information constitutes one node in the graph. The nodes are, figuratively speaking, the elements of the lexicon world. Each of the nodes in the LG can be connected to any number of other nodes of the graph. Hence, the edges of the graph are the connections of the nodes. The connection does not have the same interpretation in both directions, hence the edges, or arcs need to be directed, and as they have an interpretation they can be labeled.

A label is also required to define the type of lexical information that constitutes the nodes. The reason for this is that every node is supposed to be unique, but there are unlikely but possible events, where one node in its form is part of two different types, e.g. an orthographic form can have the same form as a phonemic transcription according to the SAMPA alphabet. In the case of not typing the nodes a problem could be that one node has to be updated but only for one type, while for the other type the node should not be changed. As the nodes exist independently of each other, this would cause side effects, which can be avoided by typing the nodes as `orthography` and having a second node typed `SAMPA transcript` for example.

With this verbose description it is possible to define a lexicon graph formally. The definitions use the following conventions:

- natural numbers used in the subscripts to differentiate nodes, arcs and types are given with the letters i, j, k, l, g, h, m, n usually appearing in pairs as needed.
- sets are named by calligraphic capital letters such as $\mathcal{T}$
- nodes are named by the Greek letter eta η with an index for their type using the Greek letter tau τ
- arcs are named by the script letter a with arc-types t
- structures will receive three letter capitalized calligraphic names such as $\mathcal{MIC}$

Definition 1 Let $\mathcal{T}$ be the set of types τ of lexical information; let $\mathcal{N}$ be the set of nodes η_τ of type τ; let $\mathcal{A}$ be the set of directed arcs $a_t(\eta_{\tau_i k}, \eta_{\tau_j l})$ of arc-(or relation-)type t connecting $\eta_{\tau_i k}$ to $\eta_{\tau_j l}$, i.e. one node of one type with a different node of another type. Then a *Lexicon Graph* $\mathcal{LG}$ is the combination of all those a_t and η_τ.

Example 1 Figure 9.4 shows an LG with five nodes, that could be used for some arbitrary orthographic forms `grill` and `unit`, with part of speech nodes V and N and a SAMPA transcription /'ju:nIt/. The arcs are labeled accordingly.

With this definition the traditional lexicographic structures can be specified formally, starting with the microstructure.

Definition 2 A microstructure $\mathcal{MIC}$ for a lexicon L is a subset of the set of arcs $\mathcal{A}$ by selecting a subset of arc types t of the set of all arc types T.

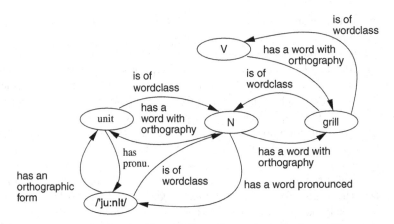

Fig. 9.4 Five node Lexicon Graph with typed directed arcs, types of nodes not illustrated

Example 2 Targeting at a part of speech lexicon one might think of using orthographic forms and part-of-speech labels. The subset from Fig. 9.4 would be all nodes
and arcs besides the transcription node /ˈjuːnɪt/ with all its arcs.

Definition 3 A macrostructure $\mathcal{MAC}$ for a lexicon L is hence the selection of one
$\tau \in \mathcal{T}$, i.e one type of lexical information, as primary nodes and an optional ordering
principle. If the ordering principle is not given, the lexicon is unordered.

Example 3 Using the orthography as primary nodes, the result would be a subgraph
of Fig. 9.4 as seen in Fig. 9.5. This graph starts with all orthography nodes and lists
all arcs from the microstructure starting at these arcs and the nodes they end at.

Definition 4 A lexicon entry LE with the microstructure $\mathcal{MIC}$ and $\mathcal{MAC}$ is the
selection of one node $\eta_{\tau i}$ of primary type τ according to $\mathcal{MAC}$, with all arcs in the
microstructure $\mathcal{MAC}$ that start at node $\eta_{\tau i}$ and their end nodes.

Example 4 The lexicon entry for the orthographic form unit according to the
microstructure and macrostructure defined before would be unit-N; for grill
it would be more problematic: it could be grill-N and grill-V or only one of
them, but the decision which one of them is not defined.

This example leads to the next issue that is often considered problematic, namely
what happens if the answer for the lexicon entry is not unique, i.e. ambiguous. With
the LG this can be described in formal terms:

Fig. 9.5 Lexicon Graph with
a micro- and macrostructure

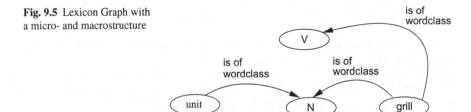

Definition 5 A lexicon entry LE_i is ambiguous iff for the start node $\eta_{\tau_i k}$ of type i $\exists$ $\eta_{\tau_j g}$, $\eta_{\tau_j h}$, which are end nodes to arcs $a_t(\eta_{\tau_i k}, \eta_{\tau_j g})$ and $a_t(\eta_{\tau_i k}, \eta_{\tau_j h})$ respectively, i.e. two different target nodes for two different arcs, where both the target node type and the arc type are the same.

Example 5 The lexicon entry for the orthography–wordclass lexicon for `grill` in Fig. 9.5 is ambiguous.

Definition 6 An ambiguous lexicon entry LE_i can be *disambiguated* iff

- there is a start node $\eta_{\tau_i k}$ of type i
- there are nodes $\eta_{\tau_j g}$ and $\eta_{\tau_j h}$ of the same type that are end nodes of arcs of the same type starting at the start node
- there are (at least) two nodes η_m and η_n, both being connected to the start node, where there is an arc connecting η_m with $\eta_{\tau_j g}$ but not with $\eta_{\tau_j h}$ and η_n with $\eta_{\tau_j h}$ but not with $\eta_{\tau_j g}$.

Example 6 The ambiguity of `grill` in the previous example could be disambiguated or *resolved* by introducing two definitions, one `Act of preparing food which is done over a fire`, which is connected to `grill` and `V`, the other with `Item for preparing food, which can contain a fire`, connected to `grill` and `N`; although the types of arcs would be the same, the nodes would be distinct, hence allowing disambiguation.

These definitions are sufficient for defining a self-contained lexicon, without any rules, inferences and sources such as external media or knowledge. After looking at the mesostructure before with references between lexicon entries, the question remains, what happens to crossreferences, references to external information and other media. The answer is easy: crossreferences are special types of arcs, hence already covered by the previous definitions. References to external information is not sufficiently covered, yet; it is possible to cover references with formal pointers such as URIs, which can also be used for other media which is stored outside of the lexicon base and be referred to.

The interpretation of pointers to external information is different from the directed graph structures in the self contained lexicon in the sense that the extension does not allow the independent parsing including these pointers. The interpretation needs to provide for the fact that the information is not embedded. In other words, the arcs pointing to external information cannot be arcs in the graph. To avoid this undefined state, virtual nodes are introduced that are distinctly marked as pointers to items outside of the graph. This is especially relevant for rule and inheritance systems such as inflectional patterns that need a logic for interpretation, while simple objects, such as multimedia items, are referred to by identifiers. These identifiers as such are the nodes, especially if they are typed as pointers to multimedia units.

The mesostructure of the lexicon is covered by the LG model by the node definition and by introducing virtual nodes representing rule based systems and pointers that receive explicit semantics to distinguish those pointers from regular internal arcs, which are also used for internal references.

This section introduced and defined a graph model for the lexicon, called the *Lexicon Graph*, defined the structures of the lexicon in formal terms and introduced the formal background for the lexicon articles. The Lexicon Graph was defined formally similar to the Annotation Graph (Bird and Liberman 2001), which is also discussed with an application in Schmidt (in this volume). Such a graph is also an extension of the restricted Multi-Rooted-Trees discussed in Goecke et al. (in this volume). The next section will show an implementation of this Lexicon Graph.

9.7 Lexicon Graph Implementation

Having a formal model for the lexicon available that covers the different requirements for a lexicon allows to implement this lexicon, using the explicit information given in the definitions of the previous section. This section describes the concrete grammar for the LG, a way of traversing the graph and an example how to disambiguate a lexicon entry.

9.7.1 LG Grammar

The data model used for the implementation is based on XML, which immediately allows to use widely available tools for syntax parsing, transformation, querying and storing, while explicitly including the information of every node and arc required by the definition in a basically legible way, allowing portability as defined by Bird and Simons (2003). After the formal definition of the LG the implementation is straight forward, using the grammar of Listing 9.6. Other implementations for example in RDF(S) are possible as well.

```
LG --> Nodes, Arcs, External Pointers
Nodes --> Node+
Node --> type, content
Arcs --> Arc+
Arc --> type, start, end
External Pointers --> Pointers*
Pointers -->type, pointer
```

Listing 9.6 Simplified Lexicon Graph grammar

Listing 9.7 shows a DTD for an XML document which represents a concrete implementation of the LG. The nodes are called `lexitem` for *lexicon item*, the arcs `relation` which is short for *relation between lexicon items*; the external pointers are called `know` as reference that these are pointers to knowledge required to interpret them. For easier reference the arcs, nodes and pointers receive an identifier as well.

The nodes can have either textual content or be objects outside of the lexicon, which are then interpreted with the URI given. The pointers to the knowledge are defined in reminiscence of concept hierarchies in terminology by a concept name

```
<!-- LG is the root element -->
<!ELEMENT LG
         (lexitems,relations,knowledge?)>
<!-- 3 basic elements per lexicon -->
<!ELEMENT lexitems     (lexitem+)>
<!ELEMENT relations    (relation+)>
<!ELEMENT knowledge    (know+)>
<!-- lexitems -->
<!ELEMENT lexitem (#PCDATA|object)*>
<!ELEMENT relation (source,target)>
<!ELEMENT know (conceptname*, knowcat+)>
<!ELEMENT object EMPTY>
<!ELEMENT source EMPTY>
<!ELEMENT target EMPTY>
<!ELEMENT conceptname (#PCDATA)*>
<!ELEMENT knowcat (#PCDATA|like)*>
<!ELEMENT like EMPTY>
<!-- ATTRIBUTES -->
<!ATTLIST lexitem id ID #REQUIRED
                  lextype CDATA #REQUIRED>
<!ATTLIST relation type CDATA #REQUIRED>
<!ATTLIST source idref IDREF #REQUIRED>
<!ATTLIST target idref IDREF #REQUIRED>
<!ATTLIST know id ID #REQUIRED>
<!ATTLIST like idref IDREF #REQUIRED>
<!ATTLIST object
                  type CDATA #IMPLIED
                  uri CDATA #REQUIRED>
```

Listing 9.7 DTD for the Lexicon Graph implementation in XML

and a knowledge category, which can either be an interpretable description such as a grammar, or a reference to another knowledge element defined in the same document. In an implementation it is intended to use pointers to knowledge for hypertextual lexicon presentation as well, see Storrer (in this volume). Knowledge can also represent connections to ontologies, for linguistic information in a lexicon this could be GOLD for example, which is discussed in Farrar and Langendoen (in this volume).

The transformation of the examples at the beginning of this chapter and others into the LG-format and the traversing of the LG-format to produce the examples was conducted in previous work (Trippel 2006). Each mentioned format was transformed into the LG format, the different sources were unified into one graph. The merged graph then provided the basis for the creation of lexicon entries encoding in the same way as the original examples. By merging the different sources, the size of the resulting lexicon, i.e. the amount of lexical information, could in some cases be increased. There was no data loss in the tested cases.

9.7.2 Example for Traversing the Graph

The following example is taken from a prototype lexicon which was developed on the basis of a corpus of multimodal annotations, including a transcript of gestures according to the CoGesT system (Trippel et al. 2004), wordlevel annotations and a meaning to describe a part of an utterance. The idea for this lexicon entry is to get to the meaning of a gesture. At present traversing such a graph does not address the question of effective, i.e., fast, queries, which is addressed in Chapter 13.

The content of the lexicon is in an ASCII based transcription of the gesture. The transcription contains a decomposition of (hand)gestures into the hand position at the beginning of the gesture with a distinct handform according to a prototype model. The gesture which contains a movement is then described by the direction, speed and form of the movement, all according to prototypes and the position and handform at the end of the gesture. The semantics of the gesture is originally described on a separate tier of a score as frequently used in phonetics, using software such as Praat, Wavesurfer, SPSS waves+, TASX-annotator, etc. Based on a signal based corpus, a basic lexicon, or in Gibbon's terminology in defining a continuum from a corpus to a sophisticated lexicon, a *first order* or *corpus lexicon* can be defined (Gibbon 2005).

In the LG a corpus lexicon can be represented easily and hence the microstructure of meaning and gesture can be extracted. In this case all nodes of the type $gesture_{cogest}$ and `meaning` would be kept as well as all arcs that combine those two types. The macrostructure would then define that the primary key would be gestures, as the meaning – unknown – is accessed from the gesture, which is known. A specific query to the LG in natural language would be the following:

"For the gesture transcribed as `15m,5A,ri,ci,1B,1,r(0),me,15m,5A,rp` give me the meaning that it is associated with."

A natural language query to the LG needs to be translated into a formal query language, in this case XQuery is used as a universal query language for XML data (Boag et al. 2007). The query can be seen in Listing 9.8. This query would be hidden from potential users behind a user interface, but it clearly shows the three phases of lexical lookup:

1. The start node is identified by content,
2. based on the start node the arcs of a specific type are identified, and
3. the target node is identified and returned.

In this case the node types can be ignored as the nodes are unique in this LG without further specification.

```
for $LG in doc("lexgraph.xml")/LG,
    $startnode in $lg/lexitems/lexitem,
    $arc in $lg/relations/relation,
    $resultnode in $lg/lexitems/lexitem
where $startnode=
    "15m,5A,ri,ci,1B,1,r(0),me,15m,5A,rp"
    and
    $arc/source/¢idref= $startnode/¢id and
    $arc/¢type = "has_meaning" and
    $arc/source/¢idref = $resultnode/¢id
return $resultnode/text()
```

Listing 9.8 XQuery for a lexicongraph querying for the meaning associated with a gesture transcription

9.7.3 Disambiguation

The formal definition of ambiguity was given above, the traversing of a non-ambiguous graph was shown in the previous section; to make it more complex, an ambiguous entry could be used. The following ambiguities are quite frequent:

- one form, such as a gesture, a word, or some other string with two (or more) associated meanings, which are usually called homonyms or cases of polysemy
- one meaning with two associated meanings: synonymy
- one wordclass with thousands of associated orthographies

In all these cases at least one additional node is needed for all ambiguous items to disambiguate them. However, the absence of a relation to another feature could also count as a differentiating feature. The question left is how such a procedure could be understood and implemented. For this purpose an example is considered that is usually classified as a homonym, namely the English orthographic form bank. Figure 9.6 shows an LG with three definitions taken and two parts of speech, all relevant for this particular orthographic form. For clarity the labels of the nodes and arcs, for the arcs also the directions are left out, assuming that there is a relation in both directions though each direction may have a separate label. Listing 9.9 visualizes a part of the LG for the previous graph in XML.

The form bank is ambiguous both in meaning and in wordclass, i.e. a query for the wordclass of bank will result in N and V, while the query for the definition will give the three definitions for the financial institution, dealing with the institution and the land next to a river. Specifying the question to combine those features will have a different result, such as the natural language question "What is the definition of bank if it is a verb?", which would result in the definition of doing business with a financial institution.

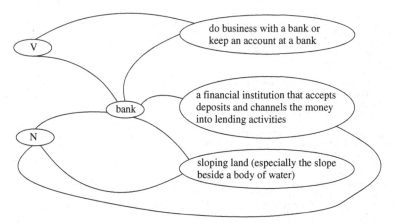

Fig. 9.6 Part of the Lexicon Graph for the English orthographic form bank, definitions taken from WordNet (Miller et al. 2006). The labels and directions of arcs are left out for simplicity

```
<LG>
  <lexitems>
    <lexitem id="node1" lextype="orthography">
          bank</lexitem>
    <lexitem id="node2" lextype="POS">V</lexitem>
    <lexitem id="node3" lextype="POS">N</lexitem>
    <lexitem id="node4" lextype="WordnetDef">do
          business with a bank or keep an
          account at a bank</lexitem>
    <lexitem id="node5" lextype="WordnetDef">a
          financial institution that accepts
          deposits and channels the money
          into lending activities</lexitem>
    <lexitem id="node6" lextype="WordnetDef">
          sloping land (especially the slope
          beside a body of water)</lexitem>
  </lexitems>
  <relations>
    <relation type="hasPOS">
      <source idref="node1"/>
      <target idref="node2"/>
    </relation>
...
    <relation type="hasDef">
      <source idref="node1"/>
      <target idref="node4"/>
    </relation>
...
```

Listing 9.9 Part of an LG in XML

Listing 9.10 is a query on the LG for the previous graph, answering the question: "what is the part of speech of bank when it has the meaning do business with a financial institution". Again, the query is complex and it is based on looking at the primary node (startnode), the secondary node (in this case containing the definition) and the node asked for, namely the node containing the part of speech information. Additionally, the arcs between those nodes are looked at. For disambiguation, arcs have to exist in the correct direction for the three nodes involved.

```
for $LG in  doc("bank_part.xml")/LG,
$startnode in $LG/lexitems/lexitem,
$relationdef in $LG/relations/relation,
$posrel in $LG/relations/relation,
$nodedef in $LG/lexitems/lexitem,
$posdefrelation in  $LG/relations/relation,
$pos in  $LG/lexitems/lexitem
where $startnode="bank" and
$relationdef/source/@idref=$startnode/@id and
       $relationdef/@type="hasDef" and
$nodedef/@id=$relationdef/target/@idref and
  $nodedef="do business with a bank or keep an
            account at a bank" and
  $posrel/source/@idref=$startnode/@id and
       $posrel/@type="hasPOS" and
$posdefrelation/source/@idref=$nodedef/@id and
     $posdefrelation/target/@idref=
                  $posrel/target/@idref and
$pos/@id=$posrel/target/@idref
return $pos/text()
```

Listing 9.10 XQuery allowing to query an LG for the wordclass of the word bank with the meaning do business with a financial institution

9.8 Model Characterization and Consequences

The data model of the Lexicon Graph is fundamentally data-centered, which implies that all bits of information represented in it need to be interpreted by an enabled application, rather than to interpret the graph as a linear document to be processed according to its marked up structure. The lexicon itself is not stored in logical order but according to the structure defined by the document grammar. The lists of nodes and arcs are separated and without any other specified order.

With the data centered approach that needs an application, the whole logics is part of the applications in querying the Lexicon Graph. As seen with the XQuery examples mentioned previously, this means that those queries can become rather complex, depending on the microstructure and especially the hierarchies of data categories that are defined. This is especially relevant in the case of transitive relations, where not only the microstructure is defined but also the values of specific data categories are to be followed as sub-headwords.

The model itself, independent of the complexity of possible queries, has a very important additional feature as it is extensible, which means that different kinds of lexicons can be used to combine their lexical information, independent of a common microstructure. A number of overlapping data categories are sufficient to allow the extension of one lexicon by the other by adding nodes of a second lexicon to a first lexicon if they are not already in there. The same is true for the arcs and external pointers. The result is a real unification, without added doublets if the data categories are termed differently if they denote something different or the same if they refer to the same logical category.

After extending one lexicon by another, the lexical information is available. Based on previously defined queries, which can be interpreted as views or perspectives on the graph, an extended lexicon in another format can be generated automatically, such as some data structure to be used as the basis for print layout. Even when using completely different kinds of lexicons as that basis, i.e. without common data categories or nodes, the information exchange is lossless, hence it is a real combination of lexical resources. The reason why this is possible is that the Lexicon Graph is a generic model for lexicons. The LG can be used for all lexical structures independently of data categories and lexical structures or data types. This covers data types that are not represented textually by pointers to external objects, so that multimodal data can actually be included in the Lexicon Graph.

Another advantage of the Lexicon Graph is that it is possible to avoid restrictive assumptions on the lexicon, such as assigning a special status to one data category. Assigning a special status is relevant for the microstructure definition, but not for the data repository. Hence, the latter can be used for different microstructures, using the same query process independent of the data category used as a primary key, giving the same status to all data categories. This means that the same LG and query mechanisms can be used for a pronunciation dictionary based on the transcription, an encyclopedia, orthographic dictionary, spellchecker dictionary, even an inference lexicon. However, this does not imply that the whole available information is used for every type of lexicon.

What is more about the data categories is that new data categories introduced result in new types of nodes and arcs of the graph, but not a fundamentally new structure, hence it is not necessary to define workarounds to stretch the specifications to allow for these new categories.

Something fundamentally different from the assumption of a unique form–meaning correspondence is also the realization that disambiguation is not a special feature for a very limited number of special cases such as homographs, but that this ambiguity is in fact a lexical ambiguity that can occur on every data category of the lexicon. That implies that disambiguation is the rule, not the pathologic case, required on every level. Therefore, workarounds such as sense enumeration are not an appropriate disambiguation strategy in a generic model.

9.9 Future Work and Further Development

The Lexicon Graph was implemented on a small set of lexicon articles based on various types of lexicons. For running performance and usability tests it would be necessary to implement larger lexicon databases, using existing lexicons and implementing various access functions, for example one for every existing lexicon used to extend the Lexicon Graph.

An extended Lexicon Graph is intended to be used by an enabled application such as a Web-based lexicon with interfaces for end users or applications to be used. This requires not only a larger lexicon to be useful for users but also a high performance and quick response by an enabled system. It would even be possible to precompile different views and include those in another structure if performance requires it.

The vague statements about the performance also imply that studies on the complexity of the graph and possible queries are still pending, but need to be conducted in order to reliably estimate required computing power. The previous examples illustrate the amount of complexity that is involved when adding nodes, and it seems obvious that the amount of arcs to be processed can be very large. The question remains if the complexity can be handled for large but finite lexicons or if the complexity increases beyond measure, so that the complexity becomes too high to be processable. The current implementation described in Trippel (2005, 2006) is not optimized for performance, neither for the write functionality (inserting, updating, and deletion operations) nor for the read functionality, i.e. individual queries. Subjectively the processing times for lexicons of some thousand nodes are fast. The investigation of complexity has to take into account that nodes of different classes typically have different numbers of arcs attached to them. As the frequency distribution of words is Zipfian (see for example Zipf 1935) it can be assumed that the number of arcs for nodes behaves similarly, which should reduce the complexity significantly.

9.10 Summary

Based on a number of lexicons and lexicon models a generic formal model for lexicons was introduced with the Lexicon Graph. In the Lexicon Graph model all different types of lexical information are represented as typed nodes which are related to each other by typed directed arcs. This data centered model for lexicons can serve as the underlying data structure for a variety of the most different types of lexicons with different structures including feature structures, dictionaries modeled by the lexicon microstructures, mesostructures and macrostructures. The graph structure allows even new types of lexicons with different keywords and microstructures. The Lexicon Graph model is generic in a way that all of these different lexicon resources can be combined, if they have common elements to even form one connected graph.

Examples were given for an implementation of the Lexicon Graph in XML with sample queries to traverse the Lexicon Graph using the standard XML technique XQuery. This was used for a lexicon with a simple microstructure of two data categories but also for a slightly more complex example including disambiguation.

A final discussion of future work has been added aiming at extending the lexicons and investigating the complexity involved in processing Lexicon Graphs.

References

Atkins, Sue; Bel, Nuria; Bouillon, Pierrette; Charoenporn, Thatsanee; Gibbon, Dafydd; Grishman, Ralph; Huang, Chu-Ren; Kawtrakul, Asanee; Ide, Nancy; Lee, Hae-Yun; Li, Paul J. K.; McNaught, Jock; Odijk, Jan; Palmer, Martha; Quochi, Valeria; Reeves, Ruth; Sharma, Dipti Misra; Sornlertlamvanich, Virach; Tokunaga, Takenobu; Thurmair, Gregor; Villegas, Marta; Zampolli, Antonio; and Zeiton, Elizabeth. Standards and best practice for multilingual computational lexicons and MILE (the multilingual ISLE lexical entry). Deliverable d2.2-d3.2 isle computational lexicon working group, International Standards for Language Engineering (ISLE), Pisa. undated.

Bird, Steven and Liberman, Mark (2001). A formal framework for linguistic annotation. *Speech Communication*, 33(1,2):23–60.

Bird, Steven and Simons, Gary (2003). Seven dimensions of portability for language documentation and description. *Language*, 79(3):557–582.

Boag, Scott, Chamberlin, Don, Fernandez, Mary F., Florescu, Daniela, Robie, Jonathan, and Siméon, Jérôme (2007). XQuery 1.0: An XML query language. URL: http://www.w3.org/TR/xquery/, accessed 2009-06-05. W3C Recommendation 23 January 2007.

Bozsahin, Cem, Kruijff, Geert-Jan M., and White, Michael (2005). Specifying grammars for OpenCCG: A rough guide.

Crowther, Jonathan, editor (1995). *Oxford Advanced Learner's Dictionary of Current English*. Oxford University Press, Oxford, fifth edition edition.

Gibbon, Dafydd (2005). Spoken language lexicography: an integrative framework. *Translatologie – Neue Ideen und Ansätze.*, pages 247–289.

Hartmann, Reinhard R. K. (2001). *Teaching and Researching Lexicography*. Applied Linguistics in Action. Pearson Education, Harlow.

ISO 12620 (1999). Computer applications in terminology – data categories. International Standard.

ISO 24610-1 (2006). Language resource management—feature structures—part 1: Feature structure representation. International Standard.

ISO-FDIS 12620:2009 (2009). Terminology and other content and language resources – data categories – specification of data categories and management of a data category registry for language resources. Final Draft International Standard.

ISO 16642:2003 (2003). Computer applications in terminology—Terminology markup framework (TMF) International Standard.

ISO-DIS 24612:2009 (2009). Language resource management—Linguistic annotation framework (LAF) Draft International Standard.

ISO 24613:2008 (2008). Language resource management—Lexical markup framework (LMF). International Standard.

ISO 30042:2008 (2008). Term-base exchange (TBX) format specification. International Standard.

Miller, George A., Fellbaum, Christiane, Tengi, Randee, Wolff, Susanne, Wakefield, Pamela, Langone, Helen, and Haskell, Benjamin (2006). Wordnet 3.0. URL: http://wordnet.princeton.edu/ accessed 2009-06-05. Cognitive Science Laboratory at Princeton University.

Pustejovsky, James (1995). *The Generative Lexicon*. MIT Press, Cambridge (Ma), London.

Sag, Ivan A., Wasow, Thomas, and Bender, Emily M. (2003). *Syntactic Theory*. CSLI Publications, Stanford, 2nd edition.

TEI P5 (2008). Dictionaries. In *TEI P5: Guidelines for Electronic Text Encoding and Interchange*. Section 9.

Trippel, Thorsten (2005). *The Lexicon Graph Model: A Generic Model for Multimodal Lexicon Development*. PhD thesis, Universität Bielefeld, Bielefeld.

Trippel, Thorsten (2006). *The Lexicon Graph Model: A Generic Model for Multimodal Lexicon Development*. AQ Verlag, Saarbrücken.

Trippel, Thorsten; Thies, Alexandra; Milde, Jan-Torsten; Looks, Karin; Gut, Ulrike; and Gibbon, Dafydd (2004). CoGesT: a formal transcription system for conversational gesture. In *Proceedings of LREC 2004*, Lisbon. ELRA.

Zipf, George Kingsley (1935). *The Psycho-Biology of Language*. Houghton Mifflin Company, Boston.

Chapter 10
HTTL – Hypertext Transformation Language

A Framework for the Generation of Hypertext Views on XML Annotated Documents

Eva Anna Lenz

Abstract We present the *Hypertext Transformation Language* (HTTL), a special-purpose transformation language designed to generate hypertext views on XML annotated documents. Unlike other transformation languages such as XSLT, HTTL transformation rules abstract from both the source language and the target language.

Keywords Hypertext linking · Hypertext segmentation · Text technology · Automatic link generation · Hypertext conversion · Open standards · Electronic publishing · Markup · XLink · XML

10.1 Background and Introduction

One aim of hypertext research has always been to make use of existing textual data and to enhance them with hypertext functionalities. In the late eighties and early nineties, a major focus was placed on the conversion from existing printed text sources to hypertexts (see Rearick (1991) and Rada and Diaper (1991) for overviews, and Raymond and Tompa (1987) for a typical project). The emphasis in these early projects was placed on the end result of the transformation, not on the re-use of the textual data for different forms of presentation.

Hypertext conversion strategies were discussed and systemised by Kuhlen, who distinguishes between three basic strategies (simple, form-based and coherence-based) (Kuhlen 1991, 162ff.). Subsequent research has concentrated on automatically interlinking existing electronic documents by using link services (as described, e.g., in De Roure et al. 2000). Some link services implement generic linking by analysing document content and sometimes context, usually performing a statistical analysis and/ or exploiting metadata. The documents thus linked are typically rather

E.A. Lenz (✉)
Institut für Deutsche Sprache und Literatur, Universität Dortmund, Dortmund, Germany
e-mail: lenz@hytex.info

A. Witt, D. Metzing (eds.), *Linguistic Modeling of Information and Markup Languages*, Text, Speech and Language Technology 40,
DOI 10.1007/978-90-481-3331-4_10, © Springer Science+Business Media B.V. 2010

small and relatively unstructured, so that there is no need to further analyse their structure or sub-divide them.

Today, we not only benefit from a plethora of texts in electronic form (see also Truran et al. 2007), but also from an increasing number of text corpora, containing texts of varying length and enriched with structural, topical, rhetorical and/or linguistic information. Additionally, nearly every text ready for publication is at least convertible (automatically) to a form with the logical text structure (e.g., the division into sections and paragraphs) marked up. All this additional information is often represented in the form of generic markup (often XML, or convertible to XML). Besides, for texts that lack this information, automatic methods have been developed to extract their logical structure and provide them with XML markup, for example for PDF documents (Nojoumian 2007). This markup can be exploited to create diverse hypertext views on the underlying texts, complementing the established approaches.

While numerous established approaches and tools exist that exploit information provided in the form of markup (well-known examples being Latex2HTML or Doc-Book2HTML), the vast majority of them requires a *specific* form of markup. In this paper, we take a more general approach: We present a flexible, rule-based method for semi-automatically generating such hypertext views on XML annotated documents. These views are based upon the generation of hypertext nodes of differing granularity, one-to-many links, procedural and semantic link types, the simultaneous display of multiple hypertext nodes, and, in the case of one-to-many links, ranking of linkends. Unlike earlier approaches to hypertext conversion, we aim at a user-driven conversion process, thus meeting the requirements now typical for the electronic publication process: different input formats, publishing for different media from a single source (cross-media-publishing), and user-adapted document views. We use XML and related technologies (including XPath, XSLT, Schematron and XLink), that support the automatic generation of different views on a single data source.

The approach is developed in the context of a project named "HyTex" which is funded by the German research foundation (see Storrer in this volume).[1] The goal of this project is to identify general principles and strategies for text-to-hypertext conversion and to base them on text-grammatical structures and coherence relations between text segments (Holler et al. 2004). We tested our strategies using a German corpus of documents belonging to two specialised research domains, namely text technology and hypertext research. The corpus was annotated in XML with regard to three annotation layers:

- On the *document structure layer* we annotate structural units (such as chapters, paragraphs, footnotes, enumerated and unordered lists) using an annotation scheme derivated from DocBook (Walsh and Muellner 2003).
- On the *terms and definitions layer* we annotate occurrences of technical terms as well as text segments in which these terms are explicitly defined.
- On the *cohesion layer* we annotate text-grammatical information of various types, e.g. co-reference, connectives, text-deictic expressions (cf. Holler et al. 2004).

These annotation layers are merged using the unification method described in Witt et al. (2005), yielding a single XML document which is handy for further automatic processing.

In this article, we focus on a formal language called *Hypertext Transformation Language* (HTTL) which addresses the two issues of *segmentation* (i.e., the division of the linear text into hypertext nodes) and *linking* (reconnecting the nodes via hyperlinks). The criteria for segmentation and linking can usually be expressed in the form of conversion rules, e.g., "make each paragraph a hypertext node" or "link each occurrence of a technical term to its definition". HTTL aims at a formalisation of such rules which are part of the overall conversion strategy.

This article is complemented by the one authored by Storrer (in this volume), which focusses on the conceptual side of hypertext conversion strategies and presents the overall project context.

In the following section, we indicate the application context HTTL was developed for by giving a number of hypertext conversion rules, and describe the motivation for its development, as well as the advantages of this approach. In Section 10.3, the HTTL framework and the language itself are detailed, following the examples from the preceding section. In Section 10.4, additional features of HTTL are outlined. Related work is described in Section 10.5, and an outlook on the further development is depicted in Section 10.6.

10.2 The HTTL Application Context

HTTL, being a special-purpose programming language, was developed for hypertext experts in order to ease the creation of different hypertext views in the HyTex project. In this section, we will describe this context: We will first introduce a number of examples for hypertext conversion rules. We will then describe established solutions for this task and contrast them with the HTTL solution.

In spite of its development for a specific application context, we believe HTTL to to flexible enough to be applicable in other domains and for purposes quite different from our own. This will be considered briefly at the end of this section.

10.2.1 Hypertext Conversion Rules

Hypertext conversion strategies comprise *conversion rules* for the two tasks of segmentation and linking. We shall give examples for both of them and stick to them throughout the paper.

10.2.1.1 Segmentation Rules

Consider the following informal segmentation rule:

(1) Make each paragraph a hypertext node.

The rationale behind this rule is the expectation that paragraphs should be self-contained and can thus be used as basic "building blocks" for a hypertext (Hammwöhner 1997, p. 41). However, we found that paragraphs are not always self-contained, but often contain cohesion markers, e.g., anaphora and connectives that point to information located external to the node. In this case, we use hyperlinks in order to re-construct cohesive closedness (we will give examples below, for further details see Storrer in this volume).

In the HyTex project, we started with this simple segmentation strategy, but soon found that it had to be refined. As a first step, we added segmentation rules that match other structural elements, such as lists, which should also be treated as a unit. Moreover, we found that some kinds of paragraphs, like those in an itemized list, should not be turned into a hypertext node. The following refined rule expresses this constraint:

> (2) Make each paragraph a hypertext node, except when it is contained in a list environment.

We also found that segmentation strategies are dependent on the document type. Node granularity is dependent on document length and structure: while it is reasonable to segment an article at the paragraph level, for a monograph or dissertation a more coarse-grained segmentation is more appropriate (e.g., on the level of sections or subsections). In a document containing Frequently Asked Questions ("FAQ"), a question and its answer should be presented as a unit, regardless of their inner structure (which might consist of several paragraphs).

All of our segmentation rules act upon markup coming from the document structure layer.

10.2.1.2 Linking Rules

Consider the following informal linking rule, which uses information from the terms and definitions layer:

> (3) Create a link from each term occurrence to the corresponding term definition(s) in the same text. If there is a single definition for the term, produce a one-to-one link. If there is more than one definition,[2] generate a one-to-many link. If there is no definition for the term, do not generate any link.

There are several possible ways of presenting one-to-many links in HTML. We use a new window that pops up on clicking the link which displays a variety of choices, in this case, two or more definitions. When the user selects one of them, he or she is directed to the position in the text where the definition occurs (see Fig. 10.1).

The above linking rule is a simplified one which is part of a linking strategy based on knowledge prerequisites developed in the HyTex project (see Storrer in this volume). In the project context, we developed a pragmatic typology of definitions (cf. Beißwenger et al. 2002), and annotated the definition type for each of the definitions in our corpus accordingly. In the case of competing definitions (i.e., in the case of a one-to-many link), these are ordered and filtered according to type and

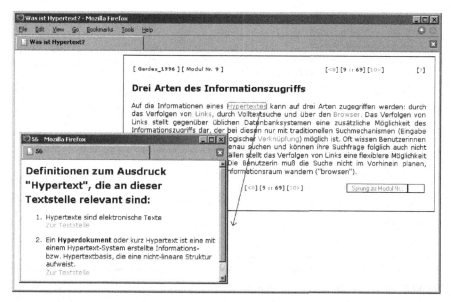

Fig. 10.1 In the case of multiple definitions of a technical term, a one-to-many link is provided from each term occurrence to its definitions

position. The aim is to rank those definitions highest which are most relevant to the text passage currently received by the user.

The following two are examples of several rules from the HyTex project which contribute to re-constructing cohesive closedness. When an anaphora is used at the beginning of a hypertext node, and the user comes upon this node not by linear reading, but by following a cross reference, he or she cannot determine the text object referenced by the anaphora (the antecedent). This case is captured in the following linking rule:

(4) Create a link from each anaphora to the corresponding antecedent(s) and show them in a pop-up window.

An example of a link created by this rule is shown in Fig. 10.2. Here, the anaphora "der Ebenen" has three antecedents, which are shown on request in the window bottom left.

Apart from *one-to-one links* and *one-to-many links* which are established features in many hypertext systems, we introduce a new feature which we call *node expansion*. When the hypertext user selects a node expansion link, the preceding or subsequent hypertext node is displayed together with the current one. The following linking rule, which evaluates the cohesion layer, uses this feature:

(5) When a connective (e.g. "furthermore") is directly bound to the preceding (subsequent) text, provide a node expansion in backwards (forwards) direction.

This rule helps reconstruct cohesive closedness by providing more context for properly understanding the node's content (see Fig. 10.3).

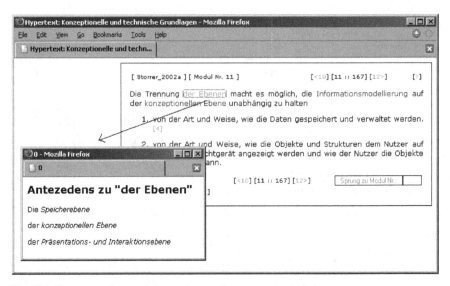

Fig. 10.2 On request, the antecedents of an anaphora are presented

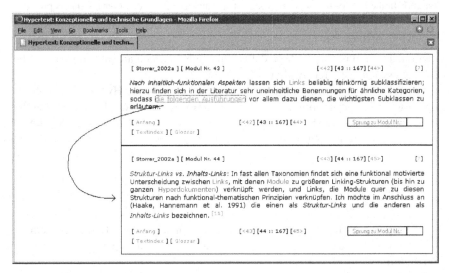

Fig. 10.3 For certain connectives, e.g. "furthermore", a node expansion link is generated. When selected by the user, a node expansion link causes the current hypertext node to be displayed together with the preceding or subsequent node

10.2.2 Established Solutions and Desiderata

There are well-established approaches to the task of generating different views and/ or output formats from a single source of information (often referred to as cross media publishing or single source publishing; see, e.g., Nicolas and Wood (1997)

and Möhr and Schmidt (1999)). These approaches enhance textual data with annotations (often using XML-based representation formats) and then transform these into a target format for a particular medium (e.g., Web, CD, or print). The programming language XSLT (Clark 1999) has been developed for these kinds of transformations.

In the first stage of the HyTex project, we adopted this approach. We specified the transformation of the XML annotated corpus documents into a hypertext in terms of verbal statements very much like the above conversion rules. We then hard-coded these rules into XSLT code which performed the transformation.

We wanted the result of the transformation to be readable by current web browsers. However, current web technologies do not yet support elaborate functionalities such as one-to-many links or procedural and semantic link types (barring XLink (DeRose et al. 2001), which current browsers implement only partially), so that these have to be emulated, using, e.g., client-side or server-side scripting languages. We chose a combination of HTML, JavaScript and Cascading Style Sheets (CSS) as our output format.

However, as the number of rules grew, the code became more complex. One rather simple rule turned out to require a long piece of code, partly because XSLT is a wordy programming language, but also because we had to generate the JavaScript code. Developing an XSLT library for hypertext segmentation and linking would have solved only part of this issue, as generating a new type of hyperlink required changing of code in more than one place, and the tasks of segmentation and linking were intertwined due to link filter rules (which are not discussed here).

Analysing our own approach, we identified the following issues for possible improvements:

Support for incremental development: One of the project's goals was to develop different conversion strategies and to *test* them by implementing them. Following the development of a new version, we often desired the refinement of rules in order to adapt them even better to the user's needs. For example, the segmentation rule "one paragraph becomes one node" was refined several times in order to add exceptions (e.g., paragraphs in a list environment, or in a pair of questions and answers in an FAQ should not produce a hypertext node boundary). This incremental procedure implied that the code had to be changed routinely, and should thus be as concise and fast to write as possible.

Support for rule sets: We have already mentioned that hypertextualization rules depend on the document type. They might even have to be adjusted to specific authors, to document length or other factors. We desired an environment where rules could be grouped into sets specific to a particular document type, author, or other criteria.

Support for changing document grammars: The corpus was being built and annotated in parallel. By looking at the result of the transformation into a hypertext, we also made refinements of the underlying annotations, and this implied changing document grammars (DTDs and XML Schemas). Furthermore, the cohesion layer was added later than the two other layers. This meant that the

XSLT code had to be revised not only in the case of changing hypertext strategies, but also in the case of changes in markup.

Readability of code: For all these reasons, it was desirable to see at all times
which rules had been implemented. However, even if writing code that fulfills a
specification is relatively easy in XSLT (or any other programming language),
guessing a hypertextualization rule from programming code is not.

In summary, we found that XSLT (or a general-purpose programming language) – even with a specialised library – was not well suited to our task of
incremental development of both hypertext strategies and document grammars, but
that we needed to write down hypertextualisation rules in a concise format. So we
decided to go one step further: We designed a formal language for describing hypertext conversion rules, namely HTTL.

10.2.3 The HTTL Approach

The Hypertext Transformation Language (HTTL) is a declarative language for
describing hypertext conversion rules. It is used in a framework together with a
code generator that translates these rules into XSLT code.

HTTL provides programming constructs specialised for writing hypertextualisation rules, which makes rules concise and self-documenting, thus meeting the
requirements for readable code and incremental development. HTTL separates
markup from hypertext strategies, using *templates*: all hypertextualisation rules
operate on templates rather than markup (detailed in Section 10.3.3). This approach
tackles the third of the above issues, i.e. changing document grammars. It also
allows us to generate different output formats from a given set of HTTL rules.
Currently, two output formats are supported: HTML augmented with JavaScript and
CSS Stylesheets, and the original XML augmented with XLink links. In principle,
other output formats can be implemented, e.g. HTML/PHP/CSS or PDF. All target-
language implementation details are hidden from the rule writer, who is provided
with abstract constructs such as one-to-many links.

The HTTL framework also allows a user to define more than one set of rules. He
or she may write several rule sets for different purposes (e.g. a rule set specific to a
document type, an author, or a particular hypertextualisation strategy).

HTTL can thus be considered a specialised, declarative transformation language
which, for the hypertext expert, is more intuitive and less time-consuming to learn
than a general-purpose programming language. The approach facilitates the generation of different hypertext views on the same linear document, and allows for
a user-driven conversion process. For example, the question of node granularity
("fragmentation problem") can be addressed – for a particular text type and a particular annotation – by experimenting with different sets of segmentation rules. For
evaluation purposes, the rule sets can be tested with different user groups.

HTTL's main application area is hypertext research, allowing the testing of conversion strategies and their incremental development, but also the production of

hypertexts tailored to specific usages. However, we can think of other application areas. We believe that HTTL will be useful for practical applications where XML documents are to be transformed into a format readable by standard web browsers, possible input document types being technical documentation or other highly structured text documents, for which no transformation implementations exist yet. For cross media publishing applications, documents in different output formats can be generated, e.g. hypertexts for different devices, or a linear version for print. It may be used to provide a browsable form for output data of various applications, e.g. SQL dumps of relational databases, in order to get an overview of their inherent structure and interrelations. Finally, HTTL may have its use as a component of adaptive hypermedia applications, as adaptive content presentation techniques such as stretchtext, dimming, scaling, or hiding of content chunks (see Bunt et al. 2007) can easily be incorporated into HTTL. The investigation of HTTL's application spectrum will be subject to further work.

10.3 The HTTL Framework

The HTTL framework consists of the HTTL language and software for processing rules written in HTTL. In this section, we will first give an overview of the framework's architecture (Section 10.3.1). We will then present the core of the HTTL language, starting with an overview of the language constructs (Section 10.3.2) and continuing with templates (Section 10.3.3) and conversion rules (Section 10.3.4). In the course of this section, we will translate most of the segmentation and linking rules given in Section 10.2.1 into a formal HTTL representation. In order to demonstrate the basic functionality, we will stick to simple examples for the time being.

10.3.1 Architecture

HTTL is a language designed to describe operations needed for the generation of hypertext views from linear documents. It consists of two parts: one part allowing to express *hypertext conversion rules* and one part allowing to express *transformation rules*. The latter produce a transformation of text from an input markup into a target markup (e.g., a transformation from DocBook to HTML), while the former effect the generation of hyperlinks and the segmentation of the text into hypertext nodes.

Figure 10.4 gives an overview of the architecture. The hypertext rules expressed in HTTL are analysed by a hypertext rule compiler and compiled into an XSLT program, the hypertext rule handler. This program takes as its input an XML document and augments it with hyperlinks (represented in XLink) and information about hypertext node boundaries, as prescribed by the hypertext conversion rules. The result is stored as an intermediate document.

In a second step, this intermediate result is transformed into the chosen target language, i.e. into a hypertext. The user can provide HTTL transformation rules,

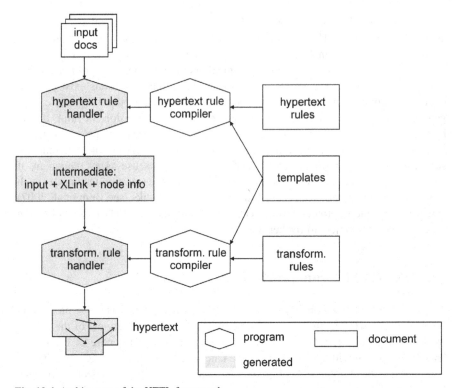

Fig. 10.4 Architecture of the HTTL framework

which are interpreted by the transformation rule compiler and compiled into an XSLT stylesheet which we call transformation rule handler. This stylesheet takes the intermediate document as its input and transforms it into the actual hypertext in the desired target language, i.e., it parses both the input markup (e.g., DocBook) and the linking and segmentation information. Instead of providing transformation rules, the user can also write his or her own XSLT stylesheet for the translation from input format to output format (which usually is a relatively simple task) or even combine both methods.

As conversion strategies are conceptually independent of both the markup of the source documents and the hypertext output format, HTTL allows for rules that do not directly operate on markup, but on *templates* representing markup. It is thus possible, by defining and using templates, to process different input and output formats, while retaining the conversion rules. Thus, the hypertext rule compiler and the transformation rule compiler also evaluate a file containing template definitions. These template definitions provide a mapping between template names and XML markup.

In the remainder of this article, we focus on the part of the HTTL language allowing to express hypertext conversion rules, neglecting the transformation part.

10.3.2 Language Constructs

The main entities of the HTTL language are the following:

Rules. HTTL rules fall into two main categories: hypertext conversion rules (segmentation and linking rules) and transformation rules (the latter will not be discussed in this article).

Templates. Templates are used to abstract from the source language (source language templates), from markup used for hypertext features such as links (hypertext templates), and from other markup in the target language (target language templates, not discussed here).

Fields. Each template has a fixed number of fields, which make template properties accessible. They are similar to object attributes in object-oriented programming languages.

Variables. Variables can be bound to templates and their fields and are used to address their instances.

Comments. The code can be interspersed with comments for human readers.

Rules operate on templates, using variables to address particular templates and their fields.

10.3.3 Templates

Owing to the uniform XML syntax, different source languages (corresponding to different document grammars, e.g., the DocBook-DTD) can be parsed and interpreted by HTTL. *Source language templates* are used to abstract from the particular, XML-based source language. They match specific XML markup in the source documents and can be defined by the HTTL user. Consider the following example:[3]

```
<def>
  As discussed in [IETF RFC 2396], a
  <definiendum><term baseForm="resource">resource</term></definiendum>
  is any addressable unit of information or service.
</def>
[...] An extended link is a link that associates an arbitrary number of
<term baseForm="resource">resources</term>.
```

This excerpt contains markup from the terms and definitions layer: the definition of the term "resource" is annotated using <def> elements, term occurrences of that term are marked by <term> elements. In the definition, the definiendum – i.e., the term defined – is also marked up.

In order to access this markup with HTTL rules, the HTTL user can define the source language templates termDefinition and termOccurrence, which match the XML markup for term definitions and term occurrences, respectively. For each template, an arbitrary number of *fields* can be declared which make properties of the markup instance accessible, e.g., attribute values or element content. In the case of the source language template `termDefinition`, we defined the following fields:

`termDefinition.defText`: the text of the definition (here: "As discussed in [IETF RFC 2396], a resource is any addressable unit of information or service.")

`termDefinition.baseForm`: the linguistic base form of the definition's definiendum (here: "resource")

In order to define source language templates, we make use of XSLT syntax. The template writer specifies an XSLT pattern to select the node(s) which are to be matched by the template, and an XSLT variable for each template field. He or she may use the full power of XSLT to compute a field's value. Additionally, HTTL provides an implicit field `location` for each template, denoting the place in the text where the current instance of the template is located.

All XML annotations which are selected by a source language template are henceforth referred to as the *instances* of that template. Source language templates and their fields are operated on by HTTL rules, as will be seen later.

Hypertext templates[4] are macros that effectuate the generation of markup and code in the chosen output format (e.g., HTML/JavaScript/CSS). There is a fixed repertoire of hypertext templates, which currently consists only of `node` (effecting the creation of a hypertext node) and `link` (producing a hyperlink). Each hypertext template has a fixed number of fields. The `link` template has ten fields which can be filled in to specify characteristics of the link. Of these ten, only one (`from`) is compulsory. Some fields are derived from similar XLink constructs. Here, we list only a few of them:

`link.from`: the link's starting point

`link.to`: the link's end point(s). Compulsory, unless `link.show` = nodeExpansionForwards or `link.show` = nodeExpansionBackwards

`link.show`: defines the desired presentation of the link end point. Possible values are `new` (ending resource is to be shown in a new window), `replace` (starting resource is to be replaced by the ending resource in the same window), `nodeExpansionForwards` and `nodeExpansionBackwards` (node expansion as introduced in 10.2.1). The default value is `replace`.

`link.arcrole`: the semantic link type. This can be an arbitrary string value, and it can be used in a Cascading Stylesheet to control the link's appearance.

10.3.4 Conversion Rules

The HTTL programmer does not state any algorithms for the hypertext conversion, but rather specifies its outcome. HTTL can thus be classified as a declarative language. In this section, we describe HTTL by showing how the examples of conversion rules from the beginning of this paper can be formally expressed.

10.3.4.1 Linking Rules

The following HTTL rule formally describes the informal linking rule (3) given in Section 10.2.1.2 which generates links from term occurrences to term definitions:

```
d/termDefinition o/termOccurrence [$d.baseForm=$o.baseForm]
=> link (from=$o.location, to=$d.location)
```

It is to be read as follows: "For all pairs of term definitions d and term occurrences o which have the same linguistic base form, generate a link from the term occurrence to the definition."

The example shows that a linking rule basically consists of two parts: the premise on the left-hand side (before the arrow) specifies when the rule matches, and the right-hand side (after the arrow) specifies the action to be executed if the rule matches. We will describe a linking rule's components by taking a closer look at this example:

instance selections: `d/termDefinition o/termOccurrence`
This part of the rule selects all pairs of instances of the stated source language templates, in our example, all pairs of term definitions (`<def>`) and term occurrences (`<term>`) of all terms in the current document. At the same time, these source language templates are bound to variables (here: d and o), so that their respective instances may be referenced within the rule as $d and $o. All source language templates involved in the link are listed here (typically, two). Note that the variables are implicitly universally quantified, so that this rule component may be read as "for all term definitions d and for all term instances o".

link condition (optional): `[$d.baseForm=$o.baseForm]`
The link condition constricts the selected pairs of template instances to a subset: only those template instances are selected that meet the condition. In the example, only those pairs of term occurrences and term definitions participate in the link whose fields "baseForm" have the same value, so that the term occurrence "resource" will be linked to definitions of "resource" only, not to definitions of other terms.

The link condition is placed in square brackets and can be an arbitrary XPath 2.0 expression, possibly containing references to variables of the form `$variable.field`.

arrow: `=>`
The arrow separates the instance selections and the link condition from the action component of the rule that effects the generation of the link.

action: `link (from=$o.location, to=$d.location)`
The action component of a linking rule consists of the hypertext template `link` that operates on the selected pairs of source language template instances and generates links between them. The fields of the `link` template can be "filled" with values from the fields of the source language template

instances, using variables. In particular, the fields `from` and `to` are assigned the source and destination of the link by using the implicit source language field `location` (see Section 10.3.3).

This rule generates a link from each term occurrence to the corresponding term definition or term definitions, in the latter case generating a one-to-many link.

Recall the informal linking rule number (5) from Section 10.2.1.2: "When a connective (e.g. 'furthermore') is directly bound to the preceding (subsequent) text, provide a node expansion in backwards (forwards) direction." In order to express this rule formally, we define a source language template with the name `connective`, together with a field `connectedTo` that supplies one of the values `backward` or `forward` for each template instance.

This rule is translated into two HTTL rules (one for each direction):

```
c/connective [$c.connectedTo='forward']
=> link (from=$c.location, show="nodeExpansionForwards")

c/connective [$c.connectedTo='backward']
=> link (from=$c.location, show="nodeExpansionBackwards")
```

The latter rule may be paraphrased as follows: "For all connectives c that point backwards, create a node expansion in backwards direction."

These two rules are special in that the `to` field is omitted: In the case of a node expansion, the link's destination is the preceding or following hypertext node. Thus, there is only one source language template (and corresponding variable) in the instance selections part of the rule.

In the case of multiple matching templates or multiple matching rules, we use heuristics to solve or report conflicts.

10.3.4.2 Segmentation Rules

Reconsider the segmentation rule (2) given in Section 10.2.1.1: "Make each paragraph a hypertext node, except when it is contained in a list environment." Having marked up the logical text structure using the DocBook annotation scheme, paragraphs are enclosed in <para> elements. We define a source language template `paragraph` to match this markup together with a field `inList`, which provides a Boolean value, returning `true` if the paragraph is contained in a (DocBook) list environment, and `false` otherwise.

Segmentation rules are constructed analogously to linking rules: they contain instance selections and an optional condition on the left-hand side and the hypertext template `node` on the right-hand side. We can formally express the above segmentation rule as follows:

```
p/paragraph [$p.inList = false()] => node()
```

This may be read as "For all paragraphs p whose field inList has the value 'false', generate a hypertext node."

As mentioned in Section 10.2.1.1, this segmentation strategy is particularly appropriate for articles. For FAQ documents, it is desirable to display a question and its answer as a unit. Provided that a source language template QandAEntry for a question and its answer has been defined, we can easily express this segmentation rule as follows:

```
q/QandAEntry => node()
```

This rule can be used in conjunction with the above segmentation rule operating on paragraphs. However, when an answer or a question itself contains paragraphs, the two rules conflict with one another. In this case, a meta-rule is applied: by default, a hypertext node boundary is generated before and after each question/answer entry and also before and after each paragraph, so that the question/answer entry is split into several hypertext nodes. If this behaviour is not desired, we have to express the constraint that paragraphs within FAQs should not generate a node boundary. This is done by providing a new field inQandAEntry for the paragraph template and extending the above paragraph segmentation rule as follows:

```
p/paragraph [$p.inList=false() and $p.inQandAEntry=false()] => node()
```

Changing the granularity of segmentation can be achieved by replacing rules acting on finer structures by rules acting on coarser ones. For example, for a monograph, we could swap the above rule for the following one, which turns each section into a hypertext node:

```
s/section => node()
```

10.4 Other HTTL Features

In addition to the described language constructs, HTTL contains some more. The hypertext template link provides additional fields, allowing the user to accurately influence the link's appearance, behaviour and semantics. For example, link titles or additional text appearing in pop-up windows can be generated. The field link.orderBy specifies an order in which multiple link ends are presented in the case of one-to-many links. This feature can be employed to partly implement the ranking rules for multiple definitions mentioned in Section 10.2.1.2.

For many applications, a subset of HTTL is sufficient. We have developed and implemented a short-hand notation omitting the declaration of variable bindings which is applicable in many cases.

Typically, linking rules operate on exactly two hypertext templates, one representing the link's source, the other representing the link's destination. However, there are cases where the information whether two text passages are to be linked is to be found outside of either template. This is true, e.g., for XLink "third-party links", which relate two remote resources, and for linkbases in general. In the HyTex project, the relations between an anaphora and its corresponding antecedent are stated outside the markup for either the anaphora or the antecedent, conceptually analogous to third-party links. In this case, an HTTL linking rule may contain a third source language template that matches the markup containing the additional information (i.e., the markup describing the third-party link) whose fields can be used in the link condition. In so doing, the above rule (4) for linking anaphora to its antecedent (see Section 10.2.1.2) can be implemented in HTTL, as well as XLink third-party links in general.

10.5 Related Work

Closely related work can be seen in a linking engine called xlinkit by Nentwich et al. (2002), who also provide a rule-based language for interlinking XML documents, making use of their structure. Xlinkit's rule language is based on first-order logic and is used to create XLink linkbases as the result of consistency checks of distributed web content. Thus, xlinkit's rules are designed to express link consistency constraints, while HTTL rules focus on the creation of hypertext functionalities.

HTTL also allows separation of markup from hypertext strategies, while XLinkit rules operate directly on XML markup. Additionally, HTTL may generate output formats which make sophisticated link functionalities (one-to-many links, etc.) available to the end-user. Xlinkit, on the other hand, can handle distributed web content which HTTL can not.

10.6 Conclusion and Outlook

In this paper, we presented the Hypertext Transformation Language (HTTL), a rule-based declarative language designed to transform annotated XML documents into hypertexts. It currently supports the hypertext operations of linking and segmentation. Conversion rules can be expressed independently of the actual markup, thus being able to parse different input formats and to generate multiple output formats without changing the rules. In order to test or change conversion strategies, only the HTTL rules have to be changed, not the hand-crafted, harder-to-maintain source code.

In the future, we will further develop HTTL. For example, for rapid coding, it is desirable for linking and segmentation rules to operate directly on markup, thus omitting the source language abstraction layer altogether. This will be particularly useful for the quick testing of conversion strategies using a particular XML annotation scheme.

As we have shown, HTTL allows for segmentation rules that operate on individual structural elements, e.g. paragraphs or lists. However, sometimes it is desirable to keep particular structural elements together with the preceding or subsequent hypertext node, for example, to display a figure or a code example together with the preceding text. This feature will be incorporated into future versions of HTTL.

An important feature that is currently being implemented is link filtering. This will enable HTTL users to tackle the well-known problem of over-linking which occurs mainly in automatically generated hypertexts (see, e.g. Truran et al. 2007). While HTTL already provides a basic link filtering mechanism through link conditions, it still lacks link filters which are dependent on node boundaries. For example, of links in the same node with the same destination, only the first could be presented to the hypertext user, while the others could be shown on demand as "hidden links". Link filtering will also be used in combination with link-end ordering (ranking), as in the case of the HyTex ranking principles for definitions.

Furthermore, the set of hypertext operations will be expanded to include the generation of index nodes, content filtering, and stretchtext.

Notes

1. See also http://www.hytex.info
2. Analysis of our corpus has shown that it is not unusual to have more than one definition of a technical term in the same text.
3. This is an excerpt from the XLink specification. In our German text corpus, we use the German translation.
4. Note that these differ from hypertext templates in the sense of document skeletons.

References

Beißwenger, Michael, Lenz, Eva Anna, and Storrer, Angelika (2002). Generierung von Linkangeboten zur Rekonstruktion terminologiebedingter Wissensvoraussetzungen. In Busemann, Stephan, editor, *KONVENS 2002. 6. Konferenz zur Verarbeitung natürlicher Sprache. Proceedings, Saarbrücken, 30.09.-02.10.2002*, DFKI Document D-02-01, pages 187–191, Saarbrücken.

Bunt, Andrea, Carenini, Giuseppe, and Conati, Cristina (2007). Adaptive content presentation for the web. In *The Adaptive Web*, volume 4321/2007 of *Lecture Notes in Computer Science*, pages 409–432. Springer.

Clark, James, editor (1999). *XSL Transformations (XSLT) Version 1.0. W3C Recommendation*. W3C.

De Roure, David C., Walker, Nigel G., and Carr, Leslie A. (2000). Investigating link service infrastructures. In *Hypertext '00: Proceedings of the eleventh ACM conference on Hypertext and hypermedia*, pages 67–76.

DeRose, Steve, Maler, Eve, and Orchard, David (2001). XML Linking Language (XLink) Version 1.0. W3C recommendation.

Hammwöhner, Rainer (1997). *Offene Hypertextsysteme. Das Konstanzer Hypertextsystem (KHS) im wissenschaftlichen und technischen Kontext*, volume 32 of *Schriften zur Informationswissenschaft*. Universitätsverlag Konstanz, Konstanz.

Holler, Anke, Maas, Jan Frederik, and Storrer, Angelika (2004). Exploiting coreference annotations for text-to-hypertext conversion. In *Proceedings of LREC, May 2004, Lisboa*, volume II, pages 651–654.

Kuhlen, Rainer (1991). *Hypertext. Ein nicht-lineares Medium zwischen Buch und Wissensbank.* Springer, Berlin.

Möhr, Wiebke and Schmidt, Ingrid, editors (1999). *SGML und XML. Anwendungen und Perspektiven.* Springer, Berlin u.a.

Nentwich, Christian, Capra, Licia, Emmerich, Wolfgang, and Finkelstein, Anthony (2002). xlinkit: A consistency checking and smart link generation service. *ACM Transactions on Internet Technology*, 2(2):151–185.

Nicolas, Charles and Wood, Derick, editors (1997). *Principles of Document Processing. Third International Workshop, Podp '96, Palo Alto, California, USA, September 1996, Proceedings*, Lecture Notes in Computer Science, Heidelberg. Springer.

Nojoumian, Mehrdad (2007). Document engineering of complex software specifications. Thesis, University of Ottawa.

Rada, R. and Diaper, D. (1991). Converting text to hypertext and vice versa. In Brown, H., editor, *Hypermedia/Hypertext and Object-oriented Databases*, pages 167–200. Chapman & Hall, London.

Raymond, Darrell R. and Tompa, Frank Wm. (1987). Hypertext and the new Oxford English Dictionary. In *Hypertext'87 Proceedings*, pages 143–153.

Rearick, T. C. (1991). Automating the conversion of text into hypertext. In Berk, E. and Devlin, J., editors, *Hypertext/Hypermedia Handbook*, pages 113–140. McGraw-Hill, New York.

Truran, Mark, Goulding, James, and Ashman, Helen (2007). Autonomous authoring tools for hypertext. *ACM Computing Surveys (CSUR)*, 39(3).

Walsh, Norman and Muellner, Leonard (2003). *DocBook: The Definitive Guide.* O'Reilly, Sebastopol.

Witt, Andreas, Goecke, Daniela, Sasaki, Felix, and Lüngen, Harald (2005). Unification of XML Documents with Concurrent Markup. *Lit Linguist Computing*, 20(1):103–116.

Chapter 11
Mark-up Driven Strategies for Text-to-Hypertext Conversion

Angelika Storrer

Abstract The paper describes an approach that converts the structure of sequential text types – text books, scientific papers – into hypertext networks. Using XML as the technical basis, the approach implements sets of rules which automatically generate hypertext views as additional layers while preserving the original sequence and content of the sequential documents. These rules process information of mark-up at different annotation layers: the document structure layer, the terms and definitions layer, the thematic structure layer and the cohesion layer. In addition, the semantics of technical terms in these domains are represented in a WordNet-style semantic network. This lexical representation is used to link technical terms with their definitions and for generating a glossary that is linked to the terms in the corpus documents. Feasability and performance of the approach was evaluated using a German corpus with documents from the domains of text technology and hypertext research. This paper concentrates on the conversion methodology and its linguistic background; the related paper by Lenz (in this volume) focuses on implementation issues and presents a specialized hypertext transformation language that she has developed in this framework.

Keywords Hypertext · Text-to-hypertext conversion

11.1 Introduction

Hypertext technology is not only used to build hypertext applications from scratch. It may just as well be used to transform existing material into a format that can be processed by a hypertext system. In this context of text-to-hypertext conversion one is confronted with three types of conversion issues:

1. *Segmentation issues*: What are the criteria for segmenting documents into hypertext units (henceforth called "hypertext nodes")?

A. Storrer (✉)
Institut für Deutsche Sprache und Literatur, Technische Universität Dortmund, Dortmund, Germany
e-mail: storrer@hytex.info

A. Witt, D. Metzing (eds.), *Linguistic Modeling of Information and Markup Languages*, Text, Speech and Language Technology 40,
DOI 10.1007/978-90-481-3331-4_11, © Springer Science+Business Media B.V. 2010

2. *Linking issues*: What are the guidelines and principles for reconnecting these nodes via hyperlinks?
3. *Reorganization issues*: What kinds of transformations are necessary to unchain text segments from their linkage to the reading path of the sequential document, so that they may be integrated into different user-selected pathways?

Early conversion approaches concentrated on text types that naturally profit from the linking and searching capabilities of hypertext: dictionaries and other reference works. For the conversion of such text types, reorganization issues are less important. Documents of this type are commonly composed of text blocks, e.g. dictionary articles, which are designed as "stand-alone" units that may be consulted selectively and in arbitrary sequence. In contrast, sequential text types like text books, scientific papers or monographs are designed to be read completely and in the sequence presented by the author. When these documents are transformed into hypertext nodes, they may still contain explicit and implicit cohesive markers (anaphoric expressions, connectives, text-deictic expressions) related to units of the preceding or subsequent text. Conversion approaches for such text types are thus naturally confronted with reorganization issues. This paper discusses conversion strategies that use mark-up on several annotation layers for the segmentation, linking and reorganization of sequentially organized document types.

Conversion approaches usually transform the structure of the sequentially organized documents into a new hypertext structure. The approach described in this paper does not intend to irreversibly convert sequential documents into hypertext networks. Instead, it implements a flexible set of segmentation, linking and reorganization rules which automatically generate hypertext views as additional layers while preserving the original sequence and content of the sequential documents. These rules process information of mark-up at different annotation layers in order to segment the documents into hypertext nodes, achieve their cohesive closedness and establish hyperlinks. The approach was developed and evaluated using a corpus of German scientific texts coming from two domains, namely text technology and hypertext research. The semantics of technical terms in these domains were represented in a WordNet-style semantic network. This network is used as a basis for generating glossary views that are linked to the term occurrences in the corpus.

The approach has been developed in the framework of the project HyTex.[1] This paper describes the basic concepts, guidelines and strategies that are substantial for our segmentation, linking and reorganization rules. The article by Lenz (in this volume) discusses implementation issues and presents a specialized hypertext transformation language that she has developed in this framework.

11.2 User Scenario and Conversion Guidelines

In order to simplify a later evaluation, our conversion approach is developed with the following usage scenario in mind: hypertext users are in search of information in a scientific domain in which they have previous but no expert knowledge. Their time is constrained, and they have to solve a specific type of problem. Such a scenario may occur in the course of an interdisciplinary research project, in scientific journalism and specialized lexicography. In these contexts users tend to read excursively and only perceive parts of longer documents. When these documents are sequentially organized, i.e. designed to be read from the beginning to the end, this selective reading may result in coherence problems. For example, a reader, jumping right in the middle of a sequential document, may not understand (or may misunderstand) a paragraph because he lacks the prerequisite knowledge given in the preceding text. The objective of our conversion approach is to avoid such coherence problems and make selective reading and browsing more efficient and more convenient than it would be possible with printmedia. To accomplish this objective our approach follows two guidelines, namely (1) recoverability and (2) coherence-based conversion.

(ad 1) By *recoverability* we mean that we generate hypertext views as additional layers while preserving the original sequence and content of the sequential documents. In this way, the reader still has the option to perceive the text in its original sequential form, provided he has the time to do so. The hypertext views mark an offer for those readers who only have the time to scan the text. Our goal is to offer this sort of reader a better support in text understanding than it would be possible while reading printmedia excursively.

(ad 2) *Coherence-based conversion* means that the way in which the documents are split up into nodes and linked to other nodes is governed by the concept of coherence. The guideline was introduced in Kuhlen (1991, 163ff) as an alternative to purely form-based conversion approaches. Below, I want to outline the main differences between form- and coherence-based approaches and explain how this guideline is implemented in our approach.

Form-based approaches segment a sequentially organized text according to its structure of chapters, sections, subsections and paragraphs. In many cases, paragraphs are regarded to be the smallest units, and the segmentation follows the principle "one paragraph is one node". The nodes generated by such form-based principles are then re-connected via hyperlinks.

Common strategies for form-based linking may be explained on the basis of the hypertext structure visualized in Fig. 11.1:

1. Form-based hierarchical linking: This principle creates hyperlinks that reconstruct the hierarchical relations between chapters, sections, subsections and paragraphs. In hypertext navigation bars, links of this type are usually represented by up(ward)- and down(ward)-arrows. In addition, most hyperdocuments provide links from all nodes to an index page – typically a "clickable" table of contents in which the headings are linked to the first nodes of the respective sections and subsections.
2. Form-based sequential linking: This principle reconstructs the sequence of the original sequential text by creating a reading path leading in a depth-first-strategy through the hierarchy of nodes. In navigation bars these links are typically represented by left- and right-arrows. Users that follow this reading path will perceive the document in exactly the sequence that the author of the sequential document had in mind.

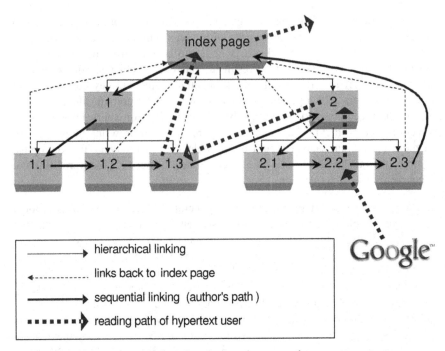

Fig. 11.1 Resulting structure of a form-based conversion approach

Reading paths created by the sequential linking principle are only an option. Most hypertext users will select their own paths. Browsing the web with a search engine, a user may directly be ushered to a node. From there, he may click to a higher level, climb down again in order to pick an interesting detail, then jump to the homepage and afterwards surf to a different site. A user path of this type is illustrated in Fig. 11.1. The crucial point for our discussion is that users of form-based hypertexts which do not follow the author's path but search their own paths may be faced with two types of problems that are both related to the concept of coherence:

1. Some problems are located on the *micro-level* and are related to the concept of cohesive closedness (cf. Kuhlen 1991, 33f and 87f). These problems are caused by the fact that paragraphs in sequential documents may contain cohesion markers (anaphoric and text-deictic expressions; connectives) related to information that is located in the preceding or in the subsequent text. Coherence-based conversion strategies that cope with this problem aim at liberating cohesive markers from their linkage to the reading path of the sequential document. These strategies will be described in Section 11.4.
2. Other problems are located on the *macro-level*. They are caused by the fact that an author of sequential text, who verbalizes its content, presupposes that the reader is already acquainted with the content in the preceding text (cf. Foltz 1996, Fritz 1999, Storrer 2002). Hence, he may not repeat information that has been

given in the preceding text. The selective reader, who is sent directly to a node, like in the example illustrated in Fig. 11.1, may, therefore, lack important knowledge prerequisites. Our solution to problems like these is linking according to knowledge prerequisites. That means that – by creating hyperlinks – we offer those knowledge units that a selective reader needs for properly understanding the current node. The strategies that we have developed in this context will be described in Section 11.5.

11.3 Project Architecture: Information Levels and Annotation Layers

Our conversion approach processes information from two levels:

1. On the *document level* we annotate the documents in our corpus on different linguistic and text-grammatical annotation layers which will be described below. This mark-up is then used for automatic segmentation, linking and reorganization.
2. On the *domain knowledge level*, we represent the main concepts of our subject domains in a WordNet style semantic net, called TermNet. The technical basis for this representation is XML Topic Maps (cf. Pepper and Moore 2001, Lenz and Storrer 2002). All technical terms are represented as word topics and related to their definitions and term occurrences in the documents.

A dynamic-adaptive component which processes logs of user paths is planned for the second phase of our project. This *hypertext usage level* would supply information about the hypertext nodes already visited by a user and, with this, about the knowledge prerequisites that he already has.

The following subsections give an outline of the annotation layers on the document level (Section 11.3.1) and of the semantic net on the domain knowledge level (Section 11.3.2). In Sections 11.4 and 11.5 we will explain how these levels and layers are used in conversion rules that we have implemented in the first phase of our project. Implementation issues are discussed in more detail in Lenz (this volume).

11.3.1 Annotation Layers on the Document Level

In the first phase of our project, we gathered a corpus with documents from two domains: hypertext research and text technology. We developed XML document grammars to annotate this corpus on different linguistic and text-grammatical information layers: the document structure layer, the terms and definitions layer, the thematic structure layer and the cohesion layer. Additional linguistic information was provided by *morphosyntactic annotations* automatically assigned by the *KaRoPars* (v.0.36) technology developed at the University of Tübingen (cf. Müller 2004).[2] The *KaRoPars* output provides part-of-speech information,[3] lemmatization and a "flat" syntactic analysis. This syntactic analysis includes the demarcation of "topological fields" ("Vorfeld", "Mittelfeld", "Nachfeld") relevant for German word order regularities.

Below we illustrate the mark-up used in these annotation layers using the following text segment as an example:

Example text 1:

Tochtermann (1995) spezifiziert einen Anker als eine eineindeutige Zuordnung zwischen einem Identifikator und einem Ankerobjekt, das sich durch fünf Felder charakterisieren lässt:
– das Hyperdokument,
– das betreffende Modul,
– die Komponente,
– der Ankerbereich,
– Attribute zum Anker (z.B. für Informationen zur Gewichtung oder zu Zugriffsrechten).

Engl.: *Tochtermann specifies an anchor as a reversibly unambiguous assignment between an identifier and an anchor object, which is characterized by five positions:*
– the hyperdocument
– the respective hypertext node
– the node component
– the position of the anchor
– further anchor attributes (e.g. information on relevance ranking, or on access rights)

On the *document structure layer* we annotate structural units (such as chapters, paragraphs, footnotes, enumerated and unordered lists) using an annotation scheme derivated from DocBook. On this layer our example text would be annotated in the following way:

```
<doc:para>
    Tochtermann (1995,76) spezifiziert einen Anker als eine
    eineindeutige Zuordnung zwischen einem Identifikator und einem
    Ankerobjekt, das sich durch fünf Felder charakterisieren lässt:
    <doc:itemizedlist>
      <doc:listitem>
        <doc:para>das Hyperdokument,</doc:para>
      </doc:listitem>
      <doc:listitem>
        <doc:para>das betreffende Modul,</doc:para>
      </doc:listitem>
      <doc:listitem>
        <doc:para>die Komponente,</doc:para>
      </doc:listitem>
      <doc:listitem>
        <doc:para>der Ankerbereich,</doc:para>
      </doc:listitem>
      <doc:listitem>
        <doc:para>Attribute zum Anker (z.B. für Informationen zur
        Gewichtung oder zu Zugriffsrechten).</doc:para>
      </doc:listitem>
    </doc:itemizedlist>
</doc:para>
```

On the *terms and definitions layer* we annotate occurrences of technical terms as well as text segments in which these terms are explicitly defined. Definitions typically consist of three functional components: the *Definiendum* (the term to be defined), the *Definiens* (meaning postulates for the term) and the *Definitor* (the verb which relates the definiens component to the definiendum component). Our document grammar specifies mark-up for each of these components. In addition, we explicitly annotate the occurrences of all terms that are included in our semantic net described in Section 11.3.2. The definition in our example text is annotated in the following way:

```
<definitions>
  [...]
  <defSegment>
    <def type="Fremdzuschreibung">
      Tochtermann (1995,76)
      <dfnSegment> spezifiziert </dfnSegment>
      <definiendum> einen
      <term normalForm="Anker" baseForm="Anker">Anker</term>
      </definiendum>
      <dfnSegment> als </dfnSegment>
      <definiens> eine eineindeutige Zuordnung zwischen einem
      Identifikator und einem Ankerobjekt, das sich durch fünf
      Felder charakterisieren lässt: das
      <term normalForm="Hyperdokument" baseForm="Hyperdokument">
      Hyperdokument </term>, das betreffende
      <term normalForm="Modul" baseForm="Modul">Modul</term>, die
      <term normalForm="Komponente" baseForm="Komponente">
      Komponente
      </term>, der Ankerbereich, Attribute zum <term normalForm="
      Anker"
      baseForm="Anker">Anker</term> (z.B. für Informationen zur
      Gewichtung oder zu Zugriffsrechten)
      </definiens>.
    </def>
  </defSegment>
</definitions>
```

On the *thematic structure layer* we want to capture the way in which topics are introduced, elaborated in the subsequent text and related to subordinate topics (subtopics) or more general topics (macro-topics). The annotation schema is based on the typology of thematic progression proposed by Ludger Hoffmann (cf. Zifonun et al. (1997, Chapter C6, 535–591) and Hoffmann 2000). This typology presents five basic patterns of thematic progression: topic continuation, topic splitting, topic composition, topic subsumption and topic association. These basic patterns can be combined into more complex clusters representing the thematic structure of paragraphs. The basic idea of our schema is to segment each paragraph in a top-down-fashion into thematic clusters and basic patterns. According to this document grammar, the first part of our example text is annotated in the following way:

```
<tCluster type="associate">
   (...)
   <tCluster role="associatedTopic" type="compose">
      <tsegment role="compoundTopic">
         (Tochtermann 1995,76) spezifiziert einen
         <topic type="word" topicConceptName="Anker"> Anker </topic>
         als eine eineindeutige Zuordnung zwischen einem
            Identifikator und einem Ankerobjekt, das sich durch fünf
            Felder charakterisieren lässt:
      </tsegment>
      <tsegment role="componentTopic">
         das <topic type="concept"> Hyperdokument </topic>,
      </tsegment>
      <tsegment role="componentTopic">
         das betreffende
         <topic type="concept" topicConceptName="Modul"> Modul </
            topic>,
      </tsegment>
      <tsegment role="componentTopic"> die
      <topic type="concept" topicConceptName="Komponente">
       Komponente
      </topic>,
      </tsegment>
      <tsegment role="componentTopic">
          der <topic type="concept"> Ankerbereich </topic>,
      </tsegment>
      <tsegment role="componentTopic">
         <topic type="concept">Attribute zum Anker</topic>
            (z.B. für Informationen zur Gewichtung oder zu
            Zugriffsrechten).
      </tsegment>
   </tCluster>
</tCluster>
```

This annotation implies that the compound topic "anchor" is composed of five subordinate component topics. When topic words are included in our semantic net, we specifiy their word forms as values of the optional attribute topicConceptName (e.g. the topic words "Anker", "Modul" and "Komponente" in our example). Accordingly, the thematic structure on the document level is linked to the topic map representation on the domain knowledge level.

On the *cohesion layer* we annotate text-grammatical information of various types, e.g. co-reference, connectives, text-deictic expressions. This layer is crucial for our reorganization strategies, i.e. for generating cohesively closed hypertext nodes. Therefore, we will describe the mark-up on this annotation level in Section 11.4.

Following the approach developed by Witt et al. (2005), we store our annotation layers in separate files. Thus, each layer can be annotated and maintained separately and can be validated against its corresponding document grammar (DTD or schema file). In a subsequent unification step, the different annotation layers of our corpus documents are merged. The resulting unified representation is the basis for an XSLT transformation, which automatically generates the hypertext views along the guidelines of our linking and segmentation strategies.

11.3.2 Structure of the Terminological WordNet on the Domain Knowledge Level

Two-level architectures of hypertext supplement the hypertext documents with a formalized knowledge representation (e.g. Mayfield 1997, Carr et al. 2001). Following this idea, our architecture connects the annotated documents on the document level with a semantic net on the domain knowledge level. This semantic net, called TermNet, represents the semantics of the technical terms that are relevant for the subject domains in our documents in a WordNet-style representation. In our approach, we use information from this domain knowledge level to automatically generate glossary views, which show how a technical term is linked to other terms and concepts of the domain. These glossary views also contain hyperlinks to text segments, in which the respective terms are explicitly defined. The glossary views are connected to all term occurrences in the documents; but the glossary can also be used as an additional stand-alone component. The interplay between the two architectural levels is illustrated in Fig. 11.2. Using an example, we will explain in Section 11.5 how information from the document and the domain knowledge level is used for our coherence-based linking strategies. In the following section we will concentrate on the main structural features of our semantic net and outline some implementation issues. More detailed descriptions (in German) are given in Beißwenger et al. (2003) and Lenz et al. 2003.

Fundamental for the structure of TermNet are the entities and relations introduced for the Princeton WordNet (Fellbaum 1998) and the German word net GermaNet (Kunze and Wagner 2001). The two main entity types in the WordNet representation model are "words" (lexical units) and "synsets", i.e. sets of synonymous word senses. Synonymy in the strong sense of interchangeability in all contexts is rare in natural language. Therefore, WordNet uses a "smoother" criterion: two word senses belong to the same synset when they may be interchanged in some context (Miller 1998). The two main entities – words and synsets – are related by lexical relations between words and conceptual relations between synsets. The number and the definition of these relations are slightly different in the Princeton WordNet and in GermaNet. In our approach we concentrated on a subset of conceptual relations used

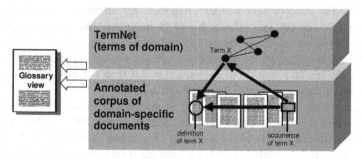

Fig. 11.2 Interplay between the two architectural levels

in both approaches. Furthermore, we introduced some additional lexical relations that we found useful for our application context.

In TermNet the two basic entities are *terms* (the equivalent to "word/ lexical unit" in the WordNet model) and *termsets* (the equivalent to "synsets" in the Word-Net model). Terms in TermNet are linguistic expressions, the technical meaning of which is explicitly defined in our corpus, i.e. a term in our TermNet is related to one or more definitions in the corpus. As described above, these definitions are explicitly annotated in our "terms and definitions layer". The version of TermNet that we developed in the first phase of the project comprises mainly nouns, many of them multiword units composed of a noun and an adjective modifier such as "bidirektionaler Link" (engl. bidirectional link). We treat these multiword units as "words-with-blanks" and provide information about the inflected forms of the nouns and adjectives in a separate list. This list is used for the automated annotation of the terms on the "terms and definition layer" described in the previous section.

Termsets contain technical terms that denote the same or a quite similar concept in different approaches to a given scientific domain. For instance, the books by Kuhlen (1991) and Tochtermann (1995) both introduced a terminology for hypertext concepts that influenced the technical terms used in German papers on hypertext research. Both authors provide definitions for the concept of a "hyperlink" and specify a taxonomy of subclasses (1:1-link, bidirectional link etc.). But Kuhlen uses the loan word "Verknüpfung" in his taxonomy (1:1-Verknüpfung, bidirektionale Verknüpfung) while Tochtermann's taxonomy uses the loan word "Verweis" (with subconcepts like 1:1-Verweis, bidirektionaler Verweis). In addition, the definitions of the concepts and subconcepts given by these authors are slightly different, and the two taxonomies are not isomorphic. As a consequence, in a scientific document on the subject domain, a term of the Kuhlen taxonomy can not be replaced by the corresponding term of the Tochtermann taxonomy. After all, the purpose of defining terms is exactly to bind their wordforms to the semantics provided in the definition. The usage of these terms in documents may serve, in contrast, as an indicator to which theoretical framework or "scientific school" the paper belongs. "Verknüpfung" and "Verweis" are, thus, not synonyms in the sense of being interchangeable in at least some contexts. For this reason, we do not use the term "synset" but introduced the term "termset": the members of termsets are terms that denote the same or very similar categories in competing taxonomies on the same scientific domain. This relationship of "Kategorienähnlichkeit" (category correspondence) is not determined by their interchangeability in corpus documents, but by their extension: two terms A and B are categorially correspondent if the set of objects in the research domain that are instances of term A has a high intersection with the set of those objects that are instances of term B.

But not all terms in a termset belong to different taxonomies. We recall two cases, in which the same technical term has alternative wordforms: (1) a multiword term has an equivalent abbreviated form (e.g. "Hyperlink" and "Link" or "hypertext markup language" and "HTML"); (2) a term has two orthographic variants (e.g.

"Hyper-Link" and "Hyperlink"). In these cases, the respective term forms are actually synonyms in the strong sense that they denote equivalent classes of instances and may be interchanged in all contexts. In TermNet we represent this strong equivalence by means of lexical relations between terms of the same termset: the relation "is-abbreviation-of" and its inverse relation "is-expansion-of", and the symmetric relation "is-orthographic-variant-of". In order to support multilingual linking in a later stage of our project, we link German technical terms to their English equivalents using the additional lexical relations "is-loanword-of" ("Link" is loanword of "link") and "is-loan-translation-of" ("Verknüpfung" is loan translation of "link").

Many concept-based terminology representations label one of the terms as the preferred term. However, when terms belong to competing approaches and schools – as it is frequently the case in scientific domains – this decision may be hard to make because all approaches have their benefits and complement each other. For this reason, we do not use the preferred term label in our representation. The objective of our representation is to connect competing technologies with each other because, in our usage scenario, it is often quite useful to know that the term A used in document x denotes merely the same category that term B used in document y. If the user is interested, he may easily reconstruct in which semantic aspects they differ because all terms of a given termset are linked to their definitions in the documents.

In addition to the lexical relations described above, TermNet represents conceptual relations between termsets: the taxonomic relation "is-hyponym-of" and its inverse relation "is-hypernym-of", the part-of relation "is-meronym-of" and its inverse relation "is-holonym-of". In addition, we relate termsets that denote opposite categories by the relation "is-antonym-of". Here we deliberately deviate from the standard WordNet model that represents antonymy as a lexical relation because we feel that, for our usage scenario, it may be important to know that the terms "monodirektionaler Verweis" and "monodirekionale Verknüpfung" both denote a category that is complementary to the category denoted by the terms "bidirektionaler Verweis" and "bidirekionale Verknüpfung". In our subject domain we found that termsets on the same hierarchical level often form groups of mutually disjoint concepts. For example, one may use multiple classification features to subdivide the general concept of a hyperlink. The class of links may be subclassified into monodirectional and bidirectional links depending on whether their underlying relation is asymmetric or symmetric. According to the position of their target, anchor links may be further subclassified into internal and external links. These subclasses are, in most cases, the same in competing taxonomies. We, thus, find a bunch of termsets with similar terms for the same specific concept, i.e. "monodirektionaler Link", "monodirektionaler Verweis", "monodirektionale Verknüpfung", that are all hyponyms to the superordinated termset for the concept "Link". If only this hyponymy relation is encoded, an aspect that is vital for inferences is concealed: an individual link in a document may be simultaneously monodirectional and external. But it cannot be simultaneously monodirectional and bidirectional, since these subclasses are defined to be mutually disjoint. In order to account for this fact, we enhanced the standard WordNet model by (optional) attributes that specify classification features for subordinate termsets. Termsets that have the same hypernym and the same classification feature are defined as denoting disjoint classes of instances.

In the first stage of our project, TermNet was represented as an XML Topic Maps (Pepper and Moore 2001) application. In order to facilitate the construction and the maintenance of TermNet, we used K-Infinity,[4] a tool for building and maintaining knowledge networks with a comfortable graphical editor. K-Infinity has an internal representation that already performs consistency checks (e.g. it prevents cycles in hyponymy relations) and is enhanced by export facitities, e.g. an XSLT stylesheet that transform the internal K-Infinity representation into an XML Topic Map representation. We conduct some additional consistency checks on this XTM representation and enrich it by relations that are not explicitly encoded but can be automatically inferred, e.g. the disjointness of subclasses with the same classification feature that we explained above (cf. Lenz et al. 2003). The resulting XTM representation forms the basis for our hypertextualisation strategies described in Section 11.5.

11.4 Coherence-Based Strategies on the Micro-Level: Cohesive Closedness in Hypertext Nodes

Form-based conversion approaches segment larger documents according to structural units, i.e. sections, subsections and paragraphs. In our approach we aim at a very "granular" segmentation that is based on the general principle that one paragraph becomes one hypertext node. The respective segmentation rules process mark-up from the document structure layer, especially mark-up indicating section, subsection and paragraph boundaries; subrules handle special cases like unordered and ordered lists, tables, figures and their respective captions. These rules construct the basic units of our hypertext view: the hypertext nodes (cf. Lenz (in this volume) for implementation details). However, these nodes quite often contain cohesion markers related to information that is located in the preceding or in the subsequent text, e.g. anaphoric pronouns or anaphoric noun phrases, text-deictic expressions like "siehe oben" (E: *see above*) and various types of connectives. This is due to the fact that sequential documents are generally designed to be read completely and in the sequence prepared by the author. A subtask in the conversion of sequential documents into hyperdocuments is to liberate cohesive markers in hypertext nodes from their linkage to a specific reading path, i.e. to achieve "cohesive closedness" in hypertext nodes (cf. Kuhlen 1991, 33f and 87f).

We transform paragraphs in cohesively closed hypertext nodes by rules that use annotations from the cohesion layer. This layer provides mark-up for anaphoric pronouns and noun phrases, text-deictic expressions and connectives. On this basis we implemented four basic operations that transform the paragraphs of sequential documents into "stand-alone" hypertext nodes that may be integrated into various reading paths:

1. *Anaphora resolution*: some paragraphs contain anaphoric pronouns or noun phrases, the antecedents of which are found in the previous paragraph. In these cases a pop up element with the antecedent is displayed above the pronoun.
2. *Node expansion*: some connectives indicate that the content of the paragraph is strongly related to the previous (or the subsequent) text, e.g. "außerdem" (*in addition*), "allerdings" (*though*), "darüber hinaus" (*furthermore*). In these cases, we provide the option to expand the current node and display the preceding or subsequent paragraph. With this option the user may accumulate as much context as he desires for properly understanding the content of the node.
3. *Linking*: in many cases we find expressions pointing to other text segments in the document. These expressions are transformed into hyperlinks that are related to their target segments. These target segments may be identified quite precisely, e.g. in expressions like "siehe Kapitel 3.4.2" (see Chapter 3.4.2). Other text-deictic expressions, e.g. "siehe oben" (see above) or "wie bereits erwähnt" (as mentioned already), are bound to the position of the current node in the author's reader path. In some of these cases, it is not easy to locate and to delimit the text segment to which the deictic expression is pointing.
4. *Deletion*: some occurrences of connective particles like "noch" or "also" seem to be stylistically motivated, i.e. they serve first and foremost the creation of a fluent text. Although they indicate how the current node is related to the previous paragraph, the content of the previous paragraph is not a prerequisite for the correct interpretation of the current node. In these cases, we decided to delete the connective particles in order to obtain a more "stand-alone" text version.

We will illustrate below how the mark-up of the cohesion layer is used to automatically obtain cohesive closedness. Example text 2 is a paragraph of a text book on hypertext.[5] According to our segmentation rules, this paragraph would constitute a hypertext node.

Example text 2:

Weiterhin unterscheidet **er noch** nach der Anzahl der in einen Link involvierten Anker in 1:1-Links, in denen ein Ausgangsanker mit genau einem Zielanker verknüpft ist, 1:n-Links, in denen ein Ausgangsanker mit mehreren Zielankern verbunden ist, und n:m-Links, in denen mehrere Anker unabhängig von der Traversierungsrichtung miteinander zu einem Linking-Muster kombiniert sind. Im Linking-Element von HTML sind nur 1:1-Links vorgesehen; **die obige Spezifikation** und das Konzept des "Extended Link" (im Sinne der Xlink-Spezifikation) sehen auch Links mit mehreren Ankern vor.

English: *According to the number of anchors that are involved in a link,* **he further** *differentiates between one-to-one-links, which connect a source anchor to exactly one target anchor, one-to-many links which connect a source anchor to several target anchors, and many-to-many-links in which several anchors are combined into a linking pattern that is independent from the direction of traversal. The link element in HTML only provides 1:1 links; the* **above-mentioned specification** *and the concept of an "extended link" (as defined in the XLINK specification) also provide links with multiple target anchors.*

This paragraph contains four cohesive markers related to elements of the preceeding text: (1) the connectives "weiterhin" (further) and "noch" (in addition), (2) the anaphoric pronoun "er", (3) the text-deictic expression "die obige Spezifikation". These markers would be annotated in the cohesion layer as follows:

```
<connective connectedTo="backward"> Weiterhin </connective>
unterscheidet
<discourseEntity deID="de_n_30" deType="nom"> er </discourseEntity>
  <connective pragType="stylistic" connectedTo="unspecified"> noch
</connective> nach der Anzahl der in einen Link involvierten Anker
  in 1:1-Links, in denen ein Ausgangsanker mit genau einem
  Zielanker verknüpft ist, 1:n-Links, in denen ein Ausgangsanker mit
  mehreren Zielankern verbunden ist, und n:m-Links, in denen
  mehrere Anker unabhängig von der Traversierungsrichtung
  miteinander zu einem Linking-Muster kombiniert sind.
<semRel>
  <cospecLink relType="propName" phorIDRef="de_n_30"
  antecedentIDRefs="de_n_27"/>
</semRel>
Im Linking-Element von HTML sind nur 1:1-Links vorgesehen;
<connective connectedTo="specifiedByID" connectedToID="caID_52">
  die obige Spezifikation </connective> und das Konzept des "
  Extended Link" (im Sinne der Xlink-Spezifikation) sehen auch Links
  mit mehreren Ankern vor.
```

Our reorganization rules process these annotations to generate the hypertext node illustrated in Fig. 11.3. In this reorganization process, all of the above-mentioned operations are applied:

1. *Anaphora resolution*: the antecedent of the anaphoric pronoun "er" is displayed in a pop up element. This operation uses the `antecedentIDRefs` attribute of the `cospecLink` element and identifies the antecedent by its value. Our antecedent assignment was annotated manually. The annotation scheme was described in Holler et al. (2004) and Holler (2003). But in principle, this operation could also be applied to documents with anaphora that were resolved automatically. Since automated anaphora resolution is not correct in all cases, we display antecedents as pop up elements (instead of replacing the pronouns by their antecedents).

2. *Node expansion (Sichtfelderweiterung)*: many connectives are directly related to the previous or the subsequent node; an example of this type is "weiterhin" (furthermore). In our annotation, we specify this relatedness by means of the values `backward` or `forward` assigned to the attribute `connectedTo`. When a connective has one of these values in its `connectedTo` attribute, it will be transformed into a link that displays the previous node (if the value is `backward`) or the subsequent node (if the value is `forward`) (cf. Fig. 11.3).

3. *Linking*: we annotate textdeictic expressions like "die obige Spezifikation" (the above-mentioned specification) as connectives which have the value

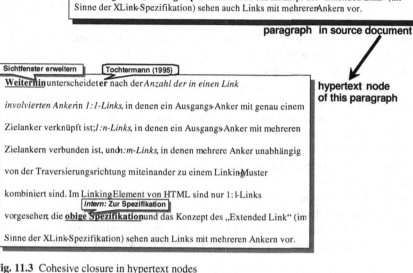

Weiterhin unterscheidet **er noch** nach der *Anzahl der in einen Link involvierten Anker* in *1:1-Links*, in denen ein Ausgangs-Anker mit genau einem Zielanker verknüpft ist; *1:n-Links*, in denen ein Ausgangs-Anker mit mehreren Zielankern verbunden ist, und *n:m-Links*, in denen mehrere Anker unabhängig von der Traversierungsrichtung miteinander zu einem Linking-Muster kombiniert sind. Im Linking-Element von HTML sind nur 1:1-Links vorgesehen; **die obige Spezifikation** und das Konzept des "Extended Link" (im Sinne der XLink-Spezifikation) sehen auch Links mit mehreren Ankern vor.

paragraph in source document

Sichtfenster erweitern | Tochtermann (1995)

Weiterhin unterscheidet **er** nach der *Anzahl der in einen Link*

involvierten Anker in *1:1-Links*, in denen ein Ausgangs-Anker mit genau einem

Zielanker verknüpft ist; *1:n-Links*, in denen ein Ausgangs-Anker mit mehreren

Zielankern verbunden ist, und *n:m-Links*, in denen mehrere Anker unabhängig

von der Traversierungsrichtung miteinander zu einem Linking-Muster

kombiniert sind. Im Linking-Element von HTML sind nur 1:1-Links

intern: Zur Spezifikation

vorgesehen; die **obige Spezifikation** und das Konzept des „Extended Link" (im

Sinne der XLink-Spezifikation) sehen auch Links mit mehreren Ankern vor.

hypertext node
of this paragraph

Fig. 11.3 Cohesive closure in hypertext nodes

`specifiedByID` assigned to the `connectedTo` attribute. The value of the additional `connectedToID` attribute identifies a text segment in the previous or subsequent text; in our example, this text segment is a specification that is annotated in the following way on our cohesion layer:

```
(...)<connectiveAnchor ID="caID_52"> Tochtermann (1995, 68)
spezifiziert einen Link als eine eineindeutige Zuordnung
zwischen einem Identifikator und einem Linkobjekt, das durch
fünf Felder charakterisiert wird: (1) einen oder mehrere
Ursprungs-Anker, (2) einen oder mehrere Ziel-Anker bzw.
Berechnungsvorschriften für Ziel-Anker, (3) die
Richtungsinformation zur Spezifikation der
Traversierungsrichtung, (4) Attribute für zusätzliche
Informationen zum Link-Typ, zur Gewichtung oder zu den
Zugriffsrechten, (5) Operationen, die bei der Aktivierung
des Verweises ausgeführt werden (optional). </
connectiveAnchor>(...)
```

Engl: *Tochtermann (1995, 68) specifies a link as a reversibly unambiguous assignment between an identifier and a link object, which is characterized by five positions: (1) one or several source anchors, (2) one or several target anchors or an algorithm for the computation of target anchors, (3) information about the direction of traversal, (4) attributes for additional information about the link*

type, about the weighting or about access rights, (5) operations which are exe-
cuted when the link is activated (optional).

When a connective has the value `specifiedByID` in its `connectedTo`
attribute, it will be transformed into a link that displays the node containing
the `connectiveAnchor` element. It should be noted that, from a linguistic
viewpoint, the expression "die obige Spezifikation" could just as well be treated
as an anaphoric expression. The decision to treat it as a text-deictic connective
is, in this case, in the first place motivated by the size of the text segment which
would not fit nicely in a pop up, and only in the second place by the adjective
"obig" and its deictic function. But in many other cases (e.g. "siehe oben") the
difference is clear, although it is not always easy to identify the boundaries of
the connective anchors to which these expressions refer. References to text segments that can automatically be identified by the document structure (e.g. "siehe
Kapitel 3.2.4") are easier to handle. In all of these cases, the basic operation is to
transform the connective into a hyperlink that is related to the node containing
the anchor element.

4. *Deletion*: some connectives and particles first and foremost serve the creation of
   a fluent text, like the connective "noch" in our example paragraph. These connectives have the value `stylistic` in the `pragType` attribute, which describes
   the pragmatic functions of connectives. Connectives with this value are deleted.

As can be seen by our example, our annotation of cohesion phenomena is
quite selective, i.e we annotate only those markers that are relevant for transforming text segments in cohesively closed hypertext nodes. A full annotation of all
cohesion phenomena would imply a complete reconstruction of anaphoric and coreference relations between text segments and an elaborate set of different types of
connectives. In the framework of our project, we did not have the means to annotate
our corpus documents in such a fine-grained manner, and German corpora with
cohesion annotations are not available yet. Our selection was made intellectually,
and the annotation was done manually; the resulting mark-up forms, thus, the basis
for the automated generation of cohesive closure in hypertext nodes.

11.5 Coherence-Based Strategies on the Macro-Level: Linking According to Terminological Knowledge Prerequisites

The conversion strategies described in the previous section are concerned with cohesion markers, i.e. with phenonema that are related to verbal units on the surface
structure of the text segment. The goal of these strategies was to revise those cohesion markers that point to segments in the previous or subsequent text in a way that
fits the resulting hypertext nodes into multiple reading paths. However, the revision
of cohesive markers on the micro level, i.e. inside the current node, does not solve
another problem that has been the focus of research on hypertext coherence (cf.
Hammwöhner 1990, Foltz 1996, Hammwöhner 1997, Fritz 1999, Storrer 2002): the
author of a sequential text assumes that the user is acquainted with the discourse
referents and information which he introduced in the preceding text. Hence, he does

not need to mention them again explicitly. For this very reason, the hypertext reader, who does not follow the author's reading path, may lack essential knowledge prerequisites.

The problem may be explained using the example hypertext structure that was illustrated in Fig. 11.1. We can imagine that the sequential text that formed the basis of this hyperdocument was a hypertext textbook. The author of the sequential document supplied a definition for a technical term in Section 1.2., e.g. he defined the term "link". He may then presuppose that the reader in the subsequent paragraphs understands this term according to this definition. But if the sequential document is converted into a hyperdocument, it will typically be read selectively and in a non-predictable sequence. Our hypothetical hypertext user in Fig. 11.1, for instance, has not "visited" node 1.2. When reading node 1.3, he may come across an occurrence of the term "link", but may not be familiar with its technical meaning – as we explained in Section 11.2, our usage scenario focuses on users with previous but no expert knowledge in the domain. In the best case, he will notice this knowledge gap and search for the definition. In the worse case, he will interpret the term in a non-technical sense or according to its technical meaning in another scientific domain (e.g. "link" as used in Artificial Intelligence). In this case, he risks missing important knowledge prerequisites and misunderstanding the content of the node.

The conversion strategies that will be discussed below aim to compensate for coherence problems of this type by generating additional links to text segments that may be prerequisite for the correct understanding of the current node. In contrast to the linking rules described in Section 11.4, these coherence phenomena are not explicitly indicated by cohesive markers (e.g. explicit references, text-deictic or anaphoric expressions), but are implicitly presupposed by the author, who verbalized his content with a fixed and predefined reading path in mind. In the first stage of our project, we concentrated on knowledge related to the meaning of technical terms because, for our user scenario, technical terms play a central role. Whoever wants to become acquainted with a particular knowledge domain has to understand the concepts denoted by the technical terms in this domain, i.e. has to be informed as to how these terms are defined.

In our hypertext views we offer two options to assist selective readers in better understanding the terms and their underlying concepts:

- Term-to-definition links: if a technical term is defined in the document, all occurrences of this term are linked to the definition segment.
- Glossary views: all technical terms are linked to glossary views, which show how a given technical term is related to other terms and concepts of the domain. The glossary view for a term also provides links to all text segments in which the term is explicitly defined. Thus, the user gets a quick survey on how the term is used and defined in the respective domain, whether all authors agree on a definition, or whether various term variations compete.

These two strategies may be illustrated by the example in Fig. 11.4.

In this example, the term "Link" is marked as an occurrence of a technical term in the hypertext node. If the user does not know the technical meaning of this term, he may activate a link button which displays its definition in a pop-up window. To get

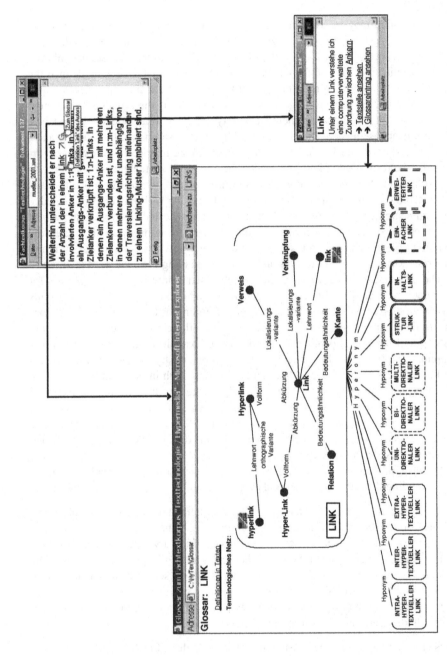

Fig. 11.4 Hypertext node enhanced by link to terminological knowledge prerequisites

more context, the definition pop up is linked to the node containing the definition. In addition, the user may activate the glossary window that visualizes the lexical and conceptual relation between the term and similar terms and concepts. Any of these terms are linked to their respective glossary entries. Each glossary entry is linked to all nodes that contain a definition for the respective term. With these linking structures, the user can, step by step, become familiar with the interrelations and differences between terms and concepts in the respective domain.

The rules that generate these linking structures process information from the "terms and definitions layer" on the document level on the one hand, and from the Topic Map Representation of our semantic net on the other hand. The XML Topic Map representation of our semantic net forms the basis to generate our glossary views (cf. Section 11.3.2). The "terms and definitions layer" (cf. Section 11.3.1) is used to explicitly mark lexical units that are used as technical terms in our domains. In order to prevent "overlinking", we only mark the first occurrence of a term in each node and filter out the other occurrences with the help of specialized rules. In addition, we rule out those special cases in which a technical term occurs in exactly the hypertext node in which this term is defined – in these cases, of course, we do not want to generate links. The "terms and definition layer" is also used to cut out the definition text segment and to display it in the definition window. This operation is quite simple when the document contains exactly one definition for the respective term. But in some cases, authors of scientific articles and textbooks discuss several definitions for the same term, e.g. definitions to be found by other authors or scientific schools, before they provide their own definition. In order to cope with this problem, we provide rules for the ranking of several definitions for the same term. This ranking is mainly based on the values of the type attribute of the def element, which classifies definitions according to their pragmatic function. One basic ranking rule is that terms that are explicitly defined by the author (the type value is "Selbstzuschreibung" = *self assignment*) are ranked higher than definitions that are assigned to other authors (when the type value is "Fremdzuschreibung" = *external assignment*). This basic ranking rule is complemented by other factors like the position of the definition in the document (cf. Beißwenger et al. 2002, Beißwenger 2004). Since our ranking results are not always adequate, we display the texts of all definitions, ordered by the results of the ranking process.

11.6 Conclusion

The conversion strategies discussed in this paper were implemented and tested using a corpus with 20 technical documents from two technical domains, namely hypertext research and text technology. In order to compare the effectiveness of our strategies, we generated four versions of our corpus:[6] The hypertext version *HyTex.1* generates hypertext views according to the rules described above: we offer cohesively closed hypertext nodes with links to related text passages, to definitions and to the glossary views. In this version external links, i.e. links that have been set by the authors in the original document, were removed. In the extended version, *HyTex.1+*, these external links are kept, although most of them are outdated or broken. The sequential text version *HyTex.0* displays the corpus documents in their original sequence and content. It provides no glossary views and no links – except for the possibility to click on a digital table of contents of the respective sections in the documents. In order to evaluate the effects of our glossary, we created an extended version, *Hytex.0+*, with the glossary as an additional stand-alone component.

Notes

1. The acronym HyTex is spelled out "Hypertextualisierung auf textgrammatischer Basis" (= Hypertextualization on a text-grammatical basis; http://www.hytex.tu-dortmund.de/). The project is funded by the German Science Foundation DFG in the framework of the research group "Texttechnologische Informationsmodellierung" (= text-technological information modelling; http://www.text-technology.de).
2. We want to thank the Erhard Hinrichs research group for their cooperation.
3. The part-of-speech categories used are those of the "Stuttgart-Tübingen-Tagset" (STTS, http://www.sfs.nphil.uni-tuebingen.de/Elwis/stts/stts.html).
4. K-Infinity is a commercial knowledge engineering software developed and distributed by Intelligent Views: http://www.i-views.de. We thank Intelligent Views for their valuable and kind support.
5. We did not find a paragraph in which all rules and procedures could be demonstrated. Therefore, the example is slightly modified – the original paragraph does not contain an anaphoric pronoun. However, our corpus contains several examples with anaphoric pronouns, the antecedents of which are placed in the previous segment. We handle these cases in the way that is described in our example.
6. These versions are available for download on http://www.hytex.tu-dortmund.de/ressourcen.html.

References

Beißwenger, M. (2004). Annotation definitorischer Textsegmente und "terminologiesensitives Linking". Arbeitsbericht, Forschergruppe Texttechnologische Informationsmodellierung.

Beißwenger, M., Lenz, E. A., and Storrer, A. (2002). Generierung von Linkangeboten zur Rekonstruktion terminologiebedingter Wissensvoraussetzungen. In Busemann, S., editor, *KONVENS 2002. 6. Konferenz zur Verarbeitung natürlicher Sprache. Proceedings, Saarbrücken, 30.09.-02.10.2002*, pages 187–191, Saarbrücken.

Beißwenger, M., Storrer, A., and Runte, M. (2003). Modellierung eines Terminologienetzes für das automatische Linking auf der Grundlage von WordNet. *LDV-Forum*, 19(1/2):95–104.

Carr, L., Hall, W., Bechhofer, S., and Goble, C. (2001). Conceptual linking: Ontology-based open hypermedia. In *Proceedings of the Tenth International World Wide Web Conference, Hong Kong*, pages 334–342.

Fellbaum, C. (1998). *WORDNET: An electronic lexical database*. MIT Press, Cambridge, MA.

Foltz, P. W. (1996). Comprehension, coherence, and strategies in hypertext and linear text. In Rouet, J.-F., Lovonen, J. J., Dillon, A., and Spiro, R. J., editors, *Hypertext and Cognition*, pages 109–136. Lawrence Erlbaum Associates Publishers, Mahwah/New Jersey.

Fritz, G. (1999). Coherence in hypertext. In Bublitz, W., Lenk, U., and Ventola, E., editors, *Coherence in Spoken and Written Discourse*, Pragmatics and Beyond New, pages 221–232. John Benjamins, Amsterdam/Philadelphia.

Hammwöhner, R. (1997). *Offene Hypertextsysteme. Das Konstanzer Hypertextsystem (KHS) im wissenschaftlichen und technischen Kontext.* Konstanzer Universitätsverlag, Konstanz.

Hammwöhner, R. (1990). Macro-operations for hypertext construction. In Jonassen, D. H. and Mandl, H., editors, *Designing Hypermedia for Learning*, pages 71–96. Springer, Berlin.

Hoffmann, L. (2000). Thema, Themenentfaltung, Makrostruktur. In Brinker, K., Antos, G., Heinemann, W., and Sager, S. F., editors, *Text- und Gesprächslinguistik – ein internationales Handbuch zeitgenössischer Forschung*, volume 16.1 of *Handbücher zur Sprach- und Kommunikationswissenschaft*, pages 344–356. de Gruyter, Berlin/ New York.

Holler, A. (2003). Spezifikation für ein Annotationsschema für Koreferenzphänomene im Hinblick auf Hypertextualisierungsstrategien. Technical report, Forschergruppe Texttechnologische Informationsmodellierung.

Holler, A., Maas, J. F., and Storrer, A. (2004). Exploiting coreference annotations for text-to-hypertext conversion. In *Proceedings of the Fourth International Conference on Language Resources and Evaluation LREC 2004, Lisboa*, pages 655–658.

Kuhlen, R. (1991). *Hypertext. Ein nicht-lineares Medium zwischen Buch und Wissensbank.* Springer, Berlin/Heidelberg/New York.

Kunze, C. and Wagner, A. (2001). Anwendungsperspektiven des GermaNet, eines lexikalisch-semantischen Netzes für das Deutsche. In Lemberg, I., editor, *Chancen und Perspektiven computergestützter Lexikographie*, pages 229–246. Niemeyer, Tübingen.

Lenz, E. A. and Storrer, A. (2002). Converting a corpus into a hypertext: An approach using XML topic maps and XSLT. In *Proceedings of the Third International Conference on Language Resources and Evaluation LREC 2002, Las Palmas*, pages 432–436.

Lenz, E. A., Birkenhake, B., and Maas, J. F. (2003). Von der Erstellung bis zur Nutzung: Wortnetze als XML Topic Maps. *LDV-Forum*, 19(1/2):113–125.

Mayfield, J. (1997). Two-level models of hypertext. In Nicholas, C. K. and Mayfield, J., editors, *Intelligent Hypertext*, volume 1326 of *Lecture Notes in Computer Science*, pages 90–108. Springer, New York.

Miller, G. A. (1998). Nouns in WordNet. In *WORDNET: An electronic lexical database*, pages 23–46. MIT Press, Cambridge, MA

Müller, F. H. (2004). Stylebook for the Tübingen Partially Parsed Corpus of Written German (TüPP-D/Z). http://www.sfb441.uni-tuebingen.de/a1/Publikationen/ stylebook-04.pdf

Pepper, S. and Moore, G. (2001). XML Topic Maps (XTM) 1.0. TopicMaps.org Specification. http://www.topicmaps.org/xtm/1.0/.

Storrer, A. (2002). Coherence in text and hypertext. *Document Design*, 3(2):156–168.

Tochtermann, K. (1995). Ein Modell für Hypermedia: Beschreibung und integrierte Formalisierung wesentlicher Hypermediakonzepte. Aachen, Shaker.

Witt, A., Goecke, D., Sasaki, F., and Lüngen, H. (2005). Unification of XML documents with concurrent markup. *Literary and Linguistic Computing*, 20(1):103–116.

Zifonun, G., Hoffmann, L., and Strecker, B., editors (1997). *Grammatik der deutschen Sprache.* de Gruyter, Berlin/New York.

Chapter 12
Structure Formation in the Web

Toward A Graph Model of Hypertext Types

Alexander Mehler

Abstract In this chapter we develop a representation model of web document networks. Based on the notion of uncertain web document structures, the model is defined as a *template* which grasps nested manifestation levels of hypertext types. Further, we specify the model on the conceptual, formal and physical level and exemplify it by reconstructing competing web document models.

Keywords Hypertext types · Web genres · Document networks · Hypertext graph · Graph model

12.1 Introduction

Approaches to web mining face an enormous challenge given the dynamics of structure formation in the WWW. On the one hand, the success of the web is partly due to the popularity of hypertext authoring based on the simplicity of HTML. On the other hand, this arguable success has the effect that reasonably persistent document patterns – which did not exist before the advent of the web – are difficult to find, since HTML does not require separating the markup of the function, content, structure and layout of documents.[1] Thus, all kinds of mixtures of content, function, structure and layout-oriented markup occur *according to a still unknown scope of fluctuation*. One reason is that web-based patterns emerge rapidly and spontaneously during the short history of the WWW, subject to the development of web document types which, compared to the abundance and binding character of text types, are still in their infancy (Rehm in this volume). This typological deficit is accompanied by the temporal dynamics of web documents whose life cycle is characterized by frequent modifications and inconsistent markup as a result of the authors' often deficient knowledge of HTML.[2] Thus, any approach to web *content* mining relies

A. Mehler (✉)
Bielefeld University, Bielefeld, Germany
e-mail: alexander.mehler@uni-bielefeld.de

A. Witt, D. Metzing (eds.), *Linguistic Modeling of Information and Markup Languages*, Text, Speech and Language Technology 40,
DOI 10.1007/978-90-481-3331-4_12, © Springer Science+Business Media B.V. 2010

on an approach to web *structure* mining which is expressive enough to master this structural dynamic.

Web structure mining starts from the observation that patterns of web documents allow reliable predictions of the functions they manifest. We have no problem distinguishing, e.g., an academic home page from a conference website in terms of their function and content. Judgments of this sort partly correlate with observations of differences in structure formation within these two webgenres. That is, the web not only manifests a tremendous set of text types which already existed before its advent, but also a vast amount of instances of newly emerging *hypertext types*, e.g., *corporate sites*, *Wikis*, *weblogs* or *home pages*. Theoretically, this makes the web the source of choice for extracting large corpora of certain genres and other linguistic varieties. It also makes the web the source of choice for studying the emergence of hypertext types as well as the growth, maturity stage and passing away of their instances manifested by websites and their constitutive pages. Thus, the web has become increasingly important as a seemingly inexhaustible resource of corpus formation (Baroni and Bernardini 2006). It apparently manifests an evolution of hypertextual patterns *in fast motion* making its various mutations accessible to corpus linguistic studies. This implies that the tremendous structural variety manifested by websites is by no means an irrelevant, needless fall-out of hypertext authoring to be abstracted away when mining hypertexts. Rather, this variety is an indispensable characteristic of this sort of *uncertain* structure formation. As a consequence, any approach to web structure mining faces the task of representing and processing aspects of structural uncertainty (Mehler et al. 2007).

This chapter is about representing patterns of web-based hypertext authoring. Its basic tenet is that *websites* and their constitutive *pages* are instances of *webgenres* (Mehler et al. 2009) and their elementary *stages* or *phases* by analogy with texts and their components are instances of genres and generic stages (Martin 1992). We hypothesize that webgenres are functionally characterized and that the respective functions can be observed, though not deterministically, in terms of structural indicators. Furthermore, we hypothesize that an appropriate webgenre model gets its validity to the degree to which it clarifies the relation of *explicit* (*visible*) or *manifesting* website structure and *implicit* (*hidden*) or *manifested* webgenre structure (cf. Mehler et al. 2007). Facing this two-mode distinction and its informational uncertain mapping, a *delimitation problem* arises. If web pages are not the largest manifestation unit of hypertext types we need to decide *where to fix their limit* in structural, functional or semantic terms. That is, other than many approaches which start from a given corpus of putative webgenre instances to perform some classification task, we have first to clarify the criteria of web corpus building. As it is hardly possible to delimit instances of hypertext types once and for all on either the page or site level (see below), we need a *template* model which is flexible enough to grasp units of varying structural resolution. This chapter is about the decision space induced by such a template model. By analogy to template programming, it presents a graph-model of hypertext types which allows for a flexible adaptation to various structural levels of web documents – including websites and pages as well as the document networks spanned by them.

In this chapter, this template model is introduced by answering the following question: *What does an appropriate representation model look like, which would allow us to annotate the structure of document networks (as instances of webgenres)?* According to the thematic focus of this book, the chapter concentrates on representational issues of annotation. Thus, in Section 12.2 we sketch our conceptual and logical data model of web documents, which is mainly based on graph theory. Its XML-based implementation is presented in Section 12.2.4. Finally, Section 12.3 concludes and lists prospects for future work.

12.2 Modeling Hypertext Graphs

Due to the problem of delimiting instances of webgenres, two fundamental issues arise when it comes to analyzing web documents as part of large document networks of hundreds or thousands of nodes:

(1) Although intertextuality is as old as literary languages, corpora of document networks in which intertextual relations are explicitly annotated do not yet exist.

With the advent of the web, networks of textual units are made accessible by hyperlinks which manifest thematic or functional relations. This includes *web fora* (Kot et al. 2003), networked *blogs* (Kumar et al. 2004), *wikis* as well as *e*-text networks which augment text collections by hyperlinks to generate value-added information (e.g., online newspapers, digital bibliographies (e.g., DBLP), *e*-print archives (e.g., arxiv.org), and digital libraries (e.g., CiteSeer)).

The digital accessibility of such document networks is only one aspect of the problem. Another is the lack of adequate representation formats:

(2) *Document Network Representation Model*s (DNRM) are needed whose instances are automatically extracted from input data. They need to be expressive enough to map varying types of networks whose complexity ranges from simple digraphs, multigraphs and r-partite graphs to hypergraphs. Instances of DNRM need to be *automatically* extractable as well as *efficiently* computable, maintainable and retrievable, as we deal with *huge* amounts of data.

In this section, document network representation is considered as a prerequisite of automatic analyzing and delimiting instances of hypertext types. This is done on four levels: Section 12.2.1 introduces a conceptual DNRM which is formalized graph-theoretically in Section 12.2.2. Further, Section 12.2.3 reconstructs alternative web models in terms of the DNRM. Finally, Section 12.2.4 considers procedural requirements of network extraction and preprocessing on the level of physical data modeling.

12.2.1 Conceptual and Formal Network Modeling

The delimitation problem includes that, *as instances of webgenres*, websites are not simply separable by exploring surface structural markers. Rather, any structure-sensitive model of webgenres has to take the networking of documents as a starting point for separating their instances. We share the epistemological conviction of the relevance of structural patterns as a source of membership to document classes (cf. Björneborn and Ingwersen 2004) and, thus, utilize graph theory to represent document networks. However, we start from the double-sided model of visible vs. hidden document structure as elaborated in Mehler and Gleim (2006) and Mehler et al. (2007). Thus, we do not simply refer to surface-structural units when defining document classes.

In order to explore diverse networks of varying genres in a generic manner, a uniform representation model is needed. As we have to distinguish the input networks from what is actually mapped within a concrete webgenre model and since the *same object network* allows for deriving *different target models* (e.g., based on functionally, semantically or structurally demarcated constituents) this representation model must be grounded in a terminology general enough to abstract from the specifics of the input networks. That is, it should be grounded in a *terminological ontology of preferably general constituents of document networking*. Thus, a first guideline for introducing the DNRM is to choose a terminology which is adaptable to different areas of document networking *as well as* to different criteria of network segmentation in order to describe heterogeneous networks in a nevertheless uniform way.

This section outlines such a DNRM on the level of *conceptual* modeling. It approaches a *graph-theoretical network model* as a prerequisite of network extraction which is a prerequisite of extracting websites as instances of webgenres. A complete linguistic grounding of this model is needed, but is not possible within the limits of the present chapter. Note that the conceptual presentation of the DNRM should neither be confused with its formal specification (in Section 12.2.2), nor with its implementation on the level of physical modeling (in Section 12.2.4). A central task of this section is to span a decision space which conditions the formation of network models to be explored within subsequent network analyses. In order to introduce this decision space, we present several guidelines as exemplified in Fig. 12.1. This is done by introducing (i) a *structural link typology*, by outlining (ii) a *layered document model* with a *kernel hierarchical structure*, by distinguishing (iii) *micro, meso and macro level units* of document networks and, finally, by spanning (iv) the *decision space* of seven modeling decisions.

The model to be presented is inspired by the alternative document model of the WWW as introduced by Björneborn and Ingwersen (2004) and Thelwall et al. (2006b). As explained in Mehler et al. (2007) we depart from this model in two respects: Firstly, we abstract from the *scope of the graph model* as we do not only focus on website external structures. Rather, we apply the same model on the level of site-external *and* internal structures so that we provide a *template model*. Secondly, we distinguish between visible layout structures and their counterpart in the form of hidden (logical document) structures as the proper reference point of functional and semantical document structuring.

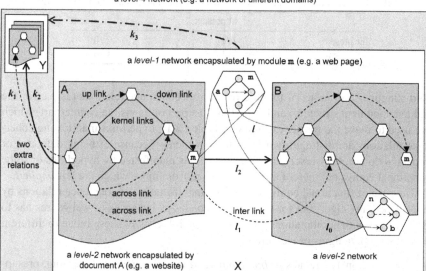

Fig. 12.1 Levels of network formation together with a structural classification of links from the point of view of the focal unit A where modules are manifested by pages, documents by websites and constituency relations by kernel links

12.2.1.1 Linguistic Grounding

A first guideline concerns the notion of *intertextuality* as a source of intertextual relations and their hypertextual manifestations. A survey of this notion is beyond the scope of this chapter. We only stress the fundamental distinction of *referential* and *typological intertextuality* (Mehler 2005) and its relation to DNRMs: whereas referential intertextuality comprises immediate text-to-text relations, which authors signal more or less explicitly by means of surface structural markers, typological intertextuality is defined by the shared usage of the same or alike patterns within different texts, which may or may not be intended. From the point of view of DNRMs, the significance of this distinction relates to the fact that referential (e.g., citation) relations induce unipartite graph models, whereas typological relations (indicating, e.g., membership to the same genre) induce *layered* models as, e.g., bipartite graphs whose top-mode manifests genres or registers and whose bottom-mode represents textual instances thereof.

To generalize our terminology, we subsume inter- and intratextual relations under the header of *coherence relations*. These include cohesion and coherence relations in the sense of surface-related relations as well as surface-distant relations (cf. Mehler 2005 for this terminology).

In the case that hyperlinks manifest referential coherence relations, we face the situation that in spite of the accessibility of their references, the coherence relation being manifested does not need to be explicit. Generally speaking, we have

Table 12.1 Hidden coherence relations (cr) vs. hyperlink-based manifestations (hl)

	hl present	hl absent
cr present	1/1	1/0
cr absent	0/1	0/0

to distinguish four cases of the interrelation of coherence relations (as part of the hidden document structure) and hyperlinks (as part of its visible counterpart) which are used to make the former explicit (cf. Table 12.1): hyperlinks manifesting coherence relations are distinguished from those which – because of being defective or broken – do not. Conversely, coherence relations manifested by hyperlinks or some functional equivalent thereof are distinguished from those which are left *implicit*.

Because of functional equivalents of the manifestation of coherence relations by hyperlinks, any algorithm for extracting websites as instances of webgenres has to deal at least with combinations 1/1 and 1/0 of Table 12.1. These relate to different algorithmic paradigms of web mining:

1. Combination 1/1 relates to *link typing* and thus to supervised learning, presupposing that the list of types of coherence relations is enumerated *ex ante* and that training examples are given.
2. Combination 1/0 relates to unsupervised *link structure mining*, as it demands exploring which functional equivalents are utilized to encode which coherence relations without presupposing the types and scopes of these equivalents *ex ante*.

A central conjecture of the present approach is that because of the implicitness of the manifestations of functional structures of web documents by functional equivalents, structure mining in the area of webgenres has to do with both of these tasks – *with an emphasis on the latter*.

12.2.1.2 A Rudimentary Link Typology

The link typology exemplified in Fig. 12.2 (cf. Haas and Grams 2000) acts as a second guideline of the DNRM. It sketches a situation of two units *A* and *B* which allow for distinguishing three types of links: *Link 0* exemplifies a link without source and target anchor as it may be used to manifest typological intertextuality. *Link 1* links source *unit A* with its target *B* by means of the source *anchor A1*. *Link 2* additionally uses a target *anchor B1*. These two types of links exemplify manifestations

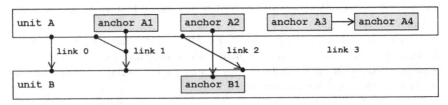

Fig. 12.2 Four types of links between textual units in document networks

of referential intertextuality. Finally, *link 3* is limited to *unit A* – it can be seen as a manifestation of an intratextual coherence relation. The type of a reflexive link from a unit to itself without a target anchor is reducible to the case of *link 1* in the sense of conflated source and target units. Note that these distinctions abstract from the status of a link whether it manifests combination 1/1 in Table 12.1 or whether it is explored and made explicit by a hyperlink (i.e. combination 1/0 in Table 12.1).

12.2.1.3 Layered Organization and Hierarchical Graphs

In order to further specify the DNRM, we switch from the level of elementary document units and their links to the encompassing level of document networks and their layered organization. We utilize the notion of a hierarchical graph, that is, a graph whose vertices denote graphs on their part, as a guideline to distinguish five levels of graph embedding, each of which represents a separate reference point of document network organization. Analogously, we distinguish five types of building blocks of the logical structure of such networks as alternative resources of extracting the vertex and edge set of corresponding graphs: that is, firstly, the level of *components* of, secondly, *document modules* as the smallest self-contained units of communication manifesting document linkage. These are interlinked to build, thirdly, *documents* as components of, fourthly, *document networks* which are finally organized into *second order networks* of networks (see Table 12.3). These reference points of structure formation uniquely induce the vertex sets of corresponding *level-0, -1, -2, -3* and *-4 graphs*, where each level-i graph, $i = 0, \ldots, 3$, is embedded into its encompassing level-$i + 1$ graph (see Fig. 12.1). As components, modules, documents and networks thereof are units of the hidden, logical structure of document networks, they are related by a many-to-many relation to their manifestations in the form of, e.g., web pages and websites. Further, whereas paragraphs, text-sentences and text-phrases can be specified as basic constituent types of document structure (cf. Power et al. 2003), modules, documents and networks extend this set in the area of web-based document networking.

12.2.1.4 Kernel Hierarchical Structures

A fourth guideline relates to the assumption that on the level of documents and their modules it is, basically, a constituency structure and, thus, a hierarchy but not a network which builds their skeleton. That is, documents and their modules are seen to be organized by *kernel hierarchies* which are superimposed by network-inducing relations. Analogously, level-1 and -2 graphs as induced by corresponding networks (cf. Fig. 12.1) are seen to consist of ordered rooted trees which are superimposed by graph-inducing edges.

In the case of web document networks that are segmented according to form- and function-oriented criteria, the notion of a kernel hierarchy is exemplified by a *conference website*. These are headed by a title and menu page referring, e.g., to the corresponding *call for papers* which in turn leads to pages on the conference's sessions etc. In this way, a hierarchical structure evolves. In this example, the kernel hierarchy reflects navigational constraints. Analogously, the DOM structure of a web page exemplifies a kernel hierarchy manifested by a single page. A third example is a Wikipedia document whose kernel hierarchy is spanned by an *article page* in conjunction with the corresponding *discussion, history* and *edit this* pages. These, taken together, form a flatly structured tree.

The notion of a kernel hierarchy can be utilized as the reference point of a structural, ontologically neutral link classification as demanded here. Since hyperlinks are form-related units, we need to clarify their counterparts on the side of the *Logical Document Structure* (LDS): kernel hierarchies are composed of constituency relations between dominating nodes and their immediately dominated nodes in terms of the kernel hierarchy. They induce subsets of the edge sets of either level-1 or -2 graphs. In the case that a constituency relation is manifested by a hyperlink, it is called *kernel link*. This is shown in Fig. 12.1 where the kernel hierarchy of node A is spanned by constituency relations all manifested by kernel links. Constituency relations may also be manifested by *inclusion relations* as functional equivalents to kernel links. This is evident when reflecting combination 1/1 and 1/0 in Table 12.1: in web documents, constituency can be manifested by a hyperlink connecting the navigationally superordinate unit A to a subordinated unit B or, alternatively, by including B into A possibly marked by an h-element of HTML. Thus, in the web, constituency is also manifested by hyperlinks, i.e., by a sort of dependency relation. This means that kernel links correspond but are not equal to what are elsewhere called *composition links* Géry and Chevallet (2001) or *inclusion links* Thüring et al. (1995).

Starting from Table 12.1 where hidden coherence relations have been distinguished from their candidate manifestations by hyperlinks we now focus on the former in order to define a structural typology of such relations. More specifically, the kernel hierarchy of either a level-1 or -2 network can be utilized as the reference point of classifying network-inducing relations and their corresponding hyperlinks (Mehler and Gleim 2006). Let $i \in \{1, 2\}$ be the focal network level:

- *Downward relations* associate nodes with one of their successor nodes in terms of the kernel hierarchy.
- *Upward relations* analogously associate nodes with one of their predecessor nodes in terms of the kernel hierarchy.
- *Cross-reference relations* associate nodes of a network which do not enter a dominance relation in terms of the kernel hierarchy.
- *Inner relations* of a network are limited to its nodes. They are distinguished from internal and external relations as follows.
- *Internal relations* are relations (as manifested by Link 3 of Fig. 12.2) whose start and end node are part of the same node of the focal network.
- *External relations* connect nodes of the focal network with nodes outside of it. More specifically: *Inter relations* connect nodes of the focal level-i network with nodes of another level i-network which is embedded *into the* same level-$i + 1$ network (e.g. relation l_1 in Fig. 12.1 from the point of view of network A). *Extra relations* associate nodes of the focal level-i network with nodes of another level i-network which is embedded *into another* level-$i + 1$ network (e.g. relation k_1

in Fig. 12.1 from the point of view of network A). Extra relations are exemplified by wiki websites with respect to document-level networks and their hyperlinks: so-called *InterWiki links* (e.g. translation links) connect articles of a focal wiki to articles of other wikis. They are distinguished from external links which connect wiki articles to non-wiki web pages.

- *Inferred relations:* An extra relation of a level-i network allows for inferring an inter relation of the corresponding level-$i + 1$ network, which implies an inner relation on the level of the corresponding level-$i + 2$ network. The latter two relations are said to be *anchored* by the first. This is exemplified by the relation l_0 in Fig. 12.1 which transitively implies the relation l_2 via l_1. In this example, the l_1 and l_2 are called *inferred* as they are *anchored* by the lower-level relation l_0. Further, the inferred inner relation is internal to the next higher embedding network so that we might build an inference chain from extra to internal relations via inter and inner relations as we approach the layered hierarchy of networks upwards. The distinction of inferred and non-inferred relations is important when it comes to inducing graphs on different levels of document networking as explained in Section 12.2.3. Note that not every inter relation (as exemplified by Link 0 in Fig. 12.2) needs to be anchored by an extra relation on the level of the embedded network. Note further, that there exist coherence relations (as exemplified by relation l in Fig. 12.1 and Link 1 in Fig. 12.2) whose start and end nodes belong to different network levels.
- Another sort of inferred relation is given by *transversal relations* (cf. Björneborn 2004) which link thematically related communities of documents to provide topic-related short-cuts between such clusters. These and related inferred relations and the paths they induce tend to belong to the area of web content mining and, thus, depart from the present focus of a structural typology.

Note that sequential relations of nodes of a level-1 or -2 network are reflected by constituency structures modeled as ordered rooted trees.

All relations distinguished so far are *perspective* in the sense that they depend on choosing a certain network unit as the reference point of their definition (e.g. network A in Fig. 12.1). This is explained in more detail by the notion of a *sampling frame* as defined below (see also Section 12.2.3 for an exemplification of this concept).

Going back to Table 12.1, we can now subclassify combination (1, 1) with regard to hyperlinks as follows: the manifestation of a downward, upward, cross-reference, inter or extra relation in the form of a *hyperlink* is called *down*, *up*, *lateral*, *inter* or *extra link*, respectively. As noted above, the hyperlink-based manifestation of these coherence relations is not mandatory. Rather, they may be manifested by some functional equivalent (cf. Mehler and Gleim 2006, Mehler et al. 2007).

12.2.1.5 Macro, Meso and Micro Level Units

Based on the guidelines presented so far, the different building blocks of structure formation in document networks can be specified in more detail as follows:

1. *Elementary components* of document modules fail as self-contained units of communication according to the segmentation criteria in use, and, thus, always occur as part of encompassing modules as the units of minimal size manifesting document linkage (this level corresponds to modules according to Rehm – cf. Rehm (in this volume)).

2. Subject to the operative criteria of network segmentation, *document modules* are the smallest self-contained unit of communication of the focal area which, in the role of candidate nodes, manifest links. That is, larger network components which are self-contained according to the same segmentation criteria consist of modules, whereas smaller network components fail to serve as self-contained communication units, that is, they are communicated as components of modules. Further, we hypothesize that modules have a kernel hierarchical constituency structure superimposed by network-inducing relations.

3. *Document units* are network components that exist between the level of modules and networks as a whole. They consist of one or more interlinked modules, but may also be recursively organized into complex documents which consist of other, less complex documents. In this sense, documents constitute a level of structural recursion in the area of network formation. This reflects the fact that, e.g., functions and topics can be seen as being recursively composed of subfunctions and subtopics, respectively. When demarcated in functional terms, documents manifest functionally closed acts of communication of, e.g., *conference organization*, *self-portrayal* or *knowledge dissemination* together with systems of dependent subfunctions (e.g. *calling for papers* or *notifying acceptances* in conference organization, *updating* or *discussing* in knowledge communication) each of which is manifested by a document or by a single module. By analogy to modules we hypothesize that documents have a kernel hierarchical constituency structure superimposed by network-inducing relations.

4. *Document networks* consist of interlinked documents which – if functionally (or topically) segmented – serve (or deal with) different functions (or topics, respectively) possibly independent of each other. The level of document networks is the level where we no longer expect to have a predominant tree-like constituency structure, but a network-like skeleton. This implies, amongst other things, that we no longer speak of a root or the leaves of a document network. Thus, document networks constitute the level of units which are reasonably input to *complex network analysis* (Mehler 2008) – in contrast to single documents and their modules. This assumption is not contradicted by the efforts of exploring hierarchical, topic-related structures of web domains (Menczer 2004) since units of this sort do not build constituency structures. Rather, the transition from the level of single documents to networks demarcates websites as the most significant manifestations of webgenres from larger-scale units outside the range of single webgenres.

5. Finally, we have to distinguish interlinked document networks which span second order *networks of document networks* as, e.g., systems of wiki websites each of which is represented as a network.

Table 12.2 Levels of representations within document networks

Level	Unit of research	Predominant methods tasks
Micro level	Module units	Classification segmentation of web pages
Meso level	Document units	Classification segmentation of web sites, Webgenre parsing
Macro level	Network units	Complex network analysis, community mining, Broad topic detection and tracking

Table 12.3 Building blocks of text networks

	Component	Module	Document	Network
Level of anchoring referential links:	+	−	−	−
Self-contained communication unit:	−	+	+	+
Recursive structure formation:	+	−	+	
Predominant inclusion hierarchy:	+	+	−	−
Predominant hierarchical organization:	+	+	+	−
Predominant network-like organization:	−	−	−	+

Table 12.2 shows how these units of document networking are mapped on 3 reference points of network analysis and their relation to web mining. See Table 12.3 which summarizes some of the distinctions made so far.

12.2.1.6 The Decision Space

Now, we specify the decision space of extracting and exploring document networks. We distinguish 7 decisions.

Decision 1. Which area of communication should be investigated?

This decision regards the distinction between networks of the different areas of web-based communication. Amongst other things, this relates to scientific, knowledge, technical, press and personal communication.

Decision 2. What criteria should be used to segment network constituents within the area under investigation?

This question asks for theoretically grounded, efficiently implementable criteria for identifying and segmenting *nodes* and *links* in target networks. At least four reference levels of such criteria can be distinguished: the *function, content,* (layout) *form* and (storage) *medium* of the units to be segmented. As we additionally distinguish the *logical* (document) *structure* (Power et al. 2003) apart from the segments' functional and topical identity, a further reference point of segmentation is attained. These reference points are obviously extended by situational parameters of the discourse situation in which the network units are produced or processed. This includes the segmentation of units produced in a certain domain in a certain period of time by a certain group of authors. With regard to processing-oriented criteria, Pirolli et al. (1996) is an early example which combines topological (hyperlink-based) with topic-related and usage-based criteria (by regarding frequencies of link traversals). Thereby, Weare and Lin (2000) distinguish technical and organizational criteria of segmentation (which relate to characteristics of the websites' authors – by sampling, e.g., pages produced by a certain community) and communication- or user-related criteria (by sampling, e.g., frequently accessed pages). Obviously, the choice of any such criteria depends on the research objective.

Note that segmentation criteria can be combined along these reference levels. Note further that Decision 2 should not be confused with the choice of surface markers to be explored in order to demarcate network constituents. Rather, it concerns the source of identifying network units as semantical, functional, structural, layout- *or* medium-oriented units.

The terminological distinction of 5 levels of network formation and building blocks introduces a parameter into network analysis to be carefully considered by any network extraction. This is reflected by the following three decisions:

Decision 3. Which network levels are relevant for graph extraction?

Deciding this question demands specifying two reference points: the *Sampling Frame* (SF) $i \in \{1, 2, 3, 4\}$ (or *sampling scope*) specifying the level of networks from which vertices are extracted and the *Level of Sampling Units* (LSU) $j < i$ identifying the level of networks to which these vertices (and their edges) belong.

In the case that $i = j + 1$ such that instances of the SF directly embed the sampling units, the focal decision can be reformulated as follows: *should we explore level-4 networks and thus links between document networks whose internal structure is abstracted away, level-3 networks of documents whose internal structure is disregarded, level-2 networks abstracting from the structuring of document modules or even level-1 networks of highest resolution in which text components serve as vertices.* Although the last of these cases seems to be implausible from the point of view of document network analysis, there exist, nevertheless, approaches to web mining which do exactly this. In the first case, we deal, amongst others, with relations of the kind of k_3 in Fig. 12.1. In the second, third and fourth case, we further distinguish relations of the kind of l_2 (and k_2), l_1 (and k_1) and l_0, respectively.

If, in contrast to this, the SF i does not directly contain the LSU j, i.e., if $i = j + k, k > 1$, nodes of different level-$j + 1, \ldots$, level-$j + k - 1$ networks and their relations may also be included as sampling units into network analysis.

This holds, e.g., for web graphs where level-4 networks are referred to as the SF (i.e. $i = 4$) and level-1 networks manifested by web pages are extracted as vertices (i.e. $j = 1$). Alternatively, sampling units may be given by level-2 networks as manifested by websites so that inferred links of the sort of l_2 in Fig. 12.1 are explored (while inner links of document A are either abstracted away or extracted as loops).

A yet unexplored alternative is to simultaneously explore several of these interleaving levels thereby reflecting the boundaries of networks, documents, modules and their components (as explained below).

Decision 4. For which graph-theoretic expressivity should we decide?

This decision chooses, amongst other things, between digraphs and undirected graphs. All graphs distinguished so far are directed. If this orientation is disregarded, i.e., if undirected graphs are considered, the question is whether simple, multi- or pseudographs should be extracted. If the decision is *multigraphs*, multiple edges are allowed (as they occur between the same pair of pages whose links are anchored by different source anchors). If the decision is *pseudographs*, even loops are extracted (as they occur by reflexive links of a web page with itself, e.g. from any position within the page to its beginning). Finally, if the decision is *simple graphs*, loops are disregarded on the corresponding graph level, whereas multiple edges are conflated to single undirected edges.

Decision 5. Should we account for informational uncertainty?

All decisions discussed so far suppose that we deal with clear-cut, segmentable nodes and their relations which straightforwardly induce vertices and their equally weighted edges. Actually, we face several, possibly combined cases of informational uncertainty of the relation of manifesting and manifested document network units (Mehler et al. 2007). Thus, the latter assumption can be violated to a large extent. Starting from a set of web pages as explicitly delimitable units of manifestation, we have to distinguish at least four aspects of informational uncertainty:

1. We need to decide whether the pages belong to documents as instances of the genres to be investigated. Further, we need to decide to which of the relevant documents these pages actually belong.
2. We need to position the pages within the constituency structure of the corresponding document. This may require us to divide pages which represent several modules or to amalgamate those which together manifest a single module (cf. Mehler et al. 2007).
3. We need to type the hyperlinks of these pages based on the typology of coherence relations presented above. According to Table 12.1, this may require us to deal with implicit coherence relations and to distinguish manifesting hyperlinks from deficient ones.
4. These tasks also demand that we decide which functional equivalents manifest which coherence relations, supposing that they are not manifested by kernel or other types of links.

In summary, it has to be decided which aspect of informational uncertainty should be processed when inducing graph models from networks. This is needed if methods of network analysis operate on weighted graphs.

Decision 6. To which extent should we include temporal variability?

Another source of informational uncertainty is temporal change. This is exemplified in Fig. 12.3 where two snapshots of the same website are made at

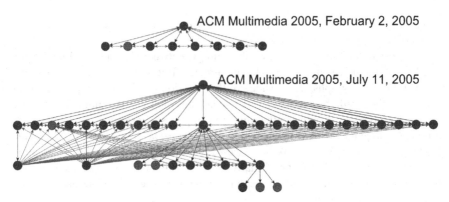

Fig. 12.3 Two snapshots of the ACM Multimedia 2005 conference website

different points in time. Koehler (1999) classifies site- and page-related types of changes in the web. They range from changes of page content via changes of link structure to changes of whole websites (cf. Mehler and Gleim 2006). Koehler points at the necessity of such classifications as the high change rates in the web affect any effort in web mining. He also hints at the domain specificity of change rates and their scopes: compared to content pages, e.g., navigation pages are likely to never go *comatose* (i.e. being unreachable for a long period of time) in commercial sites – in contrast to educational sites where he observes the opposite proportion (Koehler 2003). Koehler also observes that when a site ages, it is likely to be stable. Further, he investigates the life cycle of web units which decline their half-life after a (domain-specific) number of years (Koehler 2003). In order to include these kinds of temporal dynamics, DNRMs need to distinguish consecutive time-aligned graphs to represent the lifespan of the same document (network).

Decision 7. To which extent should the graphs be further processed?

There are two strategies (Thelwall et al. 2006a): the *purist strategy* takes the data as extracted without further processing. It tends to be restricted to media-, form- or layout-oriented segmentations. In contrast to this, the *pragmatic strategy* (which we call *explorative*) further processes the data to get content or function-oriented segmentations. Decision 7 relates to Decision 5, i.e., to handling the uncertain mapping of manifesting and manifested document (network) structures. It also relates to methods of web mining which explore form, function or content-based units on the micro, meso or macro level.

The careful examination of the seven decisions is a prerequisite for the comparability of approaches to document network analysis. It is a way out of the implicitness of web graph analyses which obscure their criteria of graph induction so that they negatively affect their repeatability.

12.2.2 A Graph Model of Document Networks

Now, we formalize our conceptual DNRM in terms of document network graphs. This is done by integrating the notion of a *Generalized Tree* (GT) with that of a bipartite hierarchical, nested graph. We redefine GTs in terms of document structures as described by Fig. 12.1:

Definition 1 Let $T = (V, E, x, \mathcal{O})$ be a directed ordered rooted tree with vertex set V, edge set E, root x and order relation $\mathcal{O} \subset V^2$ which for each vertex v linearly orders the set $\{w \mid (v, w) \in E\}$ of vertices to which v is adjacent. Let further $P_{x,v} = (v_{i_0}, e_{j_1}, v_{i_1}, \ldots, v_{i_{n-1}}, e_{j_n}, v_{i_n})$, $v_{i_0} = x$, $v_{i_n} = v$, $e_{j_k} = (v_{i_{k-1}}, v_{i_k}) \in E$, $k = 1, \ldots, n$, be the unique path in T from x to $v \in V$. We denote the set of all vertices of $P_{x,v}$ by $V(P_{x,v})$. A Generalized Tree (GT) GT $= (V, E_{[1]}, E_{[2]}, E_{[3]}, E_{[4]}, E_{[5]}, E_{[6]}, E_{[7]}, x)$ induced by T is a graph whose partitioned edge set is defined as follows:

$$
\begin{aligned}
\text{kernel edges:} \quad & E_{[1]} = E \\
\text{up edges:} \quad & E_{[2]} \subseteq E_u = \{(v, w) \mid w \in V(P_{x,v}) \setminus \{v\}\} \\
\text{down edges:} \quad & E_{[3]} \subseteq E_d = \{(v, w) \mid v \in V(P_{x,w}) \setminus \{w\}\} \\
\text{reflexive edges:} \quad & E_{[4]} \subseteq E_r = \{(v, v) \mid v \in V\} \\
\text{lateral edges:} \quad & E_{[5]} \subseteq V^2 \setminus (E \cup E_u \cup E_d \cup E_r) \\
\text{sequential edges:} \quad & E_{[6]} = \mathcal{O} \\
\text{external edges:} \quad & E_{[7]} = \emptyset
\end{aligned}
$$

We write $(V, E_{[1..7]}, x)$ when denoting generalized trees. Further, we write $e \in E_{[1..7]}$ if $e \in \cup_{i=1}^{7} E_{[i]}$. Note that we do not claim all sets $E_{[1..7]}$ to be pairwise disjunct. Obviously, each generalized tree GT $= (V, E_{[1..7]}, x)$ uniquely induces a rooted directed tree $T(\text{GT}) = (V, E_{[1]}, x)$.

Definition 2 Extended Graphs & Generalized Trees. Let $\mathbb{G}$ be a set of graphs and $G = (V, E) \in \mathbb{G}$. $\bar{G} = (\bar{V}, \bar{E})$ is called an extension of G w.r.t $\mathbb{G}$ if there exists a subset $X \subseteq \{(v, w) \mid \exists (V', E') \in \mathbb{G} \setminus G : v \in V \wedge w \in V'\}$ so that $\bar{E} = E \cup X$ and $\bar{V} = V \cup (\cup_{(v,w) \in X} \{w\})$. Elements of X are called external edges of $\bar{G}$. In the case that $G = (V, E_{[1..7]}, x)$ is a GT we set $E_{[7]} = X$, write $\bar{G} = (\bar{V}, E_{[1..7]}, x)$ and call it extended.

Note that this definition guarantees that the set of external edges of an extended GT is disjunct with respect to $\cup_{i=1}^{6} E_{[i]}$. Note that the set X of external edges extending a graph's edge set may be empty so that graphs are seen to extend themselves. This manner of speaking is needed in order to correctly formalize a hierarchical graph model as follows (a remark on notation: we write $G^{i\cdot} = (V^{i\cdot}, E^{i\cdot})$, $i \in \mathbb{N}$, for level-i graphs with vertex set $V^{i\cdot}$ and edge set $E^{i\cdot}$, that is, the superscript $i\cdot$ does not denote a Cartesian product, but the level of the graph:[3])

Definition 3 Layered graphs are hierarchical graphs which are recursively defined as follows:

- A level-1 graph $G^{1\cdot} = (V^{1\cdot}, E^{1\cdot}_{[1..7]})$ is a GT according to Def. 1.
- A level-2 graph $G^{2\cdot} = (V^{2\cdot}, E^{2\cdot}_{[1..7]})$ is a generalized tree whose vertex set $V^{2\cdot} = \{\bar{G}^{1\cdot}_i \mid i \in \mathcal{I}\}$ consists of generalized trees $\bar{G}^{1\cdot}_i = (\bar{V}^{1\cdot}_i, \bar{E}^{1\cdot}_{[1..7]_i})$ which are extending level-1 graphs $G^{1\cdot}_i = (V^{1\cdot}_i, E^{1\cdot}_{[1..7]_i})$ with respect to $V^{2\cdot}$ such that for any $(\bar{G}^{1\cdot}_i, \bar{G}^{1\cdot}_j) \in E^{2\cdot}_{[1..7]}$ there exists exactly one external edge $(v, w) \in \bar{E}^{1\cdot}_{[7]_i}$ with $v \in V^{1\cdot}_i$ and $w \in V^{1\cdot}_j$.
- A level-3 graph $G^{3\cdot} = (V^{3\cdot}, E^{3\cdot})$ is a directed graph whose vertex set $V^{3\cdot} = \{\bar{G}^{2\cdot}_i \mid i \in \mathcal{I}\}$ consists of generalized trees $\bar{G}^{2\cdot}_i = (\bar{V}^{2\cdot}_i, \bar{E}^{2\cdot}_{[1..7]_i})$ which are extending level-2 graphs $G^{2\cdot}_i = (V^{2\cdot}_i, E^{2\cdot}_{[1..7]_i})$ w.r.t $V^{3\cdot}$ such that for any $(\bar{G}^{2\cdot}_i, \bar{G}^{2\cdot}_j) \in E^{3\cdot}$ there exists exactly one external edge $(v, w) \in \bar{E}^{2\cdot}_{[7]}$ for which $v \in \bar{V}^{2\cdot}_i$, $w \in \bar{V}^{2\cdot}_j$ and where all level-1 graphs in $V^{2\cdot}_i$ are extended w.r.t $\cup_{i \in \mathcal{I}} V^{2\cdot}_i$.
- A level-k graph $G^{k\cdot} = (V^{k\cdot}, E^{k\cdot})$, $k > 3$, is a directed graph whose vertex set $V^{k\cdot} = \{\bar{G}^{k-1\cdot}_i \mid i \in \mathcal{I}\}$ consists of graphs $\bar{G}^{k-1\cdot}_i = (\bar{V}^{k-1\cdot}_i, \bar{E}^{k-1\cdot}_i)$ which extend level-$k-1$ graphs $G^{k-1\cdot}_i = (V^{k-1\cdot}_i, E^{k-1\cdot}_i)$ w.r.t $V^{k\cdot}$ so that for any $(\bar{G}^{k-1\cdot}_i, \bar{G}^{k-1\cdot}_j) \in E^{k\cdot}$ there is exactly one external edge $(v, w) \in \bar{E}^{k-1\cdot}_i$ for which $v \in \bar{V}^{k-1\cdot}_i$, $w \in \bar{V}^{k-1\cdot}_j$ and where all level-$k-2$ graphs $G^{k-2\cdot}_{i_h} \in V^{k-1\cdot}_i$ are extended w.r.t $\cup_{i \in \mathcal{I}} V^{k-1\cdot}_i$.

Edges of a level-k graph, $k > 1$, which are based on external edges of level $k - 1$ graphs are called inferred. For level-k graphs $G^{k\cdot}$, $k > 1$, whose vertex sets consist of level-$k-1$ graphs $G^{k-1\cdot}$, these vertices are called embedded into $G^{k\cdot}$ and we write $G^{k-1\cdot} \sqsubset G^{k\cdot}$ in order to denote this embedding. $\sqsubset^*$ denotes the transitive closure of $\sqsubset$.

Note that this recursive definition allows for mapping relations of the kind of l_1, l_2, k_1, k_2 and k_3 in Fig. 12.1. Now, we define a bipartite graph model together with a mapping of both part graphs in order to distinguish the visible from the hidden document structure of a network.

Definition 4 A Document Network Graph Model (DNGM) is a tuple $\mathbb{A} = (\mathbb{V}^{4\cdot}, \mathbb{H}^{4\cdot}, \alpha_{\mathbb{V}}, \alpha_{\mathbb{H}}, \beta_{\mathbb{V}}, \beta_{\mathbb{H}})$ of two level-4 graphs $\mathbb{V}^{4\cdot} = (V^{4\cdot}_{\mathbb{V}}, E^{4\cdot}_{\mathbb{V}})$, $\mathbb{H}^{4\cdot} = (V^{4\cdot}_{\mathbb{H}}, E^{4\cdot}_{\mathbb{H}})$ according to Definition 3 and two homomorphisms $\beta_{\mathbb{V}}, \beta_{\mathbb{H}}$ defined as follows: let $[V^{4\cdot}_{\mathbb{X}}]$, $\mathbb{X} \in \{\mathbb{V}, \mathbb{H}\}$, be the set of all vertices of all level-k graphs $G^{k\cdot}$, $1 \le k \le 3$, embedded into $\mathbb{X}^{4\cdot}$ and $[E^{4\cdot}_{\mathbb{X}}]$ be the corresponding set of edges, i.e.:

$$[V^{4\cdot}_{\mathbb{X}}] = V^{4\cdot}_{\mathbb{X}} \cup \cup_{V^{k\cdot} = (V^{k-1\cdot}, E^{k-1\cdot}) \sqsubset^* \mathbb{X}^{4\cdot}, 1 \le k < 4} V^{k-1\cdot} \quad \text{and}$$

$$[E^{4\cdot}_{\mathbb{X}}] = E^{4\cdot}_{\mathbb{X}} \cup \cup_{V^{k\cdot} = (V^{k-1\cdot}, E^{k-1\cdot}) \sqsubset^* \mathbb{V}^{4\cdot}, 1 \le k < 4} E^{k-1\cdot}.$$

Then we define $\alpha_{\mathbb{X}} : [V^{4\cdot}_{\mathbb{X}}] \to [V^{4\cdot}_{\mathbb{Y}}]$ and $\beta_{\mathbb{X}} : [E^{4\cdot}_{\mathbb{X}}] \to [E^{4\cdot}_{\mathbb{Y}}]$ such that

$$\forall (v, w) \in [E^{4\cdot}_{\mathbb{X}}] : \beta_{\mathbb{X}}((v, w)) = (\alpha_{\mathbb{X}}(v), \alpha_{\mathbb{X}}(w)) \in [E^{4\cdot}_{\mathbb{Y}}]$$

with $\mathbb{X}, \mathbb{Y} \in \{\mathbb{V}, \mathbb{H}\}$, $\mathbb{X} \ne \mathbb{Y}$.

The subscripts $\mathbb{V}$, $\mathbb{H}$ distinguish those graph models which are used to represent the visible and hidden structure of document networks, respectively. Likewise, the homomorphisms $\beta_{\mathbb{V}}$, $\beta_{\mathbb{H}}$ are used to map amalgamations and split-ups according to the specifications of Decision 5. Now, we can finally define a time-alignment of document network graph models in order to grasp the temporal dynamics of document networks:

Definition 5 A Time-Aligned Document Network Graph Model is a graph (V, E, τ) whose vertex set $V = \{\mathbb{A}'_1, \ldots, \mathbb{A}_n\}$, $n \in \mathbb{N}$, consists of n DNGMs according to Definition 4 together with an order relation E over V as its edge set and a function $\tau : V \to \mathbb{R}^+$ mapping elements of V onto scalars as representations of time values.

A graph model of time-aligned document networks defines an order relation over a set of document network models to represent their life cycle. Definitions 1–5 account for graph inducing coherence relations and hyperlinks, the nesting of networks mapped as hierarchical graphs, the opposition of visible *form* and hidden *logical* document structure and for the temporal dynamics of such networks. Thus, the present apparatus goes beyond classical models of web graphs (Chakrabarti 2002) which account for networking in terms of digraphs and related concepts. Obviously, digraphs do not sufficiently reflect the complexity of structures observable in the web which cannot be left out in modeling hypertext types (cf. Mehler et al. 2007). In any event, our graph model asks for a corresponding physical data model. This is outlined in Section 12.2.4.

12.2.3 A DNRM-Based View of Concurrent Models

To show the expressiveness of the DNRM, we reconstruct 5 models of web document networks. We start with complex network theory.

Web graphs: Adamic (1999) analyzes small worlds (Mehler 2008) of web graphs. In terms of the DNRM, he refers to crawls of search engines as the operative SF (Sampling Frame) in which websites are segmented as vertices based on storage-medium- and layout-oriented criteria. Further, he refers to the document level as the operative LSU (Level of Sampling Units) where a website A is seen to be linked with a website B if it contains a page which is linked with a page in B. The resulting graph is analyzed in three variants: as an undirected graph, as a directed graph and as a subgraph containing solely websites of a certain top level domain. Finally, Adamic explores URLs as indicators of topical relatedness – away from a semiotic understanding of these units.

Storage-medium- and layout-oriented segmentations: A hierarchical web graph model is built by distinguishing pages, directories, sites and domains up to *Top Level Domains* (TLD). This layered model relies on URLs to identify nested (sub-)domains of pages, while the directory path name of URLs is explored to specify the corresponding target computer. Under this regime, no distinction is made between visible website structure and LDS. In this framework, Björneborn and Ingwersen (2004) develop a hierarchical graph model of the WWW together with a link typology. They distinguish four nested aggregation levels of network formation which can be mapped on the DNRM by a bijection of manifesting and manifested structure: pages correspond to modules, directories and sites to documents, whereas domains, second-level domains and subdomains correspond to network units. Björneborn (2004) extracts networks of *university websites* whose nodes are identified by three rightmost suffix-segments of the DNS names of pages (i.e., nodes are sets of pages of websites whose domain names meet this criterion). This approach may unify thematically or functionally heterogeneous pages or sites which share domain name suffixes. Thus, URL-based segmentations may fail to segment sites correctly (Weare and Lin 2000) so that we get a semiotically deficient graph model. However, this model distinguishes nested levels of networking based on inferred or aggregated site and domain-level links which are finally anchored by page links.

Multilevel, multi-criteria segmentations based on form, function, storage-medium and topological criteria: Mukherjea (2000) describes a multilevel approach to web graphs which distinguishes four nested levels of representation. In terms of the DNRM, it can be described as follows. On the level of modules, Mukherjea identifies web pages as nodes of level-2 networks. On the level of documents, groups of interrelated pages are identified as so-called logical websites where the URLs of the pages are explored as indicators of site membership. Thus, Mukherjea applies storage medium-oriented segmentation criteria. On the level of document networks, he represents logical sites as nodes of level-3 networks whose links are inferred from page-based hyperlinks. Under this regime, documents are not seen to be recursively organized into documents. Finally, on the level of second order networks, Mukherjea computes strongly connected components of level-3 networks. These are referred to as the nodes of a level-4 network whose links are, as before, inferred from page-based links. Obviously, the latter segmentation criterion is topology-related.

A segmentation based on logical document network structure: Géry and Chevallet (2001) propose a multilevel network model of tree-like document-internal and graph-like document-external structures, thereby conflating the document level with the level of pages and negating the existence of hierarchical website structures. Above the level of documents, the level of clusters of, e.g., thematically similar documents is introduced. Based on this model, Tsikrika and Lalmas (2002) describe a structural link typology which distinguishes links according to the position of their source and target nodes. They explicitly refer to domain and directory-oriented segmentation criteria in the manner of Björneborn (2004). Tsikrika and Lalmas distinguish page internal links, hierarchical links (with the subtypes of horizontal, up and down links), transversal (i.e. lateral links), cross site (i.e. extra links) and outside domain links (i.e. cross site links which target websites of different domains). These types are finally classified into composition, sequence and reference links.

Networking in the wiki medium: All previous models primarily focus on networks of websites, i.e., layout units. This approach disregards that large, layered document networks also occur *below* the level of single sites. A prominent example is Wikipedia (Mehler 2008). It shows that even websites are problematic layout units of hypertext types, since Wikipedia is because of its size hardly comparable to, e.g., a personal academic home page. Generally speaking, we can think of a release of Wikipedia as a separate level-3 network. This binding implies that we need to identify *wiki documents* and *portals* with level-2 networks whose constitutive *wiki pages* span level-1 networks. This is done as follows: first, we specify the kernel hierarchy of elementary wiki documents in terms of their *article pages* together with the corresponding *discussion*, *history* and *edit this* pages to form a flatly structured tree. From that perspective, an elementary wiki document consists of at least four linearly ordered wiki pages which are modeled as level-1 graphs to map the network inducing link anchors. Above the level of these elementary documents and below the Wikipedia website exists the level of *portals*. Portals are document units which recursively consist of less complex ones down to the level of elementary document units. Remember that document units are recursively organized (cf. Section 12.2.1). Finally, above the level of Wikipedia we find level-4 networks which interlink different Wikipedia releases or non-wiki websites. Based on this model we can refer to different SFs and units when extracting wikis. We may, e.g., refer to a single level-3 network as the SF to extract level-1 networks (e.g. wiki articles) as the sampling units – *this is what the majority of wiki network analyses do* (Mehler 2008). Alternatively, we may analyze portals as sampling units of the same SF to study networking on a portal level. A completely different approach is to refer to a level-4 network as the SF in which level-3 networks (e.g. wiki websites) are analyzed as vertex inducing networks.

These examples show that the DNRM is general enough to grasp different network models. Thus, its decision space allows for comparing alternative models and extractions of instances of hypertext types.

12.2.4 Physical Network Modeling

Sections 12.2.1 and 12.2.2 introduced a conceptual network model and its formalization. In this section, we briefly describe a binding of this model by means of the *Graph eXchange Language* (GXL), which, in software engineering, is used as a format for data interchange between information systems (Holt et al. 2006). This binding is done in two steps:

Physical link modeling: Link_0 of Fig. 12.2 (cf. Table 12.4) is modeled as a hyperedge with two rel(ation)ends starting from unit_A and targeting at unit_B. Link_1 is modeled as a hyperedge too, but additionally integrates a source anchor_A1 as a relation end. Further, link_2 integrates a target anchor_B1 and, thus, maps a link with four relation ends. The links 0, 1, and 2 are typed as kernel and down links to exemplify link typing. Finally, link_3 is modeled as an internal link with regard to graph Level_i-1_Graph_1. Note that we use IDs which at runtime have to be replaced by numbers. This also holds for link types denoted by strings in Table 12.4. Note further that since relation ends can be extended by any GXL-attribute and since hyperedges of this kind are not restricted by the number of their sources and targets, hyperedges as modeled by the GXL allow mapping any relation of any valency.

Table 12.4 A GXL-model of link types (cf. Fig. 12.2) (dots indicate omitted content)

```
<!DOCTYPE gxl SYSTEM "http://www.gupro.de/GXL/gxl-1.0.dtd"><gxl>
  <graph id="Level_i_Graph" edgemode="directed" edgeids="true" hypergraph="true">
    <node id="unit_A">
      <graph id="Level_i-1_Graph_1" edgemode="directed" edgeids="true" hypergraph="true">
        <node id="anchor_A1"><!--...--></node><node id="anchor_A2"><!--...--></node>
        <node id="anchor_A3"><!--...--></node><node id="anchor_A4"><!--...--></node>
        <!--... add further nodes and edges of the present level-i-1 graph here ...-->
        <rel id="link_3">
          <attr name="types"><set><string>kernel_link</string></set></attr>
          <relend direction="in" target="anchor_A3" role="source" startorder="1"/>
          <relend direction="out" target="anchor_A4" role="target" endorder="1"/>
        </rel>
        <!--... add further edges of the present level-i-1 graph here ...-->
      </graph>
    </node>
    <node id="unit_B">
      <graph id="Level_i-1_Graph_2" edgemode="directed" edgeids="true" hypergraph="true">
        <node id="anchor_B1"><!--...--></node>
        <!--... add further nodes and edges of the present level-i-1 graph here ...-->
      </graph></node>
    <!--... add further nodes of the present level-i graph here ...-->
    <rel id="link_0">
      <attr name="types"><set><string>kernel_link</string></set></attr>
      <relend direction="in" target="unit_A" role="source" startorder="1"/>
      <relend direction="out" target="unit_B" role="target" endorder="1"/>
    </rel>
    <rel id="link_1">
      <attr name="types"><set><string>down_link</string></set></attr>
      <relend direction="in" target="unit_A" role="source" startorder="2"/>
      <relend direction="in" target="anchor_A1" role="source_anchor"/>
      <relend direction="out" target="unit_B" role="target" endorder="2"/>
    </rel>
    <rel id="link_2">
      <attr name="types"><set><string>down_link</string></set></attr>
      <relend direction="in" target="unit_A" role="source" startorder="3"/>
      <relend direction="in" target="anchor_A2" role="source_anchor"/>
      <relend direction="out" target="unit_B" role="target" endorder="3"/>
      <relend direction="out" target="anchor_B1" role="target_anchor"/>
    </rel>
    <!--... add further edges of the present level-i graph here ...-->
  </graph></gxl>
```

Physical graph modeling: Table 12.4 instantiates the nested DNRM of Section 12.2.1 by two graph levels: `Level_i_Graph` contains two nodes, `unit_A` and `unit_B`, which nest two graphs, i.e., `Level_i-1_Graph_1` and `Level_i-1_Graph_2`. This way of modeling hierarchical graphs is continued, straightforwardly, by nesting graphs into the nodes of the latter graphs. Generally speaking, in order to model links of nodes of the vertex sets of different level-i graphs, hyperedges are included into those level-j graphs with the smallest indenture number j which recursively contain all vertices affected by these links. That is, links l_0, l_1 and l_2 are modeled as hyperedges of the level-1 graph in Fig. 12.1. The same rule is applied when modeling links of nodes of graphs of different levels. The syntagmatic order of edges of the same graph is encoded differently for their respective source and target nodes by the `startorder`- and `endorder`-attribute of relation ends. Finally, in order to model the content of nodes of any level of document networking, we refer to models of the LDS of textual units (Mehler and Gleim 2006). This allows us to model the DOM of elementary web pages as level-1 graphs as well as the textual content of the nodes included.

Table 12.4 schematically presents a physical model of document networks in terms of our DNRM and, thus, grasps the variety of networks described in Section 12.2.3. It makes comparable different approaches to extracting instances of hypertext types. In this sense, the DNRM helps to solve the delimitation problem in the area of webgenre modeling.

12.3 Conclusion

This chapter introduced a template model of hypertext types. It serves as a preparatory step of a computational model of such types which reflects the two-mode distinction of visible layout and hidden logical document structure. We argued for an integrated approach which relies on the functional, semantic identity of hypertext types for which the visible structure is a deficient reference point. Thus, we rejected string based approaches which characterize such types by surface structural markers. Alternatively, we formalized a model of the multi-level structuring of document networks in conjunction with the two-mode distinction of visible and hidden structure. To operationalize this model, we described a decision space whose variable instantiation makes comparable different approaches to web document networks. This has been done in support of solutions of the delimitation problem in webgenre modeling.

Acknowledgments Financial support of the Deutsche Forschungsgemeinschaft (DFG) via the project *Induction of Web Genre Document Grammars* of the Research Group 437 *Text Technological Information Modeling* and via the Project *KnowCIT* of the Excellence Cluster 277 *Cognitive Interaction Technology* is gratefully acknowledged.

Notes

1. A reliable markup of content and function units is, e.g., missed in the case of web documents as a whole as in the case of their constituents and hyperlinks.
2. This deficiency causes the so-called *tag abuse problem* (Barnard et al. 1995).
3. Thus, the Cartesian product of the vertex set of a level-2 graph is noted as $(V^{2\cdot})^2$.

References

Adamic, Lada A. (1999). The small world of web. In Abiteboul, Serge and Vercoustre, Anne-Marie, editors, *Research and Advanced Technology for Digital Libraries*, pages 443–452. Springer, Berlin.

Barnard, D. T., Burnard, L., DeRose, S. J., Durand, D. G., and Sperberg-McQueen, C. M. (1995). Lessons for the World Wide Web from the text encoding initiative. In *Proc. of the 4th Int. WWW Conf.*

Baroni, Marco and Bernardini, Silvia, editors (2006). *WaCky! Working papers on the Web as corpus*. Gedit, Bologna, Italy.

Björneborn, Lennart (2004). *Small-World Link Structures across an Academic Web Space: A Library and Information Science Approach*. PhD thesis, Royal School of Library and Information Science, Department of Information Studies, Denmark.

Björneborn, Lennart and Ingwersen, Peter (2004). Towards a basic framework for webometrics. *JASIST*, 55(14):1216–1227.

Chakrabarti, Soumen (2002). *Mining the Web: Discovering Knowledge from Hypertext Data*. Morgan Kaufmann, San Francisco.

Géry, Mathias and Chevallet, Jean-Pierre (2001). Toward a structured information retrieval system on the web: Automatic structure extraction of web pages. In *Int. Workshop on Web Dynamics as part of the 8th Int. Conf. on Database Theory*.

Haas, Stephanie W. and Grams, Erika S. (2000). Readers, authors, and page structure. *JASIST*, 51(2):181–192.

Holt, Richard C., Schürr, Andy, Elliott Sim, Susan, and Winter, Andreas (2006). GXL: A graph-based standard exchange format for reengineering. *Science of Computer Programming*, 60(2):149–170.

Koehler, Wallace (1999). An analysis of web page and web site constancy and permanence. *JASIST*, 50(2):162–180.

Koehler, Wallace (2003). A longitudinal study of web pages continued: a consideration of document persistence. *Information Research*, 9(2).

Kot, Mark, Silverman, Emily, and Berg, Celeste A. (2003). Zipf's law and the diversity of biology newsgroups. *Scientometrics*, 56(2):247–257.

Kumar, Ravi, Novak, Jasmine, Raghavan, Prabhakar, and Tomkins, Andrew (2004). Structure and evolution of blogspace. *Communications of the ACM*, 47(12):35–39.

Martin, James R. (1992). *English Text. System and Structure*. Benjamins, Philadelphia.

Mehler, Alexander (2005). Zur textlinguistischen Fundierung der Text- und Korpuskonversion. *Sprache und Datenverarbeitung*, 1:29–53.

Mehler, Alexander (2008). Large text networks as an object of corpus linguistic studies. In Lüdeling, A. and Kytö, M., editors, *Corpus Linguistics. An International Handbook*, pages 328–382. De Gruyter, Berlin/New York.

Mehler, Alexander and Gleim, Rüdiger (2006). The net for the graphs: Webgenre representation for corpus linguistic studies. In Baroni, M. and Bernardini, S. (2006), pages 191–224.

Mehler, Alexander, Gleim, Rüdiger, and Wegner, Armin (2007). Structural uncertainty of hypertext types. An empirical study. In *Towards Genre-Enabled Search Engines: The Impact of NLP. Workshop in conjunction with RANLP 2007*, pages 13–19.

Mehler, Alexander, Sharoff, Serge, and Santini, Marina, editors (2009). *Genres on the Web: Computational Models and Empirical Studies*. Submitted to Springer, Berlin/New York.

Menczer, Filippo (2004). Lexical and semantic clustering by web links. *JASIST*, 55(14): 1261–1269.

Mukherjea, Sougata (2000). Organizing topic-specific web information. In *Proc. of the 11th ACM Conf. on Hypertext and Hypermedia*, pages 133–141. ACM.

Pirolli, Peter, Pitkow, James, and Rao, Ramana (1996). Silk from a sow's ear: Extracting usable structures from the web. In *Proc. of the ACM SIGCHI Conf. on Human Factors in Computing*, pages 118–125.

Power, Richard, Scott, Donia, and Bouayad-Agha, Nadjet (2003). Document structure. *Computational Linguistics*, 29(2):211–260.

Thelwall, M., Prabowo, R., and Fairclough, R. (2006a). Are raw RSS feeds suitable for broad issue scanning? A science concern case study. *JASIST*, 57(12):1644–1654.

Thelwall, Mike, Vaughan, Liwen, and Björneborn, Lennart (2006b). Webometrics. *Annual Review of Information Science Technology*, 6(8).

Thüring, Manfred, Hannemann, Jörg, and Haake, Jörg M. (1995). Hypermedia and cognition: Designing for comprehension. *Communications of the ACM*, 38(8):57–66.

Tsikrika, Theodora and Lalmas, Mounia (2002). Combining web document representations in a Bayesian inference network model using link and content-based evidence. In *Proc. ECIR '02*, volume 2291 of *LNCS*, pages 53–72.

Weare, Christopher and Lin, Wan-Ying (2000). Content analysis of the World Wide Web: Opportunities and challenges. *Social Science Computer Review*, 18(3):272–292.

Chapter 13
Regular Query Techniques for XML-Documents

Stephan Kepser, Uwe Mönnich, and Frank Morawietz

Abstract In this contribution we propose a query method for XML documents that provides a well chosen balance between expressive power of the query language and query complexity using methods derived from logic. Since XML documents are basically regular tree languages, it is appealing to use monadic second-order logic as a query language. But MSO is incapable of querying secondary relations in XML documents introduced via the ID-IDREF mechanism. We therefore show how a well-defined subclass of these ID-IDREF pairs can be queried using MSO, signature translations, and MSO-definable transductions. The ID-IDREF pairs will be coded by linear context-free tree grammars. And any query result is intersected with the coding of the ID-IDREF pairs to ensure only those matches are retained that respect the ID-IDREF informations contained in the document. The advantage of this method is that it uses regular techniques only. In consequence every query is computable.

Keywords Query languages · XML · Monadic second order logic · Logically definable transductions

13.1 Introduction

The mirror image of storing data is retrieving, that of documenting is querying. Documents, let alone document collections, of today's size are most likely not to be read as a book, but rather consulted, i.e., the reader extracts information he regards as important for him and only reads these extracts. In machine uses of XML documents this observation is even more to be stressed. But the relevant pieces of information have to be found, i.e., it is necessary to effectively query documents.

It is therefore no coincidence that there are several query languages proposed for XML documents. The most important ones are probably XSLT (Kay 2005)

S. Kepser (✉)
Theoretical Computational Linguistics Group, Linguistics Department, University of Tübingen, Tübingen, Germany
e-mail: kepser@sfs.uni.tuebingen.de

A. Witt, D. Metzing (eds.), *Linguistic Modeling of Information and Markup Languages*, Text, Speech and Language Technology 40,
DOI 10.1007/978-90-481-3331-4_13, © Springer Science+Business Media B.V. 2010

and XQuery (Boag et al. 2005) with XPath (Berglund et al. 2005) as an important sub-component of both. Since they are widespread and well supported the question may arise whether there is any space left for a discussion about query languages for XML documents. But we think there is, and it has to do with the notion of an effective query. Effectivity comprises on the one hand the ability to express precisely what one is querying. This is the question of the expressive power of the query language. And from a user's perspective, a query language should have a high expressive power so that everything one may want to query can be queried. On the other hand, effectivity also means that it does not require much time to evaluate a query, even if the queried document is a big one. More formally speaking, the query evaluation complexity should be low.

The problem we face here is an old insight from theoretical informatics that the two goals of high expressive power and low evaluation complexity are conflicting ones. If the query language has a high expressive power, then the evaluation complexity is high, too. If the evaluation complexity is low, then the expressive power cannot be high. Since both goals cannot be achieved simultaneously it is an important task to find query systems that balance the two goals. To find the right balance point is obviously something that cannot be done in general. It has to be done with a particular purpose or application in mind, because these may set certain demands – be they in terms of expressive power or evaluation complexity.

So, where do XSLT, XQuery, and XPath fit into this image? It turns out that they can be seen as extreme ends of the spectrum of potential compromises. Both XSLT and XQuery are designed in such a fashion that they are Turing-complete, i.e., all computable (and many incomputable) queries can be expressed in XSLT and XQuery (Kepser 2004). Consequently, they cannot have a low evaluation complexity. It is simple to write very demanding queries in these languages. XPath, on the other hand, has quite a low expressive power. Indeed, the navigational core of XPath has a lower expressive power than first-order predicate logic over the same basic navigational expressions (Marx 2004). It can hence be efficiently evaluated, but many interesting queries cannot be expressed.

Since the query languages recommended by the World Wide Web consortium are either very powerful or very weak, we believe there is space for defining query languages that are better balanced in terms of expressive power and evaluation complexity. One particular proposal as a query language for trees is monadic second-order logic (MSO). This is the extension of first-order logic by quantification over *sets* of nodes. This query language is quite powerful. All types of paths can be expressed. That means every XPath-expressible query is MSO-expressible. But also the transitive closure of every XPath-expressible relation of nodes is MSO-expressible. MSO also allows for limited counting like, e.g., counting modulo a natural number. This makes MSO a natural choice for talking about relations of nodes in a tree and properties of trees. (See, e.g., Gottlob and Koch 2004 for more arguments on this issue.)

Although the expressive power of MSO is quite a good one, the evaluation complexity of MSO is also moderate. In particular the data complexity is low. An MSO query can be evaluated in time linear in the size of the document (where a document is one tree).

In the considerations so far, a document is seen as a tree. This view is justified by the standard models for XML documents. But it leaves aside an important feature of XML, namely the ID-IDREF mechanism. Prima facie these are just additional node labels in the form of attributes. But the intended semantics is the introduction of additional secondary relations that are superimposed on the tree structure. Actually, since an arbitrary number of secondary relations can be defined and nodes can be arbitrarily connected via secondary relations, the underlying model of an XML document is a finite graph with coloured edges and labelled vertices rather than a tree.

If this is taken into consideration, evaluation complexity of query languages can rise significantly. The data complexity of MSO on a finite graph is exponential time in the size of the graph. Even if we restrict the query language to first-order predicate logic, the data complexity is still polynomial time in the size of the graph. Hence the question arises what can be done to lower the evaluation complexity. Since there is no solution in the general case, this amounts to the question whether there are substructures – more general than trees – that can be queried more efficiently. The particular substructures we are interested in here are ones where the structure inherent in the secondary relations can be described by so-called linear context-free tree grammars (LCFTGs). The expressive power of MSO over trees is identical to another grammar type, namely regular tree grammars. The tree languages generated by these grammars correspond to derivation trees of context-free string languages. LCFTGs are a proper extension of regular tree grammars. They are capable of coding relations of tree nodes which in the context of MSO or XML can only be encoded using secondary relations. The resulting string languages at the leaves are context-sensitive languages. We will give an example of a linear context-free tree language that has the context-sensitive string language $a^n b^n c^n d^n$ (for $n > 0$) as the leaf language. In other words, LCFTGs allow to code some amount of context-sensitivity in leaf languages. And they also allow to code some non-regular interrelations of internal nodes as secondary relations do. But it is not possible to encode all types of secondary relations with LCFTGs, as stated indirectly already at the beginning of this paragraph.

The choice of LCFTGs is driven by linguistic considerations. It is known that natural language as a string language is *not* context-free (see Huybregts 1984 or Shieber 1985). Linear context-free tree grammars are capable of describing and analysing all known phenomena of natural languages, whether their leaf languages be context-free or context-sensitive. On the other hand, the expressive power is not too far extended. There is still an efficient way to query the tree languages generated by LCFTGs. This efficient method is the topic of the present paper. We will show how LCFTGs can be recoded into regular tree grammars of an extended signature. We present a way of extracting the original structures out of the encoding ones. And we show how one can combine these insights to query documents using MSO as a query language and still query for non-regular structures.

We suppose the documents to be queried to consist of some basic units and that the search is a search for those basic units that display a certain interesting property in their tree structures plus secondary relations. One typical example is a linguistic treebank. The basic unit is the sentence together with its analysis – a tree plus some secondary relations. Users may seek for certain substructures of linguistic interest in their queries. Or the basic unit could be a paragraph. And the structure of the paragraph may be the discourse or rhetorical structure. Many more examples of this kind can be found. We believe these to be instances of quite a widespread schema.

Tree banks are a prime example of highly structured linguistic data repositories. They are therefore out of the range of typical query languages that were developed to extract information from large document collections that contain, e.g., corpora from newspapers annotated with lemmata, POS tags and sentence boundaries. A prominent example of a query language designed with this particular application domain in mind is the *Corpus Query Processor* of the IMS at Stuttgart University.

Another search engine, also due to the Stuttgart team, called *TIGERSearch*, is constructed for an object domain that corresponds to the application spectrum of MSO considered as a query system. TIGERSearch like MSO is meant as a tool for obtaining grammatical information from annotated text files that are coded along the lines model of finite graph structures. There are, though, two main distinguishing traits that set TIGERSearch apart from MSO. First, the expressive power of TIGERSearch is markedly weaker than that of MSO. Precisely, it corresponds to the existential fragment of first-order logic. Second, and more importantly, TIGERSearch does not fit into the mold of the two-step approach advertised in this paper. What we propose in the main part of the paper is a general translation procedure by which queries over an input structure, in our case the mildly context-sensitive tree bank, are transformed into queries over the lifted form of the input structure that now falls squarely within the definition range of MSO. This regularising technique is closly tied to the logical perspective adopted in this paper and it does not seem possible to develop a comparable general lifting method for for query engines in the TIGERSearch family.

This paper is organised as follows. The next section presents the technical preliminaries needed. Amongst other things this section contains the formal definition of LCFTGs. Section 13.3 gives an overview over the query method. Section 13.4 explains in detail a regular coding method for LCFTGs. The following section describes how the coding can be reverted to recover the original structures. Section 13.6 focuses on the query part after preprocessing is done. We close with some conclusions.

13.2 Preliminaries

13.2.1 Basic Algebraic Definitions

For any set M, $\wp(M)$ denotes the set of all subsets of M. For any set S, S^* is the set of all strings over S. ε is the empty string, $lg(w)$ is the length of a string w. $\mathbb{N}$ denotes the set $\{0, 1, 2, 3, \dots\}$ of nonnegative integers. Let M be a set and $R \subseteq M \times M$ be a binary relation. We denote the domain of R with $Dom(R)$ and the range of R with $Rng(R)$.

Let S be a finite set of *sorts*. An S-signature is a set Σ given with two mappings $\alpha : \Sigma \to S^*$ (the *arity* mapping) and $\sigma : \Sigma \to S$ (the *sort* mapping). The length of $\alpha(f)$ is called the *rank* of f, and is denoted by $\rho(f)$. The *type* of f in Σ is the pair $(\alpha(f), \sigma(f))$. The elements of $\Sigma_{\varepsilon,s}$ are also called constants (of sort s).

A Σ-*algebra* is a pair $\mathcal{A} = \langle (A_s)_{s \in S}, (f)_{f \in \Sigma} \rangle$ where A_s is a nonempty set for each $s \in S$, called the domain or universe of sort s of $\mathcal{A}$, and $f : A_{\alpha(f)} \to A_{\sigma(f)}$ is a total function for each $f \in \Sigma$. (For a sequence $\mu = (s_1, \ldots, s_n)$ in S^+, we let $A_\mu := A_{s_1} \times A_{s_2} \times \cdots \times A_{s_n}$.) A Σ-algebra is *finite* iff the carriers A_s for each $s \in S$ are finite.

In case S is a singleton set $\{s\}$, i.e., in case Σ is a *single-sorted* or *ranked alphabet (over sort s)*, we usually write Σ_n to denote the (unique) set of operators of rank $n \in \mathbb{N}$. In later sections of the paper we will mainly use the single-sorted case of alphabets. We will indicate the need for many-sorted alphabets where necessary.

Let S be a set of sorts, Σ a signature, and $\mathcal{A}$ and $\mathcal{B}$ two Σ-algebras. A family of functions $h_s : A_s \to B_s$ (for each $s \in S$) is called a Σ-*homomorphism* iff for all $f \in \Sigma$ of rank k and all $(a_1, \ldots, a_k) \in A_{\alpha(f)}$: $h_{\sigma(f)}(f_\mathcal{A}(a_1, \ldots, a_k)) = f_\mathcal{B}(h_{s_1}(a_1), \ldots, h_{s_k}(a_k))$.

Of particular interest to us is the algebra $\mathcal{T}_\Sigma$ of *trees* over a single-sorted signature Σ. It is the free algebra of Σ. The carrier T_Σ is defined recursively as follows. Each constant of Σ, i.e., each symbol of rank 0, is a tree. If f is of rank k and $t_1, \ldots, t_k$ are trees, then $f(t_1, \ldots, t_k)$ is a tree. Operations in $\mathcal{T}_\Sigma$ are syntactic, i.e., if $f \in \Sigma_k$ and $t_1, \ldots, t_k \in T_\Sigma$ then $f_{\mathcal{T}_\Sigma}(t_1, \ldots, t_k) := f(t_1, \ldots, t_k)$. $\mathcal{T}_\Sigma$ is the *free* or *initial algebra* in the class of all Σ-algebras, i.e., for each Σ-algebra $\mathcal{A}$ there exists a unique Σ-homomorphism $h_\mathcal{A} : \mathcal{T}_\Sigma \to \mathcal{A}$. This homomorphism is the *evaluation* of a term in $\mathcal{A}$.

A *tree language* $L \subseteq T_\Sigma$ over Σ is a subset of T_Σ. With each tree $t \in T_\Sigma$ we can associate a string $s \in \Sigma_0^*$ by reading the leaves of t from left to right. This string is called the *yield* of t, denoted $yd(t)$. More formally, $yd(t) = t$ if $t \in \Sigma_0$, and $yd(t) = yd(t_1) \cdots yd(t_k)$ whenever $t = f(t_1, \ldots, t_k)$ with $k \geq 1$. The yield of a tree language L is defined straightforwardly as $yd(L) = \{yd(t) \mid t \in L\}$.

If X is a set (of symbols) disjoint from Σ, then $T_\Sigma(X)$ denotes the set of trees $T_{\Sigma \cup X}$ where all elements of X are taken as constants. The elements of X are understood to be "variables".

Let $X = \{x_1, x_2, x_3, \ldots\}$ be a fixed denumerable set of *variables*. Let $X_0 = \emptyset$ and, for $k \geq 1$, $X_k = \{x_1, \ldots, x_k\} \subset X$. For $k \geq 0, m \geq 0, t \in T_\Sigma(X_k)$, and $t_1, \ldots, t_k \in T_\Sigma(X_m)$, we denote by $t[t_1, \ldots, t_k]$ the result of *substituting* t_i for x_i in t. Note that $t[t_1, \ldots, t_k]$ is in $T_\Sigma(X_m)$. Note also that for $k = 0, t[t_1, \ldots, t_k] = t$.

13.2.2 Basic Tree Grammar Definitions

We start with the definition of a context-free tree grammar quoting Engelfriet and Schmidt (1977).

Definition 1 A *context-free tree grammar* is a quadruple $G = (\Sigma, \mathcal{F}, S, P)$ where

Σ is a finite ranked alphabet of *terminals*,

$\mathcal{F}$ is a finite ranked alphabet of *nonterminals* or *function symbols*, disjoint with Σ,

$S \in \mathcal{F}_0$ is the *start symbol*, and

P is a finite set of productions (or rules) of the form
$F(x_1, \ldots, x_k) \to \tau$, where $F \in \mathcal{F}_k$ and $\tau \in T_{\Sigma \cup \mathcal{F}}(X_k)$.

We use the convention that for $k = 0$ an expression of the form $F(\tau_1, \ldots, \tau_k)$ stands for F. In particular, for $F \in \mathcal{F}_0$, a rule is of the form $F \to \tau$ with $\tau \in T_{\Sigma \cup \mathcal{F}}$. We frequently abbreviate the term context-free tree grammar by CFTG.

We define two special cases of context-free tree grammars. A production $F(x_1, \ldots, x_k) \to \tau$ is called linear, if each variable $x_1, \ldots, x_k$ occurs at most once in τ. Linear productions do not allow the copying of subtrees. A tree grammar $G = (\Sigma, \mathcal{F}, S, P)$ is called a *linear* context-free tree grammar, if every rule in P is linear.

A tree grammar $G = (\Sigma, \mathcal{F}, S, P)$ is called a *regular tree grammar* (abbreviated RTG), if $\mathcal{F} = \mathcal{F}_0$, i.e., if all nonterminals are of rank 0.

For a (context-free or regular) tree grammar $G = (\Sigma, \mathcal{F}, S, P)$ we now define three direct derivation relations: the unrestricted, the inside-out and the outside-in one. Let $n \geq 0$ and let $\sigma_1, \sigma_2 \in T_{\Sigma \cup \mathcal{F}}(X_n)$. We define $\sigma_1 \Rightarrow \sigma_2$ if and only if there is a production $F(x_1, \ldots, x_k) \to \tau$, a tree $\eta \in T_{\Sigma \cup \mathcal{F}}(X_{n+1})$ containing *exactly one* occurrence of x_{n+1}, and trees $\xi_1, \ldots, \xi_k \in T_{\Sigma \cup \mathcal{F}}(X_n)$ such that

$$\sigma_1 = \eta[x_1, \ldots, x_n, F(\xi_1, \ldots, \xi_k)]$$

and

$$\sigma_2 = \eta[x_1, \ldots, x_n, \tau[\xi_1, \ldots, \xi_k]].$$

In other words, σ_2 is obtained from σ_1 by replacing an occurrence of a subtree $F(\xi_1, \ldots, \xi_k)$ by the tree $\tau[\xi_1, \ldots, \xi_k]$. The definition of $\sigma_1 \underset{\text{IO}}{\Rightarrow} \sigma_2$ is the same as that for $\sigma_1 \Rightarrow \sigma_2$ except that the ξ's are required to be terminal trees $(\xi_1, \ldots, \xi_k \in T_\Sigma(X_n))$. The definition of $\sigma_1 \underset{\text{OI}}{\Rightarrow} \sigma_2$ is the same as that for $\sigma_1 \Rightarrow \sigma_2$ except that η is required to be such that x_{n+1} does not occur in a subtree of η of the form $G(\tau_1, \ldots, \tau_m)$ with $G \in \mathcal{F}$; i.e., x_{n+1} does not occur in the argument list of a function symbol.

As usual, $\overset{*}{\Rightarrow}$ $(\underset{\text{IO}}{\overset{*}{\Rightarrow}}, \underset{\text{OI}}{\overset{*}{\Rightarrow}})$ stands for the reflexive-transitive closure of $\Rightarrow$ $(\underset{\text{IO}}{\Rightarrow}, \underset{\text{OI}}{\Rightarrow}$, respectively). For a context-free tree grammar G, we define $L(G) = \{t \in T_\Sigma \mid S \overset{*}{\Rightarrow} t\}$. $L(G)$ is called the *tree language* generated by G. $L_{\text{IO}}(G) = \{t \in T_\Sigma \mid S \underset{\text{IO}}{\overset{*}{\Rightarrow}} t\}$ is the IO-tree language generated by G. $L_{\text{OI}}(G) = \{t \in T_\Sigma \mid S \underset{\text{OI}}{\overset{*}{\Rightarrow}} t\}$ is the OI-tree language generated by G.

The derivation mode of a tree grammar, i.e., whether one considers unrestricted derivations or OI-derivations or IO-derivations, has important consequences for the language thus generated.

Fact 2 Engelfriet and Schmidt (1977) *For any context-free tree grammar G, $L(G) = L_{OI}(G)$.*

The IO-language of a given context-free tree grammar is in general only a subset of the OI-language. But for some subclasses of context-free tree grammars the derivation mode is unimportant. The subclass we consider in this paper is the one of *linear* context-free tree grammars.

Fact 3 Kepser and Mönnich [2006] *Let G be a linear context-free grammar. Then $L_{IO}(G) = L_{OI}(G)$.*

Let us illustrate the above definitions by means of an example of a linear CFTG.

Example 4 Consider the CFTG $G = (\{a, b, c, d, \varepsilon, S_t, S_t^0\}, \{S, S', \overline{S}_1, \overline{S}_2, \overline{a}, \overline{b}, \overline{c}, \overline{d}\}, S', P)$ with P given as follows

$$
\begin{aligned}
S' &\longrightarrow S(\varepsilon) & \overline{a} &\longrightarrow a \\
S(x) &\longrightarrow \overline{S}_1(S(\overline{S}_2(x))) & \overline{b} &\longrightarrow b \\
S(x) &\longrightarrow S_t^0(x) & \overline{c} &\longrightarrow c \\
\overline{S}_1(x) &\longrightarrow S_t(\overline{a}, x, \overline{d}) & \overline{d} &\longrightarrow d \\
\overline{S}_2(x) &\longrightarrow S_t(\overline{b}, x, \overline{c})
\end{aligned}
$$

An example of a tree generated by this grammar is shown in Fig. 13.1.

One motivation behind this example is to give an impression on the expressive power of (linear) context-free tree grammars. It is well known that the yield languages of regular tree grammars are exactly the context-free string languages (see, e.g., Gécseg and Steinby 1984). The yield language of G is $\{a^n b^n \varepsilon c^n d^n \mid n \geq 0\}$, which is clearly context-sensitive.

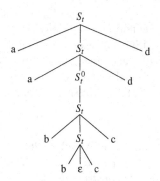

Fig. 13.1 Sample tree

13.2.3 Basic Tree Automata-Theoretic Definitions

For regular tree languages there exists an automaton model that corresponds to finite state automata for regular string languages. Let Σ be a signature. A *deterministic bottom-up tree automaton* is a pair $(\mathcal{A}_\Sigma, F)$ where $\mathcal{A}_\Sigma$ is a *finite* Σ-algebra and $F \subseteq \bigcup_{s \in \mathcal{S}} A_s$ is the set of *final states*. A tree $t \in T_\Sigma$ is recognised by $(\mathcal{A}_\Sigma, F)$ iff $h_{\mathcal{A}}(t) \in F$, i.e., the evaluation of the term t in the automaton ends in a final state. On an intuitive level, such an automaton labels the nodes in a tree with states starting from the leaves and going to the root. Suppose n is a node in the tree and f is the k-ary function symbol at node n and the k daughters of n are already labelled with states $q_1, \ldots, q_k$, and furthermore $f_{\mathcal{A}}(q_1, \ldots, q_k) = q$ is true in $\mathcal{A}$, then node n can be labelled with state q. A tree is accepted if the root can be labelled with a final state. Bottom-up tree automata are sometimes called frontier-to-root tree automata in the literature.

The language accepted by a tree automaton $(\mathcal{A}_\Sigma, F)$ is the set $\{t \in T_\Sigma \mid h_{\mathcal{A}}(t) \in F\}$. We will now report some well-known results from the theory of regular tree languages. For more information, consult Gécseg and Steinby (1984) and Gécseg and Steinby (1997).

Fact 5 *(Classical results on tree automata and regular tree languages)*

- *For every non-deterministic bottom-up tree automaton there is a deterministic tree automaton that accepts the same tree language.*
- *Bottom-up tree automata are closed under union, intersection, and complement.*
- *Both statements are constructive.*
- *A tree language L is regular if and only if there is a tree automaton that accepts L.*
- *Hence regular tree languages are closed under union, intersection, and complement.*
- *The yield language of a regular tree language is a context-free string language.*

13.2.4 Monadic Second-Order Logic

After these automata-theoretic notions, we briefly present those related to monadic second-order logic (MSO). MSO is the extension of first-order predicate logic with monadic second-order variables and quantification over them. In particular, we use MSO on trees such that individual variables $x, y, \ldots$ stand for nodes in trees and monadic second-order ones $X, Y, \ldots$ for sets of nodes (for more details see, e.g., Rogers (1998)).

Fact 6 Doner (1970) and Thatcher and Wright (1968)
A tree language is regular iff it is definable by an MSO formula. The decidability proof for MSO provides a way to construct the corresponding automaton given an MSO formula.

The particular language we will use is Rogers' variant of MSO predicate logic, $L^2_{K,P}$, with three disjoint, countable sets of *individual constants* **K**, *monadic predicate constants* **P**, and *individual and set valued variables* $\mathbf{X} = \mathbf{X}^0 \cup \mathbf{X}^1$; four binary predicates: *equality* $\approx$, plus the tree predicates *parent* $\lhd$, *dominance* $\lhd^*$, and *left-of* $\prec$, a symbol for set membership $\in$ and the usual connectives, quantifiers and brackets. As usual, the $k \in \mathbf{K}$ are interpreted as nodes, the $p \in \mathbf{P}$ as properties (or labels) of nodes, and the $x \in \mathbf{X}^0$ and $X \in \mathbf{X}^1$ range over nodes and sets of nodes, respectively. The syntax is the standard first order predicate logic syntax extended by quantification over monadic set variables: for all $X \in \mathbf{X}^1$, if φ is a formula, so are $\exists X \varphi$ and $\forall X \varphi$.

No extra n-place predicates for $n > 1$ are allowed unless they are definable. We will make use of the fact that all *explicitly* definable relations and all relations which are definable by tree-walking automata (cf. Bloem and Engelfriet 1997) are definable. In contrast, addition of monadic predicates is freely allowed since they can be added to **P**. The binary relations to navigate through a tree, parent, dominance, and left-of, correspond to basic axis steps in XPath.

The following paragraphs go directly back to Courcelle (1997). Recall that the representation of objects by means of relational structures makes them available for the use of logical description languages. Let R be a finite set of relation symbols with the corresponding arity for each $r \in R$ given by $\rho(r)$. A relational structure $\mathcal{R} = (D_\mathcal{R}, (r_\mathcal{R})_{r \in R})$ consists of the domain $D_\mathcal{R}$ and the $\rho(r)$-ary relations $r_\mathcal{R} \subseteq D_\mathcal{R}^{\rho(r)}$. In our case we choose a finite tree as our domain and the relations of immediate, proper and reflexive dominance and precedence.

The classical technique of interpreting a relational structure within another one forms the basis for MSO transductions. Intuitively, the output tree is interpreted on the input tree. E.g., suppose that we want to interpret the input tree t_1 into the output tree t_2. The nodes of the output tree t_2 will be a subset of the nodes from t_1 specified by a unary MSO relation ranging over the nodes of t_1. The daughter relation will be specified by a binary MSO relation with free variables x and y ranging over the nodes from t_1.

Definition 7 [MSO transduction] A *(non-copying) MSO transduction* Δ of a relational structure $\mathcal{R}$ (with set of relation symbols R) into another one $\mathcal{Q}$ (with set of relation symbols Q) is a tuple $(\varphi, \psi, (\theta_q)_{q \in Q})$. It consists of the formulae φ defining the domain of the transduction in $\mathcal{R}$ and ψ defining the resulting domain of $\mathcal{Q}$ and a family of formulae θ_q defining the new relations $q \in Q$ (using only definable formulae from the "old" structure $\mathcal{R}$).

The result which gives rise to the fact that we can characterise a non-context-free tree set with two devices which have only regular power is stated in Courcelle (1997). Viewing the relation of intended dominance defined later as the cornerstone of an MSO-definable transduction, our description of non-context-free phenomena with two devices with only regular power is an instance of the theorem that the image of an MSO-definable class of structures under a definable transduction is not MSO definable in general (Courcelle 1997).

13.3 Overview

In the specification of the document, the secondary relations to be coded by regular means are *not* represented using the ID and IDREF attributes. They are indirectly represented by means of a LCFTG. The LCFTG defines the admissible trees in the document. Not all of the trees that are in the language of the LCFTG must be in the document. Indeed, the language of an LCFTG is infinite in almost any interesting case. But all trees of the document must be in the language of the LCFTG. It is the structural restrictions that the LCFTG expresses that code the secondary relations. This type of grammar allows to state that certain nodes must co-occur. The co-occurrence of the nodes expresses the relation.

Since the tree structures encoded by an LCFTG are non-regular, it is not possible to directly apply regular techniques. We therefore use first a recoding technique for LCFTGs to be described in the next section that translates the LCFTG into a regular tree grammar over an extended signature. The task is, though, not to query the grammar, but the document. Since the document is a finite set of trees, it can be compactly represented by an RTG. This RTG has to be translated using the same method as the LCFTG is translated. The resulting grammar is of course again an RTG. The reason behind this step is that the signatures of the LCFTG representing the secondary relations and the RTG representing the document have to be the same after the translation step.

The aim of this tree translation process is to query the translated document using tree automata. But to do so, it is also necessary to translate queries, because a user poses his query in MSO over the original signature. The translation of the query is a simple step of replacing relations in the original signature by their more complex counterparts in the translated signature. The translated query is next coded as a tree automaton. The translated LCFTG representing the secondary relations and the translated RTG representing the document are also converted into tree automata. The query step proper now consists of intersecting the three tree automata. The result of this intersection is a tree automaton that represents those translated trees that are in the document, are compatible with the specification of the secondary relations and that are matches of the query.

This tree automaton is unfortunately not a suitable output format. It is hardly practical for users. In order to obtain a proper answer set, two steps have to be performed. Firstly the tree automaton is converted back into an RTG. And secondly, the complex signature encoding that is contained in the RTG is undone to yield a LCFTG over the original signature of the document. This final LCFTG is a compact representation of the answer set. If desired it can be unfolded by generating the language of this LCFTG.

13.4 Lifting of Grammars and Trees

In this subsection, we introduce a recoding technique for trees and tree grammars that was developed in Mönnich (1999) along the lines of Maibaum (1974, 1977) and subsequently systematically investigated and applied to questions of the formalisation of natural language in Kolb et al. (2003, 2000), Michaelis et al. (2001) and Morawietz and Mönnich (2001). It is based on ideas from Engelfriet and Schmidt (1977, 1978).

The intuition in this recoding is that the basic assumptions about the operations of a tree grammar, namely tree substitution and argument insertion, are made explicit. In the following, we will briefly describe this LIFTing in a more formal way. All technical details, in particular concerning many-sorted signatures, can be found in Mönnich (1999). Any *context-free* tree grammar G for a singleton set of sorts S can be transformed into a *regular* tree grammar G^L for the set of sorts S^*, which characterises a (necessarily regular) set of trees encoding the instructions necessary to convert them by means of a unique homomorphism h into the ones the original grammar generates (Maibaum 1974, 1977). The LIFTing is achieved by constructing for a given single S-sorted signature Σ a new, derived alphabet (an S^*-sorted signature) Σ^L, and by translating the terms over the original signature into terms of the derived one via a simple recursive procedure. The LIFT-operation takes a term in $T_\Sigma(X_k)$ and transforms it into one in $T(\Sigma^L, k)$. Intuitively, the LIFTing eliminates variables and composes functions with their arguments explicitly, e.g., a term $f(a, b) = f(x_1, x_2) \circ (a, b)$ is lifted to the term $c(c(f, \pi_1, \pi_2), a, b)$. The old function symbol f now becomes a constant, the variables are replaced with appropriate projection symbols and the only remaining non-nullary alphabet symbols are the explicit composition symbols c. The trees over the derived LIFTed signature consisting of the old symbols together with the new projection and composition symbols form the carrier of a free tree algebra $\mathcal{T}_{\Sigma^L}$.

Definition 8 [LIFT] Let Σ be a ranked alphabet of sort S and $X_k = \{x_1, \ldots, x_k\}$, $k \in \mathbb{N}$, a finite set of variables. The *derived* many-sorted S^*-sorted alphabet Σ^L is defined as follows: For each $n \geq 0$, $\Sigma'_{\varepsilon,n} = \{f' \mid f \in \Sigma_n\}$ is a new set of symbols of type (ε, n); for each $n \geq 1$ and each i, $1 \leq i \leq n$, π_i^n is a new symbol, the ith *projection symbol* of type (ε, n); for each $n, k \geq 0$ the new symbol $c_{(n,k)}$ is the (n, k)-th *composition symbol* of type $(nk_1 \cdots k_n, k)$ with $k_1 = \cdots = k_n = k$.

$$\Sigma^L_{\varepsilon,0} = \Sigma'_{\varepsilon,0}$$
$$\Sigma^L_{\varepsilon,n} = \Sigma'_{\varepsilon,n} \cup \{\pi_i^n \mid 1 \leq i \leq n\} \text{ for } n \geq 1$$
$$\Sigma^L_{nk_1 \cdots k_n, k} = \{c_{(n,k)}\} \text{ for } n, k \geq 0 \text{ and } k_i = k \text{ for } 1 \leq i \leq n$$
$$\Sigma^L_{w,s} = \emptyset \text{ otherwise}$$

For $k \geq 0$, $\text{LIFT}_k^\Sigma : T(\Sigma, X_k) \to T(\Sigma^L, k)$ is defined as follows:

$$\text{LIFT}_k^\Sigma(x_i) = \pi_i^k$$

$$\text{LIFT}_k^\Sigma(f) = c_{(0,k)}(f') \text{ for } f \in \Sigma_0$$

$$\text{LIFT}_k^\Sigma(f(t_1, \ldots, t_n)) = c_{(n,k)}(f', \text{LIFT}_k^\Sigma(t_1), \ldots, \text{LIFT}_k^\Sigma(t_n))$$
$$\text{for } n \geq 1, f \in \Sigma_n \text{ and } t_1, \ldots, t_n \in T_\Sigma(X_k)$$

Note that this very general procedure allows the translation of any term over the original signature. The left hand side as well as the right hand side of a rule of a CFTG $G = (\Sigma, \mathcal{F}, S, P)$ are terms belonging to $T_{\Sigma \cup \mathcal{F}}(X)$, but so is, e.g., any structure *generated* by G. Further remarks on the observation that the result of LIFTing a CFTG is always a regular tree grammar can be also found in Mönnich (1999). To further illustrate the techniques, we present the continuation of Example 4. Note that for better readability, we omit all the 0- and 1-place composition symbols.

Example 9 Let $G^L = (\{a, b, c, d, \varepsilon, S_t, S_t^0\}, \{S, S', \overline{S}_1, \overline{S}_2, \overline{a}, \overline{b}, \overline{c}, \overline{d}\}, S', P)$ with P given as follows

$$S' \longrightarrow c_{(1,0)}(S, \varepsilon)$$
$$S \longrightarrow c_{(1,1)}(\overline{S}_1, c_{(1,1)}(S, c_{(1,1)}(\overline{S}_2, \pi_1^1)))$$
$$S \longrightarrow c_{(1,1)}(S_t^0, \pi_1^1)$$
$$\overline{S}_1 \longrightarrow c_{(3,1)}(S_t, a, \pi_1^1, d)$$
$$\overline{S}_2 \longrightarrow c_{(3,1)}(S_t, b, \pi_1^1, c)$$

Note that we now have only nullary operatives but extra composition and projection symbols: The original non-terminals have become constants. An example tree generated by this LIFTed grammar is shown in Fig. 13.2. It is the LIFTed tree corresponding to the sample tree of Fig. 13.1. The grey shaded lines show how the intended tree is present in the LIFTed tree.

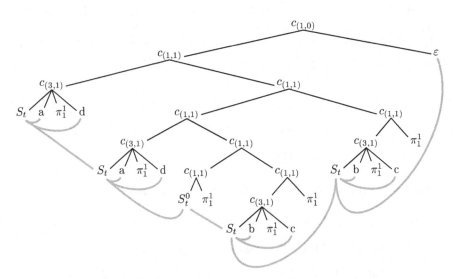

Fig. 13.2 A LIFTed tree with intended relations

13.5 Reconstructing the Intended Trees

As Fig. 13.2 shows, a LIFTed tree is a complex encoding of the tree we originally started with. We will now show how the encoding can be undone, i.e., how
the intended tree can be "read" off a LIFTed tree. Informally speaking, this is
done by interpreting the compositions (the c's) and the projections (the π's) the
way the names we have given them suggest, *viz.* as compositions and projections,
respectively.

More formally, we define a Σ^L-algebra, the *tree substitution algebra* TS_{Σ^L}, that
provides the denotational side of the reconstruction. Let Σ be a ranked alphabet of
single sort s. For each sort s^k with $k \in \mathbb{N}$ of Σ^L, the range of s^k is $T_\Sigma(X_k)$, i.e.,
trees in the intended signature with free variables $\{x_1, \ldots, x_k\}$. For each $n \in \mathbb{N}$, the
interpretation of $f' \in \Sigma^L_{\varepsilon,n}$ is $f(x_1, \ldots, x_n)$ where $f \in \Sigma_n$. For $n \geq 1$ and $1 \leq i \leq$
n, the interpretation of π^n_i is x_i. For $n, k \geq 0$, $t \in T_\Sigma(X_n)$, and $t_1, \ldots, t_n \in T_\Sigma(X_k)$,
the interpretation of $c_{n,k}(t, t_1, \ldots, t_n)$ is $t[t_1, \ldots, t_n]$, the substitution of $t_1, \ldots, t_n$
into t (see last part of Section 13.2.1).

Now, since T_{Σ^L} is the free algebra of Σ^L, there is a unique homomorphism
$Yield : T_{\Sigma^L} \to TS_{\Sigma^L}$. This homomorphism $Yield$ evaluates each tree in the LIFTed
signature to the intended tree. It is the inverse of LIFTing.

As was shown in Kolb et al. (2003), the homomorphism $Yield$ can be expressed
by means of a monadic second-order definable transduction (see Section 13.2.4).

As mentioned in the preliminaries, Rogers (1998) has shown the suitability of an
MSO description language $L^2_{K,P}$ for linguistics which is based upon the primitive
relations of immediate ($\lhd$), proper ($\lhd^+$) and reflexive ($\lhd^*$) dominance and proper
precedence ($\prec$). We will show how to define these relations with an MSO transduction thereby implementing the unique homomorphism mapping the terms into
elements of the corresponding context-free tree language.

Put differently, it should be possible to define a set of relations $R^I = \{\blacktriangleleft, \blacktriangleleft^+, \blacktriangleleft^*$
(dominance), c-command, $\lhd$(precedence), $\ldots$} holding between the nodes of the
LIFTed tree T^L which carry a label from the original label set L in such a way, that
when interpreting $\blacktriangleleft^* \in R^I$ as a tree order on the set of L-labelled nodes and $\lhd \in R^I$
as the precedence relation on the resulting structure, we have a "new" description
language on the intended structures.

Kolb et al. (2000) have shown how to give an operational account of an MSO
transduction to recover the intended relations via so called tree-walking automata
with MSO tests.[1] In this paper, we present the logical aspect of this transduction
without going into the details of how to generate the relevant formulas. The interested reader is referred to the reference given above.

We will use $\mathrm{trans}_{W_\blacktriangleleft}(x, y)$ as the formula denoting immediate dominance ($x \blacktriangleleft y$)
on the intended structures. This formula was constructed recursively from the walk-
ing language of a tree-walking automaton linking the appropriate nodes in the
lifted tree. An example of these relations is displayed graphically in Fig. 13.2. The
intended dominance relation marks the endpoints of these tree walks. Using the
defined formula $\mathrm{trans}_{W_\blacktriangleleft}(x, y)$ for $\blacktriangleleft$, the specific MSO transduction Δ, which we
need to transform the LIFTed structures into the intended ones, looks as follows:

$$\Delta = (\varphi, \psi, (\theta_q)_{q \in Q})$$

$$Q = \{\blacktriangleleft, \blacktriangleleft^*, \blacktriangleleft^+, \vartriangleleft, \dots\}$$

$$
\begin{aligned}
\varphi &\equiv \varphi_{\mathfrak{A}_{rL}} \\
\psi(x) &\equiv \neg(\exists y)[x \blacktriangleleft y \vee y \blacktriangleleft x] \\
\theta_{\blacktriangleleft}(x, y) &\equiv \mathrm{trans}_{W_{\blacktriangleleft}}(x, y) \\
\theta_{\blacktriangleleft^*}(x, y) &\equiv (\forall X)[\blacktriangleleft\text{-closed}(X) \wedge x \in X \to y \in X] \\
\theta_{\blacktriangleleft^+}(x, y) &\equiv x \blacktriangleleft^* y \vee x \not\approx y \\
\theta_{\vartriangleleft}(x, y) &\equiv \mathrm{trans}_{W_{\vartriangleleft}}(x, y) \\
\theta_{L \in \mathrm{Labels}}(x) &\equiv L(x)
\end{aligned}
\tag{13.1}
$$

As desired, the domain of the transduction Δ is characterised by the MSO formula for the LIFTed trees. The domain, i.e., the set of nodes, of the intended tree is characterised by the formula ψ which identifies the nodes with a label which stand indeed in the new dominance relation. Building on it, we define the other primitives of our description language analogous to the MSO language $L^2_{K,P}$ used to analyse large parts of GB theory in Rogers (1998). For reasons of space, we have to leave the specification of the precedence relation $\mathrm{trans}_{W_{\vartriangleleft}}(x, y)$ open. It is more complicated than dominance, but can be achieved with another tree-walking automaton. Finally, the labeling information for the nodes is taken over from R.

The MSO transduction Δ can be read from left to right as defining how the tree relations like dominance in the original trees are to be interpreted in the LIFTed trees. Hence the MSO transduction can be used to perform the translation of an MSO query. As stated before, the query is naturally posed in the language over the original signature, talking about the original document. But the intention is to evaluate the query on the LIFTed structures. We therefore have to translate the query. The translation step consists in replacing the original definition of dominance and precedence etc. by their interpretation on the LIFTed structures. This is exactly what the MSO transduction Δ provides.

For an MSO formula ϕ (over the original signature) we define recursively the translation τ into an MSO formula in the LIFTed signature as follows (where ψ is defined in Δ).

$$
\begin{aligned}
\tau(\forall X \phi) &= \forall X \; X \subseteq \psi \wedge \tau(\phi) \\
\tau(\exists X \phi) &= \exists X \; X \subseteq \psi \wedge \tau(\phi) \\
\tau(\forall x \phi) &= \forall x \; \psi(x) \wedge \tau(\phi) \\
\tau(\exists x \phi) &= \exists x \; \psi(x) \wedge \tau(\phi) \\
\tau(\phi \wedge \chi) &= \tau(\phi) \wedge \tau(\chi) \\
\tau(\phi \vee \chi) &= \tau(\phi) \vee \tau(\chi) \\
\tau(\neg \phi) &= \neg \, \tau(\phi) \\
\tau(R(x, y)) &= \Delta(R(x, y)) \text{ for every tree relation } R \\
\tau(L(x)) &= L(x) \text{ for every node label } L
\end{aligned}
$$

The methods described in this and the previous section can be used to show that linear context-free tree languages are closed under intersection with regular tree languages.

Fact 10 Kepser and Mönnich (2006)
The family of linear context-free tree languages is closed under intersection with regular tree languages. The closure is constructive in the strong sense that there are regular, i.e., tree automata theoretic means to construct the intersection.

13.6 Querying

As stated before, we consider documents that consist of some basic unit, and this basic unit has a particular structure in form of a tree. A prototypical example is a linguistic treebank. The treebank consists of many syntactically annotated trees. And it is the structure of these trees that is the target of querying. For example one may want to find all trees that have a subordinate clause embedding another subordinate clause. The basic unit need not be a sentence. Another example would be a paragraph. The structure in the paragraph could be the discourse structure within the paragraph, i.e., the way the sentences in the paragraph connect to each other forming a discourse. Here, a query might ask for a particular discourse substructure.

The structure of the basic units is not restricted to trees. There may be secondary relations between the nodes in a basic unit. These relations must be encodable by a LCFTG. Note that if the full expressive power of an LCFTG is used, then relations thus defined are *not* expressible in MSO and hence cannot be queried directly. This is the idea behind the use of LCFTG. It is the intention to provide a means of defining secondary relations that is more powerful than MSO, because there may be interesting secondary relations that cannot be defined in MSO in the first place due to their intended semantics.

If those structures cannot be expressed in MSO queries, how can they be made accessible to query without leaving the regular realm? The document is a finite set of trees. Hence it can be represented by a regular tree grammar G_D such that the language of G_D is exactly the document. The intended secondary relations are encoded in a LCFTG G_{SR}. Both tree grammars are LIFTed as described above yielding G_{SR}^L and G_D^L. A user may then write an approximative query Q in MSO. This query is translated using τ as specified in the previous section.

In the next step, the LIFTed tree grammars G_{SR}^L and G_D^L, which are both regular, are translated into equivalent tree automata $\mathcal{A}_{G_{SR}^L}$ and $\mathcal{A}_{G_D^L}$. For the translated MSO query $\tau(Q)$ the equivalent tree automaton $\mathcal{A}_{\tau(Q)}$ is constructed. The three automata are intersected to yield a LIFTed automaton representation of the solution $\mathcal{A} := \mathcal{A}_{G_{SR}^L} \cap \mathcal{A}_{G_D^L} \cap \mathcal{A}_{\tau(Q)}$. The relevant tree automata constructions are mentioned in Facts 5 and 6.

The tree automaton $\mathcal{A}$ can be translated back into a LIFTed regular tree grammar $G_{\mathcal{A}}^L$. Using the MSO-transduction Δ we finally yield a tree grammar $G_{\mathcal{A}} := \Delta(G_{\mathcal{A}}^L)$.

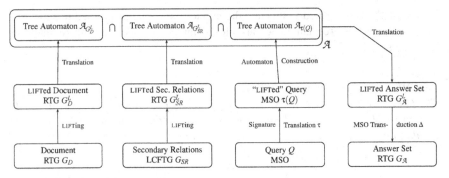

Fig. 13.3 Overview of the approach

This tree grammar G_A is a compact representation of the answer set. It generates all and only those trees from the document which are compatible with G_{SR} and for which the query Q is true. The theoretical results mentioned in Fact 10 ensure only that G_A is a LCFTG. But because the document is finite and the answer set is a subset of the document it follows that G_A is indeed an RTG. Figure 13.3 provides an overview over our approach.

Correctness of this method is based on Fact 10. Together with Facts 5 and 6 it also ensures the existence of regular means to construct the answer set.

13.7 Conclusion

In this paper we presented a method for querying documents that are enriched with secondary relations. These relations must be encodable by linear context-free tree grammars. Certainly, not every set of secondary relations can be encoded using LCFTGs. But if they can, we show how one can use monadic second-order logic as query language and tree automata as the evaluation method to query these enriched structures using regular means only. The method thus combines the advantages of sufficiently high expressive power and efficient query evaluation techniques.

Acknowledgments This research was supported by a DFG grant (SFB 441).

Note

1. A tree-walking automaton with MSO tests is a finite state automaton which can navigate through a tree by following simple directives or by testing properties of nodes via MSO formulas. In Bloem and Engelfriet 1997 it is shown that the relations between two nodes recognised by their walks is constructively MSO definable.

References

Berglund, Anders, Boag, Scott, Chamberlin, Don, Fernandez, Mary, Kay, Michael, Robie, Jonathan, and Siméon, Jérôme (2005). XML path language (XPath) 2.0. Technical report, W3C. Working draft.

Bloem, Roderick and Engelfriet, Joost (1997). Characterization of properties and relations defined in Monadic Second Order logic on the nodes of trees. Technical Report 97-03, Dept. of Computer Science, Leiden University.

Boag, Scott, Chamberlin, Don, Fernández, Mary, Florescu, Daniela, Robie, Jonathan, and Siméon, Jérôme (2005). XQuery 1.0: An XML query language. Technical report, W3C. Working draft.

Courcelle, Bruno (1997). The expression of graph properties and graph transformations in monadic second-order logic. In Rozenberg, Grzegorz, editor, *Handbook of Graph Grammars and Computing by Graph Transformation*, pages 313–400. World Scientific Publishing, Singapore.

Doner, John (1970). Tree acceptors and some of their applications. *Journal of Computer and System Sciences*, 4:406–451.

Engelfriet, Joost and Schmidt, Erik Meineche (1977). IO and OI. I. *Journal of Computer and System Sciences*, 15(3):328–353.

Engelfriet, Joost and Schmidt, Erik Meineche (1978). IO and OI. II. *Journal of Computer and System Sciences*, 16(1):67–99.

Gécseg, Ferenc and Steinby, Magnus (1984). *Tree Automata*. Akademiai Kiado, Budapest.

Gécseg, Ferenc and Steinby, Magnus (1997). Tree languages. In Rozenberg, Grzegorz and Salomaa, Arto, editors, *Handbook of Formal Languages, Vol 3: Beyond Words*, pages 1–68. Springer-Verlag, Berlin.

Gottlob, Georg and Koch, Christoph (2004). Monadic datalog and the expressive power of languages for Web information extraction. *Journal of the ACM*, 51(1):74–113.

Huybregts, Riny (1984). The weak inadequacy of context–free phrase structure grammars. In de Haan, Ger J. Trommelen, Mieke, and Zonneveld, Wim, editors, *Van Periferie naar Kern*, pages 81–99. Foris, Dordrecht.

Kay, Michael (2005). XSL Transformations (XSLT), version 2.0. Technical report, W3C. Working draft.

Kepser, Stephan (2004). A simple proof of the Turing-completeness of XSLT and XQuery. In Usdin, B. Tommie, editor, *Extreme Markup Languages 2004*.

Kepser, Stephan and Mönnich, Uwe (2006). Closure properties of linear context-free tree languages with an application to optimality theory. *Theoretical Computer Science*, 354(1): 82–97.

Kolb, Hans-Peter, Michaelis, Jens, Mönnich, Uwe, and Morawietz, Frank (2003). An operational and denotational approach to non-context-freeness. *Theoretical Computer Science*, 293: 261–289.

Kolb, Hans-Peter, Mönnich, Uwe, and Morawietz, Frank (2000). Descriptions of cross-serial dependencies. *Grammars*, 3(2/3):189–216.

Maibaum, Thomas S. E. (1974). A generalized approach to formal languages. *Journal of Computer and System Sciences*, 8(3):409–439.

Maibaum, Thomas S. E. (1977). Erratum: A generalized approach to formal languages. *Journal of Computer and System Sciences*, 14(3):369.

Marx, Maarten (2004). XPath with conditional axis relations. In Bertino, Elisa, Christodoulakis, Stavros, Plexousakis, Dimitris, Christophides, Vassilis, Koubarakis, Manolis, Böhm, Klemens, and Ferrari, Elena, editors, *Advances in Database Technology – EDBT 2004*, volume LNCS 2992, pages 477–494. Springer.

Michaelis, Jens, Mönnich, Uwe, and Morawietz, Frank (2001). On minimalist attribute grammars and macro tree transducers. In Rohrer, Christian, Roßdeutscher, Antje, and Kamp, Hans, editors, *Linguistic Form and its Computation*, pages 287–326. CSLI.

Mönnich, Uwe (1999). On cloning contextfreeness. In Kolb, Hans-Peter and Mönnich, Uwe, editors, *The Mathematics of Syntactic Structure*, pages 195–229. Mouton de Gruyter.

Morawietz, Frank and Mönnich, Uwe (2001). A model-theoretic description of tree adjoining grammars. In Kruiff, Geert-Jan, Moss, Larry, and Oehrle, Richard, editors, *Proceedings FG-MOL 2001*, volume 53 of *ENTCS*. Kluwer.

Rogers, James (1998). *A Descriptive Approach to Language-Theoretic Complexity*. CSLI Publications, Stanford.

Shieber, Stuart (1985). Evidence against the context-freeness of natural language. *Linguistics and Philosophy*, 8:333–343.

Thatcher, James W. and Wright, Jesse B. (1968). Generalized finite automata theory with an application to a decision problem of second-order logic. *Mathematical Systems Theory*, 2(1):57–81.